MW00748830

Canadian Content:

Essays for Composition from
Canada, Britain, and the
United States

SARAH NORTON
NELL WALDMAN

Holt, Rinehart and Winston of Canada, Limited   Toronto

Copyright © 1988
Holt, Rinehart and Winston of Canada, Limited
All rights reserved

It is illegal to reproduce any portion of this book except by special
arrangement with the publishers. Reproduction of this material
without authorization by any duplication process whatsoever is a
violation of copyright.

Canadian Cataloguing in Publication Data

Main entry under title:
Canadian content
ISBN 0-03-922047-8

1. College readers. 2. English language -
Rhetoric. I. Norton, Sarah, date.
II. Waldman, Nell Kozak, date.

PE1417.C36 1988   808'.0427   C87-093505-4

Cover Art: **Shop on an Island,** by Christopher Pratt. 1969. Oil on
board. 81.3 × 91.4 cm.
Reproduced by permission of Mr. C. Pratt and the London Regional
Art Gallery. This work on permanent loan from the Ontario Heritage Foundation. Gift of J.H. Moore, London.

Publisher: Susan Lilholt
Editor: Tessa McWatt
Publishing Services Manager: Karen Eakin
Editorial Co-ordinator: Edie Franks
Copy Editor: Deborah Seed
Cover and Interior Design: Gord Pronk
Typesetting and Assembly: Q Composition Inc.
Printing and Binding: Metrolitho Inc.

Printed in Canada

 2 3 4   92 91 90

Contents

By Unit

Unit Seven: Argument and Persuasion: Appealing to Reason and Emotion   256

Unit Eight: Further Reading   305

List of Useful Terms   359

Author Index   370

Contents

By Theme

On Morals and Ethics

On Politics

On Science and Technology

On the Sexes

On Sports and Leisure

On Urban Life/On Rural Life

On Work

On Writing

Miscellaneous

Preface

To the Instructor

Canadian Content is a reader designed for Canadian college students taking a first-level composition course. Arranged according to rhetorical pattern, the essays in the collection are, for the most part, by or about Canadians. Of the four traditional rhetorical modes, we have concentrated on the two most practical patterns: exposition and argument. We have omitted narration and description for two reasons: first, most students coming from high school to college have considerable experience in these modes; and second, narrative and descriptive writing are seldom required in their "pure" forms in the professional fields our students will enter. Since most of the writing they will be required to do on the job is expository, we have emphasized the six expository strategies in the various units.

We acknowledge at the outset that the six patterns we treat in isolation are usually found in combination in most expository writing. In our experience, however, students find it helpful to analyze and practise these patterns of development one by one. When all have been mastered, students can then combine the six strategies in various ways, depending on their subject and purpose.

To assist the students in their struggle to master clear, correct, and vigorous prose, we have arranged the units of this text in ascending order of difficulty. Units One to Seven deal first with exemplification, the simplest and most common pattern of development, then progress to the more complex patterns of process analysis, division and classification, comparison and contrast, cause and effect, to definition, which often requires the application of several of the preceding strategies. Unit Seven is devoted to argumentation, which also requires the command of a number of expository strategies. Finally, in Unit Eight, we include a number of fairly sophisticated essays in which the authors employ a variety of expository and persuasive techniques. Throughout the text we emphasize that there is no single, "best" way of approaching a topic; there is always a variety of choices when organizing and developing an idea—depending on one's audience, subject, and purpose. In other words, we present the various rhetorical patterns not as formulas for the purpose of restricting or confining the student's thinking, but as methods of invention, as options to explore when thinking about the most effective approach to a subject.

For those instructors who prefer to organize their course around themes rather than rhetorical modes, we have supplied an alternate table of contents, entitled By Theme.

The essays within each unit are arranged from simplest to most complex; thus an instructor can assign readings suited to the level of the class, or can lead the students through a progressively challenging series of assignments in a single rhetorical mode. In choosing the essays for this text, we kept in mind three criteria: first, the selections had to be well written and neither very formal nor highly colloquial in tone. We looked for examples of good, middle-of-the-road, all-purpose standard English prose—the kind we want our students to learn to write. Second, the selection had to exemplify one of the modes: the structure and development had to illustrate clearly the pattern being presented. Third, we looked for pieces with a high interest level, selections that would stimulate thought, provoke class discussion, and promote our students' understanding of themselves, of others, and of the world around us.

Each unit begins with an introduction written in an informal, accessible style. Where possible, examples and allusions have been drawn from the students' culture—not only to make the point clear, but also to make the writing process less intimidating. We have tried throughout the book to demystify the writing process. Each introduction encourages the student to ask specific questions about his or her subject and then to formulate a thesis statement that will summarize the whole essay in a single sentence. Whether or not the student ultimately includes this statement in the paper—a strategy we encourage—the exercise of formulating the thesis statement serves to clarify both the student's thinking and the paper's organization. Many students resist composing a traditional essay outline; the thesis statement—which is an outline in miniature—ensures that the student has done the preliminary thinking and organizing that a clearly structured paper requires. Occasionally, students object to this "blueprint" approach to composition, protesting that "real writers don't write this way!" To be sure, novelists, poets, and many other professional writers do not approach writing this way. Nevertheless, as the essays in this text clearly illustrate, "real writers" do pay particular attention to the organization and development of their work.

Most of our students, of course, do not aspire to become professional writers. Their goal is to become competent writers within a profession. The key to competent writing is organization. Yet many students arrive at college without much training or practice in the structure of clear prose—hence our emphasis on structure throughout this text. Overwhelmingly, the majority of students are interested in and grateful for a practical, no-nonsense approach to writing such as the one presented here.

Immediately following the introduction in each unit, there is a short model essay that illustrates the form being presented. These model essays, all on the subject of education, also serve to illustrate the various introductory and concluding stategies that are summarized in the List of Useful Terms at the back of the book.

The readings themselves are followed by short biographical notes and by definitions of the most difficult words and allusions in the text. Please note that our "meanings" are not intended to be exhaustive dictionary definitions; we have defined the terms specifically as they appear in the context of the selection. The terms we have chosen to define are those that many students are likely to have difficulty with, terms that do not have contextual clues as to their meaning, and terms that are necessary to the reader's understanding of the essay. We expect students to use their dictionaries to clarify the meaning of other words they may not know.

Two sets of questions follow each essay. The questions under Structure and Strategy are designed to lead the students to an understanding of *form*: how the piece is put together and why the writing strategies employed are effective. The questions under Content and Purpose are designed to encourage the students' analysis of the *content* of the piece, to deepen their understanding of meaning. Terms that are included in the List of Useful Terms at the back of the book appear in capital letters in the questions; for example, if a question refers to the purpose of an ALLUSION, the typeface serves as a cue to consult the List of Useful Terms for an explanation of the word "allusion."

We have included a few Suggestions for Writing after each essay. These suggestions lead either to a paper with a form similar to that of the essay under discussion or to one that responds in some way to the content of the piece. We have deliberately kept the number of writing suggestions small, so that students and instructors will feel free to pursue their own responses to the form and content of the selections. There are also Additional Suggestions for Writing at the conclusion of each unit.

Finally, a few words about the cover of the book: we deem Christopher Pratt's "Shop on an Island" a most appropriate cover to our text because it surrounds its outward-looking vision of sky and water with the symmetry of form. The colours are harmonious, and the effect is one of pleasingly balanced shape. It is our hope that *Canadian Content* will enable those who make use of it to lend shape to their own visions and, in so doing, focus the world of idea and imagination through the window of structure and form.

Acknowledgements

This book has been very much a team effort. We wish to thank Ruth and John Robert Colombo for their help in finding suitable selections and for suggesting stimulating and appropriate questions. We are indebted to Sheila Trant for compiling the glossary and to Holly Prue for hunting down numerous references, biographical details, and sources. To our reviewers: Mark Brubacher, York Memorial; Keith Gilley, vcc; Bobbie Goldenberg, Seneca College; and John Lucas, Dawson College, who gave us many helpful suggestions and put us firmly on the right track, our thanks. Special thanks go to Carol Baxter, who not only found and fixed numerous flaws but also laughed in all the right places. To Anthony Luengo and to our editor, Tessa McWatt, we would like to give special thanks for their encouragement and patience. And finally—in the position of prominence, as we have taught them—we thank our students who have previewed, reviewed, discussed, argued about, and endorsed our selection of essays.

INTRODUCTION

1. How to Read with Understanding

Every college student knows how to read—sort of. The trouble is that most of us don't read very efficiently. We don't know how to adapt our reading style to our purpose. Most people aren't even aware that there are different kinds of reading suited to different purposes.

Basically, there are two different kinds of reading: *surface* reading, which is casual reading for pleasure or for easy-to-find facts. This is the kind of reading we engage in when we enjoy a novel, magazine, or newspaper. The second kind of reading is *deep* reading. This is the type required in college courses or on the job: reading to acquire knowledge, facts, and ideas, which we do to *understand* a topic because we need the information. This kind of reading has practical rather than recreational purposes. Both kinds of reading can bring us personal satisfaction, but one is undeniably more difficult than the other.

Deep reading, or analytical reading, is the kind that most of us don't do as well as we would like. As with any other skill, there is a technique involved that can, with practice, be mastered. In general, there are three basic guidelines to follow: figure out as much about the piece as you can *before* reading it; identify what you don't understand *while* reading it; and review the whole thing *after* reading it.

Specifically, there are seven steps to reading with understanding:

1. Remove Distractions.

Every year teachers hear hundreds of students protest that they are perfectly able to read while listening to music, watching television, talking on the phone, or filing their nails. These students are right. They can read, but they can't read for understanding. To read analytically, you have to focus your attention completely on the text. Reading for understanding is an *active* process, requiring your full concentration and participation. For example, you should learn to read with a pencil in your hand, if you don't already do so. Only half of the task of making the meaning clear belongs to the writer; the other half belongs to you. Understanding is something you have to work at.

Find a quiet spot, with a good reading light, where you can be alone with your book, your pencil, and your dictionary. We'll get to the dictionary later.

2. Preview Before You Read.

Human beings cannot learn facts, ideas, or even words in isolation. We need a context, a sense of the whole into which the new piece of information fits. The more familiar you are with the dimensions and content of the piece before you begin to read, the better able you will be to read with understanding—whether you're reading three sentences or three volumes.

Figure out as much as you can before beginning to read. How long is the piece? You'll want to estimate how much time you'll need to complete it. What's the title? The title usually points to something significant about the writer's topic or tone. Like the label on a candy bar, the title of an article tells you something about what's inside. Who wrote it? Knowing something about the author helps you predict what the essay might be about. Is the author dead or alive? What is his or her nationality: Canadian, American, or Tasmanian? Is he a humorist or a social critic? Or is she a journalist or an academic? Is the author a specialist in a particular field?

What about the body of the work? Does it include any diagrams or illustrations? Are there any subheadings that indicate the division of the material into main ideas? Finally, for the readings in this text, don't forget the context we've provided for you: the unit in which each essay is found gives you a clue to the kind of organization and development you can expect.

3. Read the Essay All the Way Through.

This is a very important step, and it isn't always easy. Most inexperienced readers have a fairly short attention span—about eight to ten minutes, or about the length of program time between commercials—and they need to train themselves to increase it. You need to read the piece all the way through in order to get a sense of the whole; otherwise, you cannot fully understand either the essay or its parts.

As you read the essays in this text, note the words marked with a °: it signals that the meaning of the word or phrase is given in the Words and Meanings section following the essay. If you're unfamiliar with the term, check the definition we offer and continue reading. Underline any other words whose meaning you cannot figure out from the context. You'll look them up later.

This first time through, withhold judgment. Don't allow your prejudices—in the root sense of the word, "prejudgments"—to affect your response at this stage. If you decide in advance that the topic is boring ("Who cares about baked beans?") or the style is too demanding ("I couldn't possibly understand anything titled 'The Huxleyan Warning'!"), you cheat yourself out of a potentially rewarding experience. Give the writer a chance; part of his or her responsibility is to make the writing interesting and accessible to the reader. Another point to keep in mind is that reading is like any other exercise: it gets easier, or at least less painful, with practice. You'll get better at it and soon be able to tackle increasingly difficult challenges.

You haven't forgotten your pencil, have you? Here's where it comes into the act. Try to identify the main parts of the essay as you read: the INTRODUCTION, the main parts into which the body is divided, and the CONCLUSION. If they are obvious, underline the THESIS—often expressed in a thesis statement in the introduction—and each main point, usually expressed in the TOPIC SENTENCE of a PARAGRAPH. When you come across a sentence or passage you don't understand, put a question mark in the margin. Key terms that appear in CAPITALS in the introduction and in the questions are explained in the List of Useful Terms at the end of the book.

Good writers "set up" their material for you: they identify their subject early, and indicate the scope of their essay. They use various TRANSITIONS to signal to the reader that they have concluded one idea and are moving on to another. Note, however, that this first read-through is not the time to stop and analyze the structure and writing strategies in detail. You need to read the piece a second (or even a third) time to accomplish such analysis successfully.

If you've been practising what we've been suggesting here, you will *not* have stopped to look up INTRODUCTION, CONCLUSION, THESIS, TOPIC SENTENCE, PARAGRAPH, or TRANSITION in the List of Useful Terms. The time to look up the meaning of these and any other unfamiliar terms is when you have finished reading through this whole section.

4. Look Up the Meaning of Any Words You Didn't Understand.

Here's where your dictionary comes in. Look up the words you under-lined as you read through the essay—but don't just seize on the first definition given and assume this is the meaning the author intended. Read *all* the meanings given. Note that some words can be used both as nouns and as verbs; only one set of meanings will be ap-propriate in the context you are reading. When you're satisfied you've located the appropriate definition, jot it down in the margin beside the mystery word.

Now go back and reread any passages you noted with a question mark the first time through. Once you have figured out any vocabulary problems that initially bothered you, and now that you have an overview of the whole piece, you should find that the meaning of those confusing passages is much clearer.

5. Read the Questions Following the Essay.

After you've answered all your questions about the piece, go through the questions on Structure and Strategy and Content and Purpose that we have provided. You won't be able to answer them all at this point. The purpose of reading the questions now is to prepare yourself for a second, closer reading of the essay. These questions will guide you eventually to a thorough understanding of the essay. At this point, however, all you need to know is the sorts of questions you'll be considering after your second reading.

6. Read the Essay a Second Time—Slowly, Carefully.

Got your pencil ready? Identify the INTRODUCTION, the part of the essay that establishes the subject, the limits of the subject, and the writer's TONE. If you haven't already done so your first time through, underline the THESIS and main points. Make notes in the margins. Use the margins to jot down in point form an outline of the piece, to add supplementary—or contradictory—evidence, or to call attention to particularly significant or eloquently expressed ideas. Circle key TRANSITIONS. The physical act of writing as you read helps keep your attention focussed on the article and can serve to deepen your un-derstanding of both its content and its structure.

Think about the AUDIENCE the writer is addressing. Are you in-cluded in the group for whom the writer intended the essay? If not, you should remember that your reactions to and interpretations of the piece may differ from those of the intended readers. For example, if you are male, your response to Steinem's essay, "Erotica and

Pornography: A Clear and Present Difference," will probably be somewhat different from that of the committed feminists who are Steinem's primary target.

During your second reading, identify the writer's main PURPOSE. Is it to inform, to persuade, or to entertain? Notice, too, how the writer develops the main points. Be sure you distinguish between the main ideas and the supporting details—the EXAMPLES, ILLUSTRATIONS, DEFINITIONS, ANALOGIES—that the writer has used to make the ideas clear to the reader. As you read, be conscious of the writer's TONE: is it humorous or serious, impassioned or objective, formal or informal? Good writers choose their tone very carefully, since it directly affects the reader's response, probably more than any other technical aspect of writing.

Finally, consider the CONCLUSION of the essay. Does it simply restate the thesis or expand on it in some way? Are you left with a sense of the essay's completeness, a feeling that all questions raised in the piece have been satisfactorily answered? Or do you feel that you've been left dangling, that some of the loose ends have yet to be tied up?

At this point, you have a decision to make. Are you satisfied that you understand the essay? Are the writer's purpose, thesis, main ideas, and method of development all clear to you? If so, go on to step 7. If not—as often happens when you are learning to read analytically, or when you encounter a particularly challenging piece— go back and read it through a third time.

7. Answer the Questions Following the Essay.

Consider the questions carefully, one by one, and prepare your answers. Refer to the essay often to keep yourself on the right track. Most of the questions don't have simple, or single, answers! Jot down your answers in point form or in short phrases in the margins of the text.

The purpose of the questions is to engage you as deeply as possible in the structure and meaning of each essay. As you analyze *what* the writer has said (the content and purpose) and *how* he or she has said it (the structure and strategies), you will come as close as you can to full understanding. At this point you are ready to test your understanding in classroom discussion or through writing a paper of your own.

2. How to Write to Be Understood

Learning to read with understanding will help you write so that what you say is clearly understood. As you become conscious of the process readers use to make sense of a piece of writing, you will become increasingly skilful at predicting and satisfying the needs of *your* readers. For years you've probably been told, "Keep your audience in mind as you write." By itself, this is not a particularly helpful piece of advice. You need to know not only *who your audience is*, including how much they know and how they feel about your subject, but also *how readers read*. These two pieces of knowledge are the keys to writing understandable prose. (We are assuming here that you have a firm grasp of your subject matter. You cannot write clearly and convincingly about something you don't really understand.)

As long as you know what you are writing about and whom you are writing for, there are five steps you can take to ensure your readers will understand what it is you have to say. The approach we're presenting here applies to all kinds of expository and persuasive writing; that is, to any piece of writing in which your purpose is to *explain* something—a process, a relationship, a complex idea— or to *persuade* your readers to think or act in a particular way.

Writing a paper is like going on a journey: it makes sense—and it's certainly more efficient—to fix on your destination and plan your route *before* you begin. Your subject is your destination. The main points determine the route you select to get to your destination. In other words, your main points determine the kind of paper you are going to write.

In this text we explain seven of the most basic kinds of essay organization: seven different approaches to explaining a subject, seven different routes to a destination. Something we want to emphasize is that there is no *one way* to explain a subject. A **subject**, like a destination on a map, can be approached from many different directions.

Take the subject of education, for example. It is very broad, very general. Now, if you flip through the introductions to the first seven units of this book, you will see that each introduction ends with a model essay illustrating the organizational pattern explained in that unit. All of these model essays are on the subject of education, but they are all different. We've limited the subject seven different ways, chosen seven different sets of **main points**, seven different organ-izational patterns—seven different paths to the goal. Read these model essays carefully, and you'll discover how the pattern discussed in each unit can lend shape, coherence, and unity to the subject you're writing about.

As you will have discovered by now, people who are reading for information, for understanding, don't like surprises: no bumps or potholes, no sudden shifts in direction, no dead ends. They appre-ciate a well-marked, smooth path through the writer's prose. So your task is to identify the path for them, set them on it, and guide them through to the end. If you can keep them interested, even entertained, on their journey, so much the better. As you read through the essays in this book, you will encounter a variety of stylistic devices you can use to add interest and impact to your own writing.

Here are the five steps to clear, well-organized writing:
1. clarify your subject
2. identify the main points of your subject
3. write a thesis statement
4. develop the paragraphs
5. revise the paper.
If you follow these five steps carefully, in order, we guarantee that you will write papers that an attentive reader will be able to under-stand—and perhaps even enjoy!

Steps 1, 2, and 3 are the *preparation* stage of the writing process. Be warned: these three steps will take you as long as—if not longer than—steps 4 and 5, which involve the actual *writing*. There is a general rule that governs all expository and persuasive writing: the longer you spend on preparation, the less time the writing will take, and the better your paper will be.

Step 1: Clarify Your Subject.

The subject of your paper or report may be one assigned by a teacher or by your supervisor. Worse, you may have to come up with one on your own. Choosing a satisfactory subject can be the most difficult part of writing an easy-to-understand piece of prose. Inexperienced writers often choose a subject that is far bigger than either their knowledge or the space allotted to them can justify.

A suitable subject is one that is both *specific* and *supportable*. A thorough, detailed discussion of a single, specific topic is much more satisfying to read than a general, superficial treatment of a very broad topic. This is why Russell Baker chose to contrast Toronto and New York rather than Canada and the United States in his essay, "A Nice Place to Visit" (see Unit Four). You can narrow a broad subject by applying one or more limiting factors to it. Think of your subject in terms of a specific *kind*, or *time*, or *place*, or *number*, or *person* associated with it. To contrast Canadian and American lifestyles, for example, Baker limited his subject in terms of place (two contrasting cities) and time (his most recent experience).

A subject is supportable if you can develop it with examples, facts, quotations, descriptions, anecdotes, comparisons, definitions, and other supporting details. These supporting details are called EVIDENCE; we will discuss its use more fully under Step 4, below. Evidence, combined with good organization, makes your discussion of a subject both clear and convincing.

Step 2: Identify the Main Points of Your Subject.

Once you have clarified your subject, think about the approach you're going to use to explain it. There are many possible ways of thinking and writing about any subject. In a short paper, you can deal effectively with only a few aspects of a subject, even a very specific one. But how do you decide what is the best approach to take? How do you decide which aspects of your subject to discuss and what main points to make and explain?

One way to sort through these choices is to do some preliminary research. Another technique some writers use is to jot down everything they can think of about their subject until they "freewrite" or "brainstorm" their way to an organizational pattern. Perhaps the surest way to approach a subject—especially if you're stuck for ideas—is to ask yourself some specific questions about it. Apply the following list of questions, one at a time, to your subject and see which question "fits" it best—which question calls up in your mind answers that approximate what it is you want to say. **(The symbol "S" stands for your subject.)**

If this is the question that fits	Then this is the kind of paper you will be writing
1. What are some significant examples of S?	EXAMPLE
2. How is S made or done? 3. How does S work?	PROCESS ANALYSIS
4. What are the component parts of S? 5. What are the important features or characteristics of S? 6. What are the main kinds of S?	DIVISION/CLASSIFICATION

7. What are the similarities
   and/or differences between   COMPARISON/CONTRAST
   S and X?

8. What are the causes of S? ⎱
9. What are the effects or   ⎰ CAUSE/EFFECT
   consequences of S?

10. What does S mean?   DEFINITION

11. What are the main
    advantages (or
    disadvantages) of S?   ⎱ PERSUASION
12. What are the reasons for   ⎰
    (or against) S?

These questions suggest seven different ways of looking at or thinking about a subject. When you discover the question that elicits the
answers that are closest to what you know and want to write about,
then you will have discovered what kind of paper you need to write.
The answers to the best question are the aspects of the subject you
will discuss; they become the main points of your paper. The seven
different types of papers listed in the right-hand column above cor-
respond to the seven rhetorical patterns presented in this text. To
find out how to arrange and develop your main points to produce an
effective paper, turn to the introduction of the appropriate unit.

Step 3: Write a Thesis Statement.

A thesis statement in your INTRODUCTION is the clearest way to organize a short paper of 350 to 800 words. It plans your paper for
you, and it tells your reader what he or she is going to read about.
Remember: "no surprises" is the watchword when you write, unless
you're writing mystery stories. To continue the analogy between reading an essay and taking a trip, the thesis statement is a kind of map:
it identifies both your destination and the route. Like a map, it keeps
your reader (and you) on the right track.

   To be specific, a thesis statement clearly tells your reader the
subject of your paper, the main points you will discuss, and the order
in which you will discuss them. Not all essays contain thesis statements. In some of the essays in this book, for example, you will
notice that the THESIS is implied rather than explicitly stated. However,
we recommend that you include a thesis statement in every paper
you write. There is probably no writing strategy you can use that is
more helpful to your readers' understanding of what you've written.

   To write a thesis statement, you join your *subject* to the *main
points* (arranged in an appropriate ORDER) by means of a linking

word such as *are, because, since, include,* or a colon. Here is a simple formula, or blueprint, for a thesis statement (S stands for your *subject*; a, b, c, d stand for your *main points*):

> S consists of a, b, c, d . . . .

The introduction to each unit of this text contains a formula to follow when constructing a thesis statement for the particular type of paper presented in that unit.

Here are some examples of thesis statements taken from essays included in our collection:

"There are three dimensions of a complete life: length, breadth, and height." (*Dimensions of a Complete Life*)

"Three passions, simple but overwhelmingly strong, have governed my life: the longing for love, the search for knowledge, and unbearable pity for the suffering of mankind." (*What I Have Lived For*)

"In spite of ourselves, we have been changed by technology in our values, in our expectations, and in the 'needs' we feel." (*Resisting the Revolution*)

"General education is an essential part of the curriculum because it enhances one's ability to build a career and to live a full life." (*Why Are We Reading This, Anyway?*)

"Most educators agree that the principal causes of failure in school are lack of basic skills, lack of study skills, and lack of motivation." (*Why Students Fail*)

Note that the main points in a thesis statement should be expressed in PARALLEL STRUCTURE. See the List of Useful Terms for an explanation of parallel structure.

Step 4: Develop the Paragraphs.

Each of your main points will be developed in a paragraph, sometimes in two or three paragraphs. Each paragraph should contain a TOPIC SENTENCE that clearly states the main idea or topic of that paragraph. Often the topic sentence comes at the beginning of the paragraph so that the reader knows what to expect from the very beginning. The next five, six, or more sentences develop the topic. The key to making the paragraph unified (see UNITY) is to make sure that every one of the supporting sentences relates directly to the topic. An adequately developed paragraph includes enough supporting information to make the topic clear to the reader.

How do you decide what is the best way to develop a particular paragraph? How much support should you include? What kind of support should it be? To make these decisions, try putting yourself in your reader's place. What does he or she need to know in order to understand your point clearly? If you ask yourself the five questions listed below, you'll be able to decide how to develop your topic sentence.

1. Is a *definition* needed? If you're using a term that may be unfamiliar to your readers, you should define it—phrasing it in your own words, please, rather than citing a quotation from a dictionary. The Introduction to Unit Six will show you how to define terms.

2. Would two or three *examples* help clarify the point? Providing examples is probably the most common method of developing a topic. Readers may be confused or even suspicious when they read unsupported generalizations or statements of opinion. Providing specific, relevant examples will help them to understand your point. The Introduction to Unit One will show you how to use examples effectively.

3. Is a *series of steps or stages* involved? Are you explaining a process to your reader? Sometimes the most logical way to make your point clear is to explain how something is done—that is, to relate, in order, the steps involved. The Introduction to Unit Two will give you detailed directions for this kind of development.

4. Would a *comparison* or *contrast* help make your explanation clearer? Your reader will find it easier to understand something new if you explain it in terms of something he or she is already familiar with. A *comparison* points out similarities between objects, people, or ideas; a *contrast* shows how the objects, people, or ideas are different. The Introduction to Unit Four provides a detailed description of this technique.

5. Would a *quotation* or *paraphrase* be appropriate? Would your reader be convinced by reading the words of someone else who shares your opinion? Occasionally you will find that another individual—an expert in a particular field, a well-known author, or a respected public figure—has said what you want to say so well that your own paper can only benefit from including it. Quotations, so long as they are kept short and not used too frequently, can also add EMPHASIS to an idea. Sometimes you don't want to quote directly from another writer, but to rephrase the writer's idea in your own words. It's up to you to decide what the essential points

are and then word them in a way suited to the needs of your paper. This technique is called paraphrasing. (The List of Useful Terms provides a fuller explanation of PARAPHRASE.)

Whenever you use a quotation or a paraphrase, of course, you *must* acknowledge your source out of respect for the writer. Otherwise you are committing plagiarism—pretending that someone else's words or ideas are your own.

If you glance at the unit titles in the Contents, you will see that some of these methods of paragraph development are also structural principles on which whole essays can be based. Because of their multipurpose character, it is essential that you become familiar and comfortable with all five strategies.

The methods you choose to develop a point should be determined by your readers' needs and expectations. If you have a clear picture of your audience, you'll be able to choose the appropriate kinds and amount of development they require if they are to follow you with ease. You can, of course, use more than one method to develop a paragraph; sometimes a comparison can be effectively coupled with a quotation, for example. There is no fixed rule that governs the kind or number of development strategies required in any particular paragraph. The decision is yours. Your responsibility as a writer is to keep in mind what your readers know and what they need to know in order to understand the points you're making.

Once you have developed your main points, you will add two important paragraphs: the INTRODUCTION and CONCLUSION. All too often, these parts of a paper are dull, clumsy, or repetitive. But they shouldn't be and they needn't be. If carefully constructed, these paragraphs can effectively catch your reader's attention and clinch your argument. The List of Useful Terms contains specific strategies you can choose from in crafting a beginning and ending for your paper.

As you write your paragraphs, keep in mind that you want to make it as easy as possible for your reader to follow you through your paper. TRANSITIONS and TONE can make the difference between a confusing, annoying paper and an informative, pleasing one. *Transitions* are words or phrases that show the relationship between one point and the next, causing a paragraph (or a paper) to hang together and read smoothly. Transitions are like the turn signals on a car: they tell the person following you where you're going. The List of Useful Terms will give you suggestions for appropriate transitional phrases, depending on what kind of relationship between the ideas you want to signal.

Tone is the word used to describe a writer's attitude towards the subject and the reader. A writer may feel angry about a subject, or amused, or nostalgic, and this attitude is reflected in the words, examples, quotations, and other supporting details he or she chooses to explain the main points. Good writing is usually modulated in tone; the writer addresses the reader with respect, in a calm, reasonable way. Writing that is highly emotional in tone is not often very convincing to the readers: what gets communicated is the strength of the writer's feelings rather than the writer's depth of knowledge or validity of opinion about the subject.

Two suggestions may help you find and maintain the right tone. First, never insult your reader unintentionally with phrases such as "any idiot can see that . . . ," or "no sane person could believe . . . ," or even "it is obvious that. . . . " Remember that what seems obvious to you is not necessarily obvious to someone who has a limited knowledge of your subject or who disagrees with your opinion. Second, don't condescend—talk down—to your reader, and don't use heavy-handed sarcasm. On the other hand, you need not apologize for your opinion. You've thought about your subject and taken considerable time to develop it. Present your information in a positive rather than a hesitant way: avoid phrases such as "I tend to believe that . . . " or "I may be wrong, but. . . . " Have confidence in yourself and in your ideas.

Step 5: Revise the Paper.

At last you've reached the final step in the writing process. Even though you are by now probably thoroughly sick of the whole project and very eager to be rid of it, *do not* omit this important final step. Revising, which means "looking back," is essential before your paper is ready to be sent out into the world. Ideally, you should revise several days after writing the paper. After a "cooling-off" period, you'll be able to see your work more objectively. If you reread it immediately after you've finished writing, you're likely to "read" what you *think* you've written—what's in your head rather than what's really on the page.

Thorough revision requires at least two reviews of your paper. The first time you go over it, read it aloud, slowly, from beginning to end, keeping your audience in mind as you read. Is your thesis clear? Are all the points adequately explained? Has anything been left out? Are the paragraphs unified and coherent? Are there any awkward sentences that should be rephrased?

The second time you read your paper through, read it with the Editing Checklist (on the inside of the back cover) in front of you for easy reference. Pay special attention to the points that tend to give you trouble; for example, sentence fragments, verb errors, apostrophes, or dangling modifiers. Most writers know their weaknesses. Unfortunately, it's human nature to focus on our strengths and try to gloss over our weaknesses. This is the reason why editing your work can be a painful process. Nevertheless, it is an absolutely essential task. You owe it both to yourself and to your reader to find and correct any errors in your writing.

If you are a poor speller, you will need to read your paper a third time. This time, read it through from the end to the beginning to check your spelling. Reading from back to front, you're forced to look at each word individually, not in context, and thus you are more likely to spot your spelling mistakes. If you are truly a hopeless speller, ask someone to identify the errors for you. Better yet, learn to use a spell-checking program on a word processor.

A final word of advice: whether you are in school or on the job, always make a copy of your paper before you hand it in. You wouldn't want to have to go through this whole process again if your paper got misplaced!

If you follow these five steps carefully, you and your reader will arrive at your destination without any accident, mishap, or wrong turns. The journey should be relatively painless for you, and informative—perhaps even enjoyable—for your reader.

U N I T

Example: Explaining with Word Pictures

What? The Definition

If someone were to tell you that the Canadian music industry has made a major contribution to the third generation of rock'n'roll, you would probably be puzzled—even if you think you really know the rock scene. However, your confusion would quickly evaporate if the speaker were to explain by using the kind of word pictures we call **examples**. For instance, Bryan Adams and Corey Hart are two examples of contemporary Canadian rock artists who have a creative, professional approach. The idea of rock's "third generation" becomes clear if you think of Elvis Presley as the father of the first generation and of The Beatles as the leaders of the second generation. These recognizable examples make the opening statement understandable to anyone who knows even a little about the rock industry.

An *example* is something selected from a class of things and used to show the character of all of them. Examples may be briefly stated instances of people, places, ideas, or things: three examples of automobiles manufactured in Germany are BMW, Audi, and Mercedes-Benz. Examples may also be developed at greater length: an extended example is sometimes called an *illustration*—that is, it is a "word picture." Examples or illustrations are essential in effective writing because they enable the reader to visualize the concept you are explaining. Both are needed if you want to be clear—and, furthermore, they're interesting.

Why? The Purpose

Explaining a subject by offering examples of it is probably the simplest of the various strategies available to a writer. Example papers answer the question, "What are some significant examples of S?" By identifying and explaining a few significant examples of your subject, you ensure that your reader understands what you mean. The consequences of *not* including examples can be disastrous, especially when you are trying to explain a concept or principle.

Here's an example of what we mean: every student has, at one time or another, suffered through a course given by a Droner. He's the instructor who, whether lecturing on the mysteries of quantum theory, the intricacies of accounting, or the subtleties of the semicolon, drones on and on, oblivious to the snores of his slumbering students. Often the Droner has his material down cold; he knows all about physics, balance sheets, or punctuation—in theory, or what we call the ABSTRACT. But the Droner is unable or unwilling to relate these concepts to experiences that we can all understand. He cannot make the abstract principles CONCRETE for his listeners. His lectures lack specific examples that the students can picture in their minds or relate to their past experience to help them understand the concept he is trying so insensitively to explain.

Abstract words refer to ideas or qualities that we can't experience through our physical senses: words such as *love, evil, truth, justice, success*. Abstractions should be used cautiously in writing. Too many of them produce fuzzy generalities that explain little. Does the statement "Everyone needs love" refer to the "love" of a tender parent-child relationship or that of a torrid back-seat passion? Unless "love" is made concrete by the addition of examples or illustrations, the statement remains unclear. Your reader may well understand it to mean something quite different from what you intended. Good writing is a careful blend of abstract and concrete, general statement and specific examples. Thus, one important function of examples is to explain an abstraction or generality by providing vivid, familiar word pictures.

Another function of examples is to support or back up a statement, particularly a statement of your opinion about something. In this case, the use of examples becomes a persuasive strategy. If, for instance, you wanted to convince your reader that job prospects for college and university graduates are improving, you could provide statistical examples of increased hiring by major industries. Perhaps you might assemble instances of recent recruitment drives on campus by companies such as Bell Canada, Alcan, and the Bank of Montreal. Again, you use examples to clarify ideas and help persuade your reader that your opinion is valid.

Thus, examples are valuable on two counts. First, they ground your abstract concepts in concrete reality that your reader can see and understand. Second, they lend substance and credibility to your THESIS, the point you are making in your paper. If you use examples well, you'll ensure that your words don't suffer the fate of the Droner's: lost to the ears of a snoring audience.

We expect to find vivid word pictures in good writing. Examples bring ideas to life, and, therefore, we find them not just in the kind of paper we've been discussing in this chapter, but in all kinds of writing. Writers of classification, process analysis, comparison, or any other rhetorical pattern often use examples to illustrate or emphasize important points. Peter Goddard, for instance, uses examples to clarify ideas and interest the reader in his classification essay, "How to Spot Rock Types."

How? The Technique ☀

Examples may be chosen from several sources: personal experience, the experience of others, quotations, statistics, or facts you've discovered through research. Whatever kinds of examples you choose to use, organizing and developing your paper require careful thought. The overall thesis must be clear and the scope of the examples appropriate to the thesis.

Your thesis statement will probably look something like this:

> Some examples of S are a, b, c. . . .

Example: Three Canadian doctors who have made significant contributions to human welfare are Frederick Banting, Hans Selye, and Norman Bethune.

All you need to do now is develop each example in turn. At the end of this introduction we've included a short essay based on this thesis statement so you can see what the finished product looks like.

Examples are an all-purpose tool on the writer's workbench. They make your general ideas specific, your thesis convincing, and your communication interesting. Using a good example or two is also a sure-fire way to liven up an introduction or conclusion. Examples reach out and grab the reader's attention.

Now that you're aware of the usefulness of examples in your writing, you should know the three "safety rules" to follow when selecting them:

1. Make sure each example is *representative* of your subject. Gordie Howe is not a "typical hockey player," nor is Montreal's Westmount your "average Canadian neighbourhood." The examples you choose must be typical enough to represent fairly the group or the idea you are explaining.

2. Make sure all examples are *pertinent*. They must be relevant, significant, and acceptable to your audience as examples of the quality or idea they've been chosen to illustrate. For instance, most readers would recognize Donald Sutherland as a Canadian actor who is an international star. The same readers might not accept Kate Nelligan as an example of the same phenomenon, since it's debatable whether or not she is internationally renowned. And if you were to identify Madonna as your example, your whole paper would be called into question, since she's not even Canadian.

3. Make sure the range and number of your examples is *limited*. You're not writing the Sears catalogue, throwing in every colour and size in a jumbled and eventually overwhelming list. There is no set number of examples to include. How many you need depends on your purpose. The challenge is to be both selective and comprehensive, to include just enough examples to convey your idea clearly and forcefully.

Following the structural principles and the safety rules outlined here will ensure that your paper is soundly constructed and communicates exactly what you want it to, as the essay below demonstrates:

The Social Value of Education

Introduction ——————▶

Most of us think of higher education as something we engage in because it will benefit us personally. We often overlook the fact that education does more than just develop the mind and spirit or prepare us for a career. The education we acquire for personal reasons also benefits the society in which we live, some-

Thesis statement:
(S plus three examples) →

Paragraph 2 develops
first example in thesis
statement ——————

Paragraph 3 develops
second example ——————

times in surprising ways. Medical doctors, for example, are among our most highly educated citizens and are in a position to promote not only the health of their patients but also the well-being of our society. Three Canadian medical doctors who have made significant contributions to human welfare are Frederick Banting, Hans Selye, and Norman Bethune.

Frederick Banting (1891–1941) was born in Alliston, Ontario, and educated at the University of Toronto. He served in the Army Medical Corps in World War I. During the early 1920s, he joined a team of biochemical researchers at the University of Toronto. Along with physiologist Charles Best, Banting discovered the internal secretion of the pancreas, which they named "insulin." An insufficient supply of insulin causes the disease known as diabetes. The discovery and production of insulin made it possible to control the disease, thus saving or prolonging the lives of countless diabetics. Banting's contribution to this momentous medical achievement won him the Nobel Prize for Medicine and Physiology in 1923.

Hans Selye (1907–1983), a Vienna-born endocrinologist, was a physician who specialized in the study of the glands in the body that secrete hormones. After studying in Prague, Paris, and Rome, Selye joined the faculty of McGill University in 1932 and in 1945 became the first director of the Institute of Experimental Medicine and Surgery at the University of Montreal. Over the next three decades, Selye's research and publications made him the world's foremost expert on the effects of stress on the human body. Through his books and lectures, he popularized the notion that there are two kinds of stress. One, "eustress," is beneficial and leads to accomplishment and healing. The other, "distress," is the kind more familiar to us. It is destructive: it breaks down the body and leads to diseases such as high blood pressure, ulcers, mental illness, even cancer. Selye's work has thus contributed to our understanding of the effects of stress not only on the individual but also on society, since a general increase in frustration and anxiety may lead to an overall increase in the incidence of disease.

Paragraph 4 develops
third example ——→ Norman Bethune (1890–1939), who was born in Gravenhurst, Ontario, studied medicine in Toronto and in England. He had a strong social conscience and throughout his life used his medical knowledge and skill to relieve the suffering of the poor. After contracting tuberculosis in the 1920s, he moved to Quebec, where he experimented with various treatments of that disease. His research led to improvements in the technology and techniques of chest surgery. Meanwhile, Bethune's leftist political views prompted him to challenge the conservative Canadian medical establishment and eventually to join the Communist party. His political commitment led him in 1936 to fight in the Spanish Civil War. There he organized the first mobile blood-transfusion service, an innovation that saved thousands of lives. In 1938, Bethune's commitment to the anti-fascist cause took him to China, which was then defending itself against the Japanese invasion. In China he worked tirelessly to bring the benefits of modern medicine to a peasant people. Though Bethune died of blood poisoning after he had been in China only a year, his humanitarian efforts and devotion to the downtrodden made him a

hero and enhanced the reputation of Canada among the Chinese people.

Conclusion ————→

These three Canadian physicians are good examples of the social value of education. Whether a person is engaged in medicine or business, teaching or technology, the education he or she acquires helps others. Though our achievements may be less dramatic than those of Banting, Selye, or Bethune, what we learn will inevitably benefit not just ourselves but also the people around us, and, by extension, society as a whole.

By Their Foods . . .

HUGH MACLENNAN

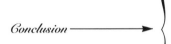

uring my life I have twice been asked by letter to tell what I like best to eat and why, my answers to be included in two separate publications. The requests were flattering, so I tried to narrow down my choices to some *pièce de résistance°* by which, gastronomically° speaking, I might become celebrated. In the end I welshed° on my answers, for you might as well publish the results of your Rorschach test as give a description of your favourite food. Favourite dishes can be as revealing as recurrent dreams; even the neophyte° traveller learns as much about a nation's character by observing what its people eat as by talking for hours to its cab drivers.

Germans, for instance, have an obsession with caraway, and caraway lurks in every dish, a fatal undertone beneath the heavy, seemingly honest surface of German food, and you get into the habit of waiting for those black, curled little seeds to catch in your teeth, for the abrupt incongruousness° of the caraway taste to shock your taste buds, just as you get into the habit of expecting a fatally recurrent behaviour-pattern to show up in German politics.

Austrians love pastries and whipped cream, succulent torten° and rich brioches, bread with little nutriment but baked with

1

2

3

From *The Other Side of Hugh MacLennan* ed. Elspeth Cameron. © 1978 by Hugh MacLennan. Reprinted by permission of Macmillan of Canada, A Division of Canada Publishing Corporation.

crunchy crusts delicious to tongue and teeth. Charming they indubitably are, these people who suffer the tragedy of living just below a nation of caraway-eaters, and wise (or infatuated) in their determination to disguise the bitterness of life wherever possible. The coffee drunk by the Austrians is a dark and heavy brew, but as your taste dwells with the whipped cream floating on top, its bitterness is revealed only in the final drops.

4   Perfect in its ardour° is the food of Italy. Not only the pizzas, spaghettis, macaronis, and raviolis with their divine harmonies of parmesan, ground meats, onions, tomatoes, and herbs, but the chianti°, so honestly rough on the tongue it forms a bridge from the pastas to the fresh figs, oranges, tangerines, and walnuts that cap a true Italian meal—such a diet breeds people of a fine but delicate vanity, opera singers, and beautifully understanding women, but few successful lusters after power.

5   Most complicated, and complicated without being subtle is the diet of that intricate people, the Swedes. Strong, contrasting textures, robust flavours implicitly critical of each other, an immense variety of carefully thought-out detail enclosed within a single central idea—that is *smorgasbord*. The smoked eels, fish, and meats of Sweden are beyond compare, the pickles blunt but seldom sour, the vegetables fresh. Neither delicate nor rich, masculine but not uneasily so, neither one thing nor the other but everything simultaneously, all excellent, *smorgasbord* is the logical calculation of Swedish life.

6   Being a Swede, Swedes tell me, is not easy, because it means being a repository° and practitioner of the best that has been taught, felt, discovered, and done in all the countries of the West, Sweden itself included. Being a successful Swede means that you have to be dynamic and static at the same time, tolerant and critical at the same time, jealous and magnanimous, virile and unaggressive all at once. The static intensity natural to Sweden can be observed in a Stockholm restaurant by anyone who watches a group of Swedes, grave and judicious, not so much attacking the *smorgasbord* as permitting their critical sense to play with this particular example of it. It is necessary for them to be sure whether the *smorgasbord* is as good as it ought to be or could be, and whether it is worthy of them and they of it, and when a foreigner sees a Swede in this condition the kindest thing he can do is to attack the *smorgasbord* himself. His enjoyment of it—or rather the fact that his enjoyment is so obvious—reassures the Swede both as regards the food of his country and his own feeling that he is more self-restrained than foreigners.

7   Of all the national diets I have sampled, the most portentous° is the Russian. Those who eat heartily in Russia are few, or were

few until very recently, but this makes no difference because these few are the only Russians who count. In 1937 I spent part of a summer in Leningrad and Moscow, eating in Intourist hotels, and even now when I remember the food and the people who enjoyed it, I tremble.

Russian food is almost exclusively protein, with a limited interlarding of fat. At breakfast, which is served any time between nine and noon, I was offered five or six boiled eggs along with caviar, bread, and tea. At lunch, which dragged on from two in the afternoon until four-thirty, caviar was followed by *borscht°* and topped by several courses of meat and fowl accompanied by tea. Dinner was more of the same except that it was much more, and the Russians who came to the hotel to eat generally settled down to their tables about midnight. After consuming huge slabs of pressed caviar, they worked their way through more *borscht*, more meat and fowl, and were offered (I can't remember whether it was before or after the meats) ponderous side dishes of head cheese, plates of smoked sturgeon, eels, and herring, and salmon pressed into shapes enriched with devilled eggs. While they chewed onward, they refreshed themselves with innumerable cups of pale tea, and most of them drank vodka and sweet Crimean champagne, and somewhere around two-thirty in the morning they at last stopped eating and went on their way. Only a people of colossal ambition and lack of subtlety could exist on such a diet, much less invent it. Churchill warned the world what to expect of Russia when he told us that Stalin, after eating a meal much larger than the one I have just described, settled down in his private quarters to an extra dinner consisting of a roast suckling pig. After eating the whole of it, he went back to work. 8

During all my time in Russia—this is the most significant note of all—I never saw a leaf of lettuce, or even a leaf of cabbage, that had not been turned into a heavy soup. One morning I woke up with the insides of my cheeks so swollen I couldn't close my jaws without biting chunks out of myself. From my boyhood reading of the life aboard sailing ships I knew this condition was caused by an excess of protein and an absence of fruit and greens. I searched for greens in vain, but I did manage to find some honeydew melons kept by the *maître d'hôtel* as decorations on his sideboard. I bought three of them at two dollars apiece, and by midafternoon I was able to sit up and eat my caviar. 9

Chinese food, in the judgment of most travellers, is the finest there is, but to me it is decadent°. Not in the way of the eating habits of the later Romans, of course; there is no record that the Chinese ever ate nightingales' tongues, or installed vomitoria as adjuncts to their banqueting halls, or that any Chinese emperor 10 followed the example of Heliogabalus in promising a consulship or a province to the cook who invented a new sauce. Yet it is obvious that a man who enjoys thirty or forty courses for dinner, no matter how sparingly he may eat of each, is in danger of declining, even though his final fall may be accomplished with grace and a conviction that his previous life has been well spent. Chinese cooks on the grand scale seem to me not cooks at all, but Toscaninis° of food, nor does anything give me more hope for the ultimate failure of Russian ambitions in China than the contrast between the tastes of these two peoples at table. Their incompatibility is total.

11   Of American cooking, apart from those restaurants in New York which offer specialities from all over the world, what can we say except that it is the most hygienic, scientifically balanced, and vitamin-conscious available? It is absolutely forthright, and no American dish above the Mason and Dixon Line ever pretends to be other than what it is. Nor is American food by any means as varied as Americans believe it to be, despite the thousands of recipes published yearly in women's magazines, for variety is bound to be limited when both cook and eater agree that what counts as the final standard of excellence is the quality of the raw materials, and when nearly everybody wants to top off with ice cream. Only in New Orleans, where a Creole tradition in decline united with a climate that often spoiled uncooked food, do you find any exaggerated development of highly flavoured sauces. Throughout the rest of the country steaks from the primest of beeves, chickens guaranteed tender by metal tags, salad-greens and vegetables scientifically grown and Cellophane-wrapped for the market, potatoes mealy and incomparable from Maine and Idaho—American food is as direct as American prose literature and (so say European connoisseurs) American love-making.

12   Of all the foods I know, the most fascinating is the English, for like everything else English, it cannot be considered apart from history, nor is its message in any sense as simple as it seems. While the empire was a-building, Englishmen ate massive meals of protein and starch, but once the empire was built, the English ruling classes tried to come to terms with a dilemma their knowledge of history told them was critical for their national existence. If they enjoyed the pleasures of the table too much (and now they could utilize all the diets known to man) they would lose their empire for the same reason the Romans lost theirs. Yet what was the use of the empire if it condemned them to living permanently on Brussels sprouts?

13   The ruling class of England thereupon came to a typically English compromise. Indifferent to the lower classes, themselves ac-

customed to spending at least a month of every year on the Continent where they could eat the delicious foods of decadence, they decided to outdo Sparta° within the home island, nor was any law necessary to guarantee the moral salubrity° of English restaurant food. By that extrasensory perception which enables the island to survive, English cooks saw their duty and did it. Hence the boiled meats and fish, the cabbages and sprouts dripping with lukewarm water, the incredible gooseberry fools°, the one all-purpose sauce that looks like ground caterpillars and is used to lubricate everything erroneously called a sweet°. But those foreigners who believe the English drink the kind of coffee they do because they lack the wit to make it any other way, have as much understanding of the English mentality as the German admiral who believed the Grand Fleet held the seas after Jutland only because the British were too stupid to know they had been beaten.

If a wise maturity accounts for the food of England, masochism   14
must be held responsible for what the Scotch eat. Believe no Scotch-man who tells you that his countrymen can afford no better. When Lord Strathcona was a millionaire many times over, oatmeal por-ridge, so I am told, remained his favourite dish. Believe no Scotch-man who attributes the national diet to the barrenness of Scottish soil. Scotland is surrounded by billions of the finest food fish in the world, and the Scotch are skilled fishermen. If they boil their salmon and halibut till no taste remains, if they bake out of their haddock the last drop of moisture, if they serve these ruined fish with a dry, grey potato and (for variation) boiled turnips and sprouts, if they offer for dessert soggy rice pudding with bloated raisins bulging out of it, if they equate a distaste for haggis° with disloyalty to Scotland herself—let nobody pity them or wonder why they eat as they do. They prefer this diet because it gives them the pleasure of being miserable.

As I neither need nor dare discuss the cooking of France, I   15
come finally to what I would call, were I Jonathan Swift, my own dear country.

A few years ago an article appeared in one of our national   16
magazines which asserted that Canadian cooking, apart from that of Montreal, is the most tasteless in the world and the most care-lessly prepared. In a later article in the same magazine statistics were paraded to establish a corollary to the previous hypothesis—namely, that Canadians are the greatest eaters of ketchup known to the Heinz company and that there are many Canadians who eat ketchup three times daily.

The only thing that astonished me about these articles, espe-   17
cially the former one, was the public response they occasioned. The editor was buried under a deluge of letters written by furious

housewives and loyal males boasting about their mothers' apple pies. Here, indubitably, was evidence that Canada is in the throes of a moral revolution.

18   A generation ago most Canadians would have been quietly pleased with a writer who told the world that their food is tasteless and carelessly prepared. Puritanism° in Canada was not on the defensive then, and the reading public would have taken "tasteless" to mean "wholesome" and "carelessly prepared" to indicate that we are a people with no nonsense about us, reserving our full energies for things higher than sensual pleasures, of which the pleasures of the table are unquestionably the lowest. Now, it seems, we are almost willing to admit that cooking is an art we may begin to practise one of these days, and that perhaps it might be interesting to climb a few steps up the slippery slope called civilization.

19   Psychologists have been heard to murmur that the desserts of our childhood are the dishes we most yearn for in our adult lives, and that this is why even middle-aged and elderly Scotchmen continue to eat rice puddings no matter how rich they are. If we don't get our childhood desserts, so they say, it is because our wives do not care for them or they have gone out of fashion. But with all respect for my own childhood, which was not an unhappy one, I harbour no nostalgic longing for the cold baked-apple and tapioca pudding which invariably made its appearance, one or the other, whenever I visited relations or dined out with a boyhood friend. In our own house these were eschewed°, at least as a rule, and personally I suffered little from the puritan theory that pleasure in food is a sin. It was the society all around me I am talking about here, not my own home, for the strength of character that made Nova Scotia great was absolutely determined to impress upon children the salutary knowledge that if they really enjoyed what they eat it was probably bad for them, while if they loathed the taste of it, they were being well nourished. So now, as I can no longer postpone answering those letters asking for my favourite menu, I shall do so in detail and with candour.

20   For breakfast I like a half-partridge, *petit pois* underdone, some light greens and a half-bottle of hock°. For lunch I will make do with a small serving of lobster Newburg or a golden-brown *soufflé* high as a chef's cap and enclosing within its airy mystery a nest of soft-boiled eggs—I ate this once in my life and have never been the same man since. Champagne is a daylight drink with me; I like it best with such a lunch at a table where no politics are discussed. Tea I dispense with unless I am in England, and as I have been in England only for a few weeks in these last many years, let's say I dispense with afternoon tea entirely, for it is a poor preparation for the dry sack° I like before dinner but almost never drink. Dinner

is, of course, the solace of a hard day, and I prefer it accompanied by a variety of wines, mostly white, and a really good dinner I like to see articulated° with some of the subtlety one looks for, but seldom finds, in a well-worked novel. The oysters should be Malpèques untouched by any sauce, and the meal should continue through vichyssoise on to Dover sole, airborne to Montreal and cooked so lightly I can still taste the North Sea (so subtly different in taste to the western Atlantic) in its incomparable flesh. For the climax to this dinner I should like roast pheasant or woodcock, and before the *demi-tasse* of Turkish coffee prepares my palate for a few dry *fines°*, I choose something light, brief, and *flambant* for a sweet, followed by a small but knowledgeable morsel of *brie* or of a soft cheese of rare delicacy native to the Ile d'Orléans. Let psychologists make of this what they will.

HUGH MACLENNAN

Hugh MacLennan, the distinguished novelist and essayist, was born in 1907 in Glace Bay, N.S., and taught for many years at McGill University in Montreal. Among his novels are *The Watch That Ends the Night*, *Two Solitudes*, *Barometer Rising*, and *Each Man's Son*.

Words and Meanings

Paragraph

pièce de résistance:	superb dish	1
gastronomically:	related to the art of good eating	
welshed:	cheated	
neophyte:	beginner	
incongruousness:	being out of place	2
torten:	German or Austrian cakes	3
ardour:	heat, passion	4
chianti	Italian wine	
repository:	place for keeping things	6
portentous	amazing, ominous	7
borscht:	beet soup	8
decadent:	morally decaying	10
Toscaninis:	Arturo Toscanini, famous Italian-American music conductor	
Sparta:	city in Ancient Greece known for its simple, hardy lifestyle	13

	salubrity:	healthfulness
	fools:	desserts made of fruit and cream
	sweet:	dessert
14	haggis:	Scottish national dish cooked in a sheep's stomach
18	Puritanism:	belief that pleasure should be denied
19	eschewed:	avoided
20	hock:	German white wine
	dry sack:	a type of sherry
	articulated:	put together
	fines:	brandies

Structure and Strategy

1. Where is MacLennan's thesis stated?
2. How many examples does MacLennan use to support his thesis? Identify the paragraphs that develop each example.
3. Why does MacLennan dismiss French cooking in one very short paragraph?
4. Why does MacLennan describe the food of his Nova Scotia childhood immediately before outlining his own favourite menu?

Content and Purpose

1. Throughout the essay, MacLennan implies that there is a close connection between cuisine and civilization. What is the tone of the essay? Do you think he intends us to take him entirely seriously?
2. Is MacLennan guilty of STEREOTYPING in this essay?
3. What do you think of MacLennan's favourite menu? (paragraph 20). How does it support (or contradict) his thesis?

Suggestions for Writing

1. Write a brief essay of example in which you refer to two or three countries not mentioned in MacLennan's essay. Use examples to show how each country's national cuisine is related to its national spirit.
2. Write a brief essay of example in which you show that individual personality is revealed through food preferences.
3. MacLennan says that psychologists claim that our childhood desserts are the ones we long for in adult life. Write a brief essay in which you support or contradict that thesis.

"The Ancient and Legendary Gods of Old"

CARL SAGAN

The sorts of scientific problems that I am 1 involved in—the environments of other planets, the origin of life, the possibility of life on other worlds—engage the popular interest. This is no accident. I think all human beings are excited about these fundamental problems, and I am lucky enough to be alive at a time when it is possible to perform scientific investigation of some of these problems.

One result of popular interest is that I receive a great deal of 2 mail, all kinds of mail, some of it very pleasant, such as from the people who wrote poems and sonnets about the plaque on *Pioneer 10*; some of it from schoolchildren who wish me to write their weekly assignments for them; some from strangers who want to borrow money; some from individuals who wish me to check out their detailed plans for ray guns, time warps, spaceships, or perpetual motion machines; and some from advocates of various arcane° disciplines such as astrology, ESP, UFO-contact stories, the speculative fiction of von Danniken°, witchcraft, palmistry, phrenology°, tea-leaf reading, Tarot cards°, the I-Ching°, transcendental meditation, and the psychedelic drug experience. Occasionally, also, there are sadder stories, such as from a woman who was talked to from her shower head by inhabitants of the planet Venus, or from a man who tried to file suit against the Atomic Energy Commission for tracking his every movement with "atomic rays." A number of people write that they can pick up extra-terrestrial intelligent radio signals through the fillings in their teeth, or just by concentrating in the right way.

But over the years there is one letter that stands out in my 3 mind as the most poignant° and charming of its type. There came in the post an eighty-five-page handwritten letter, written in green ballpoint ink, from a gentleman in a mental hospital in Ottawa.

"The Ancient and Legendary Gods of Old" from *The Cosmic Connection* by Carl Sagan. Copyright 1973 by Carl Sagan and Jerome Agel. Reprinted by permission of Doubleday & Company, Inc.

He had read a report in a local newspaper that I had thought it possible that life exists on other planets; he wished to reassure me that I was entirely correct in this supposition, as he knew from his own personal knowledge.

4   To assist me in understanding the source of his knowledge, he thought I would like to learn a little of his personal history—which explains a good bit of the eighty-five pages. As a young man in Ottawa, near the outbreak of World War II, my correspondent chanced to come upon a recruiting poster for the American armed services, the one showing a goateed° old codger° pointing his index finger at your belly button and saying, "Uncle Sam Wants You." He was so struck by the kindly visage° of gentle Uncle Sam that he determined to make his acquaintance immediately. My inform-ant boarded a bus to California, apparently the most plausible habitation for Uncle Sam. Alighting at the depot, he inquired where Uncle Sam could be found. After some confusion about surnames, my informant was greeted by unpleasant stares. After several days of earnest inquiry, no one in California could explain to him the whereabouts of Uncle Sam.

5   He returned to Ottawa in a deep depression, having failed in his quest. But almost immediately, his life's work came to him in a flash. It was to find "the ancient and legendary gods of old," a phrase that reappears many times throughout the letter. He had the interesting and perceptive idea that gods survive only so long as they have worshipers. What happens then to the gods who are no longer believed in, the gods, for example, of ancient Greece and Rome? Well, he concluded, they are reduced to the status of or-dinary human beings, no longer with the perquisites° and powers of the godhead. They must now work for a living—like everyone else. He perceived that they might be somewhat secretive about their diminished circumstances, but would at times complain about having to do menial labor when once they supped at Olympus. Such retired deities, he reasoned, would be thrown into insane asylums. Therefore, the most reasonable method of locating these defrocked° gods was to incarcerate° himself in the local mental institution—which he promptly did.

6   While we may disagree with some of the steps in his reasoning, we probably all agree that the gentleman did the right thing.

7   My informant decided that to search for all the ancient and legendary gods of old would be too tiring a task. Instead, he set his sights on only a few: Jupiter, Mercury, and the goddess on the obverse face of the old British penny—not everyone's first choice of the most interesting gods, but surely a representative trio. To his (and my) astonishment, he found—incarcerated in the very asylum in which he had committed himself—Jupiter, Mercury, and

the goddess on the obverse face of the old English penny. These gods readily admitted their identities and regaled him with stories of the days of yore when nectar and ambrosia° flowed freely.

And then my correspondent succeeded beyond his hopes. One   8
day, over a bowl of Bing cherries, he encountered "God Almighty," or at least a facsimile° thereof. At least the Personage who offered him the Bing cherries modestly acknowledged being God Almighty. God Almighty luckily had a small spaceship on the grounds of the asylum and offered to take my informant on a short tool around the Solar System—which was no sooner said than done.

"And this, Dr. Sagan, is how I can assure you that the planets   9
are inhabited."

The letter then concluded something as follows: "But all this   10
business about life elsewhere is so much speculation and not worth the really serious interest of a scientist such as yourself. Why don't you address yourself to a really important problem, such as the construction of a trans-Canadian railroad at high northern latitudes?" There followed a detailed sketch of the proposed railway route and a standard expression of the sincerity of his good wishes.

Other than stating my serious intent to work on a trans-   11
Canadian railroad at high northern latitudes, I have never been able to think of an appropriate response to this letter.

CARL SAGAN

Carl Sagan, the world's best-known astronomer, was born in 1933 in Brooklyn, N.Y. He has taught for many years at Cornell University, Ithaca, N.Y., and is the author of many books, including *The Dragons of Eden* and *Broca's Brain*. He wrote and starred in the TV series *Cosmos*.

Words and Meanings   Paragraph

arcane:	hidden, mysterious, secret	2
von Danniken:	Erich von Danniken, author of books on "ancient astronauts"	
phrenology:	pseudoscience of character-analysis through studying the shape of the head	
Tarot cards:	deck of cards used in fortune telling	
the I-Ching:	Chinese system of foretelling the future	
poignant:	piercingly sad	3
goateed:	wearing a tiny pointed beard	4
codger:	eccentric old man	
visage:	face	

5	perquisites:	customary rights and privileges
	defrocked:	fallen, exposed
	incarcerate:	lock up
7	nectar and ambrosia:	drink and food of the gods
8	facsimile:	likeness, reproduction

Structure and Strategy

1. What is the function of paragraph 1?
2. What is the topic of paragraph 2? How is the topic developed? How does paragraph 2 serve as a basis for the ILLUSTRATION that begins in paragraph 3?
3. Most of this essay (paragraphs 3 to 10) is an ILLUSTRATION. How effective is this extended example in supporting Sagan's thesis?
4. What is the dominant TONE of paragraphs 4 to 8 and of paragraphs 1 and 11?

Content and Purpose

1. Who is Uncle Sam and on what kind of posters does he usually appear?
2. Sagan considers the letter he received from the Ottawa lunatic both "poignant and charming." Why? Do you agree?
3. Can you support the idea that "gods survive only so long as they have worshipers"? In other words, do you think that your attendance at a church, synagogue, or mosque helps the deity to survive?

Suggestion for Writing

Sagan says he has "never been able to think of an appropriate response" to the letter from the Ottawa lunatic. Imagine that you are Carl Sagan—a writer, producer, actor, and astronomer—and write a response in which you give examples of the presence of two or three ancient gods on earth—perhaps Venus, Mars, or Jupiter. Find out what the deities represented or ruled over, and provide examples of their continuing influence on human behaviour.

They Also Wait Who Stand and Serve Themselves

ANDREW WARD

nyone interested in the future of Ameri-   1
can commerce should take a drive sometime to my neighborhood
gas station. Not that it is or ever was much of a place to visit. Even
when I first moved here, five years ago, it was shabby and forlorn:
not at all like the garden spots they used to feature in the commercials, where trim, manicured men with cultivated voices tipped
their visors at your window and asked what they could do for you.

Sal, the owner, was a stocky man who wore undersized, popped-   2
button shirts, sagging trousers, and oil-spattered work shoes with
broken laces. "Gas stinks" was his motto, and every gallon he
pumped into his customers' cars seemed to take something out of
him. "Pumping gas is for morons," he liked to say, leaning indelibly against my rear window and watching the digits fly on the
pump register. "One of these days I'm gonna dump this place on
a Puerto Rican, move to Florida, and get into something nice, like
hero sandwiches."

He had a nameless, walleyed° assistant who wore a studded   3
denim jacket and, with his rag and squeegee, left a milky film on
my windshield as my tank was filling. There was a fume-crazed,
patchy German shepherd, which Sal kept chained to the air pump,
and if you followed Sal into his cluttered, overheated office next
to the service bays, you ran a gauntlet° of hangers-on, many of
them Sal's brothers and nephews, who spent their time debating
the merits of the driving directions he gave the bewildered travelers
who turned into his station for help.

"I don't know," one of them would say, pulling a bag of potato   4
chips off the snack rack, "I think I would have put 'em onto 91,
gotten 'em off at Willow, and then—bango!—straight through to
Hamden."

Sal guarded the rest room key jealously and handed it out with   5
reluctance, as if something in your request had betrayed some
dismal aberration°. The rest room was accessible only through a

"They Also Wait Who Stand and Serve Themselves." Copyright 1979 by Andrew
Ward. First published in the May, 1979 issue of the *Atlantic Monthly*.

little closet littered with tires, fan belts, and cases of oil cans. Inside, the bulb was busted and there were never any towels, so you had to dry your hands on toilet paper—if Sal wasn't out of toilet paper, too.

6   The soda machine never worked for anyone except Sal, who, when complaints were lodged, would give it a contemptuous kick as he trudged by, dislodging warm cans of grape soda which, when their pop-tops were flipped, gave off a fine purple spray. There was, besides the snack rack in the office, a machine that dispensed peanuts on behalf of the Sons of Garibaldi. The metal shelves along the cinderblock wall were sparsely stocked with cans of cooling system cleaner, windshield de-icer, antifreeze, and boxed head lamps and oil filters. Over the battered yellow wiper case, below the Coca-Cola clock, and half hidden by a calendar from a janitorial supply concern, hung a little brass plaque from the oil company, awarded in recognition of Salvatore A. Castallano's ten-year business association.

7   I wish for the sake of nostalgia that I could say Sal was a craftsman, but I can't. I'm not even sure he was an honest man. I suspect that when business was slow he may have cheated me, but I never knew for sure because I don't know anything about cars. If I brought my Volvo in because it was behaving strangely, I knew that as far as Sal was concerned it could never be a simple matter of tightening a bolt or re-attaching a hose. "Jesus," he'd wearily exclaim after a look under the hood. "Mr. Ward, we got problems." I usually let it go at that and simply asked him when he thought he could have it repaired, because if I pressed him for details he would get all worked up. "Look, if you don't want to take my word for it, you can go someplace else. I mean, it's a free country, you know? You got spalding on your caps, which means your dexadrometer isn't charging, and pretty soon you're gonna have hairlines in your flushing drums. You get hairlines in your flushing drums and you might as well forget it. You're driving junk."

8   I don't know what Sal's relationship was with the oil company. I suppose it was pretty distant. He was never what they call a "participating dealer." He never gave away steak knives or NFL tumblers or stuffed animals with his fill-ups, and never got around to taping company posters on his windows. The map rack was always empty, and the company emblem, which was supposed to rotate thirty feet above the station, had broken down long before I first laid eyes on it, and had frozen at an angle that made it hard to read from the highway.

9   If, outside of television, there was ever such a thing as an oil company service station inspector, he must have been appalled by the grudging service, the mad dog, the sepulchral° john. When

there was supposed to have been an oil shortage a few years ago, Sal's was one of the first stations to run out of gas. And several months ago, during the holiday season, the company squeezed him out for good.

I don't know whether Sal is now happily sprinkling olive oil   10
over salami subs somewhere along the Sun Belt. I only know that one bleak January afternoon I turned into his station to find him gone. At first, as I idled by the no-lead pump, I thought the station had been shut down completely. Plywood had been nailed over the service bays, Sal's name had been painted out above the office door, and all that was left of his dog was a length of chain dangling from the air pump's vacant mast.

But when I got out of the car I spotted someone sitting in the   11
office with his boots up on the counter, and at last caught sight of the "Self-Service Only" signs posted by the pumps. Now, I've always striven for a degree of self-sufficiency. I fix my own leaky faucets and I never let the bellboy carry my bags. But I discovered as I squinted at the instructional sticker by the nozzle that there are limits to my desire for independence. Perhaps it was the bewilderment with which I approach anything having to do with the internal combustion engine; perhaps it was my conviction that fossil fuels are hazardous; perhaps it was the expectation of service, the sense of helplessness, that twenty years of oil company advertising had engendered°, but I didn't want to pump my own gas.

A mongrel rain began to fall upon the oil-slicked tarmac as I   12
followed the directions spelled out next to the nozzle. But somehow I got them wrong. When I pulled the trigger on the nozzle, no gas gushed into my fuel tank, no digits flew on the gauge.

"Hey, buddy," a voice sounded out of a bell-shaped speaker   13
overhead. "Flick the switch."

I turned toward the office and saw someone with Wild Bill   14
Hickok hair leaning over a microphone.

"Right. Thanks," I answered, and turned to find the switch.   15
There wasn't one. There was a bolt that looked a little like a switch, but it wouldn't flick.

"The switch," the voice crackled in the rain. "Flick the switch."   16

I waved back as if I'd finally understood, but I still couldn't   17
figure out what he was talking about. In desperation, I stuck the nozzle back into my fuel tank and pulled the trigger. Nothing.

In the office I could see that the man was now angrily pulling   18
on a slicker. "What the hell's the matter with you?" he asked, storming by me. "All you gotta do is flick the switch."

"I couldn't find the switch," I told him.   19

"Well, what do you call this?" he wanted to know, pointing   20
to a little lever near the pump register.

"A lever," I told him.   21

22   "Christ," he muttered, flicking the little lever. The digits on the register suddenly formed neat rows of zeros. "All right, it's set. Now you can serve yourself," the long-haired man said, ducking back to the office.

23   As the gas gushed into my fuel tank and the fumes rose to my nostrils, I thought for a moment about my last visit to Sal's. It hadn't been any picnic: Sal claimed to have found something wrong with my punting brackets, the German shepherd snapped at my heels as I walked by, and nobody had change for my ten. But the transaction° had dimension to it: I picked up some tips about color antennas, entered into the geographical debate in the office, and bought a can of windshield wiper solvent (to fill the gap in my change). Sal's station had been a dime a dozen, but it occurred to me, as the nozzle began to balk and shudder in my hand, that gas stations of its kind were going the way of the village smithy and the corner grocer.

24   I got a glob of grease on my glove as I hung the nozzle back on the pump, and it took more than a minute to satisfy myself that I had replaced the gas cap properly. I tried to whip up a feeling of accomplishment as I headed for the office, but I could not forget Sal's dictum: Pumping gas is for morons.

25   The door to the office was locked, but a sign directed me to a stainless steel teller's drawer which had been installed in the plate glass of the front window. I stood waiting for a while with my money in hand, but the long-haired man sat inside with his back to me, so at last I reached up and hesitantly knocked on the glass with my glove.

26   The man didn't hear me or had decided, in retaliation° for our semantic° disagreement, to ignore me for a while. I reached up to knock again, but noticed that my glove had left a greasy smear on the window. Ever my mother's son, I reflexively reached into my pocket for my handkerchief and was about to wipe the grease away when it hit me: at last the oil industry had me where it wanted me—standing in the rain and washing its windshield.

```
┌────────────────────────────┐
│                            │
└────────────────────────────┘
```

ANDREW WARD

Andrew Ward was born in Chicago in 1946. His essays and short stories appear regularly in American magazines, and he has written a number of books of humour, including *Fits and Starts: The Posthumous Memoirs of Andrew Ward* and *Bits and Pieces*.

Words and Meanings

The title is an ALLUSION to a sonnet by John Milton, a seventeenth-century English poet, on the subject of his blindness and how it had altered the way in which the poet could serve God. The poem concludes with the line, "They also serve who only stand and wait."

		Paragraph
walleyed:	having an opaque, whitish eye caused by injury or disease	3
run a gauntlet:	run between rows of armed persons who strike the runner in passing; a form of punishment	
aberration:	an abnormality	5
sepulchral:	like a sepulchre or tomb	9
engendered:	created	11
transaction:	business deal	23
retaliation:	response, revenge	26
semantic:	concerned with the meanings of words	

Structure and Strategy

1. What is Ward's thesis? Where does he state it?
2. What two ILLUSTRATIONS does Ward use to prove his point?
3. Identify some of the specific examples Ward uses to convey the impression that Sal's gas station is disorganized, decrepit, and run-down.
4. How does Ward achieve an effective TRANSITION between the description of Sal's old-style station and the new, self-service replacement?
5. What strategy does Ward use in his CONCLUSION (paragraph 26)? How does the conclusion contribute to the UNITY of the essay as a whole?

Content and Purpose

1. What is the overall purpose of this essay? Is Ward's intent to contrast the "old" and "new" ways of operating a gas station, or does he use these examples to illustrate a larger point?
2. What is Ward's attitude toward Sal and the kind of business operation he represents? What is the purpose of including Sal's nonsensical diagnosis of what is wrong with Ward's Volvo (paragraph 7)?

3. Summarize in a sentence or two the main reason Ward prefers the old-style gas station to the new.

Suggestions for Writing

1. Using two extended examples, compare the small-town corner grocery store with the large supermarket, or the small neighbourhood clothing store with the large department store, or the small advertising agency with the large agency, or any small, owner-operated organization with a large organization. Be certain to use specific details within your extended examples.
2. Use two or three extended examples to prove (or disprove) the thesis that self-service operations are advantageous to the customer.

The Cat in the Bag and Other Absolutely Untrue Tales from Our Urban Mythology

IAN PEARSON

1   There are no step dancers° in David and Karen Mills's living room. It is evening, but no mummers° peep through the windows. Instead of sea chanteys, there is Duke Ellington on the stereo. But, despite the appearances, this relatively normal dinner party in Ancaster, Ontario, is a treasure trove of folklore. After a couple of rounds of drinks are served, the stories come forth, and although shopping malls and automobiles have replaced castles and carriages, they are truly the stuff of legend.

2   The conversation has turned to cats, and David, a 31-year-old businessman, recounts with glee an incident that purportedly° happened in nearby Brantford to friends of his family: "Julie was getting married in the summer. She and her mother were going out to one of the malls on the edge of Brantford to buy some clothes at the last minute. En route, they ran over a cat. They knocked on a number of doors to try to find the owner of the cat, but no one

"The Cat in the Bag . . ." by Ian Pearson, from *Quest* magazine. Copyright November, 1984. Reprinted by permission of Ian Pearson.

was home. They figured they couldn't leave this mangled cat in the middle of the road so somehow they had to dispose of it. The only thing they had in their car that they could put this cat in was an empty Creeds° bag. They scraped the cat into the bag and put it into the trunk of the car. Then they continued to the shopping centre, intending to try again to find the owner on their way back home.

"They parked the car and, because it was a hot day, they decided they couldn't leave the festering cat remains in the hot, steamy trunk. So they put the bag on the roof of the car. They went into the mall and when they finished shopping they went for a cup of coffee in a restaurant that overlooked the parking lot. They could see the roofs of the cars and the Creeds bag perched on top of theirs. As they were looking out, a large grey Cadillac cruised by and stopped in front of their car. A well-dressed woman got out and ambled over slowly and grabbed the bag, jumped back into the car and drove away to another part of the parking lot. 3

"Julie and her mother thought this was pretty funny. But a few minutes later, the woman walked into the restaurant and sat down in a booth near them. She ordered a coffee and then she peeked into the bag to see what she had acquired. She screamed and fell over backward in a dead faint. At that point, the waitress had a conniption° and called an ambulance. The woman didn't revive when she was given smelling salts and slapped in the face. The ambulance arrived and the attendant said there was no problem, that she had just fainted. They whisked her away on a stretcher. Just as they were leaving, the waitress grabbed the Creeds bag and said, 'Excuse me, she's left this behind.' So the last Julie and her mother saw of the dead cat was it straddling the woman's chest as she was being wheeled, unconscious, into the ambulance." 4

A fine tale, and David's listeners are amused and convinced. It has strong narrative momentum. It has convincing detail. It has wonderful irony. And it's not true. 5

The dead cat in the Creeds bag is a classic example of an urban legend. Like a rumor, an urban legend is presented as the truth, contains a large number of corroborating° facts and is set in the recent past. Unlike a rumor, it has a developed plot that often results in an ironic twist. The bare-bones information of a snake biting a customer in a store (in Vancouver, it's a furrier; in Montreal, it's a sporting goods store) is a rumor. If it is elaborated into the story of a friend of a neighbor who was rushed to hospital and now is slightly paralyzed because of the snakebite, it is becoming a legend. If the same story persists for a number of years (and the dead cat tale has been traced back to 1906), it has achieved legend status. Although they are generally believed to be true by the teller, 6 the same tales are passed along by word of mouth simultaneously across North America—the state of the art of apocrypha° now.

7   In Salt Lake City, you can hear about the cat in the Creeds bag down to its most minute details, with the prestigious Castleton's store substituted for Creeds and Cottonwood Mall stepping in for the Brantford mall. Or, a few years ago, you might have heard the late Harry Chapin tell a similar story on the *Tonight* show. The singer told how his aunt was trying to dispose of her beloved German shepherd, which had died late on a Sunday night. She stuffed the corpse into a suitcase to take over to Harry's place, being unable to spend a night near the dead dog. On the subway, a man helped her with her heavy load, and then bolted away with her suitcase.

8   That black sense of irony permeates most of the legends. If everything in the legends was true, you would be well advised to arm yourself before reading any further. Because at this very moment there is an axe murderer in the house who has finished off your children and is about to call you from the upstairs extension. (Don't console yourself that such telecommunications pyrotechnics° are impossible: urban legends aren't big on logic.) The bucket of fried chicken beside your armchair contains a fried rat and at the bottom of the bottle of cola you're drinking are the remains of a dead mouse. The kitchen is a mess of fur and blood, because one of your (now deceased) family members brought in Trixie the toy poodle from the rain and attempted to dry her off in your new microwave oven. At least your other pet, a baby alligator brought back from Florida, is thriving because you flushed it down the toilet and it now marauds° the sewers.

9   Don't even think about escape. The mint condition Mercedes that you just bought for $60 last week (from an estranged wife who was seeking revenge on her runaway husband) has just been filled in with concrete by a jealous cement-truck driver. Your previous car was stolen while you were vacationing in the south: unfortunately the corpse of your grandmother (who died on the holiday) was rolled up in a rug on the roof since you were trying to sneak her past customs. (That was an extremely frantic day—just before your car was stolen you had an ugly brush with an enraged toll booth operator who had just been left with a cadaver's° arm, a dollar bill pasted to the outstretched palm, by a carload of medical students. And running down the road won't help because *out there* somewhere is the hitchhiker who vanished into *thin air* from the back seat of your car just after predicting that something awful would happen to you, yes, on this very date.

10   Brrrrr, pretty scary stuff, eh kids, as SCTV's Count Floyd would say (and Count Floyd used to be Eddie Haskell, no?). What is this

demented° mythology that we carry around in our communal consciousness like some sort of metaphysical° rubber snake? It is simply the same process of human psychology that brought us *Grimm's Fairy Tales* and Paul Bunyan. The legends give expression to some of the innermost anxieties and concerns that persist in the face of social change. "As urban men and women, we pride ourselves on our sophistication and our lack of superstition," says Dr. Martin Laba, an assistant professor of communication at B.C.'s Simon Fraser University who specializes in mass media and popular culture studies. "But clearly the existence of these legends is a testimony to the fact that the impulse for, and certainly the fascination with, the supernatural is still there."

The prevalence° of urban legends also attests to the endurance   11
of oral communication in the face of the overwhelming influence of mass media. Often, as in the case of Chapin's dead dog, the legends gain credibility and a wider audience through electronic and print media. "It's a relatively recent phenomenon that very much feeds off its relationship with the media," says Dr. Carole Carpenter, associate professor of humanities at Toronto's York University and a specialist in Canadian culture and folklore. "The urban belief tales rely on the media for their validity. You often hear, 'I heard it from someone who heard it on Johnny Carson.'"

Newspapers and films also play an important role in the trans-   12
mission of legends. "The mass media can both substantiate and be the source of legends," Laba says. "Those tiny items on the back pages of newspapers are often retold orally and get mixed up in the process. You're dealing with a process like the children's game Broken Telephone, where the original story is lost and then elaborated upon. The wonder of oral communication is that things change. There's also a degree of ambiguity between fantasy and reality. In Hitchcock's *Rear Window*, a guy chops up his wife and puts her in bags. That has now become an urban legend. Did it begin with Hitchcock or did he get it from another source? It's impossible to say. I suspect that it began with the film and has been elaborated into a legend through oral sources."

While the media generate legends, they can also be vexed by   13
apocryphal tales that are often reported to them as true incidents. Last winter, *Vancouver Sun* columnist Denny Boyd attempted to trace a story about a football player's wife who took pity on an apparently infirm old lady in Pacific Centre and submitted to her request to provide a ride home. The wife called her husband to warn him that she would be late for dinner. The husband was suspicious and called the police, who descended on the car to find the old lady was a little old man with a wig and a hatchet. Boyd could have saved his time by looking up the exact tale in *Heads*

You Lose and Other Apocryphal Tales, a 1981 collection by Francis Greig.

14   Similarly, when a story was circulating at the same time about three West Vancouver children being kidnapped in Disneyland, the *Sun* was besieged by callers wanting to know why the newspaper was suppressing the news. A call to a detective in Anaheim, California, revealed that legends about Disneyland kidnappings had been circulating for eight or nine years. Jan Harold Brunvand's groundbreaking 1981 study, *The Vanishing Hitchhiker: American Urban Legends and Their Meaning*, shows that the Disneyland legend is common across North America.

15   Of all media people, gossip columnists are probably the most frequent victims of urban legends. Gary Dunford of *The Toronto Sun* printed the cat-in-the-Creeds-bag tale as a real story four years ago. "Then over three years I heard the story three more times in three different restaurants," Dunford recalls. "And each time you hear the story, it's always somebody's best friend who swears they were there."

16   That power of testimony caught Dunford off guard on another occasion when he printed the story of the banana man of North York, Ontario. A Lothario° had been dancing at several singles bars from cocktail hour to 2 a.m. As he drove home to the suburbs, he was knocked out cold in a traffic accident. He was rushed to emergency, and when the nurses undressed the still-unconscious reveller, they discovered a banana strapped with rubber bands to his thigh. "I believed the story because the guy who called me said his girlfriend was the nurse on duty in the hospital the night it happened," Dunford explains. "Two years later I heard the same story, just like the first time, but from another hospital in Etobicoke. You have to ask, 'Is there an Etobicoke banana man or is this an urban legend?' "

17   Most definitely an urban legend and one, like many, with a meaning that is clear on first listening. The North York banana man tells us that dishonesty, especially when combined with profligate° habits, leads only to humiliation. The dead cat warns (from beyond the grave) that theft invariably leads to punishment, in this case involving the dreaded taboo of a dead body. The old man with the hatchet simply says don't pick up strangers. Other legends, such as the woman drying her poodle in the microwave, are more reflections of social or technological change. Says Carpenter: "The microwave legend is not so much a moral tale as a commentary on a social circumstance. It's not told by 35-year-olds to 11-year-olds to instruct them how to operate a microwave. The most prominent tellers are teenagers trying to shock each other."

18   Still, urban legends are not necessarily restricted to entertain-

ment value or to any age group. As Laba explains: "We tend to think that mass culture has encroached upon and destroyed the oral tradition. It's not so. Narrative is fun and it always involves entertainment value. But you have to look at legend telling within the permanent and enduring quality of storytelling. It is a fundamental means of education and communication, even in our urban society."

The permanence and endurance of many urban legends become apparent when they are compared to older, traditional legends. One recent apocryphal tale is as contemporary as today's baseball standings, but it contains oral conventions that have resonated° for centuries. Two middle-aged women from Hamilton, Ontario, embark on their first trip to New York City. Their friends have given them the direst warnings about crime in the Big Apple: if anyone accosts you, do exactly what they say and don't make any trouble. The women choose an expensive hotel, and on their first evening they are careful not to stray beyond the taxi and the Met°. After the opera, they return directly to the hotel, pleased that the evening has proceeded uneventfully. When the elevator stops at the mezzanine level, a tall black man leading a Doberman pinscher° by a leash enters. The women keep their eyes to themselves as the dog shakes nervously at the ascent of the elevator. Suddenly the black man yells, "Sit!" Instantly and obediently, the two women sit on the elevator floor. The man apologizes profusely as he gets off at the fourth floor.

The next morning the women, chastened but composed, seat themselves in the hotel's main dining room. Immediately the hotel's best breakfast appears at their table.

"There must be some mistake," protests one woman.

"No, it's all taken care of," assures the waiter. "By that gentleman in the corner banquette."

The women peer over, and spy the black man who smiles and nods. "Who is he?" asks the other woman.

"Madam, that is Mr. Reggie Jackson."

In another version, it is former football star Rosie Grier. Gary Dunford has heard the same tale set in Toronto's Royal York Hotel when the New York Yankees were in town and claims to have also read it in the *New York Post*. And now that Jackson toils in California, another New York black celebrity will surely pinch hit for him in the legend. Still, the teller of this version of the tale in Toronto insists that it is true, that it happened to her good friend Helen's aunt. When asked for verification, she replied that she had lost track of her good friend Helen.

But more fascinating than the variations of the legend is the fact that its modern dress is draped over the body of a traditional devil legend common in Quebec. "It's got all the classic elements of a supernatural legend," explains Laba. "In many Roman Catholic legends, there's always a warning at the beginning that prescribes an order of behavior. And then the devil appears and you know there's going to be a disruption. In a racist society, the devil is always portrayed as black—the prince of darkness—and he's often accompanied by the devil hound. So here, the guy of course *has* to be black and the dog *has* to be a Doberman. At the same time the story tends to parody° all that stuff. It's almost a joke because at the moment they sit down you see the absurdity of the warning and of the entire situation."

27   The sophistication of the Reggie Jackson legend is essential to its credibility. As the stories are more frequently repeated and the phenomenon of urban legends becomes better known, new twists and details must be added to convince the listener (who, of course, is the next teller of the legend). Perhaps the best-known urban legend of all tells of alligators infesting the sewers of New York. (Thomas Pynchon helped spread the tale with an Alligator Patrol in his extravagant 1963 novel *V*.) There is a kernel of truth to the legend. The February 10, 1935, *New York Times* ran an article with a headline and deck° that is almost a complete legend in itself: "Alligator Found In Uptown Sewer—Youths Shoveling Snow Into Manhole See Animal Churning in Icy Water—SNARE IT AND DRAG IT OUT—Reptile Slain by Rescuers When It Gets Vicious— Whence It Came Is Mystery." But even if there were alligators in the New York sewers in the 1930s, the legend has been officially denied so many times since then that most people now know that it is not true. In some cases, it has become what folklorists call an "antilegend," in which the denial is spread by word of mouth: "Did you know that there really *aren't* any alligators in the sewers of New York"? In other cases, the legend rejuvenates° itself with new details. In the late 1960s, stories spread among students about "New York White" marijuana, which had sprouted from seeds flushed through toilets during drug raids and flourished in the lightless sewers.

28   At the same time that old legends are being renewed, new ones are nudging their way into parlance°. A Toronto lawyer tells a story he heard in the courts of a drunk driver who was stopped by the police on a major expressway. The driver had been concentrating on his driving and was amazed that he had been pulled over.

29   "What's the matter, officer?" he asked.

30   "Do you have *any* idea how fast you were going?" came the reply.

31   "Gee, maybe 70 miles an hour. I wasn't that much over the limit."

32   "You were going *17* miles an hour!"

A sailor in Owen Sound, Ontario, relates the same story with   33
identical figures. Possibly it happened exactly as it is told. But that
does not affect its legendary character. What matters is not its
veracity but its word-of-mouth form of transmission: *My lawyer told
me about this guy who . . .* or, *This friend of Arch's was blotto and. . . .*
Inevitably, new details and variations will be added, just as inevitably as floppy disks, Michael Jackson, video games, Brian Mulroney and sushi will seep into their own legends. And in each one,
the story will be as simple and eternal as Cinderella's, as the old
world gives the new one the power to be born.

```
┌─────────────────────────┐
│                         │
└─────────────────────────┘
```

IAN PEARSON

Ian Pearson, the journalist, was born in Edmonton in 1954 and is a graduate
of the University of Toronto. His articles have appeared in such magazines
as *Maclean's*, *Canadian Business*, *Toronto Life*, and *Saturday Night*. He is
an editor of *Toronto*, a magazine published by *The Globe and Mail*.

Words and Meanings   Paragraph

step dancers:	traditional Scotch-Irish folk dancers	1
mummers:	masked folk actors	
purportedly:	said to be	2
Creeds	fashionable women's clothing store in Toronto	
conniption:	fit of hysteria	4
corroborating	supporting	6
apocrypha	stories believed to be true but actually false or doubtful	
pyrotechnics	brilliant display, like fireworks	8
marauds	preys upon, raids	
cadaver	corpse	9
demented	crazy, obsessed	10
metaphysical	philosophical, abstract	
prevalence	wide presence	11
Lothario	ridiculous lover	16
profligate	sexually indiscriminate, wasteful	17
resonated	vibrated	19
the Met	Metropolitan Opera, in New York City	
Doberman pinscher	a fashionable type of guard dog	

26	parody	mock, make ridiculous
27	deck	part of a newspaper headline
	rejuvenate	make young again
28	parlance	everyday speech

Structure and Strategy

1. What INTRODUCTORY strategy has the author used?
2. Why does the author give an example of an urban legend (paragraphs 2 to 5) before he tells the reader how an urban legend comes about?
3. Summarize the psychological basis for these grim urban legends (paragraph 10)
4. What is the effect of the direct quotations the author uses in paragraphs 10, 11, and 12?
5. How does the concluding paragraph contribute to the UNITY of the whole essay?

Content and Purpose

1. Why does the author call his examples urban legends rather than modern legends?
2. What is the implied thesis of this essay?
3. Why is the story of the cat in the bag ironic (paragraph 5)? Why does "the black sense of IRONY permeate most of the legends" (paragraph 8)?
4. Explain in your own words the first sentence of paragraph 11. Define the terms *oral communication* and *mass media*.
5. What functions do urban legends have in our culture?

Suggestion for Writing

In paragraph 6, Pearson defines an urban legend as a story that is "presented as the truth, contains a large number of corroborating facts and is set in the recent past." Write an essay in which you develop this definition using your own examples.

Canadian Wry

BARRY CALLAGHAN

1 These are strange times. I live in a country that's a hotbed of rest, where crafty lawyers argue that the holocaust° was a hoax, serious men believe they have no cash in their pockets because the poor are hoarding money, and malevolent° men, now that Pierre Trudeau is gone, want me to explain Canada.

2 Well, the first thing is this: we Canadians are never what we appear to be. Deception, sometimes self-deception, is our genius. We appear to be boring, but in fact, we're zany and make no sense at all.

3 For example, like everyone else, we have our secret police, but what other people in the world would dress up their secret cops in scarlet coats and have them ride around on horses wagging their lances at the wind, calling covert action a musical ride? What other country's serious ideologues on the radical left would call themselves the Waffle° so that absolutely no one would take them seriously? What other country could dissolve into a duality after a twelve-minute skirmish two hundred years ago on a ratty field outside Quebec City and make both inept generals who got themselves killed into heroes? And what of our national heroine—Laura Secord—our Paul Revere in drag. The fact is, that craggy face we all know from school books and chocolate boxes, is not Laura Secord at all. It's a deception, the portrait was posed for by a grandniece and was painted over a portrait of Premier George Ross. My God, George Ross in drag. In fact, the whole land as it lies on the map is a deception: huge, bigger than the United States, but almost empty because the mass of the few million folk cling to the border by their finger nails, as if the 49th parallel were a window ledge on America, on the world.

4 So, that world on the other side of the window likes to think we're boring, likes to think we win more bronze medals than anyone else on the face of the earth. We love people to think we're boring. We've raised being boring to a wacky art form. And why? Because it pays off.

5 Take William Lyon Mackenzie King, our prime minister through the war, and so it seemed, for all time until Pierre Trudeau came

"Canadian Wry" by Barry Callaghan. Copyright October, 1985. Reprinted by permission of Barry Callaghan.

along and seemed to be prime minister for all time. King held power longer than any other Western politician in this century. How did such a pudgy, mundane little man do it? The truth is, he did it deliberately. He was shrewd and self-effacing, and he told one of his friends that he made every speech as boring as possible because then no one would ever remember what he said and hold it against him. Twenty-two years in power, droning on and on over the airwaves, and meanwhile, he was as crazy as a loon.

6   He talked to his dead mother, consulted his dog, sought signs from F.D.R.° in his shaving cream in the mirror, did missionary work with local street hookers, and built his own little backyard temple from the stone remnants of old Parliament buildings. He was a choice one, *fol dol di die do*, but not so rare: after all, we're the only people anywhere who ever took the radical right-wing Social Credit economics of Ezra Pound so seriously that we've elected several Social Credit governments, and still do, in British Columbia—where the first premier's name was W.A.C. Bennett— and if such wacky right-wingers are not in power, then radical socialists are. Out East, cuddly Joey Smallwood° bossed his own fiefdom in Newfoundland for a couple of decades in a way that would have made Huey Long° green with envy. Mounties were his private strike-breaking police. And what can anyone make of our seesawing in Ottawa—from a prairie populist prime minister, John Diefenbaker, who wanted to "green" the Arctic, to the lisping internationalist, Lester Pearson who—it's true—won the Nobel Peace Prize, but it's a good thing he never had to go to war, because on the one day the Red Phone rang in his office, he couldn't find it, followed by the ascetic and acerbic Trudeau who took a flower child in tow to the marriage chamber and somehow "arranged" that two of his children actually be born on Christmas day, except his wife then ran away with all the Rolling Stones.

7   But wackiness is a rolling stone that gathers no moss, so now we have God's smooth little fixer, Brian Mulroney, bogman and bagman from Quebec. As for Quebec . . . well, not even the French from France understand the québécois, who, when they cry *vierge, hostie, ciboire, tabernacle°*, seem to be chanting tidbits from the cat- echism. In fact, they are cursing along the lines, in English, of *hot shit, suck this, my sweet ass*. The scatological is hidden inside the sacramental.

8   Who knows this? Do they want anyone to know? Not neces- sarily: who else in the world can walk up to you and, as far as he's concerned, call you a suckhole to your face and smile as you cross yourself in accord, believing yourself blessed? Clever, we're clever as we cling to the ledge of the world. And this is not just a matter of politicians cakewalking in secret. No! The determination to pre-

sent a flat face to the world crankles through our high-tone culture, too. No one but a Canadian would have carried on like Glenn Gould, the silver bullet among interpreters of Bach and Beethoven, and a great natural showman—wrapped in his scarf, playing with his winter mittens on, always seated on a dilapidated chair as if it were the abyss—the toast of the concert halls, and what did he do? Dismissed it all as vaudeville, as irrelevant as the appendix, and refused to ever play in public again, a recluse tinkling to no one but machines in closed recording studios, a powerful presence, a studied absence.

So, what's the advantage of all this dodging, all this disdain   9 for the glitter, let alone the glitz, of stardom? Well, we have—for all our lust for law and order—a remarkable freedom. In the United States, they suffer through a House Un-American Activities Committee° because they not only know who they're supposed to be, but insist on it. Such a committee in Canada would be laughable. We still refuse to agree on what the words to our national anthem are. We don't know who we are and don't want to. That way we don't have to be anybody's anything. In fact, we can pretend to be everybody else, and if we make a mistake, *they* take the rap.

Our largest corporations got very rich during the Vietnam war,   10 and several are getting rich right now in South Africa and South and Central America, but when's the last time you saw or heard of an anti-Canadian demonstration in the streets of Santiago. We're so clean we squeak, the sound of the sullen mouse beside the lumbering elephant. Haw! The Americans are our whipping boys, and if they think about us at all it's to assure us that we're lucky to be among them.

And actually, we are: not so much lucky, but among them.   11 We're insidious infiltrators inside their system. Do you know—do they know—that nearly fifty per cent of their major television reporters around the world and commentators at home are Canadian? It's true. Every night we tell millions of Americans how to see the world, how to see their wars and their movie stars and heroes and bums, their dreams achieved and broken. And if Americans ever laugh at their own insanity, Canadians control the scripts. On the loneliest night of the American week, the television program *Saturday Night Live* is a joke conceived and produced by Canadians.

As such, the archetypal Canadian is invisible—a no one who   12 is everyone from nowhere, like Rich Little . . . the most skilled impersonator in America. Having no voice of his own, he has everyone else's—male or female—and he "does" them, as they say, perfectly. People in Las Vegas and the folk in the White House prefer him to the real thing. In half an hour they get John Wayne talking to Nixon, Sylvester Stallone to Ronnie Reagan. What would

Charlie McCarthy have been without Edgar Bergen, that boring deadpan man, the perfect Canadian.

13   You see, you pick up a few tricks, clinging to the ledge of the world. You learn how to amiably draw no attention to yourself while having your own way. Canadians could be the world's greatest secret agents. Who knows? Remembering our man in Iran, perhaps we are. After all, Ken Taylor° told the world that to get the Americans out of Iran, he "disguised them as Canadians."

14   Anyway, if we fool the world, we also outfox ourselves. Margaret Atwood, the poet, once said our national mental illness is paranoid schizophrenia. That's too grim, too American. Our so-called paranoia is really nostalgia for a future we know we can never have, and the so-called schizophrenia is really the sound of two sensibilities acutely aware of each other as they rattle around inside one skull.

15   Sound and fury behind a bland face. But it was that global villager, Marshall McLuhan° (what a perfect Canadian stance—the secret conservative adored by a New York advertising world he abhorred), who came close to the point when he said that English Canada leapt directly from the eighteenth century into the twentieth century, skipping the romantic assertion of self so central to the nineteenth century. True enough, for we've got a lot of poor lost Loyalists° dragging a bogus Toryism° and a collection of coronation china around in a child's wagon in English Canada, while Quebec—as counter culture to the nation—lives in the self-aggrandizing nineteenth as if it were an *arrondissement*°, dreaming of an independent national orbit, knowing such a state can never be.

16   To live in Canada, illusion and delusion are so necessary that the "quick change artist" is commonplace, whether it's a change of hats or loyalties. We stand astride life, you see, as if it were a seesaw, balancing, waiting. The prime minister who was the master of this balancing act was Wilfrid Laurier (who of course had a "secret" mistress everyone, including his wife, knew about), and he said, "The twentieth century shall be the century of Canada." Among those who think that California is still a dream, such an idea brings hoots of derision, but he was right—that is, if Samuel Beckett° has touched any chord in the contemporary heart. We are two cultures in Canada, like the two tramps by the side of the road, watching in amazement as the Pozzos° and Luckys° of this world pass through our lives, and we wait. Bland-faced, we wait, and wait, and shrug and make sly jokes and probes—as McLuhan would have it. Trudeau's most characteristic gesture, after completing a comic pirouette behind some august person like the Queen, was a shrug. Everything may be up to date in Kansas City, but you can't get any more contemporary than that shrug.

And lest you think that this gift for deception behind the mask   17
of boredom is only a flash in the fullness of callow youth, we carry
it to the grave. I know that one of the world's favorite humorists
is Stephen Leacock, master of the comic light touch, with a tinge
of blackness around the edges, a little like a requiem mass card.
Our own secret agent of small town laughter. But did you know
how he went to his grave? It was, you see, the tradition in his
family to be buried in a plain, good old Canadian pine box, but
he'd bought a huge oak and brass-handled job and six burly men
carried it to the plot not knowing—no one knew—that he'd had
himself cremated and was only a little glass bottle of ashes cradled
in a satin puff inside the box.

Oh, wait till we really get to know our new prime minister,   18
Mulroney, for we have only heard, so far, the sound of melting
chocolate. When it comes to the temper of our times—the smooth
capacity to touch an audience's heart by saying absolutely nothing
several sweet times over—he makes Ronnie Reagan look awkward.
He's as slick as analgesic balm in Gilead°. He's a genius, a master
of mindless phrase, mindfully wrought. And he can do it in two
languages, too, with ease.

It's already the accepted wisdom that Mulroney will be in power   19
a long time. Already, no one can remember anything he's said.
Shrewd and self-effacing. Then, after he's gone, we'll all discover
he was a total secret wacko, with a fetish for changing clothes three
and four times a day—not an astringent intellectual but something
of a mystic—a man in search of the perfect press . . . just a typical
Canadian on a musical ride. Trudeau, you see, was not so special.
He just went out to lunch in foreign capitals and wore, instead of
a bronze medal, a rose in his lapel.

P.S. My favorite Trivial Pursuit question is this: *Who invented*   20
Trivial Pursuit? The answer, of course, is two Canadians, but nobody, not even masters of the game, can remember their names.

<!-- empty box -->

BARRY CALLAGHAN

Barry Callaghan, short-story writer, journalist, and editor, was born in Toronto
in 1937. He teaches at Atkinson College, York University, Toronto, where
he edits the quarterly magazine *Exile*. Callaghan originally wrote "Canadian
Wry" for *Punch*, a British humour magazine.

Words and Meanings   Paragraph

holocaust: the attempted extermination of the Jews by the   1
                              Nazis during World War II

	malevolent:	evil-minded, spiteful, mischievous
3	Waffle:	ultrasocialist and nationalist group within the NDP in the 1960s
6	F.D.R.:	Franklin Delano Roosevelt, U.S. president (1933–45)
	Joey Smallwood:	first premier of Newfoundland (1949–72)
	Huey Long:	demagogue and governor of Louisiana (1928–35)
7	*vierge, hostie, ciboire, tabernacle*:	French religious references used as swear words in Quebec
9	House Un-American Activities Committee:	U.S. Senate committee obsessed with Communist subversion in the 1950s
13	Kenneth Taylor:	Canadian ambassador to Iran (1977–80)
15	Marshall McLuhan:	theorist of the media, originator of the phrase "the global village"
	Loyalists:	Anglo-Americans loyal to Britain who left the United States in protest against the Revolution to settle in Ontario and the Maritimes
	Toryism:	doctrine of the Tory party, the Progressive Conservatives
	arrondissement:	French word for a district
16	Samuel Beckett:	playwright, author of *Waiting for Godot*
	Pozzo and Lucky:	two characters in *Waiting for Godot*
18	balm in Gilead:	Old Testament reference to comfort, consolation, or cure

Structure and Strategy

1. Look at the structure of paragraph 1. Is it an effective INTRODUCTION?
2. What is the function of paragraph 2?
3. What is the TOPIC of paragraph 3? How is the topic developed?
4. In paragraph 4, Callaghan poses a question and answers it, very briefly. What is the function of paragraphs 5 and 6?
5. Paragraph 11 provides a TRANSITION to Callaghan's point about Canadians' unique role as "infiltrators." Which paragraphs illustrate this role?
6. The CONCLUSION of this essay suggests some reasons for and provides more examples of Canadian "wackiness" disguised as blandness. Identify the concluding paragraphs. Are they effective?

Content and Purpose

1. What TONE does Callaghan adopt in this essay? Is it appropriate to his purpose? Why or why not?

2. Why does Callaghan think Canadians are deceptive? How does he think we benefit from this deceptiveness?
3. What is the price Callaghan says we pay for our deceptiveness, for being "closet wackos"?
4. Find two or three places in which Callaghan speaks of Canadians as "clinging to the ledge." Why do you think he chose this metaphor to describe the Canadian condition?
5. What is Callaghan's view of Canadian history? Do you think this view is accurate or has he twisted the facts?

Suggestions for Writing

1. Write a paper in which you provide examples of what you define as "the Canadian character."
2. Write a paper illustrating three or four differences between Canadians and Americans, or between Maritimers and Westerners, or between two other groups that suggest a similar contrast.

Mankind's Better Moments

BARBARA TUCHMAN

In this troubled world of ours, pessimism   1
seems to have won the day. But we would do well to recall some of the positive and even admirable capacities of the human race. We hear very little of them lately.

Ours is not a time of self-esteem or self-confidence as was, for   2
instance, the 19th Century, whose self-esteem may be seen oozing from its portraits. Victorians, especially the men, pictured themselves as erect, noble and splendidly handsome. Our self-image looks more like Woody Allen or a character from Samuel Beckett. Amid a mass of worldwide troubles and a poor record for the 20th Century, we see our species—with cause—as functioning very badly, as blunderers when not knaves, as violent, ignoble°, corrupt, inept, incapable of mastering the forces that threaten us, weakly subject to our worst instincts; in short, decadent.

The catalogue is familiar and valid but it is growing tiresome.   3

"Mankind's Better Moments" from a Thomas Jefferson lecture delivered in Washington by Barbara Tuchman. Copyright Autumn, 1980. Reprinted by permission of Russell & Volkening, Inc.

A study of history reminds one that mankind has its ups and downs and during the ups has accomplished many brave and beautiful things, exerted stupendous endeavors°, explored and conquered oceans and wildernesses, achieved marvels of beauty in the creative arts and marvels of science and social progress, loved liberty with a passion that throughout history has led men to fight and die for it over and over again, pursued knowledge, exercised reason, enjoyed laughter and pleasures, played games with zest, shown courage, heroism, altruism, honor and decency; experienced love, known comfort, contentment, and, occasionally, happiness. All these qualities have been part of human experience and if they have not had as important notice as the negatives nor exerted as wide and persistent an influence as the evils we do, they nevertheless deserve attention, for they currently are all but forgotten.

4   Among the great endeavors, we have in our time carried men to the moon and brought them back safely—surely one of the most remarkable achievements in history. Some may disapprove of the effort as unproductive, as too costly, and a wrong choice of priorities in relation to greater needs, all of which may be true but does not, as I see it, diminish the achievement. If you look carefully, all positives have a negative underside, sometimes more, sometimes less, and not all admirable endeavors have admirable motives.

5   Great endeavor requires vision and some kind of compelling impulse, as in the case of the Gothic cathedrals of the Middle Ages. The architectural explosion that produced this multitude of soaring vaults, arched, ribbed, pierced with jeweled light, studded with thousands of figures of the stone-carvers' art, represents in size, splendor and numbers one of the great, permanent artistic achievements of human hands.

6   What accounts for it? Not religious fervor alone. Although a cathedral was the diocesan seat° of a bishop, the decision to build did not come from the Catholic Church alone, which by itself could not finance the operation, but from the whole community. Only the common will shared by nobles, merchants, guilds, artisans, and commissioners in general could command the resources and labor to sustain such an undertaking. Each group contributed donations, especially the magnates of commerce who felt relieved thereby from the guilt of money-making. Collections were made from the public in towns and countryside, and indulgences° granted in return for gifts. Voluntary work programs involved all classes. "Who has ever seen or heard tell in times past," wrote an observer, "that powerful princes of the world, that men brought up in honors and wealth, that nobles—men and women—have bent their haughty necks to the harness of carts and like beasts of burden have dragged

to the abode of Christ these wagons loaded with wines, grains, oil, stones, timber and all that is necessary for the construction of the church?''

The higher and lighter grew the buildings and slenderer the   7
columns, the more new expedients° and techniques had to be devised to hold them up. Buttresses° flew like angels' wings against the exterior. It was a period of innovation and audacity. In a single century, from 1170 to 1260, 600 cathedrals and major churches were built in France alone. In England in that period, the cathedral of Salisbury with the tallest spire in the country was completed in thirty-eight years. The spire of Freiburg in Germany was constructed entirely of filigree° in stone as if spun by some supernatural spider. In the Sainte Chapelle in Paris the fifteen miraculous windows swallow the walls; they have become the whole.

Explanations of the extraordinary burst that produced the ca-   8
thedrals are several. Art historians will tell you that it was the invention of the ribbed vault, permitting subdivision, independence of parts, replacement of solid walls by columns, multiplication of windows and all the extrapolations° that followed. But this does not explain the energies that took hold of and developed the rib. Religious historians say these were the product of an age of faith that believed that with God's favor anything was possible. In fact, it was not a period of untroubled faith but of heresies° and Inquisition°. Rather, one can only say that conditions were right. Social order under monarchy and the towns was replacing the anarchy° of the barons so that existence was no longer merely a struggle to stay alive but allowed a surplus of goods and energies and greater opportunity for mutual effort. Banking and commerce were producing capital, roads making possible wheeled transport, universities nourishing ideas and communication. It was one of history's high tides, an age of vigor, confidence and forces converging to quicken the blood.

Even when the general tide was low, a particular group of   9
doers could emerge in exploits that still inspire awe. What of the founding of our own country? We take the Mayflower for granted, yet think of the boldness, the enterprise°, the determined independence, the sheer grit it took to leave the known and set out across the sea for the unknown where no houses or food, no stores, no cleared land, no crops or livestock, none of the equipment or settlement of organized living awaited.

Equally bold was the enterprise of the French in the northern   10
forests who throughout the 17th Century explored and opened the land from the St. Lawrence to the Mississippi, from the Great Lakes to the Gulf of Mexico. They came not for liberty like the Pilgrims,

but for gain and dominion, and rarely in history have men willingly embraced such hardship, such daunting adventure and persisted with tenacity and endurance.

11   Happily, man has a capacity for pleasure too, and in contriving ways to entertain and amuse himself, has created brilliance and delight. Pageants, carnivals, festivals, fireworks, music, dancing and drama, parties and picnics, sports and games, the comic spirit and its gift of laughter, all the range of enjoyment from grand ceremonial to the quiet solitude of a day's fishing has helped to balance the world's infelicity°. Homo ludens, man at play, is surely as significant a figure as man at war or at work. No matter what else is happening, the newspapers today give more space to the sports pages than to any other single activity. (I do not cite this as necessarily admirable, merely indicative.) In human activity the invention of the ball may be said to rank with the invention of the wheel. Imagine America without baseball, Europe without soccer, England without cricket, the Italians without bocci, China without ping pong, and tennis for no one.

12   But mankind's most enduring achievement is art. At its best, it reveals the nobility that coexists in human nature along with flaws and evils, and the beauty and truth it can perceive. Whether in music or architecture, literature, painting or sculpture, art opens our eyes and ears and feelings to something beyond ourselves, something we cannot experience without the artist's vision and the genius of his craft. The placing of Greek temples like the Temple of Poseidon on the promontory at Sunion outlined against the piercing blue of the Aegean Sea, Poseidon's home; the majesty of Michelangelo's sculptured figures in stone; Shakespeare's command of language and knowledge of the human soul; the intricate order of Bach, the enchantment of Mozart; the purity of Chinese monochrome pottery with the lovely names—celadon, oxblood, peach blossom, claire de lune; the exuberance of Tiepolo's ceiling where, without the picture frames to limit movement, a whole world in exquisitely beautiful colors lives and moves in the sky; the prose and poetry of all the writers from Homer to Cervantes to Jane Austen and John Keats to Dostoevsky and Chekov—who made all these things? We—our species—did.

13   If we have lost beauty and elegance in the modern world, we have gained much, through science and technology and democratic pressures in the material well-being of the masses. The change in the lives of, and society's attitude toward, the working class marks the great divide between the modern world and the old regime.

14   It is true, of course, that the underside of the scientific progress is prominent and dark. The weaponry of war in its ever-widening capacity to kill is an obvious negative, and who is prepared to state

with confidence that the overall effect of the automobile, airplane, telephone, television, and computer has been on balance beneficent°?

Pursuit of knowledge for its own sake has been a more certain   15
good. There was a springtime in the 18th Century when, through knowledge and reason, everything seemed possible; when reason was expected to break through religious dogma like the sun breaking through fog, and man armed with knowledge and reason would be able at last to control his own fate and construct a good society. The theory that because it exists, this is the best of all possible worlds, spread outward from Leibniz; the word "optimism" was used for the first time in 1737.

What a burst of intellectual energies shook these decades! In   16
the 20 years, 1735–55, Linnaeus named and classified all of known botany; Buffon systematized Natural History in 36 volumes; the American, John Bartram, scoured the wilderness for plants to send to correspondents in Europe; Voltaire, Montesquieu and Hume investigated the nature of man and the moral foundations of law and society; Benjamin Franklin demonstrated electricity from lightning; Dr. Johnson by himself compiled the first dictionary of the English language; Diderot and the Encyclopedists of France undertook to present all knowledge in enlightened terms; the secret of making porcelain having just previously been discovered in Europe through intensive experiments, its manufacture in a thousand forms flourished at Meissen and Dresden; clearing for the Place de la Concorde, to be the most majestic in Europe, was begun in Paris, and the fantastic cascades of Caserta constructed for the Bourbons of Naples; 150 newspapers and journals circulated in England; Henry Fielding wrote *Tom Jones*; Thomas Jefferson was born; Tiepolo painted his gorgeous masterpiece, the Four Continents, on the archducal ceilings at Wurzburg; Chardin, no less supreme, painted his gentle and affectionate domestic scenes; Hogarth, seeing a different creature in the species, exposed the underside in all its ribaldry° and squalor. It was an age of enthusiasm: At the first London performance of Handel's Messiah in 1743, George II was so carried away by the Hallelujah Chorus that he rose to his feet, causing the whole audience to stand with him. A custom was thereby established, still sometimes followed by Messiah audiences.

If the twenty-year period is stretched by another ten, it includes   17
the reverberatory° voice of Rousseau's "Social Contract," Beccaria's groundbreaking study on "Crime and Punishment," Gibbon's beginning of the "Decline and Fall," and despite the Lisbon earthquake and Voltaire's "Candide," the admission of "optimism" into the Dictionnaire de l'Académie Française.

Although the Enlightenment may have overestimated the power   18
of reason to guide human conduct, it nevertheless opened to men

and women a more humane view of their fellow passengers. Slowly the harshest habits gave way to reform—in treatment of the insane, reduction of death penalties, mitigation° of the fierce laws against debtors and poachers, and in the passionately fought cause for abolition of slave trade. The humanitarian movement was not charity, which always carries an overtone of being done in the donor's interest, but a more disinterested benevolence—altruism, that is to say, motivated by conscience. Through recent unpleasant experiences, we have learned to expect ambition, greed or corruption to reveal itself behind every public act, but it is not invariably so. Human beings do possess better impulses, and occasionally act upon them, even in the 20th Century. Occupied Denmark, during World War II, outraged by Nazi orders for deportation of its Jewish fellow citizens, summoned the courage of defiance and transformed itself into a united underground railway to smuggle virtually all 8,000 Danish Jews out to Sweden. Far away and unconnected, a village in southern France, Le Chamben-sur-Lignon, devoted itself to rescuing Jews and other victims of the Nazis at the risk of the inhabitants' own lives and freedom. "Saving lives became a hobby of the people of Le Chamben," said one of them. The larger record of the time was admittedly collaboration°, passive or active. We cannot reckon on the better impulses predominating in the world; only that they will always appear.

19   The strongest of these in history, summoner of the best in men, has been zeal for liberty. Time after time, in some spot somewhere on the globe, people have risen in what Swinburne called the "divine right of insurrection"—to overthrow despots, repel alien conquerors, achieve independence—and so it will be until the day power ceases to corrupt, which, I think, is not a near expectation.

20   The phenomenon continues today in various forms, by Algerians, Irish, Vietnamese, peoples of Africa and the Middle East. Seen at close quarters and more often than not manipulated by outsiders, contemporary movements seem less pure and heroic than those polished by history's gloss, for instance the Scots of the Middle Ages against the English, the Swiss against the Hapsburgs, Joan of Arc arousing a dispirited people against the occupier, the Albanian Scanderbeg against the Turks, the American colonies against the mother country.

21   So far I have considered qualities of the group rather than of the individual, except for art which is always a product of the single spirit. Happiness too is a matter of individual capacity. It springs up here or there, haphazard, random, without origin or explanation. It resists study, laughs at sociology, flourishes, vanishes, reappears somewhere else. Take Izaak Walton, author of *The Compleat Angler*, that guide to contentment as well as fishing of which Charles

Lamb said, "It would sweeten any man's temper at any time to read it." Although Walton lived in distracted times of revolution and regicide°, though he adhered to the losing side in the Civil War, though he lost in their infancy all seven children by his first wife and the eldest son of his second marriage, though he was twice a widower, his misfortunes could not sour an essentially buoyant° nature. "He passes through turmoil," in the words of a biographer, "ever accompanied by content."

Walton's secret was friendship. Born to a yeoman° family and apprenticed in youth as an ironmonger, he managed to gain an education and through sweetness of disposition and a cheerful religious faith, became a friend on equal terms of various learned clergymen and poets whose lives he wrote and works he prefaced. John Donne, vicar of the parish in Chancery Lane where Walton worked, was his mentor and his friend. Others were Archbishop Sheldon of Canterbury, George Morley, Bishop of Winchester, Richard Hooker, Sir Henry Wotton, George Herbert, Michael Drayton and the Royalist, Charles Cotton.   22

The Compleat Angler, published when the author was 60, glows in the sunshine of his character. In it are humor and piety°, grave advice on the idiosyncracies° of fish and the niceties° of landing them, delight in nature and in music. Walton saw five editions reprinted in his lifetime while innumerable later editions secured him immortality. The surviving son by his second wife became a clergyman; the surviving daughter married one and gave her father a home among grandchildren. He wrote his last work, a life of his friend Robert Sanderson, at eighty-five and died at ninety after being celebrated in verse by one of his circle as a "happy old man" whose life "showed how to compass true felicity." Let us think of him when we grumble.   23

Is anything to be learned from my survey? I raise the question only because most people want history to teach them lessons, which I believe it can do, although I am less sure we can use them when needed. I gathered these examples not to teach but merely to remind people in a despondent° era that the good in mankind operates even if the bad secures more attention. I am aware that selecting out the better moments does not result in a realistic picture. Turn them over and there is likely to be a darker side, as when Project Apollo, our journey to the moon, was authorized because its glamor could obtain subsidies for rocket and missile development that otherwise might not have been forthcoming. That is the way things are.   24

It is a paradox° of our time that never have so many people been so relatively well off and never has society been more troubled. Yet I suspect that humanity's virtues have not vanished,   25 although the experiences of our century seem to suggest they are in abeyance°. A century that took shape in the disillusion that followed the enormous effort and hopes of World War I, that saw revolution in Russia congeal into the same tyranny it overthrew, saw a supposedly civilized nation revert under the Nazis into organized and unparalleled savagery, saw the craven appeasement by the democracies, is understandably suspicious of human nature. A literary historian, Van Wyck Brooks, discussing the 1920s and '30s, spoke of "an eschatological° despair of the world." Whereas Whitman and Emerson, he wrote, "had been impressed by the worth and good sense of the people, writers of the new time" were struck by their lusts, cupidity° and violence, and had come to dislike their fellow men. The same theme reappeared a few months ago when a drama critic, Walter Kerr, described a mother in a play who had a problem with her two "pitilessly contemptuous" children. The problem was that "she wants them to be happy and they don't want to be." They prefer to freak out or watch horrors on television. In essence, this is our epoch. It keeps turning to look on Sodom and Gomorrah°; it has no view of the Delectable Mountains°.

BARBARA TUCHMAN

Barbara Tuchman, the well-known historian, was born in 1919 in New York, N.Y. She is the author of numerous best-selling histories, including *The Guns of August*, *A Distant Mirror*, and *The Proud Tower*.

Paragraph ## Words and Meanings

2	ignoble:	dishonorable, unworthy
3	endeavors:	strenuous efforts, attempts
6	diocesan seat:	church's diocese or bishop's district
	indulgence:	an absolution formally excusing one from punishment for a sin
7	expedients:	means to an end
	buttresses:	structural supports
	filigree:	delicate lacework
8	extrapolations:	developments, conjectures
	heresies:	false religious doctrines
	Inquisition:	religious trials often ending in torture
	anarchy:	social chaos
9	enterprise:	initiative, endeavour

infelicity:	unhappiness	11
beneficent:	positive, good	14
ribaldry:	indecency	16
reverberatory:	echoing	17
mitigation:	lessening	18
collaboration:	working together, often with the enemy	
regicide:	killing a king	21
buoyant:	cheerful, optimistic	
yeoman:	worker, small landowner	22
piety:	religious devotion	23
idiosyncracies:	individual characteristics or oddities	
niceties:	polite acts	
despondent:	dejected, downcast, not optimistic	24
paradox:	seeming contradiction	25
abeyance:	dormancy, not in use	
eschatological:	concerned with last things: death, judgment, heaven and hell	
cupidity:	greed	
Sodom and Gomorrah:	cities in the Old Testament punished by God for their wickedness	
the Delectable Mountains:	desired goal in *Pilgrim's Progress*; as close as humans can get to heaven on earth	

Structure and Strategy

1. What is the function of the first two paragraphs of this essay? Why are they so short?
2. Identify the thesis statement in paragraph 3. How does it differ from a thesis statement that you might write for an essay of example?
3. What is the topic sentence of paragraph 12, and how does Tuchman develop that topic sentence?
4. If paragraphs 16 and 17 deal with intellectual discoveries, what does paragraph 18 deal with? Why does Tuchman use these discoveries as a prelude to paragraph 18?
5. How does Tuchman effectively conclude her essay in paragraphs 24 and 25? What is the purpose of the reference to Walter Kerr at the end of the essay?

Content and Purpose

1. What is Tuchman's purpose in this essay? Do you think she has been successful or unsuccessful? Give reasons for your opinion.

2. In an essay titled "Mankind's Better Moments," why does Tuchman make the contrast she does in paragraphs 9 and 10?
3. Summarize the reasons why Tuchman considers art to be "mankind's most enduring achievement" (see paragraph 12).
4. Why does Tuchman consider Izaak Walton to be a hero? (See paragraphs 21 and 22.)
5. Tuchman is an historian. What does she believe a knowledge of history can do, and what are its limitations? (See paragraph 24.) Do you agree or disagree?

Suggestions for Writing

1. Are you optimistic or pessimistic about the human condition as we approach the end of the twentieth century? Write a brief essay defending your point of view and include two or three well-chosen illustrations to support your thesis.
2. In paragraphs 19 and 20, Tuchman declares that the strongest of mankind's better impulses has been "the zest for liberty," and she gives a number of examples of groups who have fought for liberty. However, she mentions only two individuals, Joan of Arc and Scanderbeg. Is there any individual who fought for liberty on a small or large scale whom you particularly admire? If so, write a brief essay of example explaining three of his or her accomplishments.

Additional Suggestions for Writing: Example

Choose one of the topics below and write a thesis statement based on it. Expand your thesis statement into an essay by selecting specific examples from your own experience, current events, or your studies to develop the main points.

1. Fast food is becoming a gastronomic way of life.
2. A person is not always what he or she appears to be.
3. Recent ecological disasters show how little we care for the environment that sustains us.
4. Popular tourist attractions share certain characteristics.
5. Television commercials reveal some significant characteristics of our culture.
6. A good novel is a wonderful way to escape from everyday cares.
7. Choosing a spouse is easy if one knows what to look for.
8. "Good fences make good neighbours." (Robert Frost)
9. Faith is a source of strength in one's personal life.
10. "Religion is the opiate of the people." (Karl Marx)
11. Through travel we learn about ourselves as well as about other people.
12. A good teacher is concerned for students' personal well-being as well as for their intellectual development.
13. Clothing styles reveal personality.
14. Films aimed at those between 15 and 22 share certain characteristics.
15. "The love of money is the root of all evil." (I Timothy 6:10)
16. "Money is indeed the most important thing in the world; and all sound and successful personal and national morality should have this fact for its basis." (George Bernard Shaw)
17. "Manners are more important than laws." (Edmund Burke)
18. "Feeling godless, what we have done is made technology God." (Woody Allen)
19. "Power corrupts. Absolute power corrupts absolutely." (Lord Acton)
20. "To blame others for our misfortune shows a lack of education; to blame ourselves shows the beginning of education; to blame no one shows a complete education." (Epictetus)

U N I T

Process Analysis: Explaining "How"

What? The Definition

The next time you find yourself sitting in a dentist's waiting room, pick up a copy of one of the women's magazines—*Chatelaine*, *Good Housekeeping*, or *Ladies' Home Journal*, for instance. In the table of contents you'll find a wealth of articles that are examples of process analysis: "Lose Ten Pounds in Ten Days," "Bake the Ultimate Chocolate Cheesecake," or "Raising the Perfect Child." Many of the articles in men's magazines are no different in form, only in content. Their readers learn how to choose a sports car, make a killing in the stock market, tie a Windsor knot, or meet the perfect mate. Across the land, bookstores abound with manuals on fitness, beauty, computer programming, weight control, financial planning, sexuality, and gourmet cooking. These examples of writing, all intended to teach us how to do something, attest to our interest in self-improvement and our fascination with figuring out how something is done. **Process analysis** is the kind of writing that explains how the various steps of a procedure lead to its successful accomplishment.

Why? The Purpose

Process analysis is used for two different purposes that lead to two different kinds of papers or reports. The first kind is the strictly "how-to" paper that gives the reader directions to follow. A **directional process analysis** answers one of two questions:

1. How do you do S?
2. How do you make S?

Students often need to write a directional process analysis on exams or in assignments. For example, how do you debug a COBOL program? How does a paramedic file an accident report? What are the essential steps in assembling a hydraulic valve? In directional process analysis, you are writing for the do-it-yourselfer. You must make the instructions clear so that your readers can follow along, step by step. Directions that are vague or incomplete will infuriate them. Remember the Christmas you spent struggling to assemble your supercharged, battery-operated UltraZapMobile? Remember the hopelessly confusing directions provided: "Insert Tab Square B2 firmly into Slot 5A3 while simultaneously sliding the grommetblaster into the rotating webfork . . . "? No mere mortal could possibly comprehend such GOBBLEDYGOOK.

The second kind of process analysis, on the other hand, answers these questions:

1. How does S work?
2. How does S occur?
3. How is S done?

These questions lead to **informational process analysis**. Its purpose is to explain to your reader how something is, or was, accomplished. Your readers simply want to be informed about the subject; they don't necessarily want to do the task themselves. Jessica Mitford's "Behind the Formaldehyde Curtain" is a fascinating example of informational process analysis. The subject is a process about which everyone should be informed, but few would care to try out at home. Topics such as how the greenhouse effect is developing, how Newfoundland entered Confederation, how a cell divides, how a corporate merger occurs, or how the Alberta Badlands were formed would all require the writer to produce informational process analyses.

How? The Technique

Writing a process analysis that will direct or inform your readers rather than confuse or infuriate them is not difficult if you follow these six steps:

1. Think through the whole process carefully and write down, in order, an outline of all the steps involved. If you are describing a complex process, break down each step in the sequence into substeps and group them CHRONOLOGICALLY.
2. Now write your thesis statement. Here's the formula for a thesis statement for a *directional* paper:

> To do S, you first a, then b, and finally c.

Example: To fail your year in the grand style, you must antagonize your teachers, disdain your studies, and cheat on your work.

The thesis statement for an *informational* paper also identifies the steps or stages of the process you are explaining:

> S consists of a, b, c. . . .

Example: The speech process consists of four phases: breathing, phonation, resonation, and articulation.

3. Check to be sure you have included any preparatory steps or special equipment the reader should know about before beginning, as in this example: "Make sure you have your pliers, screwdriver, table saw, and bandages handy."

4. Define any specialized or technical terms that may be unfamiliar to your reader. If you need to use words like "phonation," "resonation," or "articulation"—as we did in the example above—you must explain clearly what the terms mean. Underline the mystery words in your outline, so you'll remember to define them as you write the paper. (See Unit Six for instructions on how to write simple sentence definitions.)

5. Write your first draft. Be sure to use TRANSITIONS, or time-markers, to indicate the progression through the steps or stages. A variety of transitional words and phrases will help smooth your reader's path through your explanation of the process, as these examples illustrate:
    "*First*, assemble your tools. . . ."
    "*Next*, the legal assistant must . . . ."
    "*After* the Conservative regime was defeated, . . ."
    "The sound is *then* shaped by the tongue, lips, and teeth. . . ."
    "*Finally*, Brascan's takeover of Genstar was approved by the shareholders. . . ."

6. Revise your draft carefully. What may seem like a simple procedure to you, since you know it so well, can bewilder someone who knows little about it. Ask a friend to read through your process analysis. If it's as clear to her as it is to you, you're done—congratulations! If it isn't clear to her, back to the drawing board.

Clarify any steps that caused confusion and revise until the whole paper is both clear and interesting to whoever reads it.

The essay below, written with tongue firmly in cheek, illustrates the form and development of a directional process paper:

Flunking with Style

Introduction (challenges widely held opinion) ——→ People often remark that succeeding in school takes plenty of hard work. The remark implies that failure is a product of general idleness and zero motivation. This is an opinion I'd like to challenge. My long and checkered past in numerous educational institutions has taught me that to fail grandly, to fail extravagantly, to go down in truly blazing splendour, requires effort and imagination.

Thesis statement ——→ To fail your year in the grand style, you must antagonize your teachers, disdain your studies, and cheat on your work. Keep the following guidelines in mind.

First step (developed by example) The first step, antagonizing your teachers, isn't difficult if you keep in mind what it is that teachers like: intelligent, interested, even enthusiastic faces in front row centre. Show that you're bored before the class begins by slouching in a desk at the back of the room. Wear your Walkman, and don't forget to turn up the volume when that teacher starts to talk. Carry on running conversations with your seatmates. Aim an occasional snort or snicker in the teacher's direction when she's putting a complex point on the board. Above all, never volunteer an answer and respond sullenly with an "I dunno" if the teacher has the nerve to ask you a question. Before long, you'll have that teacher bouncing chalk stubs off your head. Once you've earned the loathing of all your instructors, you'll be well on your way to a truly memorable failure.

Second step (note the enumerated transitions)

The second step, disdaining your studies, is easy to master; they're probably B-O-R-I-N-G anyway. First, don't buy your books until close to midterm and keep them in their original condition; don't open, read, or note anything in them. Better yet, don't buy your texts at all. Second, never attempt to take notes in class. Third, stop going to class completely, but have lots of creative excuses for missed assignments: "My friend's aunt died;" "My gerbil's in a coma;" "My boyfriend was in another car wreck;" "My dog ate the lab report;" "I've got mono." You can bet your teachers will be really amused by these old stand-bys. By now, you are well on your way to disaster.

Third step (more examples)

The third step, cheating, will deliver the *coup de grâce* to your academic career. Should an instructor be so sadistic as to assign a research paper, just copy something out of a book that the librarian will be happy to find for you. Your instructor will be astonished at the difference between the book's polished, professional prose and your usual halting scrawls; you're guaranteed a zero. During your exams, sit at the back and crane your neck to read your classmate's paper. Roll up your shirt-sleeves to reveal the answers you've tattooed all over your forearms. Ask to be excused three or four times during the test so you can consult the notes you've stashed in the hall or the washroom. Be bold! Dig out your old wood-burning kit and emblazon cheat notes on the desk. If you want to ensure not just failure but actual expulsion, send in a ringer—a look-alike to write the exam for you!

Conclusion (issues a challenge)

If you follow these guidelines, you will be guaranteed to flunk your year. Actively courting failure with verve, with flair, and with a sense of drama will not only ensure your status as an academic

washout but will also immortalize you in
the memories of teachers and class-
mates alike. The challenge is yours! Become a legend—pick up the torch and
fall with it!

Baked Beans

PIERRE BERTON

ow we come to my famous (or infamous°) 1
formula for Klondike° baked beans, the one that disturbed so many
people because of its complexity. Well, winter is coming on and
these beans will be needed, no matter how complex they seem to
be. There is nothing quite like them. They are guaranteed to melt
the frostiest heart, bring warmth to the palest cheeks, satisfy the
most gnawing hunger, and rekindle the spark of hope in the coldest
breast.

The Klondikers carried baked beans frozen solid in their packs 2
and, when the trail grew weary and the stomach cried out for
succour°, they would chop pieces off with a knife and gnaw at
them as they plunged onward. For beans carry a warmth locked
within them, and when the human fire burns low, they act as hot
coals to send the blood coursing through the veins.

My beans are more exotic than the 1898 variety, and they are 3
not meant to be eaten frozen, but the principle is exactly the same.

I warn you that this is a lengthy task, so fortify° yourself in 4
any of the several ways known to cooks the world over. Step One
is the simplest: simply take the quantity of navy beans that you
require and soak them overnight in cold water.

The next morning, early, Step Two begins: simmer these soaked 5
beans very lightly. Put them over a low heat and throw in a couple
of crushed bay leaves, a handful of finely chopped parsley, some
crushed garlic, orégano, thyme, chili powder, cloves, and salt. The
idea here is to get the beans soft and to impregnate them with a
basic flavour.

Let them simmer gently for an hour or two while you go over 6
to the butcher's for some salt pork. Have him cut the pork—or

"Baked Beans" from *Pierre and Janet Berton's Canadian Food Guide* by Pierre Berton.
Copyright 1966. Reprinted by permission of McClelland and Stewart Limited.

good side bacon will do as well—into large cubes or chunks, the size of marshmallows. Get lots of pork; the makers of tinned beans skimp on the stuff, but we don't have to. There's nothing quite so good as pork or bacon cooked to a soft succulence in a frothing mass of beans and molasses.

7   You can tell if your beans are soft enough by picking a couple out of the pot and blowing on them. If the skins break, you're ready for Step Three. Turn off the heat and drain away the liquid, but for heaven's sake don't throw it away. It is nectar. What you don't use in the finished dish you can always save as soup stock.

8   Pour the drained beans in a big earthenware casserole and throw in the salt pork. I often serve beans at a party along with a good smoked ham; if you do this throw some of the ham fat in with the beans. Pour it right out of the pan, if you like.

9   Now we are into Step Three, and it is here that the boys are separated from the men, and the men from the women. Take a few cups of the liquid you poured from the beans and put it in a pot to simmer. Chop up some tomatoes and throw them in the pot with a few shots of chili sauce and a tin of tomato paste. Chop several onions, half of them very fine, so they'll disappear in the brew, and half in chunks, and throw them in. Green onion tops, chopped up, go well, too, if you can get them.

10   Now season this mixture, tasting carefully as you go, with dry mustard, freshly ground black pepper, Worcestershire sauce, crushed garlic, celery seed, a few squirts of tabasco, and some monosodium glutamate.

11   When it tastes pungent° and hot (remember that the pungency will be cut by the beans) stir in a large quantity of molasses. Most people don't put in enough molasses, and yet this is the essence of all good baked bean dishes. For there comes a critical moment when the sweetness of the molasses is wedded to the sharpness of the vegetables and herbs, and it is this subtle flavour, baked indelibly into the beans and mingling with the pork fat, that brings a sparkle to the eyes.

12   Now pour this bubbling and fragrant syrup over the pot of pork and beans. Put a lid on the pot and bake the beans for several hours in a 250 degree oven. They should bake for at least six hours, but you can bake them much longer if you want. The longer they bake, the better they taste. This gives you time to work up an appetite, shovelling snow, chopping logs for the fire and so on.

13   About half-way through the baking, pull out the pot and taste the beans. *Taste*, I said! Don't eat them all up—they're nowhere near done. But at this point you ought to check the bouquet°. Is it right? Are they too sweet or not sweet enough? Do they need more liquid? Don't let them get too dry.

Fix them up and put them back in for some more baking. One   14
hour before they're ready you perform another important rite. Pour
a cup of good sherry over them. Not cooking sherry—but the kind
you drink yourself.

Do I see a small bird-like woman in the back row rise and   15
denounce me for spreading debauchery and intoxication through
the land? Control yourself, madam. I give you my bond that before
this dish is done the alcoholic content of that fortified wine will
have vanished, leaving only its delicate flavour behind, fused in-
separably with a dish which supplies its own intoxication.

Now take some bacon strips and cover the entire top of the   16
beans. Fifteen minutes before serving, take the lid off the pot so
the bacon crispens into a thick crust.

By now you should be close to starvation, for the beans are   17
meant to be devoured only when the tortured stomach pleads for
sustenance°. Call in your friends. Get some fresh bread with a hard
crust. Tear open these loaves and rip out the soft insides. Now
open the steaming pot, plunge a ladle through the bacon crust,
spoon the bubbling brown beans, the soft globes of pork, and all
the attendant juices, into the containers of bread.

Notice that the pork is sweet to the tooth, that the beans while   18
still firm and round are infused with a delirious flavour, and that
the simmering sauce is maddening to the palate.

Provide the company with mugs of steaming coffee. Now as   19
you tear ravenously at the bread and feel the piping hot beans
begin to woo your taste buds, accept the homage° of your friends,
for you have earned it. And, as your tired muscles lose their ten-
sions, and the beans begin to come out of your ears, and the day
passes into history, give thanks to your Maker for putting beans
on this earth and giving men the wit° to bake them as they deserve.

PIERRE BERTON

Pierre Berton, the author and media personality, was born in 1920 in Dawson
City, Y.T. He is well known for his television appearances and for his best-
selling books: *Klondike*, *The National Dream*, and *Vimy*, to name a few.

Words and Meanings

Paragraph

infamous:	notorious, scandalous	1
Klondike:	a region in the southwestern part of the Yukon that includes the Klondike River and its tributaries; scene of the Klondike Gold Rush of 1896.	

2   succour: relief

4   fortify: strengthen

11   pungent: spicy, stimulating

13   bouquet: aroma produced by cooking spices

17   sustenance: food

19   homage: worship
     wit: intelligence

Structure and Strategy

1. List, in order, the steps to follow to produce Berton's dish.
2. Identify the words and phrases Berton uses to establish TRANSITION and create COHERENCE.
3. Consider the TONE of the last two paragraphs. Do you think Berton's conclusion is effective? Why or why not?

Content and Purpose

1. Why does Berton introduce his essay by justifying his recipe for baked beans? See paragraphs 1 to 4.
2. Why does Berton choose words such as "exotic" and "nectar" to describe such a simple and ordinary dish as baked beans?
3. In several places, Berton makes an association between baked beans and the gold that men sought in the Klondike. For example: "For beans carry a warmth locked within them, and when the human fire burns low, they act as hot coals to send the blood coursing through the veins."

   Why does Berton make this association?

Suggestion for Writing

Do you have a special recipe that you feel satisfies both the stomach and the spirit? Write the directions for this recipe in chronological order. In your conclusion, explain why you think this dish is food for the soul as well as the body.

A Modest Proposal for a Divorce Ceremony

PIERRE BERTON

A lot of my friends seem to be getting divorced these days. Ten years ago, a lot of my friends seem to have been getting married and I served my time as usher, best man, toastmaster, and so on. But that has all changed now and at this stage more of my friends are getting divorced than are getting married. It is the fashionable thing to do.

Yet I cannot help feeling that all these divorces are handled untidily. Half the time I don't know which of my friends are getting divorced. Or I hear they are getting divorced but I never know exactly when the divorce occurs. And sometimes they don't get divorced after all and as a result they never speak to me again because I told someone they were.

What I mean is, there is no proper ritual, no sensible code of behavior for people getting divorced as there is for people getting married. Well, why not? Why shouldn't there be a divorce ceremony laid down in the Book of Common Prayer°? The idea has considerable merit and should appeal to florists, department stores, telegraph offices, social editors, caterers, and Syd Silver's Tuxedo Rentals. Formalize divorces as we formalize weddings, I say! Send out engraved invitations in double envelopes. Invite your friends and enemies.

The ritual, in my opinion, should be held in a church and it ought to be presided over, whenever possible, by the same minister who forged the original bonds of matrimony. We will have ushers, of course, wearing white carnations in their buttonholes and conducting friends of the husband and friends of the wife down the aisle, and seating them, balefully, on opposite sides. (You'll remember that she never could abide his friends.)

The divorce itself will have been handled by the new divorce-counseling service of the Robert Simpson Company. There was a bit of trouble over that. At one point *he* swore that if he had to wear formal clothes there wouldn't be a divorce, and *she* went off

"A Modest Proposal" from *My War with the Twentieth Century* by Pierre Berton, copyright © 1965. Reprinted by permission of Doubleday and Company, Inc.

and had a good cry and said she just couldn't go through with it, there were too many details. But finally they patched it up and here he is, entering from a side door with the Worst Man (sometimes known as the Other Man). It is the job of the Worst Man to snatch the wedding ring from the little woman's hand at the appropriate moment and to fling it on the floor and stamp on it.

6   Now the church doors swing open and the wife comes down the aisle on the arm of her father who once gave her away and is now, somewhat reluctantly, taking her back. The bridal procession may also include a Matron of Honor (sometimes known as the Other Woman) and several flower girls (the children of the divorced couple), whose custody is still in doubt.

7   The ceremony itself should be simple and dignified. A few simple "I do's" in answer to the minister's question as to whether he or she rejects him or her as each other's wedded spouse, never again to have, hold, love, or cherish. Then the usual rhetorical remark: "If any here present know cause as to why these two should not be separated, ye are to declare it." It is to be hoped that there will be no sloppy speeches at this point and that the ceremony can continue with dispatch°.

8   Time now for the newly divorced couple to go into the vestry and scratch their names off the marriage register. Meanwhile, a local tenor sings some appropriate song such as "Brokenhearted." The department-store service includes photographers, not only for the social pages, but also for the Divorce Albums which are permanent mementos of the occasion. A divorce, unlike a wedding, requires two photographers, for it will be traditional that the couple leave by two separate exits. The guests throw confetti and old shoes—those shoes that he was always leaving around the house, to her annoyance.

9   A reception follows and there is the usual receiving line, congratulations from friends, a mildly intoxicating punch, and, of course, a toast to the new divorcee by her mother who says how glad she is that her little girl has finally got rid of that monster. The ex-groom replies with a few graceful remarks of his own about in-laws. Some telegrams are read, mainly salutations from old girl friends to the ex-groom, inviting him up to the family's place for a steak dinner Saturday night.

10   And now we cut the cake, while the photographers stand by. The two figures atop the divorce cake are, of course, facing resolutely away from each other. There may be a tendency for one or other of the happy pair to want to slice the head off one of these little figures, but this ought to be discouraged.

11   After the cake cutting (the guests each get a piece to keep under their pillows), it's time for the little woman to toss away her bou-

quet. All the young matrons vie for it, because there's a charming legend going the rounds, that she who catches the flowers will be the next in line at Reno°.

Did I mention the wedding gifts? They're on display in an 12 adjoining room, each marked with the name of the donor. That's right—they're giving them *back*. Some, I fear (the vases, crockery, and the like), have become a bit dented as a result of those hearty marital arguments that led to the divorce.

That's about all I can think of for a divorce ceremony, but as 13 the idea takes hold, each community no doubt, will add its own enriching refinements.

What's that, you say? This essay should not have been written? 14 Poor taste? How dare I poke fun at one of the most tragic of twentieth-century manifestations?

But I am not poking fun at all, dear lady from Richmond Hill 15 (who will be writing me tomorrow more in sorrow than in anger and signing her letter "Disgusted"). I have never been more serious, madam. The divorce ceremony is a step forward and ought to be made compulsory. Rather than go through with it, thousands will be content to stay married.

The wedding ceremony has become so complicated that scores 16 of young men and women would cheerfully remain in sober spinsterhood and bachelorhood were it not for the fact that there are simple alternatives. But there should be no alternative to the divorce ceremony. If you want to get a divorce, that's the way it ought to be done—and no other way.

Is there anyone bold enough to say that it is more foolish than 17 our present system?

```
┌─────────────────────┐
│                     │
└─────────────────────┘
```

PIERRE BERTON

Pierre Berton was born Pierre Francis de Marigny Berton in Dawson City, Y.T., in 1920. He is the author of a two-volume history of the War of 1812— *The Invasion of Canada* and *Flames Across the Border*—and many other books.

Words and Meanings   Paragraph

the Book of Common Prayer:	collection of prayers and readings used in Anglican Church services	3
with dispatch:	quickly	7
Reno:	city in Nevada, U.S.A., where divorces are readily available	11

Structure and Strategy

1. What TONE does Berton strike in paragraph 3? How does this tone make his argument more appealing?
2. Identify several examples of SATIRE in paragraphs 4, 5, and 6.
3. What concluding strategy does Berton use? Is it effective?

Content and Purpose

1. What is the function of the first two paragraphs?
2. Why do you think Berton chose to write a satiric process essay on the need for a divorce ceremony? Would he have been more successful if he had written a serious, factual essay?
3. Satire is supposed to ridicule with the object of reforming. On what serious purpose is Berton's essay based?

Suggestion for Writing

Write a process paper, satirical or serious, on a Canadian social practice that you find particularly offensive or silly.

The Way of All Flesh:

The Worm Is at Work in Us All

JUDY STOFFMAN

1   When a man of 25 is told that aging is inexorable°, inevitable, universal, he will nod somewhat impatiently at being told something so obvious. In fact, he has little idea of the meaning of the words. It has nothing to do with him. Why should it? He has had no tangible evidence yet that his body, as the poet Rilke said, enfolds old age and death as the fruit enfolds a stone.

2   The earliest deposits of fat in the aorta, the trunk artery carrying blood away from the heart, occur in the eighth year of life, but who can peer into his own aorta at this first sign of approaching debility°? The young man has seen old people but he secretly believes himself to be the exception on whom the curse will never fall. "Never will the skin of my neck hang loose. My grip will never

"The Way of All Flesh" by Judy Stoffman, copyright Sept. 15, 1979. Reprinted by permission of *The Montreal Standard* (1973) Limited.

weaken. I will stand tall and walk with long strides as long as I live." The young girl scarcely pays attention to her clothes; she scorns makeup. Her confidence in her body is boundless; smooth skin and a flat stomach will compensate, she knows, for any lapses in fashion or grooming. She stays up all night, as careless of her energy as of her looks, believing both will last forever.

In our early 20s, the lung capacity, the rapidity of motor re-   3
sponses and physical endurance are at their peak. This is the ath-
lete's finest hour. Cindy Nicholas of Toronto was 19 when she first swam the English Channel in both directions. The tennis star Bjorn Borg was 23 when he triumphed this year at Wimbledon for the fourth time.

It is not only *athletic* prowess° that is at its height between 20   4
and 30. James Boswell, writing in his journal in 1763 after he had finally won the favors of the actress Louisa, has left us this happy description of the sexual prowess of a 23-year-old: "I was in full flow of health and my bounding blood beat quick in high alarms. Five times was I fairly lost in supreme rapture. Louisa was madly fond of me; she declared I was a prodigy°, and asked me if this was extraordinary in human nature. I said twice as much might be, but this was not, although in my own mind I was somewhat proud of my performance."

In our early 30s we are dumbfounded to discover the first grey   5
hair at the temples. We pull out the strange filament and look at it closely, trying to grasp its meaning. It means simply that the pigment has disappeared from the hair shaft, never to return. It means also—but this thought we push away—that in 20 years or so we'll relinquish° our identity as a blonde or a redhead. By 57, one out of four people is completely grey. Of all the changes wrought by time this is the most harmless, except to our vanity.

In this decade one also begins to notice the loss of upper register   6
hearing, that is, the responsiveness to high frequency tones, but not all the changes are for the worse, not yet. Women don't reach their sexual prime until about 38, because their sexual response is learned rather than innate. The hand grip of both sexes increases in strength until 35, and intellectual powers are never stronger than at that age. There is a sense in the 30s of hitting your stride, of coming into your own. When Sigmund Freud was 38 an older colleague, Josef Breuer, wrote: "Freud's intellect is soaring at its highest. I gaze after him as a hen at a hawk."

Gail Sheehy in her book *Passages* calls the interval between 35   7
and 45 the Deadline Decade. It is the time we begin to sense danger. The body continually flashes us signals that time is running out. We must perform our quaint deeds, keep our promises, get on with our allotted tasks.

Signal: The woman attempts to become pregnant at 40 and   8

finds she cannot. Though she menstruates each month, menstrua-
tion being merely the shedding of the inner lining of the womb,
she may not be ovulating regularly.

9   Signal: Both men and women discover that, although they have
not changed their eating habits over the years, they are much
heavier than formerly. The man is paunchy around the waist; the
woman no longer has those slim thighs and slender arms. A 120-
pound woman needs 2,000 calories daily to maintain her weight
when she is 25, 1,700 to maintain the same weight at 45, and only
1,500 calories at 65. A 170-pound man needs 3,100 calories daily
at 25, 300 fewer a day at 45 and 450 calories fewer still at 65. This
decreasing calorie need signals that the body consumes its fuel ever
more slowly; the cellular fires are damped and our sense of energy
diminishes.

10   In his mid-40s the man notices he can no longer run up the
stairs three at a time. He is more easily winded and his joints are
not as flexible as they once were. The strength of his hands has
declined somewhat. The man feels humiliated: "I will not let this
happen to me. I will turn back the tide and master my body." He
starts going to the gym, playing squash, lifting weights. He takes
up jogging. Though he may find it neither easy nor pleasant, terror
drives him past pain. A regular exercise program can retard some
of the symptoms of aging by improving the circulation and increasing the lung capacity, thereby raising our stamina and energy
level, but no amount of exercise will make a 48-year-old 26 again.
Take John Keeley of Mystic, Connecticut. In 1957, when he was
26, he won the Boston marathon with a time of 2:20. This year he
is fit and 48 and says he is as fiercely competitive as ever, yet it
took him almost 30 minutes longer to run the same marathon.

11   In the middle of the fourth decade, the man whose eyesight
has always been good will pick up a book and notice that he is
holding it farther from his face than usual. The condition is pres-
byopia, a loss of the flexibility of the lens which makes adjustment
from distant to near vision increasingly difficult. It's harder now
to zoom in for a closeup. It also takes longer for the eyes to recover
from glare; between 16 and 90, recovery time from exposure to
glare is doubled every 13 years.

12   In our 50s, we notice that food is less and less tasty; our taste
buds are starting to lose their acuity°. The aged Queen Victoria
was wont to complain that strawberries were not as sweet as when
she was a girl.

13   Little is known about the causes of aging. We do not know if we
are born with a biochemical messenger programmed to keep the
cells and tissues alive, a messenger that eventually gets lost, or if
there is a 'death hormone,' absent from birth but later secreted by

the thymus or by the mysterious pineal gland, or if, perhaps, aging results from a fatal flaw in the body's immunity system. The belief that the body is a machine whose parts wear out is erroneous, for the machine does not have the body's capacity for self-repair.

"A man is as old as his arteries," observed Sir William Osler.   14
From the 50s on, there's a progressive hardening and narrowing of the arteries due to the gradual lifelong accumulation of calcium and fats along the arterial walls. Arteriosclerosis eventually affects the majority of the population in the affluent countries of the West. Lucky the man or woman who, through a combination of good genes and good nutrition, can escape it, for it is the most evil change of all. As the flow of blood carrying oxygen and nutrients to the muscles, the brain, the kidneys and other organs diminishes, these organs begin to starve. Although all aging organs lose weight, there is less shrinkage of organs such as the liver and kidneys, the cells of which regenerate, than there is shrinkage of the brain and the muscles, the cells of which, once lost, are lost forever.

For the woman it is now an ordeal to be asked her age. There   15
is a fine tracery of lines around her eyes, a furrow in her brow even when she smiles. The bloom is off her cheeks. Around the age of 50 she will buy her last box of sanitary pads. The body's production of estrogen and progesterone which govern menstrua-tion (and also help to protect her from heart attack and the effects of stress) will have ceased almost completely. She may suffer pal-pitations°, suddenly break into a sweat; her moods may shift ab-ruptly. She looks in the mirror and asks, "Am I still a woman?" Eventually she becomes reconciled to her new self and even ac-knowledges its advantages: no more fears about pregnancy. "In any case," she laughs, "I still have not bad legs."

The man, too, will undergo a change. One night in his early   16
50s he has some trouble achieving a complete erection, and his powers of recovery are not what they once were. Whereas at 20 he was ready to make love again less than half an hour after doing so, it may now take two hours or more; he was not previously aware that his level of testosterone, the male hormone, has been gradually declining since the age of 20. He may develop headaches, be unable to sleep, become anxious about his performance, antic-ipate failure and so bring on what is called secondary impotence— impotence of psychological rather than physical origin. According to Masters and Johnson, 25 percent of all men are impotent by 65 and 50 percent by 75, yet this cannot be called an inevitable feature of aging. A loving, undemanding partner and a sense of confidence can do wonders. "The susceptibility° of the human male to the power of suggestion with regard to his sexual prowess," observe Masters and Johnson, "is almost unbelievable."

After the menopause, the woman ages more rapidly. Her bones   17 start to lose calcium, becoming brittle and porous. The walls of the vagina become thinner and drier; sexual intercourse now may be painful unless her partner is slow and gentle. The sweat glands begin to atrophy° and the sebaceous glands that lubricate the skin decline; the complexion becomes thinner and drier and wrinkles appear around the mouth. The skin, which in youth varies from about one-fiftieth of an inch on the eyelids to about a third of an inch on the palms and the soles of the feet, loses 50 percent of its thickness between the ages of 20 and 80. The woman no longer buys sleeveless dresses and avoids shorts. The girl who once disdained cosmetics is now a woman whose dressing table is covered with lotions, night creams and makeup.

18   Perhaps no one has written about the sensation of nearing 60 with more brutal honesty than the French novelist Simone de Beauvoir: "While I was able to look at my face without displeasure, I gave it no thought. I loathe my appearance now: the eyebrows slipping down toward the eyes, the bags underneath, the excessive fullness of the cheeks and the air of sadness around the mouth that wrinkles always bring. . . . Death is no longer a brutal event in the far distance; it haunts my sleep."

19   In his early 60s the man's calves are shrunken, his muscles stringy looking. The legs of the woman, too, are no longer shapely. Both start to lose their sense of smell and both lose most of the hair in the pubic area and the underarms. Hair, however, may make its appearance in new places, such as the woman's chin. Liver spots appear on the hands, the arms, the face; they are made of coagulated melanin, the coloring matter of the skin. The acid secretions of the stomach decrease, making digestion slow and more difficult.

20   Halfway through the 60s comes compulsory retirement for most men and working women, forcing upon the superannuated worker the realization that society now views him as useless and unproductive. The man who formerly gave orders to a staff of 20 now finds himself underfoot as his wife attempts to clean the house or get the shopping done. The woman fares a little better since there is a continuity in her pattern of performing a myriad of essential household tasks. Now they must both set new goals or see themselves wither mentally. The unsinkable American journalist I.F. Stone, when he retired in 1971 from editing *I.F. Stone's Weekly*, began to teach himself Greek and is now reading Plato in the original. When Somerset Maugham read that the Roman senator Cato the Elder learned Greek when he was 80, he remarked: "Old age is ready to undertake tasks that youth shirked° because they would take too long."

21   However active we are, the fact of old age can no longer be

evaded from about 65 onward. Not everyone is as strong minded about this as de Beauvoir. When she made public in her memoirs her horror at her own deterioration, her readers were scandalized. She received hundreds of letters telling her that there is no such thing as old age, that some are just younger than others. Repeatedly she heard the hollow reassurance, "You're as young as you feel." But she considers this a lie. Our subjective reality, our inner sense of self, is not the only reality. There is also an objective reality, how we are seen by society. We receive our revelation of old age from others. The woman whose figure is still trim may sense that a man is following her in the street; drawing abreast, the man catches sight of her face—and hurries on. The man of 68 may be told by a younger woman to whom he is attracted: "You remind me of my father."

Madame de Sévigné, the 17th-century French writer, struggled   22
to rid herself of the illusion of perpetual youth. At 63 she wrote: "I have been dragged to this inevitable point where old age must be undergone: I see it there before me; I have reached it; and I should at least like so to arrange matters that I do not move on, that I do not travel further along this path of the infirmities, pains, losses of memory and the disfigurement. But I hear a voice saying: 'You must go along, whatever you may say; or indeed if you will not then you must die, which is an extremity from which nature recoils.' "

Now the man and the woman have their 70th birthday party.   23
It is a sad affair because so many of their friends are missing, felled by strokes, heart attacks or cancers. Now the hands of the clock begin to race. The skeleton continues to degenerate from loss of calcium. The spine becomes compressed and there is a slight stoop nothing can prevent. Inches are lost from one's height. The joints may become thickened and creaking; in the morning the woman can't seem to get moving until she's had a hot bath. She has os-teoarthritis. This, like the other age-related diseases, arteriosclerosis and diabetes, can and should be treated, but it can never be cured. The nails, particularly the toenails, become thick and lifeless because the circulation in the lower limbs is now poor. The man has difficulty learning new things because of the progressive loss of neurons from the brain. The woman goes to the store and forgets what she has come to buy. The two old people are often constipated because the involuntary muscles are weaker now. To make it worse, their children are always saying, "Sit down, rest, take it easy." Their digestive tract would be toned up if they went for a long walk or even a swim, although they feel a little foolish in bathing suits.

In his late 70s, the man develops glaucoma, pressure in the   24 eyeball caused by the failure of aqueous humour° to drain away; this can now be treated with a steroid related to cortisone. The lenses in the eyes of the woman may thicken and become fibrous, blurring her vision. She has cataracts, but artificial lenses can now be implanted using cryosurgery°. There is no reason to lose one's sight just as there's no reason to lose one's teeth; regular, lifelong dental care can prevent tooth loss. What can't be prevented is the yellowing of teeth, brought about by the shrinking of the living chamber within the tooth which supplies the outer enamel with moisture.

25   Between 75 and 85 the body loses most of its subcutaneous fat. On her 80th birthday the woman's granddaughter embraces her and marvels: "How thin and frail and shrunken she is! Could this narrow, bony chest be the same warm, firm bosom to which she clasped me as a child?" Her children urge her to eat but she has no enjoyment of food now. Her mouth secretes little saliva, so she has difficulty tasting and swallowing. The loss of fat and shrinking muscles in the 80s diminish the body's capacity for homeostasis, that is, righting any physiological imbalance. The old man, if he is cold, can barely shiver (shivering serves to restore body heat). If he lives long enough, the man will have an enlarged prostate which causes the urinary stream to slow to a trickle. The man and the woman probably both wear hearing aids now; without a hearing aid, they hear vowels clearly but not consonants; if someone says "fat," they think they've heard the word "that."

26   At 80, the speed of nerve impulses is 10 percent less than it was at 25, the kidney filtration rate is down by 30 percent, the pumping efficiency of the heart is only 60 percent of what it was, and the maximum breathing capacity, 40 percent.

27   The old couple is fortunate in still being able to express physically the love they've built up over a lifetime. The old man may be capable of an erection once or twice a week (Charlie Chaplin fathered the last of his children when he was 81), but he rarely has the urge to climax. When he does, he sometimes has the sensation of seepage rather than a triumphant explosion. Old people who say they are relieved that they are now free of the torments of sexual desire are usually the ones who found sex a troublesome function all their lives; those who found joy and renewal in the act will cling to their libido°. Many older writers and artists have expressed the conviction that continued sexuality is linked to continued creativity: "There was a time when I was cruelly tormented, indeed obsessed by desire," wrote the novelist André Gide at the age of 73, "and I prayed, 'Oh let the moment come when my subjugated° flesh will allow me to give myself entirely to . . . . ' But

to what? To art? To pure thought? To God? How ignorant I was! How mad! It was the same as believing that the flame would burn brighter in a lamp with no oil left. Even today it is my carnal self that feeds the flame, and now I pray that I may retain carnal desire until I die."

Aging, says an American gerontologist°, "is not a simple slope which everyone slides down at the same speed; it is a flight of irregular stairs down which some journey more quickly than others." Now we arrive at the bottom of the stairs. The old man and the old woman whose progress we have been tracing will die either of a cancer (usually of the lungs, bowel or intestines) or of a stroke, a heart attack or in consequence of a fall. The man slips in the bathroom and breaks his thigh bone. But worse than the fracture is the enforced bed rest in the hospital which will probably bring on bed sores, infections, further weakening of the muscles and finally, what Osler called "an old man's best friend": pneumonia. At 25 we have so much vitality that if a little is sapped by illness, there is still plenty left over. At 85 a little is all we have.

And then the light goes out.

The sheet is pulled over the face.

In the last book of Marcel Proust's remarkable work *Remembrance of Things Past*, the narrator, returning after a long absence from Paris, attends a party of his friends throughout which he has the impression of being at a masked ball: "I did not understand why I could not immediately recognize the master of the house, and the guests, who seemed to have made themselves up, in a way that completely changed their appearance. The Prince had rigged himself up with a white beard and what looked like leaden soles which made his feet drag heavily. A name was mentioned to me and I was dumbfounded at the thought that it applied to the blonde waltzing girl I had once known and to the stout, white haired lady now walking just in front of me. We did not see our own appearance, but each like a facing mirror, saw the other's." The narrator is overcome by a simple but powerful truth: the old are not a different species. "It is out of young men who last long enough," wrote Proust, "that life makes its old men."

The wrinkled old man who lies with the sheet over his face was once the young man who vowed, "My grip will never weaken. I will walk with long strides and stand tall as long as I live." The young man who believed himself to be the exception.

JUDY STOFFMAN

Translator and journalist Judy Stoffman was born in Budapest, Hungary, in 1957, grew up in Vancouver, then studied in England and France. She is an editor of *Canadian Living* magazine.

Paragraph	**Words and Meanings**	
1	inexorable:	relentless, unstoppable
2	debility:	weakness
4	prowess:	courage, skill
	prodigy:	person capable of extraordinary achievement
5	relinquish:	give up
12	acuity:	sharpness
15	palpitations:	irregular heartbeats
16	susceptibility:	sensitiveness, impressibility
17	atrophy:	wither
20	shirked:	neglected
24	aqueous humour:	fluid in the interior chamber of the eyeball
	cryosurgery:	surgical technique involving freezing of the tissues
27	libido:	sexual desire
	subjugated:	conquered, subdued
28	gerontologist:	expert on aging

Structure and Strategy

1. How does the first paragraph reinforce the title and subtitle of this essay?
2. Into how many stages does Stoffman divide the aging process? Identify the paragraphs that describe each stage.
3. Why do you think Stoffman uses so many direct quotations in an essay on the subject of aging? Select two of these direct quotations and explain why they are particularly effective.
4. How does the last paragraph unify or bring together the whole essay? Why do you think Stoffman ends her essay with a sentence fragment?

Content and Purpose

1. The title of this essay is a biblical ALLUSION ("I am going the way of all the earth. . . ." 1 Kings 2:2). Why do you think Stoffman chose this title?
2. What is "the worm" referred to in the subtitle?

3. Summarize the changes, both internal and external, that occur during one's fifties (paragraphs 12 to 17).
4. On his eightieth birthday, Morley Callaghan, the celebrated Canadian novelist, declared that "everyone wants to live to be 80, but no one wants to *be* 80." Do you think Stoffman would agree or disagree with Callaghan?
5. As a result of the new Charter of Rights in Canada, many vigorous 65-year-olds are challenging the principle of compulsory retirement. Do you agree or disagree that workers should be required to retire at 65? Why?

Suggestions for Writing

1. Write a directional process essay explaining how to enjoy old age.
2. Write a directional process essay explaining how to put off the aging process for as long as possible.

Behind the Formaldehyde° Curtain

JESSICA MITFORD

The drama begins to unfold with the arrival   1
of the corpse at the mortuary.

Alas, poor Yorick°! How surprised he would be to see how his   2
counterpart of today is whisked off to a funeral parlor and is in short order sprayed, sliced, pierced, pickled, trussed, trimmed, creamed, waxed, painted, rouged and neatly dressed—transformed from a common corpse into a Beautiful Memory Picture. This process is known in the trade as embalming and restorative art, and is so universally employed in the United States and Canada that the funeral director does it routinely, without consulting corpse or kin. He regards as eccentric those few who are hardy enough to suggest that it might be dispensed with. Yet no law requires embalming, no religious doctrine commends it, nor is it dictated by considerations of health, sanitation, or even of personal

"Behind the Formaldehyde Curtain" from *The American Way of Death.* Copyright 1963, 1978 by Jessica Mitford. Reprinted by permission of Simon & Schuster, Inc.

daintiness. In no part of the world but in Northern America is it widely used. The purpose of embalming is to make the corpse presentable for viewing in a suitably costly container; and here too the funeral director routinely, without first consulting the family, prepares the body for public display.

3   Is all this legal? The processes to which a dead body may be subjected are after all to some extent circumscribed by law. In most states, for instance, the signature of next of kin must be obtained before an autopsy may be performed, before the deceased may be cremated, before the body may be turned over to a medical school for research purposes; or such provision must be made in the decedent's° will. In the case of embalming, no such permission is required nor is it ever sought. A textbook, *The Principles and Practices of Embalming*, comments on this: "There is some question regarding the legality of much that is done within the preparation room." The author points out that it would be most unusual for a responsible member of a bereaved family to instruct the mortician, in so many words, to "*embalm*" the body of a deceased relative. The very term "embalming" is so seldom used that the mortician must rely upon custom in the matter. The author concludes that unless the family specifies otherwise, the act of entrusting the body to the care of a funeral establishment carries with it an implied permission to go ahead and embalm.

4   Embalming is indeed a most extraordinary procedure, and one must wonder at the docility° of Americans who each year pay hundreds of millions of dollars for its perpetuation, blissfully ignorant of what it is all about, what is done, how it is done. Not one in ten thousand has any idea of what actually takes place. Books on the subject are extremely hard to come by. They are not to be found in most libraries or bookshops.

5   In an era when huge television audiences watch surgical operations in the comfort of their living rooms, when, thanks to the animated cartoon, the geography of the digestive system has become familiar territory even to the nursery school set, in a land where the satisfaction of curiosity about almost all matters is a national pastime, the secrecy surrounding embalming can, surely, hardly be attributed to the inherent gruesomeness of the subject. Custom in this regard has within this century suffered a complete reversal. In the early days of American embalming, when it was performed in the home of the deceased, it was almost mandatory° for some relative to stay by the embalmer's side and witness the procedure. Today, family members who might wish to be in attendance would certainly be dissuaded° by the funeral director. All others, except apprentices, are excluded by law from the preparation room.

A close look at what does actually take place may explain in 6
large measure the undertaker's intractable reticence° concerning a
procedure that has become his major *raison d'être*. Is it possible he
fears that public information about embalming might lead patrons
to wonder if they really want this service? If the funeral men are
loath to discuss the subject outside the trade, the reader may,
understandably, be equally loath to go on reading at this point.
For those who have the stomach for it, let us part the formaldehyde
curtain. . . .

The body is first laid out in the undertaker's morgue—or rather, 7
Mr. Jones is reposing in the preparation room—to be readied to
bid the world farewell.

The preparation room in any of the better funeral establish- 8
ments has the tiled and sterile look of a surgery, and indeed the
embalmer-restorative artist who does his chores there is beginning
to adopt the term "dermasurgeon" (appropriately corrupted by
some mortician-writers as "demi-surgeon") to describe his calling.
His equipment, consisting of scalpels, scissors, augers, forceps,
clamps, needles, pumps, tubes, bowls and basins, is crudely imitative of the surgeon's, as is his technique, acquired in a nine- or
twelve-month post-high-school course in an embalming school. He
is supplied by an advanced chemical industry with a bewildering
array of fluids, sprays, pastes, oils, powders, creams, to fix or soften
tissue, shrink or distend it as needed, dry it here, restore the moisture there. There are cosmetics, waxes and paints to fill and cover
features, even plaster of Paris to replace entire limbs. There are
ingenious aids to prop and stabilize the cadaver: a Vari-Pose Head
Rest, the Edwards Arm and Hand Positioner, the Repose Block (to
support the shoulders during the embalming), and the Throop Foot
Positioner, which resembles an old-fashioned stocks°.

Mr. John H. Eckels, president of the Eckels College of Mortuary 9
Science, thus describes the first part of the embalming procedure:
"In the hands of a skilled practitioner, this work may be done in
a comparatively short time and without mutilating the body other
than by slight incision—so slight that it scarcely would cause serious inconvenience if made upon a living person. It is necessary
to remove the blood, and doing this not only helps in the disin-
fecting, but removes the principal cause of disfigurements due to
discoloration."

Another textbook discusses the all-important time element: 10
"The earlier this is done, the better, for every hour that elapses between death and embalming will add to the problems and compli-
cations encountered. . . . " Just how soon should one get going on
the embalming? The author tells us, "On the basis of such
scanty information made available to this profession through its

rudimentary and haphazard system of technical research, we must conclude that the best results are to be obtained if the subject is embalmed before life is completely extinct—that is, before cellular death has occurred. In the average case, this would mean within an hour after somatic° death." For those who feel that there is something a little rudimentary°, not to say haphazard, about this advice, a comforting thought is offered by another writer. Speaking of fears entertained in early days of premature burial, he points out, "One of the effects of embalming by chemical injection, however, has been to dispel fears of live burial." How true; once the blood is removed, chances of live burial are indeed remote.

11   To return to Mr. Jones, the blood is drained out through the veins and replaced by embalming fluid pumped in through the arteries. As noted in *The Principles and Practices of Embalming*, "every operator has a favorite injection and drainage point—a fact which becomes a handicap only if he fails or refuses to forsake his favorites when conditions demand it." Typical favorites are the carotid artery, femoral artery, jugular vein, subclavian vein. There are various choices of embalming fluid. If Flextone is used, it will produce a "mild, flexible rigidity. The skin retains a velvety softness, the tissues are rubbery and pliable. Ideal for women and children." It may be blended with B. and G. Products Company's Lyf-Lyk tint, which is guaranteed to reproduce "nature's own skin texture . . . the velvety appearance of living tissue." Suntone comes in three separate tints: Suntan; Special Cosmetic Tint, a pink shade "especially indicated for young female subjects"; and Regular Cosmetic Tint, moderately pink.

12   About three to six gallons of a dyed and perfumed solution of formaldehyde, glycerin, borax, phenol, alcohol and water is soon circulating through Mr. Jones, whose mouth has been sewn together with a "needle directed upward between the upper lip and gum and brought out through the left nostril," with the corners raised slightly "for a more pleasant expression." If he should be bucktoothed, his teeth are cleaned with Bon Ami and coated with colorless nail polish. His eyes, meanwhile, are closed with flesh-tinted eye caps and eye cement.

13   The next step is to have at Mr. Jones with a thing called a trocar. This is a long, hollow needle attached to a tube. It is jabbed into the abdomen, poked around the entrails and chest cavity, the contents of which are pumped out and replaced with "cavity fluid." This done, and the hole in the abdomen sewn up, Mr. Jones's face is heavily creamed (to protect the skin from burns which may be caused by leakage of the chemicals), and he is covered with a sheet and left unmolested for a while. But not for long—there is more, much more, in store for him. He has been embalmed, but not yet

restored, and the best time to start the restorative work is eight to
ten hours after embalming, when the tissues have become firm
and dry.

The object of all this attention to the corpse, it must be re-   14
membered, is to make it presentable for viewing in an attitude of
healthy repose. "Our customs require the presentation of our dead
in the semblance of normality . . . unmarred by the ravages of
illness, disease or mutilation," says Mr. J. Sheridan Mayer in his
Restorative Art. This is rather a large order since few people die in
the full bloom of health, unravaged by illness and unmarked by
some disfigurement. The funeral industry is equal to the challenge:
"In some cases the gruesome appearance of a mutilated or disease-
ridden subject may be quite discouraging. The task of restoration
may seem impossible and shake the confidence of the embalmer.
This is the time° for intestinal fortitude° and determination. Once
the formative work is begun and affected tissues are cleaned or
removed, all doubts of success vanish. It is surprising and gratifying to discover the results which may be obtained."

The embalmer, having allowed an appropriate interval to elapse,   15
returns to the attack, but now he brings into play the skill and
equipment of sculptor and cosmetician. Is a hand missing? Casting
one in plaster of Paris is a simple matter. "For replacement purposes, only a cast of the back of the hand is necessary; this is within
the ability of the average operator and is quite adequate." If a lip
or two, a nose or an ear should be missing, the embalmer has at
hand a variety of restorative waxes with which to model replace-
ments. Pores and skin texture are simulated by stippling with a
little brush, and over this cosmetics are laid on. Head off? Decap-
itation cases are rather routinely handled. Ragged edges are trimmed,
and head joined to torso with a series of splints, wires and sutures.
It is a good idea to have a little something at the neck—a scarf or
a high collar—when time for viewing comes. Swollen mouth? Cut
out tissue as needed from inside the lips. If too much is removed,
the surface contour can easily be restored by padding with cotton.
Swollen necks and cheeks are reduced by removing tissue through
vertical incisions made down each side of the neck. "When the
deceased is casketed, the pillow will hide the suture incisions . . .
as an extra precaution against leakage, the suture may be painted
with liquid sealer."

The opposite condition is more likely to present itself—that of   16
emaciation. His hypodermic syringe now loaded with massage
cream, the embalmer seeks out and fills the hollowed and sunken
areas by injection. In this procedure the backs of the hands and
fingers and the under-chin area should not be neglected.

Positioning the lips is a problem that recurrently challenges   17 the ingenuity of the embalmer. Closed too tightly, they tend to give a stern, even disapproving expression. Ideally, embalmers feel, the lips should give the impression of being ever so slightly parted, the upper lip protruding slightly for a more youthful appearance. This takes some engineering, however, as the lips tend to drift apart. Lip drift can sometimes be remedied by pushing one or two straight pins through the inner margin of the lower lip and then inserting them between the two front upper teeth. If Mr. Jones happens to have no teeth, the pins can just as easily be anchored in his Armstrong Face Former and Denture Replacer. Another method to maintain lip closure is to dislocate the lower jaw, which is then held in its new position by a wire run through holes which have been drilled through the upper and lower jaws at the midline. As the French are fond of saying, *il faut souffrir pour être belle°*.

18   If Mr. Jones has died of jaundice, the embalming fluid will very likely turn him green. Does this deter the embalmer? Not if he has intestinal fortitude. Masking pastes and cosmetics are heavily laid on, burial garments and casket interiors are color-correlated with particular care, and Jones is displayed beneath rose-colored lights. Friends will say "How *well* he looks." Death by carbon monoxide, on the other hand, can be rather a good thing from the embalmer's viewpoint: "One advantage is the fact that this type of discoloration is an exaggerated form of a natural pink coloration." This is nice because the healthy glow is already present and needs but little attention.

19   The patching and filling completed, Mr. Jones is now shaved, washed and dressed. Cream-based cosmetic, available in pink, flesh, suntan, brunette and blond, is applied to his hands and face, his hair is shampooed and combed (and, in the case of Mrs. Jones, set), his hands manicured. For the horny-handed son of toil° special care must be taken; cream should be applied to remove ingrained grime, and the nails cleaned. "If he were not in the habit of having them manicured in life, trimming and shaping is advised for better appearance—never questioned by kin."

20   Jones is now ready for casketing (this is the present participle of the verb "to casket"). In this operation his right shoulder should be depressed slightly "to turn the body a bit to the right and soften the appearance of lying flat on the back." Positioning the hands is a matter of importance, and special rubber positioning blocks may be used. The hands should be cupped slightly for a more lifelike, relaxed appearance. Proper placement of the body requires a delicate sense of balance. It should lie as high as possible in the casket, yet not so high that the lid, when lowered, will hit the nose. On the other hand, we are cautioned, placing the body too low "creates the impression that the body is in a box."

Jones is next wheeled into the appointed slumber room where   21
a few last touches may be added—his favorite pipe placed in his
hand or, if he was a great reader, a book propped into position.
(In the case of little Master Jones a Teddy bear may be clutched.)
Here he will hold open house for a few days, visiting hours
10 A.M. to 9 P.M.

All now being in readiness, the funeral director calls a staff   22
conference to make sure that each assistant knows his precise duties. Mr. Wilber Kriege writes: "This makes your staff feel that they
are a part of the team, with a definite assignment that must be
properly carried out if the whole plan is to succeed. You never
heard of a football coach who failed to talk to his entire team before
they go on the field. They have drilled on the plays they are to
execute for hours and days, and yet the successful coach knows
the importance of making even the bench-warming third-string
substitute feel that he is important if the game is to be won." The
winning of *this* game is predicated upon glass-smooth handling of
the logistics°. The funeral director has notified the pallbearers whose
names were furnished by the family, has arranged for the presence
of clergyman, organist, and soloist, has provided transportation
for everybody, has organized and listed the flowers sent by friends.
In *Psychology of Funeral Service* Mr. Edward A. Martin points out:
"He may not always do as much as the family thinks he is doing,
but it is his helpful guidance that they appreciate in knowing they
are proceeding as they should. . . . The important thing is how
well his services can be used to make the family believe they are
giving unlimited expression to their own sentiment."

The religious service may be held in a church or in the chapel   23
of the funeral home; the funeral director vastly prefers the latter
arrangement, for not only is it more convenient for him but it
affords him the opportunity to show off his beautiful facilities to
the gathered mourners. After the clergyman has had his say, the
mourners queue up to file past the casket for a last look at the
deceased. The family is *never* asked whether they want an open-
casket ceremony; in the absence of their instruction to the contrary,
this is taken for granted. Consequently well over 90 per cent of all
American funerals feature the open casket—a custom unknown in
other parts of the world. Foreigners are astonished by it. An English
woman living in San Francisco described her reaction in a letter to
the writer:

I myself have attended only one funeral here—that of an
elderly fellow worker of mine. After the service I could not
understand why everyone was walking towards the coffin (sorry,
I mean casket), but thought I had better follow the crowd. It
shook me rigid to get there and find the casket open and poor

old Oscar lying there in his brown tweed suit, wearing a suntan makeup and just the wrong shade of lipstick. If I had not been extremely fond of the old boy, I have a horrible feeling that I might have giggled. Then and there I decided that I could never face another American funeral—even dead.

24   The casket (which has been resting throughout the service on a Classic Beauty Ultra Metal Casket Bier) is now transferred by a hydraulically operated device called Porto-Lift to a balloon-tired, Glide Easy casket carriage which will wheel it to yet another conveyance, the Cadillac Funeral Coach. This may be lavender, cream, light green—anything but black. Interiors, of course, are color-correlated, "for the man who cannot stop short of perfection."

25   At graveside, the casket is lowered into the earth. This office, once the prerogative° of friends of the deceased, is now performed by a patented mechanical lowering device. A "Lifetime Green" artificial grass mat is at the ready to conceal the sere° earth, and overhead, to conceal the sky, is a portable Steril Chapel Tent ("resists the intense heat and humidity of summer and the terrific storms of winter . . . available in Silver Grey, Rose or Evergreen"). Now is the time for the ritual scattering of earth over the coffin, as the solemn words "earth to earth, ashes to ashes, dust to dust" are pronounced by the officiating cleric. This can today be accomplished "with a mere flick of the wrist with the Gordon Leak-Proof Earth Dispenser. No grasping of a handful of dirt, no soiled fingers. Simple, dignified, beautiful, reverent! The modern way!" The Gordon Earth Dispenser (at $5) is of nickel-plated brass construction. It is not only "attractive to the eye and long wearing"; it is also "one of the 'tools' for building better public relations" if presented as "an appropriate non-commercial gift" to the clergyman. It is shaped something like a saltshaker.

26   Untouched by human hand, the coffin and the earth are now united.

27   It is in the function of directing the participants through this maze of gadgetry that the funeral director has assigned to himself his relatively new role of "grief therapist." He has relieved the family of every detail, he has revamped° the corpse to look like a living doll, he has arranged for it to nap for a few days in a slumber room, he has put on a well-oiled performance in which the concept of *death* has played no part whatsoever—unless it was inconsiderately mentioned by the clergyman who conducted the religious service. He has done everything in his power to make the funeral a real pleasure for everybody concerned. He and his team have given their all to score an upset victory over death.

JESSICA MITFORD

Essayist Jessica Mitford was born to a prominent family at Batsford mansion, England, in 1917. She settled in the United States in 1939. Mitford began her writing career in the 1950s; among her best known works are *Hons and Rebels*, *The Trial of Dr. Spock*, and *Kind and Unusual Punishment*.

Words and Meanings

Paragraph

formaldehyde:	chemical used to embalm bodies	
Alas, poor Yorick:	famous line from Shakespeare's *Hamlet*, addressed to a skull	2
decedent:	dead person	3
docility:	lamblike trust and willingness	4
mandatory:	necessary	5
dissuaded:	persuaded against	
intractable reticence:	unwillingness to discuss	6
stocks:	wooden shackles used to punish offenders	8
somatic:	bodily	10
rudimentary:	basic	
intestinal fortitude:	"guts," courage	14
il faut souffrir pour être belle:	French for "you have to suffer to be beautiful"	17
horny-handed son of toil:	cliché for a labourer	19
logistics:	arrangements	22
prerogative:	privilege	25
sere:	dry	
revamped:	altered	27

Structure and Strategy

1. Consider the title and first paragraph of this essay. What ANALOGY is introduced? How does the analogy help establish Mitford's TONE?
2. Look at the last paragraph. How is the analogy introduced in paragraph 1 reinforced in the conclusion? What words specifically contribute to the analogy?
3. The process of preparing a corpse for burial involves two main procedures: embalming and restoration. Identify the paragraphs in which Mitford explains these two procedures.
4. Identify the substeps which make up the final stage in the burial process (paragraphs 20 to 25).

Content and Purpose

1. In paragraphs 2 and 8, without saying so directly, how does Mitford imply that she disapproves of embalming? Can you find other examples of her implied disapproval?
2. What medical justification for embalming is offered in paragraph 10? How does Mitford undercut this argument?
3. Why does Mitford refer to the corpse as "Mr. Jones"?
4. What reason does Mitford suggest is behind the "secrecy surrounding embalming"? If the details of the procedure were common knowledge, what do you think the effect would be on the mortuary business?
5. What was your reaction to Mitford's essay? Do you think your response was what the author intended?

Suggestions for Writing

1. Mitford's essay explains the funeral director's job as a process. Write a process analysis explaining a job or task with which you are familiar.
2. Research another means of disposing of the dead, such as cremation (burning a dead body) or cryonics (freezing a dead, diseased body in the hope of restoring it to life when a cure has been found). Write an informational process paper explaining it.
3. Write an informational process analysis explaining the ceremony or ritual behaviour associated with the birth of a baby, a child's birthday, or the initiation of a child into the religious community (such as a bar mitzvah or confirmation).

Writing, Typing & Economic$

JOHN KENNETH GALBRAITH

1   Six or seven years ago, when I was spending a couple of terms at Trinity College, Cambridge, I received a proposal of more than usual interest from the University of California. It was that I resign from Harvard and accept a chair° there

"Writing, Typing, and Economics" (which appeared in *The Atlantic Monthly*) is from *Annals of an Abiding Liberal* by John Kenneth Galbraith. Copyright 1979 by John Kenneth Galbraith. Reprinted by permission of Houghton Mifflin Company.

in English. More precisely, it was to be the chair in rhetoric; they assured me that rhetoric was a traditional and not, as one would naturally suppose, a pejorative° title. My task would be to hold seminars with the young on what I had learned about writing in general and on technical matters in particular.

I was attracted by the idea. I had spent several decades attempting to teach the young about economics. And the practical consequences were not reassuring. When I entered the field in the early 1930s, it was generally known that the modern economy could suffer a serious depression, and that it could have a serious inflation. In the ensuing forty years my teaching had principally advanced to the point of telling that it was possible to have both at once. This was soon to be associated with the belief of William Simon and Alan Greenspan, the gifts of Richard Nixon and Gerald Ford to our science, that progress in this subject is measured by the speed of the return to the ideas of the eighteenth century. A subject where it can be believed that you go ahead by going back has many problems for a teacher. Things are better now. Mr. Carter's economists do not believe in going back. But they are caught in a delicate balance between their fear of inflation and unemployment and their fear of doing anything about them. It is hard to conclude that economics is a productive intellectual and pedagogical° investment.

Then I began to consider what I could tell about writing. My experience was certainly ample. I had been initiated by two inspired professors in Canada, O.J. Stevenson and E.C. McLean. They were men who deeply loved their craft and who were willing to spend endless hours with a student, however obscure his talent. I had been an editor of *Fortune*, which in my day meant mostly being a writer. Editor was thought a more distinguished title and justified more pay. Both as an editor proper and as a writer, I had had the close attention of Henry Robinson Luce. Harry Luce is in danger of being remembered for his political judgments, which left much to be desired; he found unblemished merit in John Foster Dulles, Robert A. Taft, and Chiang Kai-shek. But more important, he was an acute businessman and a truly brilliant editor. One proof is that while Time, Inc. publications have become politically more predictable since he departed, they have become infinitely less amusing.

Finally, as I reflected, among my qualifications was the amount of my life that I have spent at a typewriter. Nominally I have been a teacher. In practice I have been a writer—as generations of Harvard students have suspected. Faced with the choice of spending time on the unpublished scholarship of a graduate student or the unpublished work of Galbraith, I have rarely hesitated. Superficially, at least, I was well qualified for that California chair.

5   There was, however, a major difficulty. It was that I could tell everything I knew about writing in approximately half an hour. For the rest of the term I would have nothing to say except as I could invite discussion, this being the last resort of the empty academic mind. I could use up a few hours telling how a writer should deal with publishers. This is a field of study in which I especially rejoice. All authors should seek to establish a relationship of warmth, affection, and mutual mistrust with their publishers. This is in the hope that the uncertainty will add, however marginally, to compensation. But instruction on how to deal with publishers and how to bear up under the inevitable defeat would be for a very advanced course. It is not the sort of thing that the average beginning writer at Berkeley would find immediately practical.

6   So I returned to the few things that I could teach. The first lesson would have to do with the all-important issue of inspiration. All writers know that on some golden mornings they are touched by the wand—are on intimate terms with poetry and cosmic truth. I have experienced those moments myself. Their lesson is simple: [i]t's a total illusion. And the danger in the illusion is that you will wait for those moments. Such is the horror of having to face the typewriter that you will spend all your time waiting. I am persuaded that most writers, like most shoemakers, are about as good one day as the next (a point which Trollope made), hangovers apart. The difference is the result of euphoria°, alcohol, or imagination. The meaning is that one had better go to his or her typewriter every morning and stay there regardless of the seeming result. It will be much the same.

7   All professions have their own ways of justifying laziness. Harvard professors are deeply impressed by the jeweled fragility of their minds. More than the thinnest metal, these are subject terribly to fatigue. More than six hours teaching a week is fatal—and an impairment of academic freedom. So, at any given moment, they are resting their minds in preparation for the next orgiastic act of insight or revelation. Writers, in contrast, do nothing because they are waiting for inspiration.

8   In my own case there are days when the result is so bad that no fewer than five revisions are required. However, when I'm greatly inspired, only four revisions are needed before, as I've often said, I put in that note of spontaneity° which even my meanest critics concede°. My advice to those eager students in California would be, "Do not wait for the golden moment. It may well be worse." I would also warn against the flocking tendency of writers and its use as a cover for idleness. It helps greatly in the avoidance

of work to be in the company of others who are also waiting for the golden moment. The best place to write is by yourself, because writing becomes an escape from the terrible boredom of your own personality. It's the reason that for years I've favored Switzerland, where I look at the telephone and yearn to hear it ring.

The question of revision is closely allied with that of inspiration. There may be inspired writers for whom the first draft is just right. But anyone who is not certifiably a Milton had better assume that the first draft is a very primitive thing. The reason is simple: [w]riting is difficult work. Ralph Paine, who managed *Fortune* in my time, used to say that anyone who said writing was easy was either a bad writer or an unregenerate° liar. Thinking, as Voltaire avowed, is also a very tedious thing which men—or women—will do any-thing to avoid. So all first drafts are deeply flawed by the need to combine composition with thought. Each later draft is less de-manding in this regard. Hence the writing can be better. There does come a time when revision is for the sake of change—when one has become so bored with the words that anything that is different looks better. But even then it may be better.   9

For months in 1955–1956, when I was working on *The Affluent°* *Society*, my title was "The Opulent° Society." Eventually I could stand it no longer: the word opulent had a nasty, greasy sound. One day, before starting work, I looked up the synonyms in the dictionary. First to meet my eye was the word "affluent." I had only one worry; that was whether I could possibly sell it to the publisher. All publishers wish to have books called *The Crisis in American Democracy.* My title, to my surprise, was acceptable. Mark Twain once said that the difference between the right adjective and the next-best adjective is the difference between lightning and a lightning bug.   10

Next, I would stress a rather old-fashioned idea to those students. It was above all the lesson of Harry Luce. No one who worked for him ever again escaped the feeling that he was there looking over one's shoulder. In his hand was a pencil; down on each page one could expect, any moment, a long swishing wiggle accompanied by the comment: "This can go." Invariably it could. It was written to please the author and not the reader. Or to fill in the space. The gains from brevity are obvious; in most efforts to achieve brevity, it is the worst and dullest that goes. It is the worst and dullest that spoils the rest.   11

I know that brevity is now out of favor. The *New York Review* *of Books* prides itself on giving its authors as much space as they want and sometimes twice as much as they need. Even those who have read only Joyce must find their thoughts wandering before   12 the end of the fortnightly article. Writing for television, I've learned in the last year or two, is an exercise in relentless condensation. It has left me with the feeling that even brevity can be carried to extremes. But the danger, as I look at some of the newer fashions in writing, is not great.

13   The next of my injunctions°, which I would impart with even less hope of success, would concern alcohol. Nothing is so pleasant. Nothing is so important for giving the writer a sense of confidence in himself. And nothing so impairs the product. Again there are exceptions: I remember a brilliant writer at *Fortune* for whom I was responsible, who could work only with his hat on and after consuming a bottle of Scotch. There were major crises in the years immediately after World War II, when Scotch was difficult to find. But it is, quite literally, very sobering to reflect upon how many good American writers have been destroyed by this solace—by the sauce. Scott Fitzgerald, Sinclair Lewis, Thomas Wolfe, Ernest Hemingway, William Faulkner—the list goes on and on. Hamish Hamilton, once my English publisher, put the question to James Thurber: "Jim, why is it so many of your great writers have ruined themselves with drink?" Thurber thought long and carefully and finally replied: "It's this way, Jamie. They wrote these novels, and they sold very well. They made a lot of money and so they could buy whiskey by the case."

14   Their reputation was universal. A few years before his death, John Steinbeck, an appreciative but not compulsive drinker, went to Moscow. It was a triumphal tour; and in a letter that he sent me about his hosts, he said: "I found I enjoyed the Soviet hustlers pretty much. There was a kind of youthful honesty about their illicit intentions that was not without charm. And their lives are difficult under their four-party system [a reference that escapes me]. It takes a fairly deft° or very lucky man to make his way upward in the worker's paradise." I later heard that one night after a particularly effusive celebration, he decided to make his way back to the hotel on foot. On the way he was overcome by fatigue and the hospitality he had received and sat down on a bench in a small park to rest. A policeman, called a militiaman in Moscow, came along and informed John, who was now asleep, and his companion, who spoke Russian, that the benches could not be occupied at that hour. His companion explained, rightly, that John was a very great American writer and that an exception should be made. The militiaman insisted. The companion explained again, insisted more strongly. Presently a transcendental light came over the policeman's face. He looked at Steinbeck asleep on the bench, inspected his condition more closely, recoiled slightly from the fumes, and said, "Oh, oh, Gemingway." Then he took off his cap and tiptoed carefully away.

We are all desperately afraid of sounding like Carry Nation°.   15
I must take the risk. Any writer who wants to do his best against
a deadline should stick to Coca-Cola. If he doesn't have a deadline,
he can risk Seven-Up.

Next, I would want to tell my students of a point strongly pressed,   16
if my memory serves, by Shaw. He once said that as he grew older,
he became less and less interested in theory, more and more interested in information. The temptation in writing is just the reverse. Nothing is so hard to come by as a new and interesting fact.
Nothing is so easy on the feet as a generalization. I now pick up
magazines and leaf through them looking for articles that are rich
with facts; I do not care much what they are. Richly evocative° and
deeply percipient° theory I avoid. It leaves me cold unless I am the
author of it. My advice to all young writers is to stick to research
and reporting with only a minimum of interpretation. And especially this is my advice to all older writers, particularly to columnists. As the feet give out, they seek to have the mind take their
place.

Reluctantly, but from a long and terrible experience, I would   17
urge my young writers to avoid all attempts at humor. It does
greatly lighten one's task. I've often wondered who made it im-
polite to laugh at one's own jokes: it is one of the major enjoyments
of life. And that is the point. Humor is an intensely personal, largely
internal thing. What pleases some, including the source, does not
please others. One laughs; another says, "Well, I certainly see
nothing funny about that." And the second opinion has just as
much standing as the first, maybe more. Where humor is concerned, there are no standards—no one can say what is good or
bad, although you can be sure that everyone will. Only a very
foolish man will use a form of language that is wholly uncertain
in its effect. That is the nature of humor.

There are other reasons for avoiding humor. In our society the   18
solemn person inspires far more trust than the one who laughs.
The politician allows himself one joke at the beginning of his speech.
A ritual. Then he changes his expression, affects an aspect of mor-
bid solemnity signaling that, after all, he is a totally serious man.
Nothing so undermines a point as its association with a wisecrack—
the very word is pejorative.

Also, as Art Buchwald has pointed out, we live in an age when   19
it is hard to invent anything that is as funny as everyday life. How
could one improve, for example, on the efforts of the great men
of television to attribute cosmic significance to the offhand and
hilarious way Bert Lance combined professed fiscal conservatism
with an unparalleled personal commitment to the deficit financing
of John Maynard Keynes°? And because the real world is so funny,

there is almost nothing you can do, short of labeling a joke a joke, to keep people from taking it seriously. A few years ago in *Harper's* I invented the theory that socialism in our time was the result of our dangerous addiction to team sports. The ethic of the team is all wrong for free enterprise. The code words are cooperation; team spirit; accept leadership; the coach is always right. Authoritarianism is sanctified; the individualist is a poor team player, a menace. All this our vulnerable adolescents learn. I announced the formation of an organization to combat this deadly trend and to promote boxing and track instead. I called it the C.I.A.—Congress for Individualist Athletics. Hundreds wrote in to *Harper's* asking to join. Or demanding that baseball be exempted. A batter is on his own. I presented the letters to the Kennedy Library.

20   Finally, I would come to a matter of much personal interest, intensely self-serving. It concerns the peculiar pitfalls of the writer who is dealing with presumptively difficult or technical matters. Economics is an example, and within the field of economics the subject of money, with the history of which I have been much concerned, is an especially good case. Any specialist who ventures to write on money with a view to making himself intelligible works under a grave moral hazard. He will be accused of oversimplification. The charge will be made by his fellow professionals, however obtuse° or incompetent. They will have a sympathetic hearing from the layman. That is because no layman really expects to understand about money, inflation, or the International Monetary Fund. If he does, he suspects that he is being fooled. One can have respect only for someone who is decently confusing.

21   In the case of economics there are no important propositions that cannot be stated in plain language. Qualifications and refinements are numerous and of great technical complexity. These are important for separating the good students from the dolts. But in economics the refinements rarely, if ever, modify the essential and practical point. The writer who seeks to be intelligible needs to be right; he must be challenged if his argument leads to an erroneous conclusion and especially if it leads to the wrong action. But he can safely dismiss the charge that he has made the subject too easy. The truth is not difficult.

22   Complexity and obscurity have professional value—they are the academic equivalents of apprenticeship rules in the building trades. They exclude the outsiders, keep down the competition, preserve the image of a privileged or priestly class. The man who makes things clear is a scab. He is criticized less for his clarity than for his treachery.

23   Additionally, and especially in the social sciences, much un-

clear writing is based on unclear or incomplete thought. It is possible with safety to be technically obscure about something you haven't thought out. It is impossible to be wholly clear on something you do not understand. Clarity thus exposes flaws in the thought. The person who undertakes to make difficult matters clear is infringing on the sovereign right of numerous economists, sociologists, and political scientists to make bad writing the disguise for sloppy, imprecise, or incomplete thought. One can understand the resulting anger. Adam Smith, John Stuart Mill, John Maynard Keynes were writers of crystalline clarity most of the time. Marx had great moments, as in *The Communist Manifesto*. Economics owes very little, if anything, to the practitioners of scholarly obscurity. If any of my California students should come to me from the learned professions, I would counsel them in all their writing to keep the confidence of their colleagues. This they should do by being always complex, always obscure, invariably a trifle vague.

You might say that all this constitutes a meager yield for a   24
lifetime of writing. Or that writing on economics, as someone once said of Kerouac's° prose, is not writing but typing. True.

☐

JOHN KENNETH GALBRAITH

John Kenneth Galbraith, the famous economist, was born in 1908 at Iona Station, Ont., and educated at the Ontario Agricultural College, now the University of Guelph. He emigrated to the United States, where he taught at Harvard University, served as an editor of *Fortune Magazine*, as well as the American ambassador to India. Among his many books are *The Affluent Society* and *The Scotch*, a memoir of his early years.

Words and Meanings

Paragraph

chair:	university teaching position	1
pejorative:	negative	
pedagogical:	educational	2
euphoria:	feeling of great joy	6
spontaneity:	naturalness	8
concede:	admit, acknowledge	
unregenerate:	unrepentant, incapable of reform	9
affluent:	wealthy	10
opulent:	very wealthy, lavish	
injunction:	strong recommendation	13

14	deft:	skilful
15	Carry Nation:	axe-wielding crusader against alcohol
16	evocative: percipient:	thought-provoking full of insight
19	John Maynard Keynes:	major twentieth-century economic theorist
20	obtuse:	stupid
24	Kerouac:	Jack Kerouac, novelist known for his highly in- dividual, offbeat prose style

Structure and Strategy

1. How many paragraphs make up the INTRODUCTION to this essay? Why do you think Galbraith spends so long introducing his subject?
2. List in order the steps Galbraith recommends that the would-be writer follow.
3. How does Galbraith achieve COHERENCE? Consider his use of TRANSITIONS and TONE.
4. Has Galbraith written a directional or an informational process analysis?

Content and Purpose

1. Against what does Galbraith especially warn the beginning writer? (See paragraphs 13, 14, and 15.) Summarize in a sentence or two his reasons for this lengthy warning.
2. What does Galbraith suggest about writers and writing in this sentence (paragraph 8)?: "The best place to write is by yourself, because writing becomes an escape from the terrible boredom of your own personality."
3. Why does Galbraith advise the beginning writer to avoid humour (paragraphs 17 and 18) and then include an example of his own humour (paragraph 19)?
4. After writing an essay on how to write clearly and concisely, Galbraith concludes with a discussion of economics and scholarly obscurity and advises his students from the learned professions to write obscurely. Why? Consider Galbraith's overall purpose and TONE.

Suggestion for Writing

Write a directional process essay, either humorous or serious, in which you explain to a new college student how to write his or her first English essay.

Additional Suggestions for Writing: Process Analysis

I.   Choose one of the topics below and develop it into an informational process analysis.
1. How a computer (or any other mechanical device) works.
2. How a child is born.
3. How a particular rock group, sports personality, or political figure appeals to the crowd.
4. How a bill is passed in parliament.
5. How a company plans the marketing of a new product.
6. How a particular chemical reaction takes place.
7. How alcohol (or any other drug) affects the body.
8. How microwaves cook food.
9. How learning takes place.
10. How a particular process in nature occurs: for example, how coral forms, a spider spins a web, salmon spawn, lightning happens, or a snowflake forms.

II. Choose one of the topics below and develop it into a directional process analysis.
1. How to buy (or sell) something: a used car, a house, a piece of sports equipment, a stereo system, junk.
2. How to perform a particular life-saving technique: for example, mouth-to-mouth resuscitation or the Heimlich manoeuvre.
3. How to play roulette, blackjack, poker, or some other game of chance.
4. How to get attention.
5. How to prepare for a job interview.
6. How to choose a mate (or roommate, friend, or pet).
7. How to make or build something: for example, beer, a kite, a radio transmitter, bread.
8. How to survive English (or any other subject you are studying).
9. How to get your own way.
10. How to talk your way out of a traffic ticket, a failing grade, a date, a conversation with a bore, a threatened punishment, or keeping a promise.

U N I T

Division and Classification: Explaining Parts and Kinds

What? The Definition

In **analysis**, we separate something into its parts in order to determine their essential features and study their relationship to each other. A research chemist, for example, analyzes a substance by breaking it down into its component elements. We speak of trying to "analyze someone's motives" in an effort to understand what prompts a person to behave in a certain way. Some people undergo years of psychoanalysis in an attempt to identify and explore their unconscious mental processes. In Unit Two, we used the term *process analysis* to describe a writing pattern in which the subject is divided into steps or stages: the steps involved in baking beans or in embalming a body, for instance. In Unit Five, we will look at subjects that are analyzed in terms of their causes or effects, an organizational pattern called *causal analysis*. The subjects of this unit, **division** and **classification**, are also forms of analysis.

The various kinds of analysis all involve dividing or sorting—breaking a complex whole into its parts or categories.

In the rhetorical pattern called *division*, a single subject is divided into its component parts. For example, a Big Mac consists of two all-beef patties, special sauce, pickles, cheese, lettuce, and onions on a sesame seed bun. A newspaper can be divided into its various sections: news, sports, features, entertainment, and classified ads. In one of the reading selections that follows, Martin Luther King, Jr. divides a "complete life" into three dimensions: length, breadth, and height. In division, the subject is always a single entity: one hamburger, one newspaper, or one life. The writer's task is to identify and explain the parts that make up the whole.

In *classification*, on the other hand, the subject is a whole group of things, and the writer's task is to sort the group into classes or categories on the basis of some shared characteristic. For example, fast-food hamburgers can be classified according to the chains that serve them: McDonald's, Wendy's, Harvey's, and Burger King. Then the writer would explain the distinctive features of the burgers in each category. Newspapers can be classified into tabloids like the *Toronto Sun*, which aim for a working-class audience; broad-based, general circulation papers like the *Toronto Star*, which aim for a middle-class audience; and upscale, business-oriented papers like *The Globe and Mail*, which appeal to professional, upper-middle-class readers. Singles could be classified into the kinds of dates they represent: divine, dull, or disastrous.

Classification is a familiar strategy. It is used so often that there is even an old joke that relies on popular knowledge of the technique for its point: "There are two kinds of people in the world—those who sort the world into two kinds of people and those who don't."

Why? The Purpose

Division and classification are methods by which we can isolate, separate, and sort things. They are essential ways of making sense out of the world around us. Both strategies appeal to the reader's need for order in the way information is presented.

A *division paper* usually answers one of two questions:

1. What are the component parts of S?
2. What are the important characteristics or features of S?

Once you have reduced the subject to its constituent parts, you can examine each part in turn to discover its distinctive features and its function within the whole. Division can be used to explore and clarify many kinds of subjects. You can analyze an organization (a college, for instance), a geographical location (such as the city of Winnipeg), a musical group (perhaps a rock band), an idea (equal pay for work of equal value), or a part of the body (such as the heart), by dividing it into its parts.

Classification, as we've seen, is a sorting mechanism. It is the pattern to choose when you find yourself writing a paper that answers the question, "What are the main kinds or types of S?"

Classification is useful when you need to examine a group of similar things with meaningful differences between them. You could classify colleges: CEGEPs in Quebec, CAATs in Ontario, and university-transfer institutions in British Columbia. You could classify people: various kinds of musicians or actors or athletes, for example. In one of the essays in this unit, Max Eastman classifies all the people of the world into two types: practical and poetic. Ideas (such as economic theories), places (such as resorts, slums, amusement parks), and events (such as golf tournaments, weddings, elections) can all be sorted into kinds and explained in terms that your readers will find informative, useful, and even—when appropriate—entertaining.

Division and classification are used to give shape and order to the welter of information that surrounds us. In the business world, for example, papers and reports are too often a hodgepodge of data or opinion that fails to provide the reader with an orderly explanation of the subject. Dividing or classifying the material organizes it into logically related units that the reader can grasp and understand.

Besides giving form and focus to shapeless chunks of information, division and classification are useful for evaluation purposes. A real estate company might divide a city into its residential areas so that prospective home buyers can choose where they want to live. Consumers' magazines classify different kinds of dishwashers, stereo turntables, automobiles, or dandruff shampoos, in order to recommend which brand is the best buy. Whether the writer's purpose is to organize a mass of data or to evaluate the relative merits of several items or ideas, division and classification can help to ensure a clear, coherent piece of communication.

How? The Technique

Writing a good *division paper* involves three steps: clarifying the principle of division, identifying the appropriate components of the subject, and constructing a clear thesis statement.

Most subjects can be divided in a number of different ways. For instance, you could divide a college into its physical areas: classrooms, offices, cafeteria, recreational facilities, and plant services. Or you could divide a college into its human components: faculty, students, administrators, and support staff. How you choose to divide something will determine the parts that you analyze and the relationship between those parts that you explore. Choose your dividing principle carefully, keeping your audience in mind: what specific aspects of your subject do you want your readers to know more about?

Second, decide whether your division is to be *exhaustive* (that is, to include *all* the component parts of the subject) or *representative* (to include *a few* of the major component parts). Sometimes the nature of your subject determines which approach you will take: if there are only two or three component parts, for example, it makes good sense to include them all. But if there are a dozen or more, a carefully chosen representative sampling will give your readers the information they require without trying their patience in the process.

Third, include a thesis statement that maps out the scope and arrangement of your paper. It will probably look something like this:

> The component parts of S are a, b, c, and d.

Example: Blood is made up of plasma, red cells, white cells, and platelets.

On the other hand, it may read like this:

> The significant characteristics of S are a, b, and c.

Example: A good business letter is one that is concise, clear, and courteous.

Classification papers involve similar steps. To begin with, make sure your classification is both complete and logical. For instance, classifying the Romance languages (those descended from Latin since 800 A.D.) into French, Italian, and Portuguese would be incomplete because there are many more Romance languages than these three. However, if your purpose were to classify the Romance languages most frequently spoken in Canada today, the list above would be complete.

Your classification will be logical as long as your categories do not overlap: they must all be different from each other. To test your classification for logical soundness, check to be sure no example can be included under more than one category. For instance, if you were to classify your favourite kinds of movies into the categories of science fiction, comedy, and war films, where would you put *Catch-22*, a comic film about war, or *Star Wars*?

Of course, a classification paper must be based on a clear thesis statement:

> The kinds (or categories) of S are a, b, c, and d.

Example: Most teachers fit into one of three categories: Bumblers, Martinets, and Pros.

Division and classification are useful rhetorical strategies by themselves, but they can be used together effectively, too. In "What I Have Lived For," for example, Bertrand Russell divides his life's purpose, his reason for living, into what he calls "three passions": the longing for love, the search for knowledge, and pity for the suffering of mankind. Then he classifies his search for knowledge into the three kinds of knowledge he sought: the social sciences, the natural sciences, and mathematics.

Whether you choose to apply them separately or together, division and classification are two of the most useful strategies you can use to explain a complex subject to your readers. They can help you create order out of chaos in many different situations. Both strategies have practical and professional applications. Division is used on the job in organizational analyses, cost breakdowns, and technical reports. Classification is frequently the logical pattern on which performance appraisals, market projections, or product assessments are based. The ability to analyze through division and classification is obviously a useful skill for any writer to acquire.

The sample essay below is a paper that classifies into three categories a subject dear to the hearts of all students: teachers.

Bumblers, Martinets, and Pros

Introduction (uses quotations) ———→

The playwright George Bernard Shaw provided us with the memorable definition, "Those who can, do. Those who can't, teach." The film director Woody Allen took the definition one step farther, "Those who can't teach, teach phys ed." At one time or another, most of us have suffered these truisms. We've all encountered teachers who fit Shaw's definition, as well as some who manage to do their jobs successfully, even cheerfully. Overall, most teachers fit into one of three categories: Bumblers, Martinets, and Pros.

Thesis statement ———→

First category (developed with descriptive details)

Every student gets a Bumbler at least once. She's the teacher who trips over the doorjamb as she makes her first entrance. She looks permanently flustered, can't find her lesson plan, and dithers as she scrambles through her mess of books and papers. The Bumbler can't handle the simplest educational technologies: chalk self-destructs in her fingers, overhead projectors blow up at her touch, and filmstrips snap if she so much as looks in their direction. Organization isn't Ms. Bumbler's strong point, either. She drifts off in mid-sentence, eyes focused dreamily out the window. Students can easily derail her with off-topic questions. She'll forget to collect assignments or to give the test that everyone has studied for. The Bumbler is an amiable sort, but her mind is on a perpetual slow boat to nowhere. Students can learn in her class, but only if they are willing to take a great deal of initiative.

Second category (note the definition of an unfamiliar term)

Martinet was the name of a seventeenth-century French general who invented a particularly nasty system of military drill. Thus, the word itself has come to mean a strict disciplinarian, a stickler for the rules, a tough "drill sergeant." As a teacher, the Martinet is an uptight, rigid authoritarian who sends shivers down students' spines. He rarely smiles, certainly not during the first month. His voice is harsh, biting, and he specializes in the barbed response and the humiliating putdown. His classes unfold in a precise and boring manner. Each minute is accounted for, as he scouts the room for any disruptive or slumbering captives to be brought to heel. He tolerates no searching questions or interesting digressions. His assignments are lengthy and tedious; his tests are notoriously fearsome. Instead of the critical inquiry into ideas, rote learning takes place in the Martinet's classroom. And it takes place at the expense of the patience and self-esteem of his students.

Third category (note the implied contrast to the previous two categories)

Every once in a while, a student is blessed with the teacher who can be described as a Professional. The Pro is characterized by a genuine liking and respect for students and is motivated by enthusiasm for the subject matter. This teacher is organized enough to present lessons clearly, but not so hidebound as to cut off questions or the occasional excursion along an interesting sideroad of learning. The Pro's classroom is relaxed, friendly, yet stimulating enough to keep students concentrating on the task at hand. Assignments are designed to enhance learning; tests are rigorous but fair. Landing in the Pro's class is a stroke of luck. Such a teacher is a gift, for the Pro imparts the desire and ability to learn to the students he or she encounters.

Conclusion (asks a rhetorical question)

These characterizations of the Bumbler, the Martinet, and the Pro are, of course, extreme portraits of some of the worst and best qualities a teacher can possess. Indeed, some teachers, in Jekyll-and-Hyde fashion, display characteristics of two or more types, sometimes in a single class period! In an ideal world and a perfect course, the student would be given a choice of instructors. Who would opt for a Bumbler or a Martinet, given the chance to sign up for a Pro?

Practical and Poetic People

MAX EASTMAN

1   A simple experiment will distinguish two types of human nature. Gather a throng of people and pour them into a ferry-boat. By the time the boat has swung into the river

"Practical and Poetic People" from *Enjoyment of Poetry: With Other Essays on Aesthetics* by Max Eastman, copyright 1939. Reprinted by permission of Charles Scribner's Sons.

you will find that a certain proportion have taken the trouble to climb upstairs, in order to be out on deck and see what is to be seen as they cross over. The rest have settled indoors, to think what they will do upon reaching the other side, or perhaps lose themselves in apathy° or tobacco smoke. But leaving out those apathetic, or addicted to a single enjoyment, we may divide all the alert passengers on the boat into two classes—those who are interested in crossing the river, and those who are merely interested in getting across. And we may divide all the people on the earth, or all the moods of people, in the same way. Some of them are chiefly occupied with attaining ends, and some with receiving experiences. The distinction of the two will be more marked when we name the first kind practical, and the second poetic, for common knowledge recognizes that a person poetic or in a poetic mood is impractical, and a practical person is intolerant of poetry.

We can see the force of this intolerance too, and how deeply   2
it is justified, if we make clear to our minds just what it means to be practical, and what a great thing it is. It means to be controlled in your doings by the consideration of ends yet unattained. The practical man is never distracted by things, or aspects of things, which have no bearing on his purpose, but, ever seizing the significant, he moves with a single mind and a single emotion toward the goal. And even when the goal is achieved you will hardly see him pause to rejoice in it; he is already on his way to another achievement. For that is the irony of his nature. His joy is not in any conquest or destination, but his joy is in going toward it. To which joy he adds the pleasure of being praised as a practical man, and a man who will arrive.

In a more usual sense, perhaps, a practical man is a man occu-   3
pied with attaining certain ends that people consider important. He must stick pretty close to the business of feeding and preserving life. Nourishment and shelter, money-making, maintaining respectability, and if possible a family—these are the things that give its common meaning to the word "practical." An acute regard for such features of the scenery, and the universe, as contribute or can be made to contribute to these ends, and a systematic neglect of all other features, are the traits of mind which this word popularly suggests. And it is because of the vital importance of these things to almost all people that the word "practical" is a eulogy°, and is able to be so scornful of the word "poetic."

"It is an earnest thing to be alive in this world. With compe-   4
tition, with war, with disease and poverty and oppression, misfortune and death on-coming, who but fools will give serious attention to what is not significant to the business?"

"Yes—but what is the *use* of being alive in the world, if life is   5
so oppressive in its moral character that we must always be busy

getting somewhere, and never simply realizing where we are? What were the value of your eternal achieving, if we were not here on our holiday to appreciate, among other things, some of the things you have achieved?"

6   Thus, if we could discover a purely poetic and a purely practical person, might they reason together. But we can discover nothing so satisfactory to our definitions, and therefore let us conclude the discussion of the difference between them. It has led us to our own end—a clearer understanding of the nature of poetic people, and of all people when they are in a poetic mood. They are lovers of the qualities of things. They are not engaged, as the learned say that all life is, in becoming adjusted to an environment, but they are engaged in becoming acquainted with it. They are possessed by the impulse to realize, an impulse as deep, and arbitrary, and unexplained as that "will to live" which lies at the bottom of all the explanations. It seems but the manifestation°, indeed, of that will itself in a concrete and positive form. It is a wish to experience life and the world. That is the essence of the poetic temper.

MAX EASTMAN

Max Eastman (1883–1969) was a poet, philosopher, and social critic who taught at Columbia University. Co-founder and editor of various socialist periodicals and an editor of Karl Marx's works, Eastman is best known for his social criticism, including such works as *The Literary Mind: Its Place in an Age of Science* and *The End of Socialism in Russia*.

Paragraph   **Words and Meanings**

1   apathy: indifference, lack of interest

3   eulogy: praise, positive expression

6   manifestation: demonstration, display

Structure and Strategy

1.   Eastman introduces his thesis with an ANALOGY. Why? How does it help the reader to understand his point?
2.   What method of development does Eastman use in paragraphs 2 and 3? What is the function of these two paragraphs?
3.   What unusual method does Eastman use to develop paragraphs 4 and 5? Why?
4.   Where does Eastman explain what he means by the "poetic" personality? Why does he devote comparatively little space to this topic?

Content and Purpose

1. In paragraph 1, Eastman regards "a person . . . in a poetic mood as impractical, and a practical person as intolerant of poetry." Do you agree?
2. Which sort of person does Eastman prefer—the practical or the poetic? How do you know?
3. On the basis of Eastman's classification, would you describe yourself as a "practical" or a "poetic" person? Why?

Suggestions for Writing

1. Write a short paper in which you classify the members of a familiar group such as parents, police officers, friends, salespersons, bosses, or car drivers.
2. Write a short paper in which you explore some of the relationships in your life. How many different roles do you play? Explain three or four of the several roles or identities you have.

How to Spot Rock Types

PETER GODDARD

It might appear to the uninitiated° or un-   1
involved that pop music fans, like the followers of British football, are all alike and all equally unruly.

The truth is quite the opposite. There are more factions°, sub-   2
factions and sub-sub-factions going to this summer's bumper crop of concerts than there are garrulous sects° among Protestants. And as with theological disputes, the differences between one kind of fan and another, although barely noticeable to the outsider, can be enormous indeed.

Music has something to do with it, of course. Someone who   3
finds their heart enraptured by Engelbert Humperdinck is not likely to get much out of a punk performance at which the singer is graphically describing nine ways he's going to tear off your face. And vice versa.

"How to Spot Rock Types" by Peter Goddard. Copyright 1983. Reprinted with permission—The Toronto Star Syndicate.

4   The real differences, the kinds that often end up with a collision of fist and teeth, go beyond the musical. Social distinctions are as jealously guarded among rockers as they are at any country club. Often they are just as petty. It is permissible to wear a Black Sabbath T-shirt to an AC/DC concert. To arrive at the same event wearing a Kenny Rogers T-shirt would be considered hopelessly wimpy, however.

5   For many of the same reasons, there are certain concerts certain people should not attend. They may be discovered. Excuses may be needed. If you're discovered at a hard-core punk event, wall-to-wall in black leather, by your company's lawyer, for instance, you may have to hastily explain that it was a disgusting habit picked up in an impoverished youth and you can't break it.

6   Better still, whack him with your chain. Then ask him what *he's* doing there.

7   To help everyone better identify the various crowds who are going to pop concerts these days and nights, we've prepared the following collection of profiles. Study it. It may help you avoid getting lumped in with a loud, sweaty lot of heavy metal freaks. Or with Engelbert Humperdinck devotees. Whichever seems worse.

Reggae

8   There are, in fact, two reggae crowds. The original and basic following for this danceable roots music from Jamaica is, not surprisingly, made up of Jamaicans. The other crowd is not made up of Jamaicans—although many in it wish they were. They are usually white, middle-class, somewhat political and very concerned about community. They are, in short, hippies 10 or 15 years down the road. They can tell you everyone who ever played with singer Peter Tosh and can spell the name of the trio Black Uhuru. What they often can't do is discern a great reggae song from something that's awful. Just as often what they're smoking makes the issue fuzzy. They dance at the drop of a bass note. They eat good, organic natural foods. "Herb" is their favorite word after "man." They're worried about their health, yet they often look wan. They are generally harmless and would only want tea, not your 12-year-old scotch, should you invite them home. They regularly head to Jamaica and, with reggae songs in their head, feel they've made a radical advancement over their parents, who used to head to Jamaica humming Harry Belafonte songs. They haven't.   '

New wave

9   Although occasionally given to dyed hair, shocking colors in shocking combinations, and/or high-camp styles, the new wave

crowd usually looks like a convention of computer programmers—which it often is. Until recently it was the fashionable group until it was discovered that the secret new bands the insiders kept talking about—Heaven 17, Haircut 100, Ultra-vox—were just as boring as all the ratty familiar bands even the most lumpen° outsider knew. Still, this crowd retains some of its social superiority over the other crowds mainly because no one else can figure out what it's all about. For the neophyte°, a copy of *Wet* magazine, a smattering of German tossed into the conversation, and complete up-to-the-second knowledge of the latest technological gimmick help. Don't worry, though, about being caught up in a new wave crowd. You'll never know it—and they'll never tell.

Middle of the road

A mysterious and proud race, middle-of-the-roaders can be   10
downright militant about their sheer, blatant averageness. The most enraged heavy-metal crowd is no match for a group of Anne Murray fans whom someone has called "kooky." Wally Crouter°, on CFRB radio, is their main man and for music they tend to Billy Joel, Neil Diamond, Diana Ross (when she's not being too funky), Carly Simon, and James Taylor—any of the 1960s singers who, over the years, have come to show their true, middle-of-the-road colors. This crowd is into health; not a whiff of smoke of any kind could be smelled at the recent John Denver concert at Maple Leaf Gardens. They jog, play racket sports, and often eat good, organic natural foods. They're contemporaries of the reggae crowd but lost their sense of commitment about the time the mortgage rates started going up. They, too, are generally harmless but should you invite them home, it'll be your 12-year-old scotch, not tea, they'll be after.

Heavy metal

There's nothing too loud for a heavy-metal crowd. Uriah Heep   11
played at full volume? A train wreck? A dead cat thrown through a plate glass window? Kaaa-rang. More. Gimme more. As you may have guessed, heavy metal is not merely a matter of music but a question of faith—the belief that no excess can ever be too much. Women tend not to be attracted by this. As a result, it's the last completely male bastion° this side of the York Club. And in its way, it has clubby rules. There's a uniform—tight jeans, the more worn the better; T-shirt advertising one heavy-metal combo or another; boots; and long hair. And there are certain codes of behavior to follow. If, for instance, you are going to fall down roaring drunk, taking at least one usher with you, only do so after the 15-minute guitar solo, which because of its intensity and sheer repetitiveness,

will likely be the only thing you'll remember anyway. One rather caustic critic said that certain heavy-metal crowds weren't exactly comprised of future nuclear physicists. "They couldn't spell 'Jimi Hendrix' if you spotted them the first 10 letters," was the way he put it. This was unfair and not true. For example, no crowd knows more ways of smuggling illicit booze past police into Maple Leaf Gardens.

Jazz

12   As it is with reggae, there are two jazz crowds. The division here is generational, not racial. The older crowd likes its jazz in bars, is known to take a drink or a dozen while in these bars, and gets misty-eyed when someone mentions such quaint-sounding names as Mezz Mezzrow, Miff Mole, Lucky Millinder, or anything about Kansas City. To this crowd, jazz was—and still is, on occasion—an entertainment. That Earl Hines may be the most gifted pianist in any style in the entire 20th century means less to this crowd than the fact he can swing like a tropical forest before a hurricane.

13   The new jazz crowd takes it all much more seriously. It rarely gets misty-eyed. Rather, it gets angry when certain names are mentioned: Cecil Taylor or Charlie Mingus or Albert Ayler—men who suffered because they played "black classical music," or what many new jazz fans have come to call jazz. The younger crowd wants the music out of the bars and into the concert halls; it doesn't want to pay concert-hall prices yet.

14   The old crowd prides itself on being able to name the most obscure sideman and the most obscure record ("Frankie Newton? Didn't he play trumpet for John Kirby back in '40?"). Not the new crowd. It's into theory. It can tell you which inversion of the dominant ninth pianist McCoy Tyner played just before the augmented sixth. I mean, this crowd takes its jazz *seriously*.

Punks

15   The most maligned group of them all, the punks went completely out of style a while back, after it was discovered they really didn't want to cut themselves, but were only looking for a better record deal. They're back and back in force, though, at places like Club Domino, off Yonge Street, pale kids in from the suburbs, drenched in leather and beating the stuffing out of each other doing something called slam dancing. Now, slam dancing is jitterbugging for sadists and masochists. Punks and punkettes bob up and down and, when the moment is right, literally slam into one another.

And this is where the misunderstanding comes in. Psychologists, sociologists, musicologists° and, in all probability, tree surgeons all think this behavior indicates severe emotional/social/musical or ringworm° problems. It indicates nothing of the sort. It is, in fact, fun. And it keeps you in shape, which is more than you can say for bingo.

Funk

The old funk crowd was cool. The new one is aggressively cool.   16
It's not into Marvin Gaye, but Rick James, king of "punk funk" or rhythm 'n' blues with a rocket in the rhythm section. Punk funk is a street style with designer overtones. You should look as if you're perfectly capable of making it behind enemy lines in Iran and at the same time, finish no lower than third in the weekly soul train dance contest. The radio is optional. The "I've-got-you-covered-turkey" look is absolutely essential.

Country

If Nancy Reagan, clothes designer Ralph Lauren, and the pro-   17
ducers of *Urban Cowboy* had their way, we would all be wearing $300 western boots, drinking Jim Beam bourbon and, in just about every other way, acting as if we were all good ole boys in the good ole city. But the fake urban-cowboy country crowd went the way of so many other fads and what's left is the real country crowd, which is to say people who look like everyone else but who listen to country music. Well, that's not entirely true. Bring a country music show into town and you're likely to see more pantsuits there than anywhere else. And the belts tend to be more handsome and everyone seems to have a Kodak camera attached to their hands. They are generally harmless—unless you say something untoward about George Jones—and should you invite them home, they won't want your tea or your 12-year-old scotch. Most likely they will have brought an even better scotch with them.

Big bands

The older big-band crowd tends to be nostalgic every chance   18
it gets and you can always fob off the latest incarnation of the "Tommy Dorsey Orchestra" on it. The young crowd, the ones who ignored the Beatles for Stan Kenton and have some musical train-ing, is made up of fanatics. There's no other word for them. They know the names of sidemen in bands that decent, common folk didn't know even existed yet. They think rock is trite, punks are ridiculous, jazz is for snobs, and they're ready to fight to prove

their point. They have a hungry look about them and they tend to be thin. They look like they couldn't beat up a pillow, but many have secretly trained in karate. A lot of them carry pocket calculators. If they've had musical training, they're that kind of musician who can play anything—a note, fly speck, grease-drop from a Big Mac—that's on paper. They will probably end up ruling the world.

PETER GODDARD

Peter Goddard, the journalist, was born in Toronto in 1942 and has written on popular music for the *Toronto Star* since 1973. He has published a thriller about modern technology and is working on a history of pop music since the 1940s.

Words and Meanings

Paragraph

1	uninitiated:	people who lack inside information
2	factions:	cliques, groups
	garrulous:	talkative, wordy
	sect:	group that follows a particular doctrine or leader
9	lumpen:	(from German) lowest class, low status
	neophyte:	beginner, recent convert
10	Wally Crouter:	Toronto radio personality
11	bastion:	part of a fortress
15	musicologists:	specialists in music
	ringworm:	skin disease characterized by ring-shaped patches

Structure and Strategy

1. How many paragraphs make up the INTRODUCTION to this essay?
2. Identify the sentence fragments in these introductory paragraphs. Can you spot any examples of nonstandard pronoun usage? What TONE does Goddard establish by using ungrammatical constructions?
3. Which three groups of music fans does Goddard divide into two subgroups?
4. What is the purpose of Goddard's repeated references to "your 12-year-old scotch" (paragraphs 8, 10, and 17)? To what sort of reader is he addressing this essay?
5. Paragraph 18 is both Goddard's profile of "big band fans" and

the concluding paragraph of this essay. Is it effective as a CONCLUSION?

Content and Purpose

1. Is Goddard's purpose really to show his readers "how to spot rock types"? Why do you think he treats his "rock types" humorously rather than seriously?
2. Does Goddard distinguish clearly between "punk" and "funk" (paragraphs 15 and 16)? What additional information could be added to make the distinction clear to someone unfamiliar with modern music?
3. Why has Goddard chosen to classify fans rather than the different types of rock music?

Suggestions for Writing

1. Write an essay in which you classify rock music into three or four major categories.
2. Choose another kind of entertainment, such as dance or films, or a category of sports, such as wrestling or racing, and classify the fans into three or four categories.

What I Have Lived For

BERTRAND RUSSELL

Three passions, simple but overwhelm-   1
ingly strong, have governed my life: the longing for love, the search for knowledge, and unbearable pity for the suffering of mankind. These passions, like great winds, have blown me hither and thither, in a wayward° course, over a deep ocean of anguish, reaching to the very verge° of despair.

I have sought love, first, because it brings ecstasy°—ecstasy so   2
great that I would often have sacrificed all the rest of life for a few hours of this joy. I have sought it, next, because it relieves lone-

"What I Have Lived For" from *The Autobiography of Bertrand Russell* by Bertrand Russell. Copyright 1967. Reprinted by permission of The Bertrand Russell House, George Allen and Unwin Limited.

liness—that terrible loneliness in which one shivering consciousness looks over the rim of the world into the cold unfathomable
lifeless abyss°. I have sought it, finally, because in the union of
love I have seen, in a mystic miniature, the prefiguring° vision of
the heaven that saints and poets have imagined. This is what I
sought, and though it might seem too good for human life, this is
what—at last—I have found.

3   With equal passion I have sought knowledge. I have wished
to understand the hearts of men. I have wished to know why the
stars shine. And I have tried to apprehend the Pythagorean° power
by which number holds sway above the flux°. A little of this, but
not much, I have achieved.

4   Love and knowledge, so far as they were possible, led upward
toward the heavens. But always pity brought me back to earth.
Echoes of cries of pain reverberate° in my heart. Children in famine,
victims tortured by oppressors, helpless old people a hated burden
to their sons, and the whole world of loneliness, poverty, and pain
make a mockery of what human life should be. I long to alleviate°
the evil, but I cannot, and I too suffer.

5   This has been my life. I have found it worth living, and would
gladly live it again if the chance were offered me.

BERTRAND RUSSELL

Bertrand Russell (1872–1970), the philosopher, mathematician, and social
reformer, was awarded the Nobel Prize for Literature in 1950. His progressive
views on the liberalization of sexual attitudes and the role of women led to
his dismissal from the University of California at Los Angeles in the 1920s.
Russell was a leading pacifist and proponent of nuclear disarmament. Among
his many books are *Principia Mathematica*, *Why I Am Not a Christian*, and
History of Western Philosophy.

Paragraph   **Words and Meanings**

1	wayward:	unpredictable, wandering
	verge:	edge, brink
2	ecstasy:	supreme joy
	abyss:	bottomless pit, hell
	prefiguring:	picturing to oneself beforehand
3	Pythagorean:	relating to the Greek philosopher Pythagoras and his theory that through mathematics one could understand the relationship between all things and the principle of harmony in the universe
	flux:	continual motion, change

reverberate:	echo	4
alleviate:	relieve, lessen	

Structure and Strategy

1. Identify Russell's thesis statement and the topic sentences of paragraphs 2, 3, and 4.
2. How does the structure of the second sentence in paragraph 1 reinforce its meaning?
3. The number three is the basis for the structure of Russell's essay. Three is an ancient symbol for unity and completeness and for the human life cycle: birth, life, death. Find as many examples as you can of Russell's effective use of three's. (Look at paragraph and sentence structure as well as content.)
4. What is the function of the first sentence of paragraph 4?
5. How does Russell's concluding paragraph contribute to the UNITY of the essay?
6. Refer to the introduction to this chapter and show how paragraph 1 sets up a DIVISION essay and how paragraph 5 is actually a CLASSIFICATION.
7. Analyse the order in which Russell explains his three passions. Do you think the order is chronological, logical, climactic, or random? Does the order reflect the relative importance or value that Russell ascribes to each passion? How?

Content and Purpose

1. Love, to Bertrand Russell, means more than physical passion. What else does he include in his meaning of love (paragraph 2)?
2. What are the three kinds of knowledge Russell has spent his life seeking?
3. Which of Russell's three "passions" has he been least successful in achieving? Why?

Suggestions for Writing

1. What goals have you set for yourself for the next ten years? Write a short paper in which you identify and explain two or three of your goals.
2. In what ways are you different from other people? Write a short paper in which you identify and explain some of the qualities and characteristics that make you a unique human being.
3. Imagine that you are 75 years old. Write a short paper explaining what you have lived for.

Anarchy Around the Corner?

JOHN KETTLE

1   The once solid rule of church and state that made nineteenth-century Canada work is now so weakened that it is hard to imagine what, if anything, will structure society in the twenty-first century.

2   It is clear that we are in transition from a world run by authority to something very different.

3   As viewed from 1985, the society of 2010 looks close to anarchy°. The institutions that still impose some order on the way we live in 1985 are all changing fast. Some of them are approaching their end.

4   Take organized religion. A little more than 25 years ago, 43 per cent of Canadian Protestants went to church at least once a week. Now, fewer than 30 per cent do.

5   At the same time, the percentage of Catholics attending church weekly dropped to 43 from 87. Even as Catholicism is about to become the religion of the majority of Canadians, today's Catholics are no more observant churchgoers than the Protestants of 1957.

6   Regular church attendance was part of a system of beliefs and practices that was intended to keep people on the straight and narrow path, and generally it succeeded.

7   The behavior of a community in which most people were regular churchgoers conformed more closely to agreed norms. That was because the priest or minister praised the "right" behavior and deplored the bad. Many priests did not hesitate to name offenders in the congregation and hold them up to scorn, thus bringing considerable pressure on them to conform.

8   The same characteristic seems to have belonged to farming and fishing communities, bound as they were by a shared work and lifestyle as well as by the parish church in many cases.

9   Farming communities learned to support members in need. The farmer whose barn burned down could count on his neighbors' help in rebuilding[;] the farm wife whose husband died could expect her neighbors' support as well as sympathy.

"Anarchy Around the Corner?" by John Kettle. From *The Globe and Mail*. Copyright Friday Oct. 4, 1985. Reprinted by permission of John Kettle.

The price exacted for community support was conformity with   10
community standards, and this holds true in most Canadian communities where farming or fishing remains the major activity.

In 2010, few people will be living in farm or fishing commu-   11
nities, and it is a reasonable guess that fewer than one-third of
Catholics, and maybe only one Protestant in six, will go to church
regularly.

Instead, the great majority of people will say something like,   12
"I don't need a church to tell me what's right[;] I can decide for
myself." Many young people already implicitly determine their
own private ethic.

Nothing we can see in society suggests that this tendency away   13
from shared morality toward personal morality is going to be turned
back, at least not before 2010.

There seem to be two causes for the collapse of community   14
ethics and conformity. One is education, the other affluence.

Until several years after the Second World War, the average   15
Canadian quit school at the end of Grade 8. As late as 1961, half
the adult population had no more than elementary education.

People left school with a shared stock of knowledge, straight-   16
forward ideas of how the world worked, black and white issues,
agreed questions, answers in the back of the book. Independent
inquiry was not encouraged.

But the early sixties were about the last time it was possible to   17
talk of national goals, the last time there was anything that most
Canadians agreed on.

Formerly, for those who went on after Grade 8, the process of   18
developing independence began in high school. Now projects requiring use of the library or resource centre show up even before
high school, bringing the beginnings of independent thought and
judgment—and nonconformity.

Affluence liberates the mind from worry about survival and   19
security. Only now are large numbers of Canadians getting far
enough away from the struggle for survival to be concerned with
self-actualization, the theoretical peak of human development in
the theory of values that Abraham Maslow, the U.S. psychologist,
published 30 years ago.

Another institution that once held society together, the family,   20
is also crumbling fast.

Today's couples are producing an average of fewer than two   21
children each, compared with four in 1960. There are good reasons
to think that the typical family of 2010 will have only one child and
that the typical marriage will last fewer than 20 years.

The extended family of brothers and sisters, aunts, uncles, and   22
cousins, so characteristic of the nineteenth century, helped to

impose rules and standards on all its members, but it is likely to be in splinters by the twenty-first century.

23 Everything we know suggests that is a situation that will breed independence and nonconformity.

24 The old role of nurturing wife and mother bound many women together in a kind of social union that developed a uniform approach to child-rearing, family values, acceptable social behavior.

25 For the parents of the last big generation of Canadians, born in the fifties and early sixties, Dr. Benjamin Spock's° *Common Sense Book of Baby and Child Care* was a bible. Between the mid-forties and mid-seventies, Dr. Spock sold about 30 million copies, roughly one to a household throughout North America.

26 No such mass penetration of a single set of ideas about family life and behavior is ever likely again.

27 Instead, child-raising is just one of the things the modern parent does. It stands about even with going out to work, going to night school, going out for the ski team or the chess team, and a whole menu of other activities now blended into millions of unique lifestyles.

28 Politics, too, has fallen into a new and less conformist pattern, and government along with it. Although few politicians like to acknowledge it, the last time politics worked well was in the years after the Second World War, when politics was based on class, which in Canada meant income.

29 The central issue of politics was the haves versus the have-nots. It influenced taxation policies, social security programs, even industrial policy. It redefined the positions of left and right, firmly and for the last time.

30 Since then Canada has become rich. The average income of every man, woman and child was $15 a week in 1945. Today it is about $260 a week.

31 Prices, too, have gone up in the intervening 40 years, but if inflation is discounted, the average weekly income in 1945 still bought only $90 worth of groceries and socks at today's prices.

32 And there is no doubt the poor are less poor, if not exactly rich. The poverty line was first set in 1961; it said you were poor if you spent 70 per cent or more of your income on the three necessities: food, shelter and clothing. More than 20 per cent of the population were poor.

33 In 1969 the poverty definition was dropped to 62 per cent of income spent on the necessities, and in 1978 it was dropped again to 58.5 per cent of income. By that definition, 14 per cent were poor in 1983, but it wasn't the poverty defined in 1961.

34 No more than 5 or 6 per cent of families today spend 70 per cent of their income on the necessities.

35 Significant numbers of the post-war generation are entrepre-

neurs at heart, far more than any earlier generation. This is apparent in the increasing proportion of people who are self-employed, now about one worker out of seven.

It can be seen in the rising number of small companies. More than half the new jobs created since 1975 are in concerns that employ fewer than 20 people.   36

Union leaders notice the change in the attitude of their younger members, who don't automatically think that "owner" or "manager" or even "capitalist" is a dirty word. Many young union members harbor ambitions to run their own companies.   37

So politics is no longer concerned with the confrontation between the haves and the have-nots, except in a few special cases such as renters versus landlords.   38

Much more it is concerned with cutting the taxes that now hit almost every worker.   39

It is also focused on dozens of separate issues: the environment, day care, international nuclear politics, energy supplies, pollution, free trade, animal rights and so on.   40

What could bring back the politics of haves versus have-nots is jobs.   41

The year 2010 may well see a political confrontation over income distribution that pits those who have jobs against those without them. It seems almost certain there will be enough money to go around, but not so certain that Canadians will agree how it should be shared.   42

The death of the institutions has been accompanied by the rise of individual choice and responsibility. Independence and self-actualization are by no means universal yet, but all the trends indicate that we're moving in that direction.   43

The depression-recession of 1981-83 slowed the trends, mostly by reducing employment and income, but they should pick up again in the second half of the eighties.   44

With few big institutions, few broad issues, no national goals or interests, little sense of community, no shared ethic or political programs, the society of 2010 will seem close to anarchy to those who remember the orderly days of 1985.   45

But there's a very good chance that the people of 2010 will be happier living with anarchy than we are today with the crumbling remnants of nineteenth-century institutions and authority.   46

JOHN KETTLE

John Kettle is one of Canada's few professional futurists. He has been writing about the future since 1966 and is the editor of The Future Letter.

Paragraph # Words and Meanings

3   anarchy: social chaos

25   Benjamin Spock (1903–):   controversial pediatrician and social activist

Structure and Strategy

1. Why has Kettle written this piece in such short paragraphs? Who are his intended readers?
2. Paragraphs 1 to 3 are the introduction to this article. In which sentence does Kettle state his thesis? After reading the whole article, expand that sentence into a complete thesis statement.
3. What is the function of paragraphs 4, 8, 14, 20, and 28?
4. Identify at least two places where transition is needed in this article.
5. What concluding strategies does Kettle use in paragraphs 43 to 46? Is his conclusion effective? Can you improve it?

Content and Purpose

1. What three social institutions does Kettle identify as "changing fast" or "approaching their end"?
2. Why does Kettle believe that education and affluence are causing the collapse of community ethics and conformity (paragraphs 14 to 19)? Does Kettle believe conformity to be desirable? Why?
3. What reasons does Kettle offer for the collapse of the family as a social institution?
4. How has "the central issue of politics" changed from the 1940s to the 1980s? What does Kettle predict the "central issue" will be in the early part of the next century?
5. Do you agree with Kettle, or do you think most people need a certain measure of authority to be happy? Give your reasons.

Suggestion for Writing

A utopia is an imaginary society with a perfect political and social system. A dystopia is an imaginary society in which living conditions are bleak and terrible. Write a short paper in which you identify and develop three or four significant aspects of either a utopia or a dystopia. (You might begin by looking up the etymology of the word "utopia" in your dictionary.)

After Hiroshima: The Shift to Nuclear Technology

ROBERT MALCOLMSON

War," observes Field Marshal Lord Carver, "is the final resort in the struggle for power."[1] It is the ultimate arbiter° in relations between states. The making of war has, as we know, been a central reality in the ongoing pursuit of political ends; and the outcome of battle, and the nature of victory and defeat, have been undoubtedly affected, at various times and to various degrees, by the presence of new technologies. Certainly the custodians of sovereign power throughout the ages have been keenly interested in new military technologies—technologies that offered them improved capabilities for attacking enemies or for defending already-secured positions. Established weapons have been improved, new weapons have been invented. The crossbow, gunpowder, cannons on sailing ships, fast-loading rifles, heavy metal armaments, machine guns, aerial bombers—all these technological innovations have been enthusiastically adopted at various times in the past. Nuclear weaponry has sometimes been regarded as essentially the latest in a long line of breakthroughs in the technology of armaments, but this latest manifestation of force is a breakthrough of a new order of magnitude. For there are at least four major ways in which nuclear weapons are fundamentally different from those of all previous ages. These differences underlie and deeply reinforce the sense that we are, inescapably and undeniably, inhabiting a truly revolutionary age—that, as one of the scientists engaged in the Manhattan Project recalls feeling at the time of the Alamogordo test°, "this was the end of one world and the beginning of another."[2] What, then, are these extraordinary implications of the weapons that now surround us?

[1] Field Marshal Lord Carver, *A Policy for Peace* (London: Faber and Faber, 1982), 13.
[2] Isador Rabi, as quoted in Gregg Herken, "Mad about the Bomb," *Harper's*, December 1983, 51.

"After Hiroshima: The Shift to Nuclear Technology" from *Nuclear Fallacies: How We Have Been Misguided Since Hiroshima* by Robert W. Malcolmson. © McGill–Queen's University Press 1985. Reprinted by permission of McGill–Queen's University Press.

2   First, nuclear weapons permit not merely the defeat of an adversary° state, they make possible the total annihilation° of that state and its society. Destruction can now be made virtually limitless—and essentially instantaneous. Distinctions between civilians and combatants°, between military and non-military targets, are almost certain in any nuclear war to be largely or entirely meaningless. (One recalls that, in 1945, Hiroshima was regarded by American policy-makers as a centre of military importance, and was targeted partly for that reason.) Nuclear weapons, then, are not only vastly powerful, they are also by their very nature extremely blunt and undiscriminating instruments of destruction.

3   Second, not only is there no credible° defence against nuclear weapons, it is virtually inconceivable that any such defence will ever exist. In order to inspire confidence, any plausible° defence system would have to be essentially leakproof; for even if only a small fraction of an attacker's warheads were able to penetrate a defender's "shield," the resultant slaughter for that defender would be colossal. Moreover, defensive weapons are themselves vulnerable to attack, and it is difficult to see how even the most elaborate and sophisticated defence system could avoid being overwhelmed by sheer numbers, that is, by the addition of more and more offensive warheads to the arsenal of an adversary. Much thought has certainly been given, in military and engineering circles, to the possibility of constructing a defence against nuclear attack. But this thinking has led nowhere. Nor is it likely to yield fruit in the future. We are, in all likelihood, now at the end of the road in the long-standing struggle between offence and defence. Offensive force has triumphed definitively over defensive resistance. Universal vulnerability° is now a fundamental fact of life.

4   Third, when nuclear weapons are possessed in abundance by at least two states, their use by any nuclear power is potentially suicidal. The first-use of nuclear weapons by one power will invite nuclear retaliation by another power, whether that initial use was "limited" and purportedly "restrained" or whether it was massive and pre-emptive in intent. In the former set of circumstances the momentum of warfare, the breakdown in communications, and the "fog of battle" are likely to make it extremely difficult for a nation's rulers to keep control of their huge nuclear arsenal and to prevent the conflict from becoming total; in circumstances of a pre-emptive° attack, total war would exist from the start. Whatever the particular circumstances, the users of nuclear weapons risk destroying themselves along with their enemies.

5   Fourth, if nuclear weapons were used on a large scale, the natural environment might be so severely damaged that this planet would become largely uninhabitable—perhaps even totally unin-

habitable—for most complex forms of life, our own species included. Here, of course, we are on very uncertain intellectual terrain.
Our thinking about such matters is inevitably speculative. But many
competent scientists have been studying the possible and likely
consequences for our biosphere° of varying levels of nuclear warfare, and the results of their inquiries point unequivocally° to the
manifold risks and dangers that would assuredly confront us. For
we not only must think about the immediate destruction of life and
those human institutions that have been built up over generations;
we also have to consider the long-term implications for survival
and recovery: the contamination of food and water supplies; the
huge firestorms that would consume large areas; the probable spread
of disease with the breakdown of public health; the collapse of
agriculture in many regions because of the persistent cover of soot
and dust clouds that would block out sunlight and cause a drop
in temperature (a kind of "nuclear winter," whatever the season,
with consequent widespread starvation); the possibility of long-
term climatic changes resulting from damage to the protective
atmosphere, especially the ozone layer°.[3] The consequences of a
major nuclear war could be with the world and its human survivors
(let us assume some survivors) for centuries, perhaps even millen-
nia°. Nature is not likely to forgive quickly such an assault on its
integrity.

The destructive possibilities here outlined are unique to the   6
second half of this century. And it is clear that these possibilities
are a consequence of the unrelenting industrialization of the means
of making war. Machinery of increasing sophistication has been
entering the armouries of nation states, with growing rapidity, for
over a century. These machines have made killing much more
efficient; they have allowed their possessors to fulfil the traditional
objective of the soldier's enterprise—the successful application of
force against opponents—with greater effect; and their presence in
modern warfare has ensured that the casualties of battle are now
much more numerous than ever before. Nuclear weapons, of course,
are the most dramatic and starkly potent of the military products
of industrialization. But even the non-nuclear weapons that are
now with us—the fragmentation bombs, the undetectable mines,
the guided missiles with deep-penetration capabilities—have

[3]See, for example, the essays on "Nuclear War: The Aftermath," published in
AMBIO: A Journal of the Human Environment 11, nos 2–3 (1982); and Carl Sagan,
"Nuclear War and Climatic Catastrophe: Some Policy Implications," *Foreign Affairs*
62, no. 2 (Winter 1983/4), 257–92. Military planners, in assessing the damage likely
to be caused by nuclear war, have systematically underestimated the collateral
destruction (especially from fire and radiation) that would result from nuclear
explosions.

achieved unparalleled levels of destructiveness. Conventional fire-power in the twentieth century has taken tens of millions of lives. The consequences of this relentless process of industrialization compel us to face, as one distinguished historian has put it, "the dilemma of modern military power: that its destructiveness is now so great, in the conventional as well as the nuclear field, that its unleashing would certainly devastate what it is intended to preserve."[4]

```



```

ROBERT MALCOLMSON

Robert Malcolmson, a professor of history at Queen's University in Kingston, Ontario, is the author of *Popular Recreations in English Society, 1700–1850* (1973), *Life and Labour in England, 1700–1780* (1981), and *Nuclear Fall-acies: How We Have Been Misguided Since Hiroshima* (1985).

Paragraph

Words and Meanings

1 arbiter: judge, referee
   the Alamogordo test: first explosion of the atom bomb at Alamogordo, New Mexico, 1945

2 adversary: enemy
   annihilation: total destruction
   combatants: those engaged in battle

3 credible: believable
   plausible: reasonable, convincing
   vulnerability: weakness

4 pre-emptive: striking first to destroy an enemy before the enemy can strike you

5 biosphere: atmosphere that supports life
   unequivocally: without question
   ozone layer: atmospheric level required for life
   millennia: a millennium is a period of a thousand years

Structure and Strategy

1. What introductory strategy has Malcolmson used?
2. Identify Malcolmson's thesis statement (paragraph 1) and the topic sentences in paragraphs 2, 3, 4, and 5. How do paragraphs 2 to 5 support the thesis?

---

[4]John Keegan, "The Specter of Conventional War," *Harper's*, July 1983, 14.

3. Study the use of sentence variety in paragraph 3. How
   combination of long and short sentences contribute to tl
   of that paragraph?

Content and Purpose

1. Summarize in your own words the unique characteristics of nuclear weapons. What makes them "fundamentally different from
   those weapons of all other ages"?
2. How does Malcolmson show that nuclear weapons have become
   a moral problem as well as a military one?
3. Part of the difficulty we face in confronting the issue of nuclear
   war is "thinking about the unthinkable." The potential devastation
   is so awesome as to be incomprehensible. How does Malcolmson's essay deal with this dilemma? What is its TONE? How would
   you characterize its DICTION? How do these factors combine with
   the logic of the argument to make it a persuasive piece of prose?

Suggestions for Writing

1. What is it like to grow up in the shadow of the bomb? Write a
   paper analyzing your own or your generation's response to the
   threat of nuclear annihilation.
2. Identify and explain some of the beneficial uses of nuclear power.
3. How can the nuclear time bomb be defused? Suggest several
   ways that the superpowers might explore to decrease the chances
   of a nuclear confrontation.

The Dimensions of a Complete Life

MARTIN LUTHER KING, JR.

Many, many centuries ago, out on a lonely, 1
obscure island called Patmos°, a man by the name of John° caught
a vision of the new Jerusalem descending out of heaven from God.
One of the greatest glories of this new city of God that John saw
was its completeness. It was not partial and one-sided, but it was
complete in all three of its dimensions. And so, in describing the
city in the twenty-first chapter of the book of Revelation, John says

"The Dimensions of a Complete Life" from *The Measure of a Man* by Martin Luther
King, Jr. Copyright 1959. Reprinted by permission of Christian Education Press.

this: "The length and the breadth and the height of it are equal." In other words, this new city of God, this city of ideal humanity, is not an unbalanced entity but it is complete on all sides.

2   Now John is saying something quite significant here. For so many of us the book of Revelation° is a very difficult book, puzzling to decode. We look upon it as something of a great enigma° wrapped in mystery. And certainly if we accept the book of Revelation as a record of actual historical occurrences it is a difficult book, shrouded with impenetrable mysteries. But if we will look beneath the peculiar jargon of its author and the prevailing apocalyptic° symbolism, we will find in this book many eternal truths which continue to challenge us. One such truth is that of this text. What John is really saying is this: that life as it should be and life at its best is the life that is complete on all sides.

3   There are three dimensions of any complete life to which we can fitly give the words of this text: length, breadth, and height. The length of life as we shall think of it here is not its duration or its longevity, but it is the push of a life forward to achieve its personal ends and ambitions. It is the inward concern for one's own welfare. The breadth of life is the outward concern for the welfare of others. The height of life is the upward reach for God.

4   These are the three dimensions of life, and without the three being correlated, working harmoniously together, life is incomplete. Life is something of a great triangle. At one angle stands the individual person, at the other angle stand other persons, and at the top stands the Supreme, Infinite Person, God. These three must meet in every individual life if that life is to be complete.

5   Now let us notice first the length of life. I have said that this is the dimension of life in which the individual is concerned with developing his inner powers. It is that dimension of life in which the individual pursues personal ends and ambitions. This is perhaps the selfish dimension of life, and there is such a thing as moral and rational self-interest. If one is not concerned about himself he cannot be totally concerned about other selves.

6   Some years ago a learned rabbi, the late Joshua Liebman, wrote a book entitled *Peace of Mind*. He has a chapter in the book entitled "Love Thyself Properly." In this chapter he says in substance that it is impossible to love other selves adequately unless you love your own self properly. Many people have been plunged into the abyss° of emotional fatalism° because they did not love themselves properly. So every individual has a responsibility to be concerned about himself enough to discover what he is made for. After he discovers his calling he should set out to do it with all of the strength and power in his being. He should do it as if God Almighty called him at this particular moment in history to do it. He should seek to do

his job so well that the living, the dead, or the unborn could not do it better. No matter how small one thinks his life's work is in terms of the norms of the world and the so-called big jobs, he must realize that it has cosmic significance if he is serving humanity and doing the will of God.

To carry this to one extreme, if it falls your lot to be a street- 7 sweeper, sweep streets as Raphael painted pictures, sweep streets as Michelangelo carved marble, sweep streets as Beethoven composed music, sweep streets as Shakespeare wrote poetry. Sweep streets so well that all the hosts of heaven and earth will have to pause and say, "Here lived a great street-sweeper who swept his job well." In the words of Douglas Mallock:

If you can't be a highway, just be a trail;
If you can't be the sun, be a star,
For it isn't by size that you win or you fail—
Be the best of whatever you are.

When you do this, you have mastered the first dimension of life— the length of life.

But don't stop here; it is dangerous to stop here. There are 8 some people who never get beyond this first dimension. They are brilliant people; often they do an excellent job in developing their inner powers; but they live as if nobody else lived in the world but themselves. There is nothing more tragic than to find an individual bogged down in the length of life, devoid of the breadth.

The breadth of life is that dimension of life in which we are 9 concerned about others. An individual has not started living until he can rise above the narrow confines of his individualistic concerns to the broader concerns of all humanity.

You remember one day a man came to Jesus and he raised 10 some significant questions. Finally he got around to the question, "Who is my neighbor?" This could easily have been a very abstract question left in mid-air. But Jesus immediately pulled that question out of mid-air and placed it on a dangerous curve between Jerusalem and Jericho. He talked about a certain man who fell among thieves. Three men passed; two of them on the other side. And finally another man came and helped the injured man on the ground. He is known to us as the good Samaritan. Jesus says in substance that this is a great man. He was great because he could project the "I" into the "thou."

So often we say that the priest and the Levite were in a big 11 hurry to get to some ecclesiastical meeting and so they did not have time. They were concerned about that. I would rather think of it another way. I can well imagine that they were quite afraid.

You see, the Jericho road is a dangerous road, and the same thing that happened to the man who was robbed and beaten could have happened to them. So I imagine the first question that the priest and the Levite asked was this: "If I stop to help this man, what will happen to me?" Then the good Samaritan came by, and by the very nature of his concern reversed the question: "If I do not stop to help this man, what will happen to him?" And so this man was great because he had the mental equipment for a dangerous altruism°. He was great because he could surround the length of his life with the breadth of life. He was great not only because he had ascended to certain heights of economic security, but because he could condescend° to the depths of human need.

12   All this has a great deal of bearing in our situation in the world today. So often racial groups are concerned about the length of life, their economic privileged position, their social status. So often nations of the world are concerned about the length of life, perpetuating their nationalistic concerns, and their economic ends. May it not be that the problem in the world today is that individuals as well as nations have been overly concerned with the length of life, devoid of the breadth? But there is still something to remind us that we are interdependent°, that we are all involved in a single process, that we are all somehow caught in an inescapable network of mutuality. Therefore whatever affects one directly affects all indirectly.

13   As long as there is poverty in the world I can never be rich, even if I have a billion dollars. As long as diseases are rampant and millions of people in this world cannot expect to live more than twenty-eight or thirty years, I can never be totally healthy even if I just got a good check-up at Mayo Clinic. I can never be what I ought to be until you are what you ought to be. This is the way our world is made. No individual or nation can stand out boasting of being independent. We are interdependent. So John Donne placed it in graphic terms when he affirmed, "No man is an island entire of itself. Every man is a piece of the continent, a part of the main." Then he goes on to say, "Any man's death diminishes me because I am involved in mankind, and therefore never send to know for whom the bell tolls; it tolls for thee." When we discover this, we master the second dimension of life.

14   Finally, there is a third dimension. Some people never get beyond the first two dimensions of life. They master the first two. They develop their inner powers; they love humanity, but they stop right here. They end up with the feeling that man is the end of all things and that humanity is God. Philosophically or theologically, many of them would call themselves humanists°. They seek to live life without a sky. They find themselves bogged down

on the horizontal plane without being integrated on the vertical plane. But if we are to live the complete life we must reach up and discover God. H. G. Wells was right: "The man who is not religious begins at nowhere and ends at nothing." Religion is like a mighty wind that breaks down doors and makes that possible and even easy which seems difficult and impossible.

In our modern world it is easy for us to forget this. We so often find ourselves unconsciously neglecting this third dimension of life. Not that we go up and say, "Good-by, God, we are going to leave you now." But we become so involved in the things of this world that we are unconsciously carried away by the rushing tide of materialism° which leaves us treading in the confused waters of secularism°. We find ourselves living in what Professor Sorokin of Harvard called a sensate° civilization, believing that only those things which we can see and touch and to which we can apply our five senses have existence.

Something should remind us once more that the great things in this universe are things that we never see. You walk out at night and look up at the beautiful stars as they bedeck the heavens like swinging lanterns of eternity, and you think you can see all. Oh, no. You can never see the law of gravitation that holds them there. You walk around this vast campus and you probably have a great esthetic experience as I have had walking about and looking at the beautiful buildings, and you think you see all. Oh, no. You can never see the mind of the architect who drew the blueprint. You can never see the love and the faith and the hope of the individuals who made it so. You look at me and you think you see Martin Luther King. You don't see Martin Luther King; you see my body, but, you must understand, my body can't think, my body can't reason. You don't see the me that makes me me. You can never see my personality.

In a real sense everything that we see is a shadow cast by that which we do not see. Plato° was right: "The visible is a shadow cast by the invisible." And so God is still around. All of our new knowledge, all of our new developments, cannot diminish his being one iota°. These new advances have banished God neither from the microcosmic compass of the atom nor from the vast, unfathomable ranges of interstellar space. The more we learn about this universe, the more mysterious and awesome it becomes. God is still here.

So I say to you, seek God and discover him and make him a power in your life. Without him all of our efforts turn to ashes and our sunrises into darkest nights. Without him, life is a meaningless drama with the decisive scenes missing. But with him we are able to rise from the fatigue of despair to the buoyancy of hope. With

19   Love yourself, if that means rational, healthy, and moral self-interest. You are commanded to do that. That is the length of life. Love your neighbor as you love yourself. You are commanded to do that. That is the breadth of life. But never forget that there is a first and even greater commandment, "Love the Lord thy God with all thy heart and all thy soul and all thy mind." This is the height of life. And when you do this you live the complete life.

20   Thank God for John who, centuries ago, caught a vision of the new Jerusalem. God grant that those of us who still walk the road of life will catch this vision and decide to move forward to that city of complete life in which the length and the breadth and the height are equal.

MARTIN LUTHER KING, JR.

Dr. Martin Luther King, Jr. (1929–1968), the American civil rights leader, was a Baptist minister who advocated racial equality and non-violent resistance against discriminatory laws and practices. He was awarded the Nobel Prize for Peace in 1964. In 1968, he was assassinated in Memphis, Tennessee.

Paragraph   Words and Meanings

1	John of Patmos:	Christian saint, author of the book of Revelation
2	the book of Revelation:	last book of the New Testament, concerned with the end of the world and other mysteries
	enigma:	puzzle, mystery
	apocalyptic:	concerned with the Apocalypse, the last day
6	abyss:	bottomless pit, hell
	fatalism:	belief that a predetermined fate rules our lives
11	altruism:	selfless concern for others
	condescend:	stoop, bend down to
12	interdependent:	dependent on each other
14	humanists:	people interested in human nature and concerns
15	materialism:	concern only for the goods of this world
	secularism:	social and nonreligious concern for the world
	sensate:	perceived by the senses
17	Plato:	ancient Greek philosopher, idealist
	iota:	smallest particle

Structure and Strategy

1. What ANALOGY are paragraphs 1 and 2 based on? What analogy is introduced in paragraph 4?
2. Identify King's thesis statement. What question of division does it answer? (See the introduction to this unit.)
3. What is the function of paragraph 3? How does King begin to develop his three points in this paragraph?
4. Identify the paragraphs that develop each of the three dimensions of life. In what ORDER has King arranged his points?
5. How does paragraph 8 contribute to COHERENCE? Paragraphs 9 and 14?
6. Paragraphs 19 and 20 form the conclusion of this piece. What is the function of paragraph 20? How does it round off or conclude the essay effectively?
7. Writers and speakers often use PARALLEL STRUCTURE to emphasize key ideas. King's thesis statement is, of course, an example of parallelism, but there are other examples. Identify parallel structures in paragraphs 7 and 18. What do they emphasize? How effective are they? (Hint: read the paragraphs aloud.)

Content and Purpose

1. King originally wrote "Dimensions" as a speech. As you read through the piece, what clues can you find that indicate it was designed to be heard rather than read?
2. King regards the length of life as "selfish," but, nevertheless, the basis of the other dimensions of life. How does King convince the reader that this "selfishness" is a positive rather than a negative quality?
3. What is a parable? What is the purpose of the parable in paragraphs 11 and 12?
4. King's purpose in this piece is to demonstrate that the complete life is one in which the personal, social, and spiritual dimensions are integrated. Study King's development of one of these dimensions and show how he has carefully selected his examples to reinforce his thesis.

Suggestions for Writing

1. Write an essay of division in which you analyze your own vision of the complete life. What will bring you happiness and satisfaction?
2. Though it lasted only 39 years, King's own life fulfilled the dimensions of a "complete life." After doing some research, write a short paper describing his accomplishments.
3. Think of someone you know or have read about and write a paper explaining how that person's life satisfies King's criteria for completeness.

Humour As I See It

STEPHEN LEACOCK

1   Personally . . . I do not mind making the admission, however damaging it may be, that there are certain forms of so-called humour, or, at least, fun, which I am quite unable to appreciate. Chief among these is that ancient thing called the Practical Joke.

2   "You never knew McGann, did you?" a friend of mine asked me the other day. When I said, "No, I had never known McGann," he shook his head with a sigh, and said:

3   "Ah, you should have known McGann. He had the greatest sense of humour of any man I ever knew—always full of jokes. I remember one night at the boarding house where we were, he stretched a string across the passageway and then rang the dinner bell. One of the boarders broke his leg. We nearly died laughing."

4   "Dear me!" I said. "What a humourist! Did he often do things like that?"

5   "Oh, yes, he was at them all the time. He used to put tar in the tomato soup, and beeswax and tin-tacks on the chairs. He was full of ideas. They seemed to come to him without any trouble.

6   McGann, I understand, is dead. I am not sorry for it. Indeed I think that for most of us the time has gone by when we can see the fun of putting tacks on chairs, or thistles in beds, or live snakes in people's boots.

7   To me it has always seemed that the very essence of good humour is that it must be without harm and without malice. I admit that there is in all of us a certain vein of the old original demoniacal° humour or joy in the misfortune of another which sticks to us like our original sin°. It ought not to be funny to see a man, especially a fat and pompous man, slip suddenly on a banana skin. But it is. When a skater on a pond who is describing graceful circles and showing off before the crowd, breaks through the ice and gets a ducking, everybody shouts with joy. To the original savage, the cream of the joke in such cases was found if the man who slipped broke his neck, or the man who went through the ice never came up again. I can imagine a group of prehistoric men standing round the ice-hole where he had disappeared and laugh-

"Humour As I See It" from *Laugh with Leacock* by Stephen Leacock. Copyright 1968. Reprinted by permission of McClelland and Stewart Limited.

ing till their sides split. If there had been such a thing as a pre-historic newspaper, the affair would have been headed up: "*Amusing Incident. Unknown Gentleman Breaks Through Ice and Is Drowned.*"

But our sense of humour under civilisation has been weakened. Much of the fun of this sort of thing has been lost on us.   8

Children, however, still retain a large share of this primitive sense of enjoyment.   9

I remember once watching two little boys making snowballs at the side of the street and getting ready a little store of them to use. As they worked there came along an old man wearing a silk hat, and belonging by appearance to the class of "jolly old gentlemen." When he saw the boys his gold spectacles gleamed with kindly enjoyment. He began waving his arms and calling, "Now, then, boys, free shot at me! free shot!" In his gaiety he had, without noticing it, edged himself over the sidewalk on to the street. An express cart collided with him and knocked him over on his back in a heap of snow. He lay there gasping and trying to get the snow off his face and spectacles. The boys gathered up their snow-balls and took a run towards him. "Free shot!" they yelled. "Soak him! Soak him!"   10

I repeat, however, that for me, as I suppose for most of us, it is a prime condition of humour that it must be without harm or malice, nor should it convey even incidentally any real picture of sorrow or suffering or death. There is a great deal in the humour of Scotland (I admit its general merit) which seems to me, not being a Scotchman, to sin in this respect. Take this familiar story (I quote it as something already known and not for the sake of telling it).   11

A Scotchman had a sister-in-law—his wife's sister—with whom he could never agree. He always objected to going anywhere with her, and in spite of his wife's entreaties° always refused to do so. The wife was taken mortally ill and as she lay dying, she whispered, "John, ye'll drive Janet with you to the funeral, will ye no?" The Scotchman, after an internal struggle, answered, "Margaret, I'll do it for ye, but it'll spoil my day."   12

Whatever humour there may be in this is lost for me by the actual and vivid picture that it conjures up—the dying wife, the darkened room and the last whispered request.   13

No doubt the Scotch see things differently. That wonderful people—whom personally I cannot too much admire—always seem to me to prefer adversity° to sunshine, to welcome the prospect of a pretty general damnation, and to live with grim cheerfulness within the very shadow of death. Alone among the nations they have converted the devil—under such names as Old Horny—into a familiar acquaintance not without a certain grim charm of his own. No doubt also there enters into their humour something of   14 the original barbaric attitude towards things. For a primitive people who saw death often and at first hand, and for whom the future world was a vivid reality, that could be *felt*, as it were, in the midnight forest and heard in the roaring storm—for such a people it was no doubt natural to turn the flank of terror° by forcing a merry and jovial acquaintance with the unseen world. Such a practice as a wake, and the merrymaking about the corpse, carry us back to the twilight of the world, with the poor savage in his bewildered misery, pretending that his dead still lived. Our funeral with its black trappings and its elaborate ceremonies is the lineal descendant of a merrymaking. Our undertaker is, by evolution, a genial master of ceremonies, keeping things lively at the death-dance. Thus have the ceremonies and the trappings of death been transformed in the course of ages till the forced gaiety is gone, and the black hearse and the gloomy mutes betoken the cold dignity of our despair.

15   But I fear this article is getting serious. I must apologise.

16   I was about to say, when I wandered from the point, that there is another form of humour which I am also quite unable to appreciate. This is that particular form of story which may be called, par excellence, the English Anecdote°. It always deals with persons of rank and birth, and, except for the exalted nature of the subject itself, is, as far as I can see, absolutely pointless.

17   This is the kind of thing that I mean.

18   "His Grace the Fourth Duke of Marlborough was noted for the openhanded hospitality which reigned at Blenheim, the family seat, during his régime. One day on going in to luncheon it was discovered that there were thirty guests present, whereas the table only held covers for twenty-one. 'Oh, well,' said the Duke, not a whit abashed, 'some of us will have to eat standing up.' Everybody, of course, roared with laughter."

19   My only wonder is that they didn't kill themselves with it. A mere roar doesn't seem enough to do justice to such a story as this.

20   The Duke of Wellington has been made the storm-centre of three generations of wit of this sort. In fact the typical Duke of Wellington story had been reduced to a thin skeleton such as this:

21   "A young subaltern° once met the Duke of Wellington coming out of Westminster Abbey. 'Good morning, your Grace,' he said, 'rather a wet morning.' 'Yes,' said the Duke, with a very rigid bow, 'but it was a damn sight wetter, sir, on the morning of Waterloo.' The young subaltern, rightly rebuked, hung his head."

22   Nor is it only the English who sin in regard to anecdotes.

23   One can indeed make the sweeping assertion that the telling of stories as a mode of amusing others, ought to be kept within

strict limits. Few people realise how extremely difficult it is to tell a story so as to reproduce the real fun of it—to "get it over" as the actors say. The mere "facts" of a story seldom make it funny. It needs the right words, with every word in its proper place. Here and there, perhaps once in a hundred times, a story turns up which needs no telling. The humour of it turns so completely on a sudden twist or incongruity° in the dénouement° of it that no narrator however clumsy can altogether fumble it.

Take, for example, this well known instance—a story which,   24 in one form or other, everybody has heard.

"George Grossmith, the famous comedian, was once badly run   25 down and went to consult a doctor. It happened that the doctor, though, like everybody else, he had often seen Grossmith on the stage, had never seen him without his make-up and did not know him by sight. He examined his patient, looked at his tongue, felt his pulse and tapped his lungs. Then he shook his head. 'There's nothing wrong with you, sir,' he said, 'except that you're run down from overwork and worry. You need rest and amusement. Take a night off and go and see George Grossmith at the Savoy.'

" 'Thank you,' said the patient, 'I *am* George Grossmith.' "   26

Let the reader please observe that I have purposely told this   27 story all wrongly, just as wrongly as could be, and yet there is something left of it. Will the reader kindly look back to the beginning of it and see for himself just how it ought to be narrated and what obvious error has been made. If he has any particle of the artist in his make-up, he will see at once that the story ought to begin:

"One day a very haggard and nervous-looking patient called   28 at the office of a fashionable doctor, etc., etc."

In other words, the chief point of the joke lies in keeping it   29 concealed till the moment when the patient says, "Thank you, I am George Grossmith." But the story is such a good one that it cannot be completely spoiled even when told wrongly. This particular anecdote has been variously told of George Grossmith, Coquelin, Joe Jefferson, John Hare, Cyril Maude, and about sixty others. And I have noticed that there is a certain type of man who, on hearing this story about Grossmith, immediately tells it all back again, putting in the name of somebody else, and goes into new fits of laughter over it, as if the change of name made it brand new.

But few people, I repeat, realise the difficulty of reproducing   30 a humorous or comic effect in its original spirit.

"I saw Harry Lauder last night," said Griggs, a Stock-Exchange   31 friend of mine, as we walked up town together the other day. "He came onto the stage in kilts" (here Griggs started to chuckle) "and he had a slate under his arm" (here Griggs began to laugh quite heartily), "and he said, 'I always like to carry a slate with me' (of course he said it in Scotch, but I can't do the Scotch the way he does it) 'just in case there might be any figures I'd be wanting to put down' " (by this time Griggs was almost suffocated with laughter)—"and he took a little bit of chalk out of his pocket, and he said" (Griggs was now almost hysterical), " 'I like to carry a wee bit chalk along because I find the slate is (Griggs was now faint with laughter), " 'the slate is—is—not much good without the chalk.' "

32   Griggs had to stop, with his hand to his side and lean against a lamp post. "I can't, of course, do the Scotch the way Harry Lauder does it," he repeated.

33   Exactly. He couldn't do the Scotch and he couldn't do the rich mellow voice of Mr. Lauder and the face beaming with merriment, and the spectacles glittering with amusement, and he couldn't do the slate, nor the "wee bit chalk"—in fact he couldn't do any of it. He ought merely to have said, "Harry Lauder," and leaned up against a post and laughed till he had got over it.

34   Yet in spite of everything, people insist on spoiling conversation by telling stories. I know nothing more dreadful at a dinner table than one of these amateur raconteurs°—except perhaps, two of them. After about three stories have been told, there falls on the dinner table an uncomfortable silence, in which everybody is aware that everybody else is trying hard to think of another story, and is failing to find it. There is no peace in the gathering again till some man of firm and quiet mind turns to his neighbour and says—"But after all there is no doubt that whether we like it or not prohibition is coming." Then everybody in his heart says, Thank Heaven! and the whole tableful are happy and contented again, till one of the story tellers "thinks of another," and breaks loose.

35   Worst of all perhaps is the modest story teller who is haunted by the idea that one has heard his story before. He attacks you after this fashion:

36   "I heard a very good story the other day on the steamer going to Bermuda"—then he pauses with a certain doubt in his face— "but perhaps you've heard this?"

37   "No, no, I've never been to Bermuda. Go ahead."

38   "Well, this is a story that they tell about a man who went down to Bermuda one winter to get cured of rheumatism—but you've heard this?"

39   "No, no."

40   "Well, he had rheumatism pretty bad and he went to Bermuda to get cured of it. And so when he went into the hotel he said to the clerk at the desk—but, perhaps you know this."

41   "No, no, go right ahead."

"Well, he said to the clerk I want a room that looks out over   42
the sea—but perhaps—"

Now the sensible thing to do is to stop the narrator right at   43
this point. Say to him quietly and firmly, "Yes, I have heard that
story. I always liked it ever since it came out in *Titbits* in 1878, and
I read it every time I see it. Go on and tell it to me and I'll sit back
with my eyes closed and enjoy it."

No doubt the story-telling habit owes much to the fact that   44
ordinary people, quite unconsciously, rate humour very low: I
mean, they underestimate the difficulty of "making humour." It
would never occur to them that the thing is hard, meritorious° and
dignified. Because the result is gay and light, they think the process
must be. Few people would realise that it is much harder to write
one of Owen Seaman's "funny" poems in *Punch* than to write one
of the Archbishop of Canterbury's sermons. Mark Twain's *Huckle-
berry Finn* is a greater work than Kant's *Critique of Pure Reason,* and
Charles Dickens' creation of Mr. Pickwick° did more for the ele-
vation of the human race—I say it in all seriousness—than Cardinal
Newman's "Lead, Kindly Light, Amid the Encircling Gloom'"°.
Newman only cried out for light in the gloom of a sad world.
Dickens gave it.

But the deep background that lies behind and beyond what   45
we call humour is revealed only to the few who, by instinct or by
effort, have given thought to it. The world's humour, in its best
and greatest sense, is perhaps the highest product of our civilisation. One thinks here not of the mere spasmodic° effects of the
comic artist or the blackface expert of the vaudeville show, but of
the really great humour which, once or twice in a generation at
best, illuminates and elevates our literature. It is no longer dependent upon the mere trick and quibble of words, or the odd and
meaningless incongruities in things that strike us as "funny." Its
basis lies in the deeper contrasts offered by life itself: the strange
incongruity between our aspiration° and our achievement, the
eager and fretful anxieties of to-day that fade into nothingness
tomorrow, the burning pain and the sharp sorrow that are softened
in the gentle retrospect° of time, till as we look back upon the
course that has been traversed° we pass in view the panorama° of
our lives, as people in old age may recall, with mingled tears and
smiles, the angry quarrels of their childhood. And here, in its larger
aspect, humour is blended with pathos till the two are one, and
represent, as they have in every age, the mingled heritage of tears
and laughter that is our lot on earth.

STEPHEN LEACOCK

Stephen Leacock (1869–1944), the humorist, is well known for his collection of funny sketches called *Sunshine Sketches of a Little Town*, based on the Ontario town of Orillia, where he had his summer home. When not writing humour and speaking across the country, he taught economics at McGill University, Montreal.

Paragraph ## Words and Meanings

7	demoniacal	fiendish, evil
	original sin:	Christian belief that every child is born tainted with the sin of Adam and Eve's disobedience to God
12	entreaties:	pleas, urgent requests
14	adversity:	misfortune, disaster
	turn the flank of terror:	cope with fear
16	anecdote:	humorous story
21	subaltern:	junior officer
23	incongruity:	inconsistency, absurdity
	dénouement:	final unravelling of the plot of a story
34	raconteur:	story teller
44	meritorious:	deserving praise or reward
	Mr. Pickwick:	character in Charles Dickens's comic masterpiece, *Pickwick Papers*
	"Lead, Kindly Light . . . ":	title of a hymn by Cardinal Newman, a well-known late nineteenth-century convert to the Catholic church
45	spasmodic:	irregular, in fits and starts
	aspiration:	aim or goal
	retrospect:	backward view, survey of past events
	traversed:	travelled
	panorama:	continuous passing scene

Structure and Strategy

1. In this essay, Leacock classifies into five categories jokes and anecdotes that he doesn't think are funny. His first category is practical jokes (paragraphs 2 to 6) and the last is poorly told jokes (paragraphs 23 to 43). Identify the other three kinds of unfunny humour and the paragraphs in which each kind is developed.

2. Leacock divides poorly told jokes (paragraphs 23 to 43) into two kinds. What are they?

3. What is the IRONY in paragraph 8?
4. Study the conclusion of this essay, paragraph 45. Compared to the rest of the piece, it is difficult to read. Why? Consider Leacock's SYNTAX, DICTION, and TONE.

Content and Purpose

1. What, in Leacock's opinion, are the characteristics of *genuine* humour? Why does Leacock dislike practical jokes?
2. According to Leacock, the George Grossmith joke (paragraphs 24 to 29) is an example of a story that is intrinsically funny: it "cannot be completely spoiled even when told wrongly." Do you agree? What makes it funny?
3. Summarize paragraph 45 in your own words. What examples of humour as "the highest product of our civilization" can you think of?

Suggestions for Writing

1. What is humour as *you* see it? Write a short paper in which you classify genuine humour into three or four categories.
2. Think of a book or film you found genuinely funny. What made it funny? Write a paper based on a thesis statement of division developed with examples.
3. Analyze the humour of movies aimed at what's called "the youth market." What standard characters and plot devices can you identify? Write an essay explaining the humour and why it works for its audience.

Additional Suggestions for Writing: Division and Classification

Use division or classification, whichever is appropriate, to analyse one of the topics below into its component parts, or characteristics, or kinds. Write a thesis statement based on your analysis and then develop it into a detailed, interesting essay.

part-time jobs
marriages
films
pop singers
role-playing games
popular novels
radio stations
TV game shows
families
dreams
college students
cameras

advice
morality
friendship
an unforgettable event
parenting
a winning team
a short story, poem, or play
shopping malls
a religious or social ritual (such as a wedding, funeral, bar mitzvah, birthday celebration)

UNIT

Comparison and Contrast: Explaining Similarities and Differences

What? The Definition

Why does a person choose to go to college rather than find a full-time job? How does that same person choose between attending Douglas College and B.C. Institute of Technology in Vancouver, or between Laurentian University and the Haileybury School of Mines in Sudbury? Which Canadian hockey team deserves the title of dynasty: the Toronto Maple Leafs or the Montreal Canadiens? Who will be remembered as the better prime minister: Pierre Trudeau or Brian Mulroney? What's for lunch: chicken wings and potato skins, or a plate of nachos and a wet burrito? Every day of our lives we are called upon to make choices, to evaluate alternatives. Sometimes, as in the "what's-for-lunch?" question, the decision may have few consequences (other than indigestion). But sometimes our decisions have far-reaching effects, as in the college-or-job dilemma. Fortunately our minds quite naturally work in a way that helps us to assess the options and to choose between the alternatives.

First, we consider what the two subjects we are comparing have in common; in other words, how are they alike? The Leafs and the Canadiens both skate, shoot, and occasionally score, and both teams have illustrious pasts. Then we consider how the two teams are different; in other words, what distinguishes one from the other? Montreal has good scouting, consistent coaching, and solid owner-ship. The Leafs? Well, perhaps the less said, the better.

Pointing out similarities is called **comparing**; pointing out differences is called **contrasting**. When we assess both similarities and differences, we are engaging in **comparison and contrast**. Often, however, people use the term "comparison" to mean comparing, or contrasting, or both. In this chapter, we will use *comparison* to cover all three approaches.

Why? The Purpose

Comparison is a natural mental process; it's something we do, con-sciously or unconsciously, all the time. In writing, we use comparison to answer these questions:

1. What are the main similarities between S_1 and S_2?
2. What are the main differences between S_1 and S_2?
3. What are the main similarities and differences between S_1 and S_2?

Using such a pattern in written communication can be useful in sev-eral ways. First, an essay or report structured to compare various items can be highly informative. It can explain two subjects clearly by putting them alongside each other. Second, a comparison paper can evaluate as well as inform. It can assess the relative merits of two subjects and provide reasons on which a reader can base a judgment, or reasons to explain the writer's preference for one item over the other.

In school, you use the comparison pattern for both purposes: to *inform* and to *evaluate*. An exam may ask, "What similarities and differences are there between analog and digital computers?" A research paper, on the other hand, may require you to focus on the parallels and divergences between health-insurance plans in Ontario and Alberta, while a test question may take the comparison a step further, by requiring you to evaluate the merits of the two health-care plans. Your field placement, for instance, may require a judgment as to the overall competence of two engineering firms. Each case calls for a *comparison*. It serves as the structural principle of your exam answer, your paper, or your report.

How? The Technique

Organizing a paper according to the principle of comparison isn't difficult if you approach the task by asking three questions. First: are the two items really comparable? Second: what are the terms of comparison? Third: what is the most appropriate pattern of organization to use?

Comparing Wayne Gretzky to Dolly Parton has, at first glance, at least comic potential. It's true they are both highly paid entertainers. But there is no sustained or significant basis for drawing a comparison between them because their talents are just too different. The writer of a comparison, then, must be sure that a meaningful similarity exists between the two subjects. They must have something *significant* in common. For instance, Wayne Gretzky could be compared in an interesting manner to another hockey legend like Bobby Orr. Dolly Parton would best be compared to another high-camp vamp of the silver screen—Mae West, perhaps—or another country singer such as Loretta Lynn.

After deciding that your two subjects are comparable in a meaningful way, you should then carefully consider the terms of the comparison. If, for instance, you were asked to assess two engineering firms, it would make little sense to compare the management structure and computer systems of one firm to the washrooms and cafeteria food of the other. Resemblances and differences must be assessed in the same terms or categories. Your report should be organized to assess both firms in identical terms: management structure, computer systems, and employee facilities, for example.

Your final step is to decide on an appropriate structure for your comparison. There are two effective patterns to choose from: subject-by-subject and point-by-point. Like pineapples, comparison papers can be processed into *chunks* or *slices*. (Pineapples also come crushed, but this form is precisely what you're trying to avoid.)

Structuring a comparison according to the *chunk* pattern involves separating the two subjects and discussing each one separately, under the headings or categories you've chosen to consider. If you were asked, for example, to compare the novel and film versions of Mordecai Richler's *The Apprenticeship of Duddy Kravitz*, you might decide to focus your analysis on the characters, the setting, and the plot of the two versions. You would first discuss the novel in terms of these three points, then you would do the same for the film. Here is a sample chunk outline for such an essay:

Paragraph 1   Introduction and thesis statement
Paragraph 2 S_1 Novel
                a. characters in the novel
                b. setting of the novel
                c. plot of the novel
Paragraph 3 S_2 Film
                a. characters in the film
                b. setting of the film
                c. plot of the film
Paragraph 4   Conclusion summarizing the similarities and differences and possibly stating your preference

The chunk pattern does not rule out a discussion of the two subjects in the same paragraph. In this example, particularly in your analysis of the film, some mention of the novel might be necessary. However, the overall structure of the chunk comparison should communicate the essentials about Subject 1, then communicate the essentials about Subject 2.

The chunk style works best with fairly short papers (essay questions on exams, for instance) where the reader does not have to remember many intricate details about Subject 1 while trying to assimilate the details of Subject 2.

Structuring a comparison according to the *slice* pattern involves setting out the terms or categories of comparison, then discussing both subjects under each category heading. The *Duddy Kravitz* essay structured in slices could communicate the same information as the chunked paper, yet its shape and outline would be quite different:

Paragraph 1   Introduction and thesis statement
Paragraph 2   Characters
                S_1 in the novel
                S_2 in the film
Paragraph 3   Setting
                S_1 in the novel
                S_2 in the film
Paragraph 4   Plot
                S_1 in the novel
                S_2 in the film
Paragraph 5   Conclusion with, perhaps, a statement of your preference

The slice pattern makes the resemblances and differences between the two subjects more readily apparent to the reader. It's the type of structure that is ideally suited to longer reports and papers, where the terms of comparison are complex and demand high reader recall.

Because comparing and contrasting is a natural human thought process, organizing written communication in this pattern is not very difficult. It does, however, require clear thinking and preparation. Before you even begin to write, you need to study the subjects themselves, decide on the terms of comparison, and choose the appropriate structure.

A good thesis statement is essential to a well-written comparison paper (as it is, indeed, to any piece of writing). Because comparison involves considering two different items in terms of several aspects, writing the thesis statement presents an interesting challenge.

Here are three models for you to choose from in drafting thesis statements for comparison papers.

> S_1 and S_2 can be compared in terms of a, b, and c.

Example: Trudeau and Mulroney can be compared in terms of their power bases, religious backgrounds, and family ties.

> S_1 and S_2 can be contrasted in terms of a, b, and c.

Example: College and university can be contrasted in terms of cost, instruction, and orientation.

> Although S_1 and S_2 are different in terms of a, b, and c, they are alike in terms of d.

Example: Although Canada and Scotland are different in terms of size, geography, and culture, they are alike in terms of their relationship with their southern neighbours.

Be prepared to spend time shaping and perfecting your thesis statement. The effort you invest at this stage will pay off by providing a solid framework on which you can construct and then communicate what it is you want to say.

Here is a comparison essay that illustrates the slice pattern of organization, based on the second example above.

College or University?

Introduction (makes use of a contrast)

{ In the United States, the word "college" is used to designate all formal education that takes place after high school. Whether people attend a local two-year

Thesis statement ──────→ junior college or a university as renowned as Harvard, they are described
as "going to college." In Canada, however, the word "college" is contrasted
with the word "university." Here, "going
to college" denotes a different educational experience from that of "going to
university." The college experience and
the university experience in Canada can
be contrasted in terms of cost, instruction, and orientation.

*First point (developed
with examples and
statistics)*

A college education is less costly
than a university education, partly because it takes less time to complete. For
instance, a student can complete an engineering technology program at most
community colleges in three years; the
technician's program takes only two. An
engineering degree from a university requires an investment of four years, or in
some cases even five, if the particular
institution offers a co-op program. Each
extra year in school costs the student
money in lost wages as well as in living
expenses and tuition. Tuition is, of
course, another reason for the difference in cost. By and large, university
fees are about four times as high as
those of a college. Although statistics
indicate that the average university
graduate earns, over a lifetime, approximately twice as much as the average
college graduate, going to university
costs considerably more than going to
a community college.

*Second point (again,
note the well-chosen
examples)*

The methods of instruction are different at university and college. At many
universities, especially in the first two
years, students attend large lecture
classes for their introductory courses.
They may participate in smaller seminar
groups led by graduate students, yet the
fundamentals of the undergraduate curriculum, whether in mathematics, psychology, or literature, are often presented

in classes containing hundreds of people. Colleges offer a more "hands-on" approach and smaller-group interaction between students and instructors. Students who require psychology to complete a correctional worker program, for instance, will probably find themselves in a small class in which dialogue between students and teacher is encouraged.

The transition here connects the first and second points to the third point — the topic of this paragraph.

The above example points to the third and most important difference between university and college: their orientation toward career learning. Though professional studies—those aimed at a particular career—may be part of a university education, the curriculum is largely based on theoretical learning—learning for its own sake. Often a student must complete postgraduate work in order to qualify for a particular profession, such as law, teaching, or medicine. Universities aim at providing students with a background in arts, sciences, and languages in addition to their chosen discipline. Colleges, on the other hand, are usually oriented toward providing a career education that will prepare students for jobs in such fields as data processing, recreation leadership, or fashion design. Hence, while there is an element of general education in most college programs, much of the learning is practical and job-specific.

Conclusion (restates the thesis in different words)

Canadian students interested in post-secondary education thus have an important choice to make. After considering the differences in time and cost and weighing the advantages of the broader academic study offered by a university as opposed to the more career-specific training provided by a college, they can decide which kind of institution best suits their needs, aptitudes, and goals.

People and Their Machines and Vice Versa

PETER GZOWSKI

1   If I have remembered my own history correctly, it is exactly thirty years ago this week that I arrived in Timmins, Ontario, to begin my life as a newspaperman. Almost every day for those thirty years, I have opened my working procedures the same way. I have cranked a piece of paper into my typewriter, banged out what newspapermen call a slug at the top of the page, usually followed, for reasons I don't know but by a habit I can't break, by the page number typed four or five times, and started pounding away with as many fingers as seemed to fit. Like most old newspapermen, I am as fast as a Gatling gun° at my machine, and almost as noisy. I make mistakes—which is like saying Wayne Gretzky gets scoring points—but I strike them out: xxxxxxx or, if I'm really flying, mnmnmnmnmnmn, *m* with the right forefinger, *n* with the left. Afterward, I go over what I've done with the heaviest pencil I can find, changing a word here, a phrase there. I cross out some more, with a bold, black stroke and a flourishing delete sign. I add. Sometimes I make what one of my editors called chicken tracks from the place I had the first thought out into the margin. Out there, I create anew. I scribble up into the bare space at the top, up by the stammering page numbers, and on good days, when my juices are flowing and the ghost of Maxwell Perkins° is looking over my shoulder, I carry on from there, turning the page under my pencil, down the outer edges, filling the bottom and off, off into virgin territories, leaving my inky spoor° behind me. When I am pleased with what I have done, or when the chicken tracks get too dense to follow, I put a new page in the typewriter and start again. This is not the way anyone taught me to work. But it is the way I have done things. It has served me through five books, more magazine articles than you could shake an art director's ruler at and enough newspaper pieces to line the cage of every eagle that ever flew.

"People and Their Machines and Vice Versa" from *The Morningside Papers* by Peter Gzowski, copyright 1985. Reprinted by permission of McClelland and Stewart Limited.

But no more. I am a word-processor man now, or trying to become one. I made the change at the end of this summer. The words I am reading to you now first appeared to my eye etched in green on a dark screen. Or, rather, some *version* of the words I am reading to you now so appeared. "Green," for instance, was "gereen," or perhaps "jereen," until I danced my cursor around the screen (the "screeen?") and obliterated the extra *e*. "Etched," too, is probably the wrong word. The process by which these words appear is too sophisticated for my manually operated mind, and I no more understand it than I understand what really happens when I turn on the ignition of my car. All I know, in fact, are two things: one, I can do it. If I take my time, and think my way through such delicate differences as that between the "control" key and the shift lock, and resist the urge to hit the space bar (which makes sense to me) and instead hit a simultaneous "control" and *d* (which doesn't) when I want to move my little cursor over one notch, I can, however painstakingly, make the words come out in prose. That's one. Two is that I hate doing it. Over the years, the relationship I have built up with my various manuals° is an emotional one. I pound them and they respond, as the Steinway° responded to Glenn Gould. I knew I was working because I could hear it, and the measure of what I had accomplished in a working day was often the pile of out-takes that grew in my wastepaper basket, like tailings at a mine. Now, I work silently. I wrote what you are hearing now while my daughter slept in the next room. This was convenient for Alison, but it did not seem to me to be what I have always done for a living. It neither sounded nor felt like *writing*. God, it seems to me, no more meant words to appear in fluorescent electronic letters than he meant pool tables to be pink, or golf balls orange.

2

[   ]

PETER GZOWSKI

Peter Gzowski, broadcaster and journalist, was born in Toronto in 1934 but was raised in Galt, Ont. He is the regular host of the CBC radio program *Morningside* and the author or editor of numerous books, including *Spring Tonic* and *The Game of Our Lives*, a study of hockey.

Words and Meanings   Paragraph

Gatling gun:	early form of machine gun	1
Maxwell Perkins:	well-known New York book editor	
spoor:	track or scent of an animal	

2   manuals: manually operated (non-electric) typewriters
     Steinway: make of concert piano

Structure and Strategy

1. First review the different patterns for comparison and contrast thesis statements in the introduction to this unit and then write a thesis statement for Gzowski's essay.
2. Has Gzowski used the *slice* or *chunk* method to organize his essay?
3. What effective ALLUSIONS and FIGURES OF SPEECH has Gzowski used in paragraph 1?
4. How has Gzowski achieved TRANSITION between paragraphs 1 and 2? Why is the first sentence of paragraph 2 so short?
5. How does the contrast in DICTION in paragraphs 1 and 2 help reinforce Gzowski's thesis?
6. Gzowski uses two particularly effective comparisons in paragraph 2. What are they, and why are they appropriate to convey his attitude toward writing?

Content and Purpose

1. What are the implications of the title? How does the title prepare the reader for Gzowski's thesis?
2. What is the essential difference, according to Gzowski, between composing at a typewriter and composing on a word processor?
3. Why does Gzowski make the following revelation about himself and his method of writing: "This is not the way anyone taught me to work. But it is the way I have done things. It has served me through five books . . . "? Is he just bragging, or does the statement communicate something the reader needs to know?

Suggestions for Writing

1. Write thesis statements comparing and/or contrasting the following: two cars, two sports, two fashion designers, two celebrities, two political leaders, two teachers.
2. Compare and/or contrast an old and a new way of performing a task with which you are familiar, such as playing a game, operating a machine, raising a child, or preparing a meal.

A Nice Place to Visit

RUSSELL BAKER

Having heard that Toronto was becoming one of the continent's noblest cities, we flew from New York to investigate. New Yorkers jealous of their city's reputation and concerned about challenges to its stature have little to worry about.   1

After three days in residence, our delegation noted an absence of hysteria that was almost intolerable and took to consuming large portions of black coffee to maintain our normal state of irritability. The local people to whom we complained in hopes of provoking comfortably nasty confrontations declined to become bellicose°. They would like to enjoy a gratifying big city hysteria, they said, but believed it would seem ill-mannered in front of strangers.   2

Extensive field studies—our stay lasted four weeks—persuaded us that this failure reflects the survival in Toronto of an ancient pattern of social conduct called "courtesy."   3

"Courtesy" manifests itself in many quaint forms appalling to the New Yorker. Thus, for example, Yankee fans may be astonished to learn that at the Toronto baseball park it is considered bad form to heave rolls of toilet paper and beer cans at players on the field.   4

Official literature inside Toronto taxicabs includes a notification of the proper address to which riders may mail the authorities not only complaints but also compliments about the cabbie's behavior.   5

For a city that aspires to urban greatness, Toronto's entire taxi system has far to go. At present, it seems hopelessly bogged down in civilization. One day a member of our delegation listening to a radio conversation between a short-tempered cabbie and the dispatcher distinctly heard the dispatcher say, "As Shakespeare said, if music be the food of love, play on, give me excess of it."   6

This delegate became so unnerved by hearing Shakespeare quoted by a cab dispatcher that he fled immediately back to New York to have his nerves abraded° and his spine rearranged in a real big-city taxi.   7

What was particularly distressing as the stay continued was the absence of shrieking police and fire sirens at 3 A.M.—or any other hour, for that matter. We spoke to the city authorities about this. What kind of city was it, we asked, that expected its citizens   8

"A Nice Place to Visit" by Russell Baker. Copyright © April 17, 1979 by The New York Times Company. Reprinted by permission.

to sleep all night and rise refreshed in the morning? Where was the incentive° to awaken gummy-eyed and exhausted, ready to scream at the first person one saw in the morning? How could Toronto possibly hope to maintain a robust urban divorce rate?

9   Our criticism went unheeded, such is the torpor° with which Toronto pursues true urbanity°. The fact appears to be that Toronto has very little grasp of what is required of a great city.

10   Consider the garbage picture. It seems never to have occurred to anybody in Toronto that garbage exists to be heaved into the streets. One can drive for miles without seeing so much as a banana peel in the gutter or a discarded newspaper whirling in the wind.

11   Nor has Toronto learned about dogs. A check with the authorities confirmed that, yes, there are indeed dogs resident in Toronto, but one would never realize it by walking the sidewalks. Our delegation was shocked by the presumption of a town's calling itself a city, much less a great city, when it obviously knows nothing of either garbage or dogs.

12   The subway, on which Toronto prides itself, was a laughable imitation of the real thing. The subway cars were not only spotlessly clean, but also fully illuminated. So were the stations. To New Yorkers, it was embarrassing, and we hadn't the heart to tell the subway authorities that they were light-years away from greatness.

13   We did, however, tell them about spray paints and how effectively a few hundred children equipped with spray-paint cans could at least give their subway the big-city look.

14   It seems doubtful they are ready to take such hints. There is a disturbing distaste for vandalism in Toronto which will make it hard for the city to enter wholeheartedly into the vigor of the late twentieth century.

15   A board fence surrounding a huge excavation for a new high-rise building in the downtown district offers depressing evidence of Toronto's lack of big-city impulse. Embedded in the fence at intervals of about fifty feet are loudspeakers that play recorded music for passing pedestrians.

16   Not a single one of these loudspeakers has been mutilated. What's worse, not a single one has been stolen.

17   It was good to get back to the Big Apple. My coat pocket was bulging with candy wrappers from Toronto and—such is the lingering power of Toronto—it took me two or three hours back in New York before it seemed natural again to toss them into the street.

RUSSELL BAKER

Born in Virginia in 1925, humorist Russell Baker has been a columnist for
The New York Times for the past twenty-five years. The winner of two Pulitzer
Prizes, Baker has written numerous books, including *Baker's Dozen* (1964)
and *So This Is Depravity* (1980).

Words and Meanings

Paragraph

bellicose:	warlike	2
abraded:	scraped, injured	7
incentive:	motive	8
torpor:	slowness, dullness	9
urbanity:	quality of being civilized, sophisticated	

Structure and Strategy

1. This piece was written as a column for *The New York Times*.
   What are some of the differences between a newspaper column
   and an essay?
2. Is Baker being serious in this piece? Find several examples
   showing how he has made effective use of IRONY.
3. What are three of the categories that Baker uses to contrast
   Toronto and New York? Is his article organized in *slices* or in
   chunks? (See introduction to this unit.)
4. What is the function of paragraph 9? How does it contribute to
   COHERENCE?
5. The DICTION and SYNTAX of this piece are, for the most part,
   highly formal. In what sort of writing would you expect to find
   expressions such as "extensive field studies," "the local people,"
   or "the survival of an ancient pattern of social conduct"? What
   role does Baker assume in this article? Is the TONE of the piece
   as formal as its DICTION?

Content and Purpose

1. Why has Baker chosen this particular title?
2. Baker does not tell us what New York is like, but he does tell us
   what Toronto is *not* like. How, then, does he communicate to his
   readers a vivid picture of life in New York?
3. What does Baker really think about life in Toronto? Find specific
   examples in his article to support your answer.

Suggestions for Writing

1. Write a short paper comparing two countries, jobs, schools, or neighbourhoods with which you are familiar. Decide beforehand whether you intend to be serious or ironic in your comparison and try to maintain a consistent tone.
2. Write a short essay comparing two cities, two close friends, or two kinds of vacation. Use the *slice* method to organize your paper.
3. Read Tom Wolfe's essay "O Rotten Gotham: Sliding Down into the Behavioral Sink" in Unit Five. Then compare Wolfe's and Baker's views of life in New York.

If You Drop a Stone . . .

HUGH MACLENNAN

1   If you drop a stone into the ocean the impact is as great as if you drop it into a farmer's pond. The difference is that the ocean doesn't seem to care. It swallows the stone and rolls on. But the pond, if the stone is large enough, breaks into waves and ripples that cover its surface and are audible in every cranny along its banks.

2   So it is with life in a metropolis and life in a small town. It takes a colossal event to affect a city. After the bombing of Hamburg in which eighty thousand people were killed, the city was functioning within a few days. Grief did not paralyse it because, to the survivors, most of the casualties were people they had never met. But a single murder can convulse a small town for the reason that in such a community people care who lives and who dies. They care because they know each other. All knowledge is relative to our capacity to grasp its details, and no matter what the communists and industrial organizers may say, no man can think humanly if he thinks in terms of masses. In the small town, and not in the metropolis, human life is understood in fundamental terms.

3   Because I grew up in a smallish town, this idea struck me with

"If You Drop a Stone . . ." from *The Other Side of Hugh MacLennan*, ed. Elspeth Cameron. © 1978 by Hugh MacLennan. Reprinted by permission of Macmillan of Canada, A Division of Canada Publishing Corporation.

the force of a shock the first time I saw a play in London about London life. I marvelled how any audience could believe in it. Apparently, I thought, Londoners don't know each other and the playwright has taken advantage of their ignorance. A play as superficial as this, I said to myself when I left the theatre, could never succeed in Halifax.

My youthful reaction was naïve°, but it was not stupid. I did not know then, as I have learned since, that practically no creative ideas have ever originated in a megalopolis°. The prelude° to creation, as every parent knows, is intimacy. I had come straight to London from an intimate town, and what we knew about each other in that town could have kept a Balzac° supplied with material for life. Small-town gossip may be notorious, but by no means all of it is malicious°. It has one virtue which its metropolitan imitators, the newspapers, cannot claim. Most of it has personal significance for the people who listen to it.

We knew in our town, for example, and we knew in detail, how our wealthiest citizens had made their money. Although we did not know a neurosis° from a psychosis°, we understood, and made allowances for, the family conditions which caused one man to be aggressive and another subservient, one woman to be charming and another to be a shrew°. We had a sixth sense which the more intelligent city-dwellers lack—a sense of time. We knew that a family, like Rome, is not built in a day.

We would look at one family and remember hearing about the grandfather, now dead, who used to sit in his galluses° on a stool outside the livery stable chewing a straw and occasionally reaching up with the thumb of his left hand to scratch his head. It had been a matter of interested speculation whether he scratched because he was nervous or because he was lousy°. The father, still with us, was a middle-aged man doing fairly well in a hardware business. He never scratched his head, but it was noticed that he had a curious habit of stopping suddenly while walking down the street to lift the right leg of his trousers and scratch the back of his calf. As the hardware merchant was certainly not lousy, this gesture was assumed to be hereditary; as such, it cleared the grandfather's reputation from all suspicion of uncleanliness. The merchant's son raised the family one notch higher. He went to college, did well, and now was laying the foundations of a solid career in the administration in Ottawa. Perhaps he might even rise to cabinet rank and make us all proud, for rumour had it that the Prime Minister's eye was on him. Incidentally, he was never seen to scratch himself at all.

This kind of small-town knowledge may seem petty, but the sum of it is vast. Through a multitude of intimate details people

4

5

6

7

come to know the best and the worst about each other, and concealment of character is impossible over a lifetime. A ruthless° or a cunning° man can ride roughshod° over his neighbours and cop° most of the money in the place. In every small town there are always a few who try this, and at least one who succeeds. They make bad bargains, for they spend the rest of their days knowing exactly what their neighbours think and say about them. In the small town, since everyone knows the sins of everyone else, each man must live as best he can with the knowledge that his faults and weaknesses are part of the lore of the whole community. That is what I mean by saying that in a small town people know life as it really is. That is why Halifax or Peterborough has a better chance of producing a Balzac than London or New York, and why a little place like Bermuda, where the stakes are really high, could produce a second Shakespeare if some Bermudian had the genius and the nerve to write as Shakespeare did.

8   But for the past two hundred years the small towns have failed in what should be their mission, which is the illumination of life. Only to a very small extent has their unrivalled knowledge of life been used for artistic purposes. They have given the world nearly all its famous writers and artists, but the moment their gifted children are ready to produce they are compelled to leave home and emigrate to the city. "Appearances must be maintained," a small-town friend said to me not long ago; "otherwise life couldn't go on." But to maintain appearances is the one thing no creative artist can ever do. If he tries, his work shows as much liveliness and veracity° as the average obituary column. So, for freedom's sake, he moves to the big city and there he tends to stay. That is why for the past two hundred years art has always been associated in people's minds with the life of the metropolis.

9   But the metropolis—London, Paris, New York, Rome—does not nurture° art. It merely gives the immigrant artist or writer freedom to paint or write as he pleases. And it exacts a bitter price for this freedom, the loss of the small-town intimacy from which all life-knowledge derives. That is why so many writers over the past two hundred years have done their best work before they were forty. In their early years in the big city, they availed themselves of the freedom it offered to be themselves. They wrote, generally, of the life they had lived in their native regions. But as they grew older they inevitably consumed their vital material, and in middle age they tended to run dry. The metropolis which was now their home failed to provide them with the life-giving material they required.

10   The very freedom the big city grants is based on a kind of indifference to the individual, an indifference that springs from

ignorance. The city has no real gossip. In the city a man is a name or a career, a unit in a factory or the occupant of an office desk. There is no universal folk-memory of the grandfather who scratched his head or the son who hoisted his trouser to scratch the back of his leg. The emotional upheavals which shatter families are swallowed up by the city as the ocean swallowed the *Titanic*, and to the onlooking artist they seem almost as meaningless as traffic accidents because he cannot possibly know, much less feel, the forces which caused them.

When modern writers attempt to use metropolitan life as the   11
material for tragedy their work is usually cold and dry. This has been especially notable in the English-speaking centres of London and New York. It is true that Dickens was a Londoner; it is equally true that he saw only the surface of things. As for New York, in the whole of American literature not a single great book has been based on its life.

How could it be? In New York, who cares who commits sui-   12
cide? The crowds massed in the street to see if the stranger will jump from the skyscraper window are not interested in the man, because they do not know him. They are interested only in the spectacle. In New York, who cares who cheats whom? Or who survives through endurance? Or who, by a denial of himself, wins spiritual greatness? This does not imply that New York is less noble than a small town. It merely implies that in terms of art it is too large for any individual artist to handle.

Far different was the situation in the days when no cities were   13
immense and a few small or medium-sized towns were the life-centres of a whole people. Ancient Athens at the height of her glory had a voting list somewhat smaller than that of modern Halifax. But she had a spirit which Halifax and all modern smallish towns entirely lack—she preferred excitement to caution and greatness to respectability. She invented tragic and comic drama, the art of history, and the democratic method of government. All these stupendous inventions arose out of her own experience. The characters in her great comedies were living Athenian citizens, and when Socrates° was satirized in *The Clouds* by Aristophanes he rose in the theatre so that everyone would know that he was enjoying the play, too. Plato's° *Republic* had its origin in a dinner party which assembled after a late-afternoon walk just as casually as Joe Smith gets together his cronies for a poker game by the simple expedient of walking the length of the main street from the barber shop to the Maple Leaf Hotel.

It has always been the same—without intimacy, there can be   14
no creation. Republican Rome was a relatively small town. Florence, Genoa, Venice, and Pisa, in the days of their glory, were

about a quarter the size of Ottawa. In Shakespeare's London everyone who mattered knew everyone else, and we can be pretty certain
that the characters who live in Shakespeare's plays were modelled
on people the playwright knew personally or had heard about from
the intimate gossip of others who did.

15   But these wonderful small towns had one thing in common
besides the intimate knowledge of life which all small towns share.
It never occurred to them that their knowledge should be re-
pressed° "in order that life might go on". There was no conspiracy
of silence when it came to writing books and plays. The citizens
were not afraid of gossip. In such communities a man like Mackenzie King could never have become Prime Minister, nor would a
generation of public servants have admired his theory that a leader
should veil his thoughts in the stuffiest language possible lest the
public become sufficiently interested to make an effort to find out
what he was talking about.

16   It seems to me, thinking along these lines, that the cultural
future of Canada is opposed only by fear of what the neighbours
will say. For Canada, by and large, is still a nation of small towns.
Toronto, for all its sprawling size, has a small-town psychology.
So, when it comes down to it, does Montreal; in this city we still
have a great deal of the intimate small-town knowledge of life
which New York and London lack. It has made us shrewder than
we realize. We know, for example, that our present material prosperity does not mean, in itself, that we are a great country. We
know intuitively° that we will become great only when we translate
our force and knowledge into spiritual and artistic terms. Then,
and only then, will it matter to mankind whether Canada has
existed or not.

HUGH MACLENNAN

Hugh MacLennan, the essayist and novelist, was born in 1907 in Glace Bay,
N.S., and has won five Governor General's awards for his writing. Among
his many publications are *Barometer Rising*, *Return of the Sphinx*, *The
Watch that Ends the Night*, *The Rivers of Canada*, and *Voices in Time*.

Paragraph   **Words and Meanings**

4   naïve: unsophisticated, inexperienced
     megalopolis: huge city
     prelude: condition that precedes, or comes before
     Balzac: Honoré de Balzac, great nineteenth-century
                               French novelist
     malicious: evil-minded, harmful

neurosis:	an emotional disorder; anxiety	5
psychosis:	a serious mental illness	
shrew:	nagging, scolding woman	
galluses:	suspenders	6
lousy:	infested with lice (plural of louse)	
ruthless:	without pity	7
cunning:	shrewd, clever	
ride roughshod over:	show no consideration for	
cop:	grab (slang)	
veracity:	truthfulness	8
nurture:	nourish, provide environment in which something can grow	9
Socrates:	ancient Greek philosopher	13
Plato:	ancient Greek philosopher, student of Socrates	
repressed:	silenced, not expressed	15
intuitively:	instinctively, without thinking about it	16

Structure and Strategy

1. With what ANALOGY does MacLennan introduce his subject?
2. What is the topic sentence of paragraph 2, and how does MacLennan use a contrast to develop it?
3. Where does MacLennan state his thesis?
4. Has MacLennan used the *chunk* or *slice* method of organizing his material? (See the introduction to this unit.)
5. What is the function of paragraphs 5, 6, and 7? What point do they develop?
6. What concluding strategy does MacLennan use in paragraph 16? Is it effective?

Content and Purpose

1. MacLennan believes that "practically no creative ideas have ever originated in a megalopolis." Do you agree? Or can you cite examples to disprove his thesis?
2. Why does MacLennan feel that small-town dwellers develop "a sense of time" that city dwellers lack?
3. What are the reasons underlying MacLennan's belief that the big cities have failed to produce great art?
4. According to MacLennan, is Canada likely to produce great artists? Why or why not?

Suggestions for Writing

1. Write a short paper using the *chunk* method of organization (see the introduction to this unit) in which you compare high school

and college. You may want to adapt some of MacLennan's ideas: think of the high school as a small town and college as a big city.

2. Write a paper, using either the *chunk* or the *slice* method of organization, that compares two different ways of life: rural and urban, single and married; living with and without children, or with and without a strong religious belief.

How the West Was Lost

ROBERT FULFORD

1   They may never have seen each other's faces, but the two most famous non-whites in late nineteenth-century Canada—Louis Riel and Big Bear—were linked by history and by the events of the crisis year 1885. They were dissimilar in many ways—Riel a Montreal-educated Métis who travelled widely and was three times elected to the Canadian parliament, Big Bear a Plains Cree who knew no world beyond the Prairies. But they were also alike: both were mystics and prophets and both were charismatic°, leaders of peoples doomed by the westward thrust of the Canadian empire. At the beginning of 1885 Riel was a towering figure in the West, feared as well as respected, and Big Bear was a chief of considerable reputation. By the end of the year Riel was dead, hanged for high treason°: and Big Bear was in prison, an object of hatred to the whites and of contempt to the Indians. They were defeated by a process they only dimly understood and could do nothing to resist.

2   This year [1985] Canada is marking the hundredth anniversary of the North-West Rebellion with a TV documentary, radio programmes, books, a large exhibition of Métis crafts in Calgary, and half a dozen academic conferences. These events can't be construed° as a celebration, because not even the most blissfully unaware Canadian white can regard the destruction of the Métis and Indian societies as an accomplishment. But it isn't exactly an occasion for mourning either; only total hypocrites would pretend to mourn a series of events by which we have all handsomely profited. Perhaps

"How the West Was Lost" by Robert Fulford. © July 1985. Reprinted by permission of *Saturday Night* magazine.

the centenary of the rebellion can serve us best if it broadens our understanding of how we came to be what we are, and of the human price that was paid for modern Canada.

Both Louis Riel and Big Bear were products as well as victims   3
of the Europeanization of North America. Descendants of fur traders who married Indian women, the Métis built the brief prosperity
of their society (it lasted about seven decades) by feeding the European and white North American markets with buffalo hides and
other skins. Big Bear led an Indian community that was heavily
influenced by Europe: in the middle of the nineteenth century he
and his followers were hunting buffalo on horses brought by the
Europeans and shooting them with European guns. In many ways
the Europeans were a curse to the Indians—they brought smallpox
(which Big Bear survived in childhood while many of his contemporaries died)—but at times they must also have seemed a blessing.
In the short term, Europeans made possible the greatest mobility   ·
and freedom the Plains Cree had ever enjoyed.

The events of 1885 brought that period of intense and some-   4
times happy collaboration to an end. By the beginning of that year,
Riel was already a legend. He had behind him the abortive rebellion
of 1869–70, which failed to establish a Métis political jurisdiction
but nevertheless led to the creation of Manitoba. He had survived
his years of exile in Montana and been called back, to the leadership
of his people. But what the Métis in general had in mind, and what
Riel dreamed, were different. They wanted their land rights; he
wanted not only land rights but a new Roman Catholicism in which
everyone would be a priest, the pope would be a Canadian, the
Métis would be the chosen people, and he himself would be the
"Prophet of the New World." Riel's eighteen months in a mental
hospital were now years behind him but his old illness—a kind of
megalomania°—was upon him again. The man who was about to
become one of the central myths of our history was (the evidence
seems clear) in the throes of madness.

Riel interpreted the Gospels in a way that made violence   5
acceptable and necessary. "Justice commands us to take up arms,"
he told his followers. On March 18, at Batoche, in what is now
Saskatchewan, he and about sixty supporters ransacked the stores
and seized a number of people, including the Indian agent. The
next day he formed a provisional government and a few days later
took part in a battle in which twelve Mounties and five Métis were
killed. It was only a matter of time before the soldiers arrived from
the East, defeated the Métis (in early May), and arrested Riel. The
war seemed to be over almost before it began. Soon the soldiers
were returning to the East, and—as Bob Beal and Rod Macleod
write in their absorbing new book, *Prairie Fire: The 1885 North-West*

Rebellion (Hurtig)—it was a time of national triumph for the young Dominion of Canada: "Every city and town that had sent a unit greeted their return with ecstatic crowds, and an orgy of banquets, church services, speeches, and plans for memorials followed. By the end of July all the troops were home and the last military operation in which Canadians shot and killed each other was over."

6   It could be argued that in pursuing their grievances the Métis were blindly impetuous°. In 1885 only fools could have imagined that violent action by a tiny, isolated community would win an argument with the government of Canada. And perhaps Riel knew this all along. George Woodcock, in his 1975 book on Riel's general, *Gabriel Dumont*, suggested that Riel was courting martyrdom, consciously or not: "He belonged to a people against whose characteristic culture almost all the forces of the nineteenth century were aligned; even if he had survived, the way of life he defended could hardly have done so, and perhaps that was one of the reasons . . . he decided to die and even made sure of doing so by disputing his defence lawyers' pleas of insanity when he was tried at Regina." But if the Riel rebellion was a kind of madness, the course of patient and peaceful negotiation was no more profitable. The experience of Big Bear was proving that point forcefully.

7   The year 1885 is mainly remembered for Riel's defeat, but it was also the year the Plains Cree finally collapsed into the arms of white civilization and began their long decades of servitude as wards of the Canadian state. The end of their free civilization on the Prairies was at least as melancholy as the destruction of the Métis.

8   Big Bear's life—described recently in Hugh A. Dempsey's richly informative *Big Bear: The End of Freedom* (Douglas & McIntyre)— encompassed the whole story of nineteenth-century prairie Indians, from triumph on the open plains to humiliation on the reserves. A chief's son, Big Bear won his own reputation in adolescence as a buffalo hunter and a warrior. Like the Métis, the Plains Cree built their lives around the buffalo, which provided most of what they needed—not only food but skins that could be made into clothes and tents, even bones to be made into implements. But the buffalo, while plentiful enough to serve the Indians who hunted them with bow and arrow, didn't last long when attacked by Indians, Métis, and whites with fast horses and repeater rifles. It was said that in the peak years 160,000 buffalo were killed every season, and by the late 1870s they had all but disappeared.

9   The Cree knew no other way to live, and in 1878 Big Bear explained to Lieutenant-Governor David Baird: "The Great Spirit has supplied us with plenty of buffalo for food until the white man

came. Now as that means of support is about to fail us, the government ought to take the place of the Great Spirit, and provide us with the means of living in some other way." His statement sounded absurd at the time, but it turned out to be a summary of government policies for native peoples for at least the next century.

It was commonly said of Big Bear that if he had been white he 10 would have been a great statesman. He approached the whites in a spirit of friendliness and brotherhood, but he was the last major chief in the West to sign a treaty with the government. Other chiefs, promised a few dollars and some provisions, signed away their rights to the land without knowing what their acquiescence meant for the future. Big Bear somehow knew. He never understood the complexities of white power—he seems always to have thought that "government" was the name of a man in Ottawa who controlled everything—but he realized that the whites were taking away all that the Indians had. His dreams often guided the Plains Cree; in his youth, shortly after the smallpox attack, a vision had told him that eventually the whites would come in great number, bearing gifts, and take away the Indian land. That process was set in motion in 1869 when the Hudson's Bay Company sold the West to the new Dominion of Canada for £300,000. The news of this transaction baffled and distressed the Indians, who had believed until then that no-one owned the land.

Their reaction illustrated the mutual incomprehension° that 11 made a reconciliation between Indians and whites impossible. The whites were bound by their view of the world as something to be owned and conquered. The Indians, as pre-agrarians°, knew the world only as something to live with. In the nineteenth century no white man could understand a view so fundamentally alien to his own—or even admit that it existed. Given this profound difference, there was nothing for the whites to do except convert the Indians to Christianity, British justice, and farming.

Big Bear never imagined that a war against the whites would 12 be profitable; he counselled peace while he practised the tactics of delay. His followers were not so patient, and in the 1880s his authority began to slip away. Younger men, more attracted to violent action, pushed him aside. In the spring of 1885, when Big Bear and his people were camped near the Frog Lake settlement—north of the North Saskatchewan River, in what is now Alberta—the younger men were in control. When word came that Louis Riel and the Métis had taken control of Batoche, the Plains Cree were ready to join.

At this point, the history of my own family intersected with Ca- 13 nadian history in a way that has always made 1885 a compelling date for me. The Canadian government had decided that the Indians should be taught to farm. In 1879, John Delaney, until then an Ottawa Valley lumberman, went to work as a farm instructor in the North-West. He settled at Frog Lake and built a house. In 1882 he went back to the Ottawa Valley to marry his fiancée, Theresa Fulford, my great-aunt. The journey to Frog Lake, the last 400 miles by buckboard, was their wedding trip.

14   As my great-aunt later told the story, her husband was an exemplary figure, "generous to a fault. He was liked by all the bands." But then, she took that view of the whites in general. *"The Indians have no grievances and no complaints to make,"* she reported, emphasizing her opinion with italics in *Two Months in the Camp of Big Bear*, the book she wrote with another Frog Lake survivor, Theresa Gowanlock. "Their treatment is of the best and most generous kind. The government spares no pains to attempt to make them adopt an agricultural life. . . . " Hugh Dempsey's book describes Indians starving within sight of white settlements, where food was doled out to them in minuscule amounts; Dempsey believes the government consciously used starvation to subdue the Indians. Aunt Theresa didn't see that, or didn't care to recall it.

15   Before they left the Ottawa Valley, John Delaney must have told her a great deal about Frog Lake. But there was one part of his life in the West that he almost certainly didn't mention to her. Writing some sixty-five years after the events of 1885, an Anglican clergyman, the Reverend Edward Ahenakew, set down a cryptic remark about Frog Lake: "The reason for the bad feeling entertained by some of these individual Indians I need not mention at this late date, though I can do so. It is enough to say that there was some slight reason for trouble at this particular place." Ahenakew was probably referring, in his discreet way, to John Delaney's sexual relations with Indian women.

16   In 1885, two months after the massacre, an article in the Stratford *Beacon* described Delaney as one of those government employees "who prostituted their authority to the debauchery of young Indian women." In the archives Hugh Dempsey has found a letter written in 1881 from one government official to another. According to the letter, Delaney was accused of stealing the wife of an Indian named Sand Fly. When Sand Fly protested, Delaney charged him with assault. When this didn't lead to a jail sentence, Delaney brought a theft charge and had him sent to jail for two-and-a-half years. The letter says that there was a general feeling that "Mr. Delaney had the man arrested in order to accomplish his designs." He lived with the prisoner's wife all that winter. For these and other reasons, such as his sternness, Delaney was disliked in the Frog Lake settlement.

On the night of April 1, the Indians at Frog Lake—made bitter   17
by hunger, possibly enraged by Delaney's behaviour, certainly em-
boldened by the news of Riel's uprising—put on war paint and
gathered for a dance. Wandering Spirit, the most militant° of them
all and now in effect Big Bear's successor, announced, "Tomorrow
I am going to eat two-legged meat"—an expression that meant
killing someone. During the night and the early morning, Wandering Spirit and others broke into the stores and seized the whites'
guns. They apparently drank two cases of Perry Davis's Pain Killer,
which was ninety per cent alcohol. In the morning they took the
twelve whites in the community prisoner and went with them to
the Roman Catholic Church for Holy Thursday services. In church,
the Indians shouted and otherwise made evident their new-found
confidence. Outside, after the service, they began shooting. Big
Bear, some distance away, cried, "Stop! Stop! Don't do it!" But
they went on shooting, and in a few minutes killed nine men,
including two Oblate priests. John Delaney fell dead at his wife's
side. The only whites who escaped were a Hudson's Bay Company
clerk and the two women—Theresa Delaney and Theresa Gowanlock, the wife of a man who was constructing a mill nearby. She
too was widowed.

The Indians took the women hostage but apparently treated   18
them with considerable kindness. Finally the women escaped, at
about the time the Indians' brief armed struggle against the whites
was ending in defeat. They then went east and wrote their book,
published the same year by the Parkdale Times in Toronto (and
republished in 1976 in Stuart Hughes's compilation, *The Frog Lake
"Massacre"*). My great-aunt settled again in the Ottawa Valley,
never remarried, taught school for a while, and lived well into the
twentieth century.

Six Indians, including Wandering Spirit, were hanged for the   19
killings. The jury that heard Big Bear's trial recommended mercy
and he was sentenced to three years in Stony Mountain Peniten-
tiary; after two years he was released on grounds of sickness. Back
among his people, he was a failure and an outcast. His visions,
his preaching, his leadership, his moderation had done no-one
good. Another chief visited him one day and Big Bear, after a long
silence, said, "You must wonder why I don't speak. My heart is
broken. All I can think of are my past deeds and the misfortunes
which have happened to me. . . . " He died in January, 1888. Hugh
Dempsey, in the last sentence of his biography, provides an epitaph
for both Big Bear and the policies of the Canadian government:
"Big Bear had tried to sow the seeds of communication and cooperation between Indians and whites, but the seeds had fallen
on barren ground."

20   A century ago, Canada was imposing a grid of European rationalism on the West, carefully dividing up the land and preparing it for farming. Hunting and trapping were no longer to be important, were even to be discouraged—Aunt Theresa probably reflected official opinion when she declared her hatred of the Hudson's Bay Company, whose continued presence encouraged Indians to hunt when (in her view) they should have been farming. The force that struck down both Louis Riel and Big Bear was western civilization, with its urgent need to expand and develop. The landscape, created over millions of years by natural forces, was now to yield in a couple of generations to surveyors and government agents. Neither Riel's violence nor Big Bear's hopeful arguments could face down a power as tragic as it was splendid.

21   In the early days of Indian-white contact, Indian skills were essential to explorers and fur traders. But in 1885 no-one needed them any more, and no-one needed the Métis either. This story of acceptance followed by rejection was enacted again and again throughout North America, as Ramsay Cook remarked a few years ago in *The Frontier in History*: "As the fur trade was succeeded by agricultural settlement and industry, the American Indian was gradually pressed to the margins of North American society. His way of life was an obstacle to agricultural production organized through private land ownership. His technology and skills, so important in the fur trade, were no longer in demand in the more diversified society. He rarely fitted into the new capitalist economy, even at the lowest level."

22   Mad Louis Riel, the most hated man in the West a century ago, is now a kind of hero: westerners who resent the power of the East join their grievances with his and see him as a pioneer spokesman for western alienation (some even want a posthumous° pardon bestowed on him by the government). But there's something perverse° in our tendency to idolize him (as we also increasingly idolize Big Bear). It requires us to stand history on its head. Riel and Big Bear remain the natural enemies of those who now populate the West and indeed of all prosperous modern Canadians; it was only after the defeat of the Métis and the Indians that easterners could move west and begin the settlements that laid the foundations of Saskatchewan and Alberta.

23   But of course Riel has lived on in another way, his story woven into the larger story of Canadian politics. Sir John A. Macdonald's decision to let him hang (when there were good grounds to commute° his sentence) profoundly alienated Quebec and helped Sir Wilfrid Laurier's Liberals seize that province in a grip so powerful it would not be broken until 1958. Riel had his posthumous revenge, if not on all Canadians then at least on the Conservatives.

24   The criminal trials of the Indians and the Métis in the autumn

of 1885 seem, in retrospect, outrageously illogical—the rebels were convicted of treason against an empire that had conscripted° them as citizens without consulting them. But the North-West Rebellion also produced a trial that was merely bizarre. Shortly after the rebellion ended, an article in the Toronto *News* said that Montreal's Sixty-fifth Battalion had conducted itself during the hostilities in a way that was mutinous, reckless, disorderly, and drunken. Officers of the battalion sued, and eventually the editor of the *News*—a notorious enemy of French Canadians and the French language—was summoned to Montreal to stand trial for criminal libel. Convicted and fined $200, he emerged from the courtroom, barely escaped with his life from a howling mob of outraged Montrealers, and went home to be greeted by a torchlight parade of 4,000 cheering supporters in Toronto. Two years later, fed up with the stresses of daily newspaper work, the editor, Edmund E. Sheppard, founded a new periodical, *Saturday Night*.

ROBERT FULFORD

Robert Fulford, writer and former editor of *Saturday Night* magazine, was born in 1932 in Ottawa into a family of journalists. He has written on books, culture, and public affairs for *Maclean's*, *The Canadian Forum*, and the *Toronto Star*, and has also been a television broadcaster.

Words and Meanings

Paragraph

charismatic:	possessing a quality that inspires others	1
high treason:	betrayal of one's country in wartime	
construed:	interpreted	2
megalomania:	inflated sense of self-importance; a form of insanity	4
impetuous:	hot-headed, thoughtless	6
incomprehension:	lack of understanding	11
pre-agrarians:	early peoples who made their living from hunting, not farming	
militant:	warlike	17
posthumous:	occurring after death	22
perverse:	unreasonable	
commute:	set aside a severe sentence in favour of a lesser sentence	23
conscripted:	drafted, compelled into service	24

Strategy and Structure

1. How does PARALLEL STRUCTURE help make Fulford's opening paragraph so effective?
2. What is the function of paragraph 2?
3. How does paragraph 6 provide TRANSITION?
4. What METAPHOR does Fulford use in paragraph 7, the introduction to the history of the Plains Cree?
5. Has Fulford organized his essay according to the *chunk* or the *slice* pattern? Why do you think he chose this organizational pattern for this essay?

Content and Purpose

1. How does Fulford establish that Riel and Big Bear were both products as well as victims of the Europeanization of North America?
2. How does Fulford convey to the reader Big Bear's stature, nobility and tragic doom (paragraphs 9 and 10)?
3. What is the purpose of Fulford's account of his ancestor's behaviour among the Plains Cree (paragraphs 13 to 18)?
4. To what extent were the Plains Cree and Louis Riel the agents of their own destruction?
5. In paragraph 20, the beginning of the last section of this essay, Fulford states that "Neither Riel's violence nor Big Bear's hopeful arguments could face down a power as tragic as it was splendid." If Fulford is neither mourning nor celebrating the fate of Riel and Big Bear, what is the purpose of his essay?

Suggestions for Writing

1. In 1837, nearly 50 years before Riel and Big Bear led their rebellions, there was a rebellion in Upper Canada (now Ontario) and in Lower Canada (now Quebec) against the government of each province. Canada was not yet a confederation. William Lyon Mackenzie led the revolt in Upper Canada and Louis-Joseph Papineau led the rebellion in Lower Canada. Both revolutionaries were defeated, but, unlike Riel and Big Bear, both returned to the political scene after a period of exile.

    Check a reference book or *The Canadian Encyclopedia* in your library and write an essay, using the *chunk* method of organization, in which you compare and contrast the careers of Mackenzie and Papineau.
2. Compare two public figures of your choice. Select two individuals whose careers intersected with interesting results, illuminated each other's accomplishments, or represented opposing forces

of their particular time (such as Pierre Trudeau and Brian Mulroney, Ronald Reagan and Jesse Jackson, Betty Friedan and Hugh Hefner).

Love and Lust

HENRY FAIRLIE

Lust is not interested in its partners, but only in the gratification of its own craving: not even in the satisfaction of our whole natures, but in the appeasement merely of an appetite which we are unable to subdue. It is therefore a form of self-subjection; in fact of self-emptying. The sign it wears is: "This property is vacant." Anyone may take possession of it for a while. Lustful people may think that they can choose a partner at will for sexual gratification. But they do not really choose; they accept what is available. Lust accepts any partner for a momentary service; anyone may squat in its groin.   1

Love has meaning only insofar as it includes the idea of its continuance. Even what we rather glibly° call a love affair, if it comes to an end, may continue as a memory that is pleasing in our lives, and we can still renew the sense of privilege and reward of having been allowed to know someone with such intimacy and sharing. But Lust dies at the next dawn and, when it returns in the evening, to search where it may, it is with its own past erased. Love wants to enjoy in other ways the human being whom it has enjoyed in bed. But in 'the morning Lust is always furtive. It dresses as mechanically as it undressed, and heads straight for the door, to return to its own solitude. Like all the sins, it makes us solitary. It is a self-abdication° at the very heart of one's own being, of our need and ability to give and receive.   2

Love is involvement as well as continuance; but Lust will not get involved. This is one of the forms in which we may see it today. If people now engage in indiscriminate° and short-lived relationships more than in the past, it is not really for some exquisite sexual pleasure that is thus gained, but because they refuse to become involved and to meet the demands that love makes. They are asking for little more than servicing, such as they might get at a gas station. The fact that it may go to bed with a lot of people is less its offense   3

"Love and Lust" from "Lust or Luxuria" by Henry Fairlie. Reprinted by permission of The New Republic, Inc., © 1977.

than the fact that it goes to bed with people for whom it does not care. The characteristic of the "singles" today is not the sexual freedom they supposedly enjoy, but the fact that this freedom is a deception. They are free with only a fraction of their natures. The full array of human emotions is hardly involved. The "singles bar" does not have an obnoxious° odor because its clients, before the night is over, may hop into bed with someone whom they have just met, but because they do not even consider that, beyond the morning, either of them may care for the other. As they have made deserts of themselves, so they make deserts of their beds. This is the sin of Lust: just as it dries up human beings, so it dries up human relationships. The word that comes to mind, when one thinks of it, is that it is parched. Everyone in a "singles bar" seems to have lost moisture, and this is peculiarly the accomplishment of Lust, to make the flesh seem parched, to deprive it of all real dewiness, shrivelling it to no more than a husk.

HENRY FAIRLIE

Henry Fairlie, political correspondent and writer, was born in England in 1924 and has lived in the United States since 1966. He has contributed to *Punch*, the *New Statesman*, and *The New Yorker*. His books include *The Spoiled Child of the Western World* and *The Seven Deadly Sins Today*.

Paragraph   **Words and Meanings**

2   glibly: smoothly, thoughtlessly
     self-abdication: renunciation, rejection

3   indiscriminate: promiscuous
     obnoxious: unpleasant, foul

Structure and Strategy

1. Has Fairlie structured his essay in *chunks* or in *slices*? (See the introduction to this unit.)
2. What words does Fairlie choose to show how repugnant lust is? Find some examples of the effective use of DICTION in paragraph 1.
3. How does Fairlie's use of PERSONIFICATION contribute to the effect of his essay?
4. How does Fairlie effectively conclude his essay? (See ANALOGY.)

Content and Purpose

1. What are the major differences between love and lust that Fairlie identifies?
2. Why does Fairlie regard lust as selfish?

3. Later in the essay from which "Love and Lust" has been ex-
    cerpted, Fairlie writes:

    The managers of our society much prefer that we are infatuated with
    our sexuality than that we look long and steadily at what they contrive
    from day to day. . . . They have discovered that, now that religion has
    been displaced, sex can be made the opiate of the masses. When the
    entire society is at last tranquilly preoccupied in the morbid practices of
    onanism, they will know that there is nothing more for them to do but
    rule forever over the dead.

    What does he mean by "opiate of the masses"? Where does
    the phrase come from? Do you agree with Fairlie that the com-
    mercialization of sex manipulates us? What examples can you
    cite to support your point of view?
4. What would Fairlie think of C.S. Lewis's thesis in "We Have No
    'Right to Happiness' " in Unit Seven?

Suggestion for Writing

Write a paper of four or five paragraphs in which you explain the
similarities and differences between any two abstract qualities—such
as optimism and pessimism; generosity and selfishness; conservatism and liberalism; bravery and cowardice; honesty and dishonesty;
professionalism and amateurism; or innocence and guilt.

Erotica and Pornography:

A Clear and Present Difference

GLORIA STEINEM

Human beings are the only animals that   1
experience the same sex drive at times when we can—and cannot—
conceive.

Just as we developed uniquely human capacities for language,   2
planning, memory, and invention along our evolutionary path, we

"Erotica and Pornography" from *Outrageous Acts and Everyday Rebellions* by Gloria
Steinem. Copyright 1983 by Gloria Steinem. Reprinted by permission of Henry Holt
and Company, Inc.

also developed sexuality as a form of expression; a way of communicating that is separable from our need for sex as a way of perpetuating ourselves. For humans alone, sexuality can be and often is primarily a way of bonding, of giving and receiving pleasure, bridging differentness, discovering sameness, and communicating emotion.

3   We developed this and other human gifts through our ability to change our environment, adapt physically, and in the long run, to affect our own evolution. But as an emotional result of this spiraling path away from other animals, we seem to alternate between periods of exploring our unique abilities to forge new boundaries, and feelings of loneliness in the unknown that we ourselves have created; a fear that sometimes sends us back to the comfort of the animal world by encouraging us to exaggerate our sameness.

4   The separation of "play" from "work," for instance, is a problem only in the human world. So is the difference between art and nature, or an intellectual accomplishment and a physical one. As a result, we celebrate play, art, and invention as leaps into the unknown; but any imbalance can send us back to nostalgia° for our primate° past and the conviction that the basics of work, nature, and physical labor are somehow more worthwhile or even moral.

5   In the same way, we have explored our sexuality as separable from conception: a pleasurable, empathetic° bridge to strangers of the same species. We have even invented contraception—a skill that has probably existed in some form since our ancestors figured out the process of birth—in order to extend this uniquely human difference. Yet we also have times of atavistic° suspicion that sex is not complete—or even legal or intended-by-god—if it cannot end in conception.

6   No wonder the concepts of "erotica" and "pornography" can be so crucially different, and yet so confused. Both assume that sexuality can be separated from conception, and therefore can be used to carry a personal message. That's a major reason why, even in our current culture, both may be called equally "shocking" or legally "obscene," a word whose Latin derivative means "dirty, containing filth." This gross condemnation of all sexuality that isn't harnessed to childbirth and marriage has been increased by the current backlash against women's progress. Out of fear that the whole patriarchal structure° might be upset if women really had the autonomous° power to decide our reproductive futures (that is, if we controlled the most basic means of production), right-wing groups are not only denouncing prochoice abortion literature as "pornographic," but are trying to stop the sending of all contraceptive information through the mails by invoking obscenity laws. In fact, Phyllis Schlafly° recently denounced the entire Women's Movement as "obscene."

Not surprisingly, this religious, visceral° backlash has a secu-   7
lar°, intellectual counterpart that relies heavily on applying the
"natural" behavior of the animal world to humans. That is ques-
tionable in itself, but these Lionel Tiger°-ish studies make their
political purpose even more clear in the particular animals they
select and the habits they choose to emphasize. The message is
that females should accept their "destiny" of being sexually dependent and devote themselves to bearing and rearing their young.

Defending against such reaction in turn leads to another temp-   8
tation: to merely reverse the terms, and declare that *all* nonpro-
creative° sex is good. In fact, however, this human activity can be
as constructive or destructive, moral or immoral, as any other. Sex
as communication can send messages as different as life and death;
even the origins of "erotica" and "pornography" reflect that fact.
After all, "erotica" is rooted in *eros* or passionate love, and thus in
the idea of positive choice, free will, the yearning for a particular
person. (Interestingly, the definition of erotica leaves open the
question of gender.) "Pornography" begins with a root meaning
"prostitution" or "female captives," thus letting us know that the
subject is not mutual love, or love at all, but domination and violence against women. (Though, of course, homosexual pornography may imitate this violence by putting a man in the "feminine"
role of victim.) It ends with a root meaning "writing about" or
"description of" which puts still more distance between subject
and object, and replaces a spontaneous yearning for closeness with
objectification and a voyeur°.

The difference is clear in the words. It becomes even more so   9
by example.

Look at any photo or film of people making love; really making   10
love. The images may be diverse, but there is usually a sensuality
and touch and warmth, an acceptance of bodies and nerve endings.
There is always a spontaneous sense of people who are there because they *want* to be, out of shared pleasure.

Now look at any depiction of sex in which there is clear force,   11
or an unequal power that spells coercion°. It may be very blatant°,
with weapons of torture or bondage, wounds and bruises, some
clear humiliation, or an adult's sexual power being used over a
child. It may be much more subtle: a physical attitude of conqueror
and victim, the use of race or class difference to imply the same
thing, perhaps a very unequal nudity, with one person exposed
and vulnerable while the other is clothed. In either case, there is
no sense of equal choice or equal power.

The first is erotic: a mutually pleasurable, sexual expression   12
between people who have enough power to be there by positive
choice. It may or may not strike a sense-memory in the viewer, or
be creative enough to make the unknown seem real; but it doesn't

require us to identify with a conqueror or a victim. It is truly sensuous, and may give us a contagion of pleasure.

13   The second is pornographic: its message is violence, dominance, and conquest. It is sex being used to reinforce some
inequality, or to create one, or to tell us the lie that pain and
humiliation (ours or someone else's) are really the same as pleasure.
If we are to feel anything, we must identify with conqueror or
victim. That means we can only experience pleasure through the
adoption of some degree of sadism° or masochism°. It also means
that we may feel diminished by the role of conqueror, or enraged,
humiliated, and vengeful by sharing identity with the victim.

14   Perhaps one could simply say that erotica is about sexuality,
but pornography is about power and sex-as-weapon—in the same
way we have come to understand that rape is about violence, and
not really about sexuality at all.

15   Yes, it's true that there are women who have been forced by
violent families and dominating men to confuse love with pain, so
much so that they have become masochists. (A fact that in no way
excuses those who administer such pain.) But the truth is that, for
most women—and for men with enough humanity to imagine
themselves into the predicament of women—true pornography
could serve as aversion therapy for sex.

16   Of course, there will always be personal differences about what
is and is not erotic, and there may be cultural differences for a long
time to come. Many women feel that sex makes them vulnerable
and therefore may continue to need more sense of personal connection and safety before allowing any erotic feelings. We now find
competence and expertise erotic in men, but that may pass as we
develop those qualities in ourselves. Men, on the other hand, may
continue to feel less vulnerable, and therefore more open to such
potential danger as sex with strangers. As some men replace the
need for submission from childlike women with the pleasure of
cooperation from equals, they may find a partner's competence to
be erotic, too.

17   Such group changes plus individual differences will continue
to be reflected in sexual love between people of the same gender,
as well as between women and men. The point is not to dictate
sameness, but to discover ourselves and each other through sexuality that is an exploring, pleasurable, empathetic part of our lives;
a human sexuality that is unchained both from unwanted pregnancies and from violence.

18   But that is a hope, not a reality. At the moment, fear of change
is increasing both the indiscriminate repression of all nonprocreative sex in the religious and "conservative" male world, and the
pornographic vengeance against women's sexuality in the secular
world of "liberal" or "radical" men. It's almost futuristic to debate

what is and is not truly erotic, when many women are again being forced into compulsory motherhood, and the number of pornographic murders, tortures, and woman-hating images are on the increase in both popular culture and real life.

It's a familiar division: wife or whore, "good" woman who is   19 constantly vulnerable to pregnancy or "bad" woman who is unprotected from violence. *Both* roles would be upset if we were to control our own sexuality. And that's exactly what we must do.

In spite of all our atavistic suspicions and training for the "nat-   20 ural" role of motherhood, we took up the complicated battle for reproductive freedom. Our bodies had borne the health burden of endless births and poor abortions, and we had a greater motive for separating sexuality and conception.

Now we have to take up the equally complex burden of ex-   21 plaining that all nonprocreative sex is *not* alike. We have a motive: our right to a uniquely human sexuality, and sometimes even to survival. As it is, our bodies have too rarely been enough our own to develop erotica in our own lives, much less in art and literature. And our bodies have too often been the objects of pornography and the woman-hating, violent practice that it preaches. Consider also our spirits that break a little each time we see ourselves in chains or full labial display for the conquering male viewer, bruised or on our knees, screaming a real or pretended pain to delight the sadist, pretending to enjoy what we don't enjoy, to be blind to the images of our sisters that really haunt us—humiliated often enough ourselves by the truly obscene idea that sex and the domination of women must be combined.

Sexuality *is* human, free, separate—and so are we.   22

But until we untangle the lethal° confusion of sex with violence,   23 there will be more pornography and less erotica. There will be little murders in our beds—and very little love.

```
┌─────────────────────────┐
│                         │
└─────────────────────────┘
```

GLORIA STEINEM

Gloria Steinem, the American journalist and feminist, was born in 1934 in Toledo, Ohio. She was co-founder in New York of the feminist magazine *Ms.* and is the author of numerous essays, including her now-famous piece on becoming a Playboy bunny.

Words and Meanings   Paragraph

nostalgia:	yearning for earlier times	4
primate:	highest order of animals, including monkeys and man	

5	empathetic:	having ability to share deeply the thoughts, feelings, and attitudes of others
	atavistic:	reversion to earlier, more primitive behaviour
6	patriarchal structure:	social system governed by males
	autonomous:	self-governing, independent
	Phyllis Schlafly:	conservative opponent of Equal Rights Amendment in the United States
7	visceral:	bodily
	secular	nonreligious
	Lionel Tiger	Montreal-born anthropologist who writes about the animality of man
8	nonprocreative:	not leading to conception and childbirth
	voyeur:	someone who gets sexual gratification by watching others
11	coercion:	force
	blatant:	obvious, offensive; unsubtle
13	sadism:	deriving pleasure through inflicting pain on others
	masochism:	deriving pleasure through pain inflicted on oneself
23	lethal:	causing death

Structure and Strategy

1. What is the function of paragraphs 1 to 5? What contrast is established in these paragraphs that serves as a basis for the whole essay?

2. Why are paragraphs 1, 9, and 22 so short? What function do they serve?

3. What is the function of paragraph 8? How does it contribute to the reader's understanding of the contrast between erotica and pornography?

4. How does Steinem structure her contrast in paragraphs 10 to 13?

5. In paragraph 12, the word "contagion" is a lapse of DICTION. Can you substitute a word that would be more consistent with the tone of the paragraph?

6. Steinem's shifts in point of view are worth studying. Why, for example, does she change from third person ("they") to first person ("we") in the middle of paragraph 16? Who are the "we" referred to in paragraphs 2 to 5? Who are the "we" in paragraphs 16 to 21? Is the change in meaning purposeful and effective, or does it lead to confusion?

Content and Purpose

1. What is Steinem's overall purpose? Summarize her thesis in your own words.

2. What link does Steinem identify between pornography and rape?
3. What is Steinem's attitude to homosexuality? How does she defend her view?
4. What attitude toward men does Steinem reveal in paragraph 15?
5. How does Steinem account for the current conservative backlash against free sexual expression and even abortion?
6. Why does Steinem believe women must reject their traditional roles of wife and whore? What role must they adopt instead?
7. The meaning of paragraphs 22 and 23 depends in part on who the "we" refers to: either to all men and women, or to women alone. How does the reader's understanding of the conclusion depend on the interpretation of the "we"?

Suggestions for Writing

1. Use your dictionary to check the etymologies of one of the following pairs of words, then compare them, using the *chunk* method of organization: philanthropy and philosophy; virility and virtue; character and charisma.
2. Compare two men's views on feminism. You could choose one man who is opposed to it and one man who supports a more powerful role for women in society. Alternatively, you could compare the views of two men who belong to different generations.
3. Compare Fairlie's concept of lust in "Love and Lust" with Steinem's concept of pornography. Or compare Fairlie's concept of love with Steinem's concept of erotica.

Additional Suggestions for Writing: Comparison and Contrast

Write a comparison and/or contrast paper based on one of the topics below. Make sure that your thesis statement clarifies the basis of your comparison or contrast, then develop it by providing sufficient and relevant examples and details.

1. People's lifestyles often reveal their personal philosophies. Choose two people of your acquaintance whose ways of life reveal very different attitudes.

2. Compare and/or contrast living in Canada with living in another country. (Be sure to limit this topic to a few specific characteristics before you begin to write.)

3. Compare and/or contrast two sports, teams, or players.

4. Compare and/or contrast men and women as consumers (or voters, or employees, or supervisors, etc.).

5. Compare and/or contrast the appearance, mood, or appeal of a specific place in the summer and in the winter: your home town, a secret hideaway, a neighbourhood park, a favourite hangout.

6. Compare and/or contrast two artists with whose work you are familiar: two painters, poets, film directors, musicians, or actors.

7. Contrast your present career goals with those you dreamed of having as a child. How do you account for the differences between the two sets of goals?

8. Choose an issue and contrast the way a typical Progressive Conservative and a typical New Democrat would respond to it: free trade, gay rights, equal pay for work of equal value, fully subsidized day-care.

9. Contrast the way in which you and your parents view a particular issue: premarital sex, post-secondary education, family life, careers for women.

10. "Love is a gambling table on which women recklessly throw dollars and men carefully place pennies." (Richard Needham)

Cause and Effect: Explaining "Why"

What? The Definition

Until about 500 years ago, human beings observed the sky, watched the sun come up and the sun go down, and remarked on the comfortable regularity of the sun's journey around our planet. Not until a Polish astronomer named Copernicus doubted the validity of this earth-centred view of the universe did people begin to see that the predictability of the sun had a completely different *cause*: it was we who were going around it! The *effects* of the Copernican theory were momentous. Its publication in 1543 caused much controversy and spurred the study of astronomy and mathematics. Less than a hundred years later, a scientist named Galileo almost lost his life at the hands of conservative religious authorities for supporting the Copernican theory. Ultimately, we earthlings had to cease viewing ourselves as the centre of all existence, and this shift has had profound consequences for religion and science, philosophy and art.

The Copernican theory is an example of the search for causes as well as the attempt to understand effects. Identifying reasons and consequences is one of the ways we try to make sense of the flow of events around us. Asking "Why?" is a fundamental human impulse—just ask the parent of any two-year-old. Finding out "What happened then?" is also part of our natural human curiosity. **Cause and effect**, sometimes called **causal analysis**, is a rhetorical pattern based on these instincts: the writer explains the reasons for something, such as an event or decision, or analyzes its consequences.

Sometimes a writer attempts to do both, which is necessarily a longer, more complex process. Taking one direction, either cause *or* effect, is usually sufficient in a paper.

Why? The Purpose

Causal analysis answers one of two questions:

1. "What are the causes of S?"
2. "What are the effects or consequences of S?"

To write a good causal analysis, you must be honest and objective in your investigation. You must analyze complex ideas carefully in order to sort out the *remote*—more distant, not immediately apparent—causes or effects and the *immediate*—direct, readily apparent—causes or effects. Don't be the prisoner of old prejudices in your causal reasoning. For instance, concluding that the reason for a strike is the workers' greed and laziness, without exploring the motives behind their demands or investigating possible management errors, is irresponsible reasoning: it will lead to an ineffective causal analysis that will convince no one.

Oversimplification is another pitfall in writing cause and effect. To claim, for example, that the increase in juvenile crime is caused by "all the violence on TV" or that women's wages are lower than men's because "men are plotting to keep women down" is an unsubstantiated simplification of complex issues. Such statements contribute nothing to your reader's understanding of causes and effects.

Similarly, you should recognize that an event can be triggered by a complex variety of things. Sometimes it is necessary to focus on several immediate reasons, while omitting what may be remote causes. For example, if you were asked to identify the causes of a social trend such as the increased consumption of light alcoholic beverages rather than hard liquor, you might have enough space to write only about the concern for fitness and the increasing awareness of the dangers of drunk driving, leaving aside the historic and demographic causes that could not be adequately explained in a short paper. Selecting your focus and scope, then, is very important when you are writing cause and effect.

A common error in causal analysis is assuming that one event that happened to occur before another is the cause of the second event. For example, you walked under a ladder yesterday morning, and that is why you got a speeding ticket in the afternoon. Mistaking coincidence for causation is called the *post hoc* error (from the Latin *post hoc ergo propter hoc*—"after this, therefore because of this"), and it is bad reasoning.

How? The Technique

After looking at some of the problems involved in sorting through cause and effect relationships, you can see that a manageable topic and a clear thesis are essential in any causal analysis. For instance, it would be impossible to explain the causes of all serious eating disorders in a 500-word paper. However, you could adequately explain why a particular person is anorexic. Similarly, you could, after some investigation, describe the effects of anorexia on the patient or on her family. In other words, limit your topic to one you can explore thoroughly. Avoid the unwieldy "Effects of Nuclear Radiation" and choose instead the more manageable "Effects of the Chernobyl Nuclear Reactor Meltdown." The more specific your topic, the more manageable it will be for you and, since you'll be able to support it with specific details, the more interesting it will be for your reader.

Once you have decided on your topic, spend some time shaping your thesis statement. The causes or effects you wish to explain usually become the main points in your thesis statement and outline. In a short paper, each main point can be developed in a paragraph. Your thesis statement may be patterned after one of these models:

> The causes of S are a, b, and c.

Example: The principal causes of failure in college are lack of basic skills, lack of study skills, and lack of motivation.

> There are three effects of S : a, b, and c.

Example: There are three consequences of minor league hockey violence: brutal playing styles, injured children, and angry parents.

To explain both causes and effects is a challenging task in a paper or report. If you choose to analyze both cause and effect in a single paper, be sure that your topic is narrow enough to enable you to develop your points adequately. In this kind of essay, to attempt too much is practically to guarantee confusing, if not overwhelming, your reader.

The final point to keep in mind when writing causal analysis is that your assertions must be fully supported. If you are trying to convince your reader that A causes B or that the inevitable effect of X is Y, you must supply compelling proof. This back-up material may take the form of statistical data, facts gleaned from research, "expert witness" quotations, or well-chosen examples. Don't rely on your audience's indulgence or intelligence; the logic of your identification of causes and effects must be apparent to the reader. Illustrate your causal analysis with sufficient—and interesting—supporting data and examples.

An example of a simple causal analysis follows:

Why Do They Fail?

*Introduction
(gets attention with a
startling statistic)*

Statistics show that most people who begin high school finish. Some drop out, of course, but approximately three-quarters earn a diploma. At the post-secondary level, however, fewer than two-thirds of the students complete their program of study. Why do so many college and university students drop out? Knowing the factors that prevent students from completing their post-secondary programs may prove crucial to you regardless of whether you are presently a college student or thinking of becoming one.

Thesis statement

Most educators agree that the principal causes of failure are lack of basic skills, lack of study skills, and lack of motivation.

*First point (developed
with facts and
examples)*

A firm grasp of basic skills—what are termed the three Rs: reading, writing, and arithmetic—is a must for college or university work. Not only are texts and research material more difficult to understand than they were in high school, but also the quantity of required reading is greater. The ability to express oneself clearly in standard written English is essential; garbled essays, ungrammatical reports, or poorly spelled and punctuated papers will be routinely failed by instructors, regardless of the ideas the writer may think he is expressing. Similarly, mathematical skills are essential to a student's success in many post-secondary programs. Business, science, technology, and some applied arts programs require sound computational skills. Post-secondary students who lack these basic skills often find little remedial help available and little instructor tolerance for poor work; hence, they fall behind and drop out.

Second point (note
continuing contrast
between high school and
college experience)

Occasionally students come to college equipped with the 3Rs but lacking the study skills necessary for success. Time management is critical; keeping up with course work when classes meet only once or twice a week is often a challenge for those accustomed to the high school routine. Students must know how to take notes from texts and lectures because college instructors, unlike high school teachers, rarely provide notes. Basically, good study skills in college or university mean taking responsibility for one's own learning. Going to class, reading and reviewing material, and preparing for assignments and tests are all up to the student. Few instructors will hound or cajole their students into learning as teachers may have done in high school.

Third point (developed
by division)

Lack of motivation is also a major cause of failure. Even with good basic skills, a student who doesn't really *want* to be in college, who doesn't possess the necessary drive to do the work, may fail. School must be a priority in the student's life. For instance, if a student works 30 hours a week in a demanding job that she finds more interesting and rewarding than school, it is almost inevitable that her school work will suffer. To be successful, the student must also have a firm commitment to the career for which the college program is preparation. Finally, the successful student is someone with genuine intellectual curiosity. Without the will to learn as well as to succeed, a student is unlikely to complete a post-secondary education.

Conclusion (points out ——————▶ Basic skills, study skills, and moti-
additional benefits) vation: all are essential to success in

college. Students who possess all three will not automatically achieve straight As, but they are on the right road to a degree or diploma. And—an important side benefit—those students will have mastered the traits that will make them as successful in their careers as they have been in school.

Reflections on My Brother's Murder

DAVID FINN

1   Several months ago, my brother, Herbert Finn, a prominent civil rights lawyer from Phoenix, Arizona, was shot and killed while visiting my family in New York. We had been to the opera—Herbert, his wife, my wife, my sister, my daughter, and I—and the six of us drove to the quiet residential neighborhood of Riverdale, where my daughter lives. I left the car for a few minutes to take her to her apartment. While I was gone, several young black men held up the rest of the family, taking pocketbooks from my wife and sister and grabbing my brother's wallet as he took out his money for them. Although no one is quite sure what happened, we think my brother reached out to retrieve the credit cards in his wallet because he was planning to leave the next day on a trip to Egypt and Israel. One impatient robber fired a single .22-caliber bullet, and all of them fled. A moment later I arrived on the scene to find the women screaming and my brother dead.

2   All that night I repeated four words— *I can't believe it*—so often that they must be imprinted on my brain. The murder took place just after midnight, and we finished with the police interrogation at 5:30 the next morning. My wife and I had a couple of drinks to try to calm our nerves, but the alcohol didn't work. I couldn't stop myself from shivering (although I wasn't cold) and repeating the four words endlessly. In desperation, I took a pad from the drawer next to my bed and wrote "I can't believe it" 26 times, as if writing it out would serve as a cathartic° for disbelief. But it was no help.

"Reflections on My Brother's Murder" by David Finn. Copyright 1980 by *Saturday Review* magazine. Reprinted by permission.

I truly could *not* believe it. I went on repeating the words to myself all through the next day as I sat with my wife, sister, and sister-in-law in three different police stations, going through hundreds of mug shots and answering questions posed by various teams of detectives. While I could not absorb the reality of what had happened, neither could I get the sight of it—the sight of my brother slumped in the back seat—out of my mind.

About two weeks later, four suspects were arrested. Their ages were 19, 17, 17, and 15. Newspaper accounts stated that three of them came from middle-class homes in Mt. Vernon, New York.   3

Two of the youths confessed. The story they told deepened the crease of incredulity° in my brain. It went something like this: One boy borrowed his mother's car to go to a high-school dance. He changed his mind and instead picked up three friends, drove to a pizzeria, then to a disco, and finally went for a ride in Riverdale. As they were cruising, the four boys thought of sticking up an ice-cream store, but by the time they got there it was closed. Later, they passed our car, saw the people in it, and thought it looked like an interesting target. They pulled into a driveway, and three of them said they'd check our car and be right back. The fourth boy waited, listening to his car radio. A minute later he heard a noise and the three ran back screaming, "Get out of here, get out of here." As they sped away, one of the boys kept asking another, "Why did you do it? Why did you shoot him?" "I had to," he answered and then said reassuringly, "Don't worry about it." They argued for a while. Finally, one of them distributed $44 to each of the others. "You shot [this guy] for less than $200? That's stupid," one of the boys remarked. "Don't worry," the murderer insisted.   4

As told by the two who confessed, the casualness of the whole incident—taking my brother's life to get some money for fun— makes the tragedy all the more unbearable. It was apparently just a matter of going after easy pickings and striking down a victim who might have been trying to hold out. It was like swatting a fly. That was all there was to it.   5

In the months that followed, the shock waves of what we initially took to be a private nightmare radiated farther than any of us could have imagined. People from all over the world called and wrote to give some expression to the pain they felt. I could almost hear the whispers echoing in the atmosphere as anybody who had the slightest connection to us passed the story on. What dumbfounded° acquaintances was the senselessness, the chilling irony, of Herbert's death. Dying from an illness is no better than dying from a robber's bullet, but we learn to accept death from disease as fate, while murder threatens to undermine the assumption that man can control societal forces.   6

7   A friend who served for many years as Chief of Police in the
Bronx, Anthony Bouza, has likened the unchecked spread of crime
to a cancer that will destroy our society unless we attack its cause—
poverty and unemployment. People who can't speak the language,
can't get jobs, and can't find decent places to live are excluded
from society. They come to feel that robbing and killing are the
only ways they can survive. Desperation, Chief Bouza believes,
overwhelms morality and the law. What is worse, he says, is the
more recent development. As the poor increasingly resort to their
desperate solutions, more fortunate youths adopt the same measures to accomplish their own ends. Robbing and killing fill the
emptiness caused, not by hunger, but by boredom and a lack of
purpose in their lives. The cancer that begins in the burned-out
buildings of our cities metastasizes° to the rest of society.

8   A number of people, reacting to my brother's death, are seeking
cures for the disease Bouza describes. Some say they will work for
stricter gun-control laws. Others want tougher sentences for convicted criminals. Still others want to reinstate the death penalty.
And some want to work for a stronger and better equipped police
force. But it seems to me that these efforts, many of which are
clearly necessary, are unlikely to rid us of the cancer; they treat
the symptoms, not the disease. The cancer itself can be arrested,
I believe, only if we minister to° its root cause. We must stop the
decay in our cities and the deterioration of our values. We must
have faith in our own power to cure the disease and the determination to exercise that power.

9   The shock of my brother's death has in itself given rise to some
innovative° ideas that illustrate the kind of determination called
for. While talking about Herbert's death, for example, a friend who
heads an influential foundation raised the question of relating education to work opportunities. He proposed an unusual plan for a
pilot project: If a small group of underprivileged students would
promise to finish their college education, he would arrange jobs
for them in advance, guaranteeing them positions on graduation.
The companies for which they would work would pay only half
their salaries, and his foundation would pay the rest. If the project
succeeds, he would encourage other foundations to do the same
thing for thousands of young people. His idea could be the small
beginning of a major accomplishment.

10   My brother's death was cruel, inhuman, personally devastat-
ing; but I do not want to believe it was futile°. Taking initiatives°
to cope with the disease rather than despairing at its ravages° is
the only sane response to our tragedy. If we who have been subjected to such horrors can show the world that we have not lost
our faith, if out of our pain we can help to awaken the forces within

our society that are capable of curing the disease, his death and the deaths of other martyrs° of the streets will not have been in vain.

DAVID FINN

David Finn, a painter, photographer, and writer, was born in 1921 in the United States. His work has been exhibited in several galleries and museums in New York and his writings have appeared in *Saturday Review* and other publications.

Words and Meanings

Paragraph

cathartic:	purging, cleansing	2
incredulity:	unwillingness or inability to believe	4
dumbfounded:	astonished; left speechless	6
metastasize:	spread of cancer cells from one part of the body to another	7
minister to:	tend to; treat	8
innovative:	new, experimental	9
futile:	useless	10
initiatives:	fresh starts	
ravages:	destructive effects	
martyrs:	people who are killed for their beliefs	

Structure and Strategy

1. In what ORDER are the ideas of paragraphs 2 to 3 arranged? What is the effect on the reader?
2. How does Finn create the effect of immediacy in paragraph 4?
3. What ANALOGY is introduced in paragraph 7?
4. Why did Finn write this essay in the first person, using the pronouns "I" and "we"? How would the effect have been different if he had written this piece in the third person?

Content and Purpose

1. According to Finn, what are the causes of crime among the poor? Among the more affluent?
2. Do you agree with Finn that the death of a loved one from disease is easier to bear than death caused by murder?
3. Why does Finn reject the solutions to crime which other well-meaning people have proposed? (paragraph 8)

4. Finn wrote this essay several months after his brother's death, describing it as "inhuman," but he never mentions the very human desire for vengeance. Why do you think he chose not to include the idea in his essay, even if he himself might have wanted to seek revenge?

Suggestions for Writing

1. Have you or has a member of your family been affected by a serious crime? Identify and explain the effects the crime had on the victim and/or his or her family.
2. Write a short paper explaining why so many teenagers commit "petty crimes" such as shoplifting or joy-riding.

Canadians: What Do They Want?

MARGARET ATWOOD

1   Last month, during a poetry reading, I tried out a short prose poem called "How to Like Men." It began by suggesting that one start with the feet. Unfortunately, the question of jackboots° soon arose, and things went on from there. After the reading I had a conversation with a young man who thought I had been unfair to men. He wanted men to be liked totally, not just from the heels to the knees, and not just as individuals but as a group; and he thought it negative and inegalitarian° of me to have alluded° to war and rape. I pointed out that as far as any of us knew these were two activities not widely engaged in by women, but he was still upset. "We're both in this together," he protested. I admitted that this was so; but could he, maybe, see that our relative positions might be a little different.

2   This is the conversation one has with Americans, even, uh, *good* Americans, when the dinner-table conversation veers round to Canadian-American relations. "We're in this together," they like to say, especially when it comes to continental energy reserves. How do you *explain* to them, as delicately as possible, why they are not categorically° beloved? It gets like the old Lifebuoy ads:

"Canadians: What Do They Want?" by Margaret Atwood. Copyright January 1982. Permission to reprint by *Mother Jones* magazine.

even their best friends won't tell them. And Canadians are supposed to be their best friends, right? Members of the family?

Well, sort of. Across the river from Michigan, so near and yet so far, there I was at the age of eight, reading *their* Donald Duck comic books (originated however by one of *ours*; yes, Walt Disney's parents were Canadian) and coming at the end to Popsicle Pete, who promised me the earth if only I would save wrappers, but took it all away from me again with a single asterisk: Offer Good Only in the United States. Some cynical members of the world community may be forgiven for thinking that the same asterisk is there, in invisible ink, on the Constitution° and the Bill of Rights°.

But quibbles° like that aside, and good will assumed, how does one go about liking Americans? Where does one begin? Or, to put it another way, why did the Canadian women lock themselves in the john during a '70s "international" feminist conference being held in Toronto? Because the American sisters were being "imperialist,"° that's why.

But then, it's always a little naïve° of Canadians to expect that Americans, of whatever political stamp, should stop being imperious. How can they? The fact is that the United States is an empire and Canada is to it as Gaul° was to Rome.

It's hard to explain to Americans what it feels like to be a Canadian. Pessimists among us would say that one has to translate the experience into their own terms and that this is necessary because Americans are incapable of thinking in any other terms— and this in itself is part of the problem. (Witness all those draft dodgers who went into culture shock when they discovered to their horror that Toronto was not Syracuse.)

Here is a translation: [p]icture a Mexico with a population ten times larger than that of the United States. That would put it at about two billion. Now suppose that the official American language is Spanish, that 75 percent of the books Americans buy and 90 percent of the movies they see are Mexican, and that the profits flow across the border to Mexico. If an American does scrape it together to make a movie, the Mexicans won't let him show it in the States, because they own the distribution outlets. If anyone tries to change this ratio, not only the Mexicans but many fellow Americans cry "National chauvinism°," or, even more effectively, "National socialism." After all, the American public prefers the Mexican product. It's what they're used to.

Retranslate and you have the current American-Canadian picture. It's changed a little recently, not only on the cultural front. For instance, Canada, some think a trifle late, is attempting to regain control of its own petroleum industry. Americans are predictably angry. They think of Canadian oil as *theirs*.

9   "What's mine is yours," they have said for years, meaning exports; "What's yours is mine" means ownership and profits. Canadians are supposed to do retail buying, not controlling, or what's an empire for? One could always refer Americans to history, particularly that of their own revolution. They objected to the colonial situation when they themselves were a colony; but then, revolution is considered one of a very few home-grown American products that definitely are not for export.

10   Objectively, one cannot become too self-righteous about this state of affairs. Canadians owned lots of things, including their souls, before World War II. After that they sold, some say because they had put too much into financing the war, which created a capital vacuum° (a position they would not have been forced into if the Americans hadn't kept out of the fighting for so long, say the sore losers). But for whatever reason, capital flowed across the border in the '50s, and Canadians, traditionally sock-under-the-mattress hoarders, were reluctant to invest in their own country. Americans did it for them and ended up with a large part of it, which they retain to this day. In every sellout there's a seller as well as a buyer, and the Canadians did a thorough job of trading their birthright for a mess°.

11   That's on the capitalist end, but when you turn to the trade union side of things you find much the same story, except that the sellout happened in the '30s under the banner of the United Front. Now Canadian workers are finding that in any empire the colonial branch plants are the first to close, and what could be a truly progressive labor movement has been weakened by compromised bargains made in international union headquarters south of the border.

12   Canadians are sometimes snippy to Americans at cocktail parties. They don't like to feel owned and they don't like having been sold. But what really bothers them—and it's at this point that the United States and Rome part company—is the wide-eyed innocence with which their snippiness is greeted.

13   Innocence becomes ignorance when seen in the light of international affairs, and though ignorance is one of the spoils of conquest—the Gauls always knew more about the Romans than the Romans knew about them—the world can no longer afford America's ignorance. Its ignorance of Canada, though it makes Canadians bristle, is a minor and relatively harmless example. More dangerous is the fact that individual Americans seem not to know that the United States is an imperial power and is behaving like one. They don't want to admit that empires dominate, invade and subjugate—and live on the proceeds—or, if they do admit it, they believe in their divine right to do so. The export of divine right is

much more harmful than the export of Coca-Cola, though they may turn out to be much the same thing in the end.

Other empires have behaved similarly (the British somewhat   14
better, Genghis Khan decidedly worse); but they have not expected to be *liked* for it. It's the final Americanism, this passion for being liked. Alas, many Americans are indeed likable; they are often more generous, more welcoming, more enthusiastic, less picky and sardonic° than Canadians, and it's not enough to say it's only because they can afford it. Some of that revolutionary spirit still remains: the optimism, the 18th-century belief in the fixability of almost anything, the conviction of the possibility of change. However, at cocktail parties and elsewhere one must be able to tell the difference between an individual and a foreign policy. Canadians can no longer afford to think of Americans as only a spectator sport. If Reagan blows up the world, we will unfortunately be doing more than watching it on television. "No annihilation with[out] representation" sounds good as a slogan, but if we run [it] up the flagpole, who's going to salute?

We *are* all in this together. For Canadians, the question is how   15
to survive it. For Americans there is no question, because there does not have to be. Canada is just that vague, cold place where their uncle used to go fishing, before the lakes went dead from acid rain.

How do you like Americans? Individually, it's easier. Your   16
average American is no more responsible for the state of affairs than your average man is for war and rape. Any Canadian who is so narrow-minded as to dislike Americans merely on principle is missing out on one of the good things in life. The same might be said, to women, of men. As a group, as a foreign policy, it's harder. But if you like men, you can like Americans. Cautiously. Selectively. Beginning with the feet. One at a time.

MARGARET ATWOOD

Margaret Atwood, the well-known poet and novelist, was born in Ottawa in 1939. She expressed the view in *Survival* that Canadians are content to "get along," unlike the Americans who must "get ahead." She has written numerous collections of poetry and such novels as *The Edible Woman*, *Surfacing*, and *The Handmaid's Tale*.

Words and Meanings   Paragraph

| jackboots: | large boots coming up above the knees, noto- | 1 |
| | rious for having been worn by Nazis | |

	inegalitarian:	not believing in equality
	alluded:	referred to, hinted at
2	categorically:	without question
3	the Constitution and the Bill of Rights:	documents setting forth the fundamental principles of law and government in the United States
4	quibbles:	minor concerns
	imperialist:	a country that exploits others
5	naïve:	silly, inexperienced
	Gaul:	ancient country in what is now France, conquered by the Romans in 58 B.C.
7	chauvinism:	extreme patriotism
10	capital vacuum:	shortage of investment money
	trading their birthright for a mess:	Esau, in the Old Testament, sold his inheritance "for a mess of pottage" (soup)
14	sardonic:	sneering, cynical

Structure and Strategy

1. With what introductory strategy does Atwood begin her essay?
2. Find three or four particularly effective examples of IRONY in Atwood's essay.
3. Atwood's thesis statement is found in paragraph 5. On what ANALOGY is it based? Do you think the analogy is a valid one?
4. What is the function of paragraph 7? How is it similar to paragraph 2?
5. Identify some of the ways paragraph 16 contributes to the UNITY of this essay.

Content and Purpose

1. The title of this essay, written for Americans and published in an American magazine, is an ALLUSION to Freud's famous question, "Women: what do they want?" Why do you think Atwood chose this title?
2. What causes of anti-Americanism does Atwood identify? (There are at least ten.)
3. According to Atwood, Americans are different from other conquering peoples, ancient and modern. How? Do you think she regards this difference as a strength or a weakness?
4. If you were an American, and therefore part of the audience this essay was written for, how would you react to Atwood's charges? As a Canadian, how valid do you think they are?

Suggestions for Writing

1. Write an essay showing the effects of American influence and domination in a part of the world with which you are familiar.
2. Is there anti-American feeling in the town or city you come from? Write an essay that explains the causes of this anti-Americanism.
3. Mavor Moore once joked that "Canada's national animal isn't the beaver; it's really the carp." What makes Canadians, in Atwood's words, so "picky and sardonic"? Write a short paper outlining the causes of Canadians' well-known tendency to complain about everything.

O Rotten Gotham°— Sliding Down into the Behavioral Sink

TOM WOLFE

just spent two days with Edward T. Hall,   1
an anthropologist, watching thousands of my fellow New Yorkers short-circuiting themselves into hot little twitching death balls with jolts of their own adrenalin. Dr. Hall says it is overcrowding that does it. Overcrowding gets the adrenalin going, and the adrenalin gets them queer, autistic°, sadistic°, barren, batty, sloppy, hot-in-the-pants, chancred-on-the-flankers°, leering, puling°, numb—the usual in New York, in other words, and God knows what else. Dr. Hall has the theory that overcrowding has already thrown New York into a state of behavioral sink. Behavioral sink is a term from ethology, which is the study of how animals relate to their environment. Among animals, the sink winds up with a "population collapse" or "massive die-off." O rotten Gotham. *(Batman)*

It got to be easy to look at New Yorkers as animals, especially   2
looking down from some place like a balcony at Grand Central° at the rush hour Friday afternoon. The floor was filled with the poor white humans, running around, dodging, blinking their eyes, making a sound like a pen full of starlings or rats or something.

"Listen to them skid," says Dr. Hall.   3

"O Rotten Gotham—Sliding Down into the Behavioral Sink" from *The Pump House Gang* by Tom Wolfe. Copyright © 1968. Reprinted by permission of Farrar, Straus and Giroux, Inc.

4   He was right. The poor old etiolate° animals were out there skidding on their rubber soles. You could hear it once he pointed it out. They stop short to keep from hitting somebody or because they are disoriented and they suddenly stop and look around, and they skid on their rubber-soled shoes, and a screech goes up. They pour out onto the floor down the escalators from the Pan-Am Building, from 42nd Street, from Lexington Avenue, up out of subways, down into subways, railroad trains, up into helicopters—

5   "You can also hear the helicopters all the way down here," says Dr. Hall. The sound of the helicopters using the roof of the Pan-Am Building nearly fifty stories up beats right through. "If it weren't for this ceiling"—he is referring to the very high ceiling in Grand Central—"this place would be unbearable with this kind of crowding. And yet they'll probably never 'waste' space like this again."

6   They screech! And the adrenal glands in all those poor white animals enlarge, micrometer by micrometer, to the size of cantaloupes. Dr. Hall pulls a Minox camera out of a holster he has on his belt and starts shooting away at the human scurry°. The Sink!

7   Dr. Hall has the Minox up to his eye—he is a slender man, calm, 52 years old, young-looking, an anthropologist who has worked with Navajos, Hopis, Spanish-Americans, Negroes, Trukese. He was the most important anthropologist in the government during the crucial years of the foreign aid program, the 1950's. He directed both the Point Four training program and the Human Relations Area Files. He wrote *The Silent Language* and *The Hidden Dimension*, two books that are picking up the kind of "underground" following his friend Marshall McLuhan° started picking up about five years ago. He teaches at the Illinois Institute of Technology, lives with his wife, Mildred, in a high-ceilinged town house on one of the last great residential streets in downtown Chicago, Astor Street; he has a grown son and daughter, loves good food, good wine, the relaxed, civilized life—but comes to New York with a Minox at his eye to record!—perfect—The Sink.

8   We really got down in there by walking down into the Lexington Avenue line subway stop under Grand Central. We inhaled those nice big fluffy fumes of human sweat, urine, effluvia°, and sebaceous secretions°. One old female human was already stroked out on the upper level, on a stretcher, with two policemen standing by. The other humans barely looked at her. They rushed into line. They bellied each other, haunch to paunch, down the stairs. Human heads shone through the gratings. The species North European tried to create bubbles of space around themselves, about a foot and a half in diameter—

9   "See, he's reacting against the line," says Dr. Hall.

—but the species Mediterranean presses on in. The hell with   10
bubbles of space. The species North European resents that, this
male human behind him presses forward toward the booth . . .
breathing on him, he's disgusted, he pulls out of the line entirely,
the species Mediterranean resents him for resenting it, and neither
of them realizes what the hell they are getting irritable about exactly. And in all of them the old adrenals grow another micrometer.

Dr. Hall whips out the Minox. Too perfect! The bottom of The   11
Sink.

It is the sheer overcrowding, such as occurs in the business   12
sections of Manhattan five days a week and in Harlem, Bedford-
Stuyvesant, southeast Bronx every day—sheer overcrowding is
converting New Yorkers into animals in a sink pen. Dr. Hall's
argument runs as follows: all animals, including birds, seem to
have a built-in inherited requirement to have a certain amount of
territory, space, to lead their lives in. Even if they have all the food
they need, and there are no predatory animals threatening them,
they cannot tolerate crowding beyond a certain point. No more
than two hundred wild Norway rats can survive on a quarter acre
of ground, for example, even when they are given all the food they
can eat. They just die off.

But why? To find out, ethologists have run experiments on all   13
sorts of animals, from stickleback crabs to Sika deer. In one major
experiment, an ethologist named John Calhoun put some domes-
ticated white Norway rats in a pen with four sections to it, connected by ramps. Calhoun knew from previous experiments that
the rats tend to split up into groups of ten to twelve and that the
pen, therefore, would hold forty to forty-eight rats comfortably,
assuming they formed four equal groups. He allowed them to
reproduce until there were eighty rats, balanced between male and
female, but did not let it get any more crowded. He kept them
supplied with plenty of food, water, and nesting materials. In other
words, all their more obvious needs were taken care of. A less
obvious need—space—was not. To the human eye, the pen did
not even look especially crowded. But to the rats, it was crowded
beyond endurance.

The entire colony was soon plunged into a profound behavioral   14
sink. "The sink," said Calhoun, "is the outcome of any behavioral
process that collects animals together in unusually great numbers.
The unhealthy connotations of the term are not accidental: a behavioral sink does act to aggravate all forms of pathology° that can
be found within a group."

For a start, long before the rat population reached eighty, a   15
status hierarchy° had developed in the pen. Two dominant male
rats took over the two end sections, acquired harems of eight to

ten females each, and forced the rest of the rats into the two middle pens. All the overcrowding took place in the middle pens. That was where the "sink" hit. The aristocrat rats at the end grew bigger, sleeker, healthier, and more secure the whole time.

16   In The Sink, meanwhile, nest building, courting, sex behavior, reproduction, social organization, health—all of it went to pieces. Normally, Norway rats have a mating ritual in which the male chases the female, the female ducks down into a burrow and sticks her head up to watch the male. He performs a little dance outside the burrow, then she comes out, and he mounts her, usually for a few seconds. When The Sink set in, however, no more than three males—the dominant males in the middle sections—kept up the old customs. The rest tried everything from satyrism° to homosexuality or else gave up on sex altogether. Some of the subordinate males spent all their time chasing females. Three or four might chase one female at the same time, and instead of stopping at the burrow entrance for the ritual, they would charge right in. Once mounted, they would hold on for minutes instead of the usual seconds.

17   Homosexuality rose sharply. So did bisexuality. Some males would mount anything—males, females, babies, senescent° rats, anything. Still other males dropped sexual activity altogether, wouldn't fight and, in fact, would hardly move except when the other rats slept. Occasionally, a female from the aristocrat rats' harems would come over the ramps and into the middle sections to sample life in The Sink. When she had had enough, she would run back up the ramp. Sink males would give chase up to the top of the ramp, which is to say, to the very edge of the aristocratic preserve. But one glance from one of the king rats would stop them cold and they would return to The Sink.

18   The slumming females from the harems had their adventures and then returned to a placid, healthy life. Females in The Sink, however, were ravaged°, physically and psychologically. Pregnant rats had trouble continuing pregnancy. The rate of miscarriages increased significantly, and females started dying from tumors and other disorders of the mammary glands, sex organs, uterus, ovaries, and Fallopian tubes. Typically, their kidneys, livers, and adrenals were also enlarged or diseased or showed other signs associated with stress.

19   Child-rearing became totally disorganized. The females lost the interest or the stamina to build nests and did not keep them up if they did build them. In the general filth and confusion, they would not put themselves out to save offspring they were momentarily separated from. Frantic, even sadistic competition among the males was going on all around them and rendering their lives chaotic. The males began unprovoked and senseless assaults upon one

another, often in the form of tail-biting. Ordinarily, rats will suppress this kind of behavior when it crops up. In The Sink, male rats gave up all policing and just looked out for themselves. The "pecking order" among males in The Sink was never stable. Normally, male rats set up a three-class structure. Under the pressure of overcrowding, however, they broke up into all sorts of unstable subclasses, cliques, packs—and constantly pushed, probed, explored, tested one another's power. Anyone was fair game, except for the aristocrats in the end pens.

Calhoun kept the population down to eighty, so that the next   20
stage, "population collapse" or "massive die-off," did not occur. But the autopsies showed that the pattern—as in the diseases among the female rats—was already there.

The classic study of die-off was John J. Christian's study of   21
Sika deer on James Island in the Chesapeake Bay, west of Cambridge, Maryland. Four or five of the deer had been released on the island, which was 280 acres and uninhabited, in 1916. By 1955 they had bred freely into a herd of 280 to 300. The population density was only about one deer per acre at this point, but Christian knew that this was already too high for the Sikas' inborn space requirements, and something would give before long. For two years the number of deer remained 280 to 300. But suddenly, in 1958, over half the deer died; 161 carcasses were recovered. In 1959 more deer died and the population steadied at about 80.

In two years, two-thirds of the herd had died. Why? It was   22
not starvation. In fact, all the deer collected were in excellent condition, with well-developed muscles, shining coats, and fat deposits between the muscles. In practically all the deer, however, the adrenal glands had enlarged by 50 percent. Christian concluded that the die-off was due to "shock following severe metabolic disturbance, probably as a result of prolonged adrenocortical hyperactivity. . . . There was no evidence of infection, starvation, or other obvious cause to explain the mass mortality." In other words, the constant stress of overpopulation, plus the normal stress of the cold of the winter, had kept the adrenalin flowing so constantly in the deer that their systems were depleted of blood sugar and they died of shock.

Well, the white humans are still skidding and darting across   23
the floor of Grand Central. Dr. Hall listens a moment longer to the skidding and the darting noises, and then says, "You know, I've been on commuter trains here after everyone has been through one of these rushes, and I'll tell you, there is enough acid flowing in the stomachs in every car to dissolve the rails underneath."

Just a little invisible acid bath for the linings to round off the   24
day. The ulcers the acids cause, of course, are the one disease people have already been taught to associate with the stress of city

life. But overcrowding, as Dr. Hall sees it, raises a lot more hell with the body than just ulcers. In everyday life in New York—just the usual, getting to work, working in massively congested areas like 42nd Street between Fifth Avenue and Lexington, especially now that the Pan-Am Building is set in there, working in cubicles such as those in the editorial offices at Time-Life, Inc., which Dr. Hall cites as typical of New York's poor handling of space, working in cubicles with low ceilings and, often, no access to a window, while construction crews all over Manhattan drive everybody up the Masonite wall with air-pressure generators with noises up to the boil-a-brain decibel level, then rushing to get home, piling into subways and trains, fighting for time and for space, the usual day in New York—the whole now-normal thing keeps shooting jolts of adrenalin into the body, breaking down the body's defenses and winding up with the work-a-daddy human animal stroked out at the breakfast table with his head apoplexed° like a cauliflower out of his $6.95 semi-spread Pima-cotton shirt, and nosed over into a plate of No-Kloresto egg substitute, signing off with the black thrombosis, cancer, kidney, liver, or stomach failure, and the adrenals ooze to a halt, the size of eggplants in July.

25   One of the people whose work Dr. Hall is interested in on this score is Rene Dubos at the Rockefeller Institute. Dubos's work indicates that specific organisms, such as the tuberculosis bacillus or a pneumonia virus, can seldom be considered "the cause" of a disease. The germ or virus, apparently, has to work in combination with other things that have already broken the body down in some way—such as the old adrenal hyperactivity. Dr. Hall would like to see some autopsy studies made to record the size of adrenal glands in New York, especially of people crowded into slums and people who go through the full rush-hour-work-rush-hour cycle every day. He is afraid that until there is some clinical, statistical data on how overcrowding actually ravages the human body, no one will be willing to do anything about it. Even in so obvious a thing as air pollution, the pattern is familiar. Until people can actually see the smoke or smell the sulphur or feel the sting in their eyes, politicians will not get excited about it, even though it is well known that many of the lethal substances polluting the air are invisible and odorless. For one thing, most politicians are like the aristocrat rats. They are insulated from The Sink by practically sultanic buffers—limousines, chauffeurs, secretaries, aides-de-camp, doormen, shuttered houses, high-floor apartments. They almost never ride subways, fight rush hours, much less live in the slums or work in the Pan-Am Building.

TOM WOLFE

Tom Wolfe, the American journalist and author, was born in 1931 in Richmond, Virginia. One of the best-known writers of New Journalism, he is the author of such books as *The Electric Kool-Aid Acid Test*, *The Right Stuff*, and *From Bauhaus to Our House*.

Words and Meanings

Paragraph

Gotham:	humorous reference to New York	
autistic:	self-absorbed	1
sadistic:	deriving pleasure from the pain of others	
chancred-on-the-flankers:	slang expression for genital infection	
puling:	crying weakly, whining	
Grand Central:	major train and subway station in New York	2
etiolate:	pale as a result of being deprived of sun	4
scurry:	run with short, quick steps, like mice	6
Marshall McLuhan:	Canadian-born philosopher of the media	7
effluvia:	exhaled odours	8
sebaceous secretions:	substances produced by skin glands	
pathology:	disease	14
status hierarchy:	order based on rank, social position	15
satyrism:	uncontrollable sexual appetite in males	16
senescent	aged	17
ravaged:	devastated, ruined	18
apoplexed:	having suffered an internal rupture as a result of a stroke	24

Structure and Strategy

1. Where and why does Wolfe use definition in paragraph 2?
2. How does Wolfe create feelings of disgust and even horror in paragraphs 8 to 10? Consider both DICTION and SYNTAX.
3. What is the function of paragraph 14? Could it be omitted without affecting the reader's understanding?
4. With what specific ANALOGY does Wolfe conclude his essay? How does the last sentence of paragraph 19 prepare us for the conclusion?
5. The DICTION, TONE, and STYLE of this essay are distinctive. Contrast the restrained, scientific language of paragraphs 21 and 22 with the vocabulary and style of paragraph 24. Find other examples of Wolfe's unique personal prose style. What is the overall effect of this style on the reader?

Content and Purpose

1. What is the thesis of this essay?
2. Wolfe constructs an elaborate ANALOGY to support his thesis. What is the analogy and how does it help to make his point clear?
3. What or who is the "species North European" and the "species Mediterranean" (paragraph 10)? What is the difference between them? Can you account for this difference?
4. Summarize anthropologist Edward Hall's explanation of behavioural sinks.
5. In the last paragraph of this essay, Wolfe suggests that while there is no single *cause* of the behavioural sinks urban dwellers live in, there is an identifiable, assignable *responsibility*. Whom does he blame for the existence of behavioural sinks, and why?

Suggestions for Writing

1. Think of a situation that leads to overcrowding: registration line-ups, rush-hour traffic, jam-packed buses or subways, or the crowds at a game, for example. Write a short paper describing the effects of this overcrowding on the people who must endure it.
2. After doing some research, write an essay explaining the causes of a particular scientific effect, such as the "greenhouse effect"; use Hall's description of the behavioural sink as your model.

My Wood

E.M. FORSTER

1   A few years ago I wrote a book which dealt in part with the difficulties of the English in India. Feeling that they would have had no difficulties in India themselves, the Americans read the book freely. The more they read it the better it made them feel, and a cheque to the author was the result. I bought a wood with the cheque. It is not a large wood—it contains scarcely any trees, and it is intersected, blast it, by a public footpath. Still, it is the first property that I have owned, so it is right that other people should participate in my shame, and should ask themselves,

"My Wood" from *Abinger Harvest* by E.M. Forster. Copyright 1936 and 1964. Reprinted by permission of Edward Arnold (Publishers) Ltd.

in accents that will vary in horror, this very important question:
What is the effect of property upon the character? Don't let's touch
economics; the effect of private ownership upon the community
as a whole is another question—a more important question, perhaps, but another one. Let's keep to psychology. If you own things,
what's their effect on you? What's the effect on me of my wood?

In the first place, it makes me feel heavy. Property does have   2
this effect. Property produces men of weight, and it was a man of
weight who failed to get into the Kingdom of Heaven. He was not
wicked, that unfortunate millionaire in the parable, he was only
stout; he stuck out in front, not to mention behind, and as he
wedged himself this way and that in the crystalline entrance and
bruised his well-fed flanks, he saw beneath him a comparatively
slim camel passing through the eye of a needle and being woven
into the robe of God. The Gospels all through couple stoutness
and slowness. They point out what is perfectly obvious, yet seldom
realized: that if you have a lot of things you cannot move about a
lot, that furniture requires dusting, dusters require servants, servants require insurance stamps, and the whole tangle of them
makes you think twice before you accept an invitation to dinner
or go for a bathe in the Jordan. Sometimes the Gospels proceed
further and say with Tolstoy° that property is sinful; they approach
the difficult ground of asceticism° here, where I cannot follow them.
But as to the immediate effects of property on people, they just
show straightforward logic. It produces men of weight. Men of
weight cannot, by definition, move like the lightning from the East
unto the West, and the ascent of a fourteen-stone° bishop into a
pulpit is thus the exact antithesis° of the coming of the Son of Man.
My wood makes me feel heavy.

In the second place, it makes me feel it ought to be larger.   3

The other day I heard a twig snap in it. I was annoyed at first,   4
for I thought that someone was blackberrying, and depreciating
the value of the undergrowth. On coming nearer, I saw it was not
a man who had trodden on the twig and snapped it, but a bird,
and I felt pleased. My bird. The bird was not equally pleased.
Ignoring the relation between us, it took fright as soon as it saw
the shape of my face, and flew straight over the boundary hedge
into a field, the property of Mrs. Henessy, where it sat down with
a loud squawk. It had become Mrs. Henessy's bird. Something
seemed grossly amiss here, something that would not have
occurred had the wood been larger. I could not afford to buy Mrs.
Henessy out, I dared not murder her, and limitations of this sort
beset me on every side. Ahab° did not want that vineyard—he only
needed it to round off his property, preparatory to plotting a new
curve—and all the land around my wood has become necessary to

me in order to round off the wood. A boundary protects. But—
poor little thing—the boundary ought in its turn to be protected.
Noises on the edge of it. Children throw stones. A little more, and
then a little more, until we reach the sea. Happy Canute!° Happier
Alexander!° And after all, why should even the world be the limit
of possession? A rocket containing a Union Jack, will, it is hoped,
be shortly fired at the moon. Mars, Sirius. Beyond which . . . But
these immensities ended by saddening me. I could not suppose
that my wood was the destined nucleus of universal dominion—
it is so very small and contains no mineral wealth beyond the
blackberries. Nor was I comforted when Mrs. Henessy's bird took
alarm for the second time and flew clean away from us all, under
the belief that it belonged to itself.

5   In the third place, property makes its owner feel that he ought
to do something to it. Yet he isn't sure what. A restlessness comes
over him, a vague sense that he has a personality to express—the
same sense which, without any vagueness, leads the artist to an
act of creation. Sometimes I think I will cut down such trees as
remain in the wood, at other times I want to fill up the gaps between
them with new trees. Both impulses are pretentious° and empty.
They are not honest movements towards money-making or beauty.
They spring from a foolish desire to express myself and from an
inability to enjoy what I have got. Creation, property, enjoyment
form a sinister trinity in the human mind. Creation and enjoyment
are both very, very good, yet they are often unattainable without
a material basis, and at such moments property pushes itself in as
a substitute, saying, "Accept me instead—I'm good enough for all
three." It is not enough. It is, as Shakespeare said of lust, "The
expense of spirit in a waste of shame"[;] it is "Before, a joy proposed; behind, a dream." Yet we don't know how to shun° it. It
is forced on us by our economic system as the alternative to starvation. It is also forced on us by an internal defect in the soul, by
the feeling that in property may lie the germs of self-development
and of exquisite or heroic deeds. Our life on earth is, and ought
to be, material and carnal°. But we have not yet learned to manage
our materialism and carnality properly; they are still entangled with
the desire for ownership, where (in the words of Dante) "Possession is one with loss."

6   And this brings us to our fourth and final point: the blackberries.

7   Blackberries are not plentiful in this meagre° grove, but they
are easily seen from the public footpath which traverses it, and all
too easily gathered. Foxgloves°, too—people will pull up the fox-
gloves, and ladies of an educational tendency even grub for toad-
stools to show them on the Monday in class. Other ladies, less
educated, roll down the bracken° in the arms of their gentlemen

friends. There is paper, there are tins. Pray, does my wood belong to me or doesn't it? And, if it does, should I not own it best by allowing no one else to walk there? There is a wood near Lyme Regis, also cursed by a public footpath, where the owner has not hesitated on this point. He had built high stone walls each side of the path, and has spanned it by bridges so that the public circulate like termites while he gorges on the blackberries unseen. He really does own his wood, this able chap. Dives° in Hell did pretty well, but the gulf dividing him from Lazarus° could be traversed by vision, and nothing traverses it here. And perhaps I shall come to this in time. I shall wall in and fence out until I really taste the sweets of property. Enormously stout, endlessly avaricious,° pseudo-creative, intensely selfish, I shall weave upon my forehead the quadruple crown of possession until those nasty Bolshies° come and take it off again and thrust me aside into the outer darkness.

```
┌─────────────────────┐
│                     │
│                     │
└─────────────────────┘
```

E.M. FORSTER

E.M. Forster (1879–1970), the English critic, essayist, and novelist, is most widely known as the author of *A Passage to India* and *A Room with a View*. His essays have been published in such collections as *Abinger Harvest* and *Two Cheers for Democracy*.

Words and Meanings

Paragraph

Tolstoy:	Count Leo Tolstoy, nineteenth-century Russian novelist, landowner, social critic, and pacifist	2
asceticism:	self-denial, rejection of physical and worldly pleasure	
fourteen-stone:	a stone is 14 pounds; 14 stone is roughly 90 kg	
antithesis:	direct opposite of	
Ahab:	Biblical king who died fighting to expand his territory	4
Canute:	early king of England who tried to command the sea	
Alexander:	Alexander the Great (356–323 BC), conqueror of the ancient Greco-Persian world	
pretentious:	self-important, conceited	5
shun:	avoid	
carnal:	physical	
meagre:	small, limited	7
foxgloves:	type of flower	
bracken:	ferns	

Dives and Lazarus:	In the Bible, Lazarus was a miserable beggar who suffered at the gates of the very rich Dives. After death Lazarus was carried to heaven by angels while Dives suffered torment in hell.
avaricious:	greedy
Bolshies:	slang form of Bolsheviks, early Russian communists

Structure and Strategy

1. With what introductory strategy does Forster begin his essay? What function does the question at the end of paragraph 1 serve?
2. What is the TOPIC SENTENCE of paragraph 2, and how does Forster develop it?
3. Paragraph 4 consists of an ANECDOTE. What is its function in the essay?
4. What cause and effect relationships does Forster discuss in paragraph 5? Why does he shift from CONCRETE to ABSTRACT language in this paragraph?
5. How does Forster's final sentence give COHERENCE to his essay?

Content and Purpose

1. What negative effects of property ownership does Forster identify? What do "the blackberries" symbolize?
2. In paragraphs 2 and 4, Forster uses Biblical and historical ALLUSIONS; in paragraph 5, he refers to Shakespeare and to Dante. Why does Forster turn to the Bible and to literature to help develop his thoughts on property ownership?
3. What is the purpose of Forster's reference to Americans at the beginning of this essay and to "Bolshies" at the end?
4. What is the implied thesis of this essay? Why do you think Forster bought a wood?

Suggestions for Writing

1. Write a short paper explaining how the ownership of—for example—a new car, stereo, or wardrobe has affected your life. Like Forster, you should consider both positive and negative effects.
2. Many people are driven to acquire things, such as grand houses, fine cars, fancy clothes, and expensive vacations. They become compulsive consumers chasing their vision of "the good life."

   What do you think are some of the causes of this obsession with material gain? Explain the causes in a short paper.

Under the Hood

DON SHARP

he owner of this 1966 Plymouth Valiant 1
has made the rounds of car dealers. They will gladly sell him a
new car—the latest model of government regulation and industrial
enterprise—for $8,000, but they don't want his clattering, emphy-
semic old vehicle in trade. It isn't worth enough to justify the
paperwork, a classified ad, and space on the used-car lot. "Sell it
for junk," they tell him. "Scrap iron is high now, and they'll give
you $25 for it."

The owner is hurt. He likes this car. It has served him well for 2
90,000-odd miles. It has a functional shape and he can get in and
out of it easily. He can roll down his window in a light rain and
not get his shoulder wet. The rear windows roll down, and he
doesn't need an air conditioner. He can see out of it fore, aft, and
abeam. He can hazard° it on urban parking lots without fear of
drastic, insurance-deductible casualty loss. His teenage children
reject it as passé, so it is always available to him. It has no buzzers,
and the only flashing lights are those he controls himself when
signaling a turn. The owner, clearly one of a vanishing tribe, brings
the car to a kindred spirit and asks me to rebuild it.

We do not discuss the cost. I do not advertise my services and 3
my sign is discreet. My shop is known by word of mouth, and
those who spread the word emphasize my house rule: "A blank
check and a free hand." That is, I do to your car what I think it
needs and you pay for it; you trust me not to take advantage, I
guarantee you good brakes, sound steering, and prompt starting,
and you pay without quarrel. This kind of arrangement saves a lot
of time spent in making estimates and a lot of time haggling over
the bill. It also imposes a tremendous burden of responsibility on
me, and on those who spread the word, and it puts a burden of
trust on those who deliver their cars into my custody.

A relationship of that sort is about as profound as any that two 4
people can enjoy, even if it lasts no longer than the time required
to reline a set of brakes. I think of hometown farmers who made
sharecropping deals for the season on a handshake; then I go into

"Under the Hood" from *Car Trouble* by Don Sharp. Copyright June 1980. Reprinted
by permission of Harper's Magazine Foundation.

a large garage and see the whitecoated service writer noting the customer's every specification, calling attention to the fine print at the bottom of the work order, and requiring a contractual signature before even a brake-light bulb is replaced. I perceive in their transaction that ignorance of cause and effect breeds suspicion, and I wonder who is the smaller, the customer or the service writer, and how they came to be so small of spirit.

5   Under the hood of this ailing Valiant, I note a glistening line of seeping oil where the oil pan meets the engine block. For thousands of miles, a piece of cork—a strip of bark from a Spanish tree—has stood firm between the pan and the block against churning oil heated to nearly 200 degrees, oil that sought vainly to escape its duty and was forced back to work by a stalwart gasket. But now, after years of perseverance, the gasket has lost its resilience and the craven oil escapes. Ecclesiastes allows a time for all things, and the time for this gasket has passed.

6   Higher up, between the block casting that forms the foundation of the engine and the cylinder-head casting that admits fresh air and exhausts oxidized air and fuel, is the head gasket, a piece of sheet metal as thin as a matchbook cover that has confined the multiple fires built within the engine to their proper domains. Now, a whitish-gray deposit betrays an eroded area from which blue flame spits every time the cylinder fires. The gasket is "blown."

7   Let us stop and think of large numbers. In the four-cycle engines that power all modern cars, a spark jumps a spark-plug gap and sets off a fire in a cylinder every time the crankshaft goes around twice. The crankshaft turns the transmission shaft, which turns the driveshaft, which turns the differential gears, which turn the rear axles, which turn the wheels. In 100,000 miles—a common life for modern engines—the engine will make some 260 million turns, and in half of those turns, 130 million of them, a gasoline-fueled fire with a maximum temperature of 2,000 degrees (quickly falling to about 1,200 degrees) is built in each cylinder. The heat generated by the fire raises the pressure in the cylinder to about 700 pounds per square inch, if only for a brief instant before the piston moves and the pressure falls. A head gasket has to contend with heat and pressure like this all the time the engine is running, and, barring mishap,° it will put up with it indefinitely.

8   This Plymouth has suffered mishap. I know it as soon as I raise the hood and see the telltale line of rust running across the underside of the hood: the mark of overheating. A water pump bearing or seal gave way, water leaked out, and was flung off the fan blades with enough force to embed particles of rust in the undercoating. Without cooling water, the engine grew too hot, and that's

why the head gasket blew. In an engine, no cause exists without an effect. Unlike a court of law, wherein criminals are frequently absolved of wrongdoing, no engine component is without duty and responsibility, and failure cannot be mitigated° by dubious explanations such as parental neglect or a crummy neighborhood.

Just as Sherlock Holmes would not be satisifed with one clue   9
if he could find others, I study the oil filter. The block and oil pan are caked with seepings and drippings, but below the filter the caking is visibly less thick and somewhat soft. So: once upon a time, a careless service-station attendant must have ruined the gasket while installing a new oil filter. Oil en route to the bearings escaped and washed away the grime that had accumulated. Odds are that the oil level fell too low and the crankshaft bearings were starved for oil.

Bearings are flat strips of metal, formed into half-circles about   10
as thick as a matchbook match and about an inch wide. The bearing surface itself—the surface that *bears* the crankshaft and that *bears* the load imposed by the fire-induced pressure above the piston— is half as thick. Bearing metal is a drab, gray alloy, the principal component of which is *babbitt*, a low-friction metal porous enough to absorb oil but so soft that it must be allowed to withstand high pressures. When the fire goes off above the piston and the pressure is transmitted to the crankshaft via the connecting rod, the babbitt- alloyed bearing pushes downward with a force of about 3,500 pounds per square inch. And it must not give way, must not be peened° into foil and driven from its place in fragments.

Regard the fleshy end joint of your thumb and invite a 100-   11
pound woman (or a pre-teen child, if no such woman be near to hand) to stand on it. Multiply the sensation by thirty-five and you get an idea of what the bearing is up against. Of course, the bearing enjoys a favorable handicap in the comparison because it works in a metal-to-metal environment heated to 180 degrees or so. The bearing is equal to its task so long as it is protected from direct metal-to-metal contact by a layer of lubricating oil, oil that must be forced into the space between the bearing and the crankshaft against that 3,500 pounds of force. True, the oil gets a lot of help from hydrodynamic action as the spinning crankshaft drags oil along with it, but lubrication depends primarily on a pump that forces oil through the engine at around 40 pounds of pressure.

If the oil level falls too low, the oil pump sucks in air. The oil   12
gets as frothy as whipped cream and doesn't flow. In time, oil pressure will fall so low that the "idiot" light on the dashboard will flash, but long before then the bearing may have run "dry" and suffered considerable amounts of its metal to be peened away

by those 3,500-pound hammer blows. "Considerable" may mean only .005 inches, or about the thickness of one sheet of 75-percent-cotton, 25-pound-per-ream dissertation bond°—not much metal, but enough to allow oil to escape from the bearing even after the defective filter gasket is replaced and the oil supply replenished. From the time of oil starvation onward, the beaten bearing is a little disaster waiting to spoil a vacation or a commute to an important meeting.

13   Curious, that an unseen .005 inches of drab, gray metal should enjoy more consequence for human life than almost any equal thickness of a randomly chosen doctoral dissertation. Life is full of ironies.

14   The car I confront does not have an "idiot" light. It has an old-fashioned oil-pressure gauge. As the driver made his rounds from condominium to committee room, he could—if he cared or was ever so alert—monitor the health of his engine bearings by noting the oil pressure. Virtually all cars had these gauges in the old days, but they began to disappear in the mid-'50s, and nowadays hardly any cars have them. In eliminating oil-pressure gauges, the car makers pleaded that, in their dismal experience, people didn't pay much attention to gauges. Accordingly, Detroit switched to the warning light, which was cheaper to manufacture anyway (and having saved a few bucks on the mechanicals, the manufacturer could afford to etch a design in the opera windows; this is called "progress"). Curious, in the midst of all this, that Chrysler Corporation, the maker of Plymouths and the victim of so much bad management over the past fifteen years, should have been the one car manufacturer to constantly assert, via a standard-equipment oil-pressure gauge, a faith in the awareness, judgment, and responsibility of drivers. That Chrysler did so may have something to do with its current problems.

15   The other car makers were probably right. Time was when most men knew how to replace their own distributor points, repair a flat tire, and install a battery. Women weren't assumed to know as much, but they were expected to know how to put a gear lever in neutral, set a choke and throttle, and crank a car by hand if the battery was dead. Now, odds are that 75 percent of men and a higher percentage of women don't even know how to work the jacks that come with their cars. To be sure, a bumper jack is an abominable contraption—the triumph of production economies over good sense—but it will do what it is supposed to do, and the fact that most drivers cannot make one work says much about the way motorists have changed over the past forty years.

16   About all that people will watch on the downslide of this cen-

tury is the fuel gauge, for they don't like to be balked in their purpose. A lack of fuel will stop a car dead in its tracks and categorically prevent the driver from arriving at the meeting to consider tenure for a male associate professor with a black grandfather and a Chinese mother. Lack of fuel will stall a car in mid-intersection and leave dignity and image prey to the honks and curses of riffraff driving taxicabs and beer trucks, so people watch the fuel gauge as closely as they watch a pubescent daughter or a bearish stock.

But for the most part, once the key goes into the ignition, people assign responsibility for the car's smooth running to someone else—to anybody but themselves. If the engine doesn't start, that's not because the driver has abused it, but because the manufacturer was remiss° or the mechanic incompetent. (Both suspicions are reasonable, but they do not justify the driver's spineless passivity.) The driver considers himself merely a client of the vehicle. He proudly disclaims°, at club and luncheon, any understanding of the dysfunctions of the machine. He must so disclaim, for to admit knowledge or to seek it actively would require an admission of responsibility and fault. To be wrong about inflation or the political aspirations of Albanians doesn't cost anybody anything, but to claim to know why the car won't start and then to be proved wrong is both embarrassing and costly.   17

Few people would remove $500 from someone's pocket without a qualm° and put it in their own. Yet, the job-lot run of mechanics do it all the time. Mechanics and drivers are alike: they gave up worrying long ago about the intricacies and demands of cause and effect. The mechanics do not attend closely to the behavior of the vehicle. Rather, they consult a book with flowcharts that says, "Try this, and if it doesn't work, try that." Or they hook the engine up to another machine and read gauges or cathode-ray-tube squiggles, but without realizing that gauges and squiggles are not reality but only tools used to aid perception of reality.   18

Mechanics, like academics and bureaucrats, have retreated too far from the realities of their tasks. An engine runs badly. They consult the book. The book says to replace part A. They replace A. The engine still runs badly, but the mechanic can deny the fact as handily as a socialist can deny that minimum-wage laws eventually lead to unemployment. Just as the driver doesn't care to know why his oil pressure drops from 40 to 30 to 20 pounds and then to zero, so the mechanic cares little for the casuistic° distinctions that suggest that part A is in good order but that some subtle conjunction of wholesome part B with defective part C may be causing the trouble.   19

20   And why should the mechanic care? He gets paid in any event. From the mechanic's point of view, he should get paid, for he sees a federal judge hire academic consultants to advise about busing, and after the whites have fled before the imperious column of yellow buses and left the schools blacker than ever, the judge hires the consultants again to find out why the whites moved out. The consultant gets paid in public money, whatever effects his actions have, even when he causes things he said would never happen.

21   Consider the garden-variety Herr Doktor° who has spent a pleasant series of warm fall weekends driving to a retreat in the Catskills; his car has started with alacrity and run well despite a stuck choke. Then, when the first blue norther of the season sends temperatures toward zero, the faithful machine must be haggled into action and proceeds haltingly down the road, gasping and backfiring. "Needs a new carburetor," the mechanic says, and, to be sure, once a new carburetor is installed, the car runs well again. Our Herr Doktor is happy. His car did not run well; it got a new carburetor and ran well again; ergo, the carburetor was at fault. Q.E.D.°

22   Curious that in personal matters the classic *post hoc* fallacy° should be so readily accepted when it would be mocked in academic debate. Our Herr Doktor should know, or at least suspect, that the carburetor that functioned so well for the past several months could hardly have changed its nature overnight, and we might expect of him a more diligent inquiry into its problems. But "I'm no mechanic," he chuckles to his colleagues, and they nod agreeably. Such skinned-knuckle expertise would be unfitting in a man whose self-esteem is equivalent to his uselessness with a wrench. Lilies of the postindustrial field must concern themselves with weighty matters beyond the ken of greasy laborers who drink beer at the end of a workday.

23   Another example will illustrate the point. A battery cable has an end that is designed to connect to a terminal on the battery. Both cable-end and battery-terminal surfaces look smooth, but aren't. Those smooth surfaces are pitted and peaked, and only the peaks touch each other. The pits collect water from the air, and the chemistry of electricity-carrying metals causes lead oxides to form in the pits. The oxides progressively insulate the cable end and battery terminal from each other until the day that turning the key produces only a single, resounding *clunk* and no more. The road service mechanic installs a new $75 battery and collects $25 for his trouble. Removing the cables from the old battery cleans their ends somewhat, so things work for a few days, and then the car again fails to start. The mechanic installs a $110 alternator, applies a $5 charge to the battery, and collects another $25; several days later he gives

the battery another $5 charge, installs a $75 starter, and collects $25 more. In these instances, to charge the battery—to send current backwards from cable end to battery terminal—disturbs the oxides and temporarily improves their conductivity. Wriggling the charger clamps on the cable ends probably helps too. On the driver's last $25 visit, the mechanic sells another $5 battery charge and a pair of $25 battery cables. Total bill: $400, and all the car needed was to have its cable ends and battery terminals cleaned. The mechanic wasn't necessarily a thief. Perhaps, like academic education consultants, he just wasn't very smart—and his ilk° abound; they are as plentiful as the drivers who will pay generously for the privilege of an aristocratic disdain of elementary cause and effect in a vehicular electrical system.

After a tolerably long practice as a mechanic, I firmly believe   24
that at least two-thirds of the batteries, starters, alternators, ignition coils, carburetors, and water pumps that are sold are not needed. Batteries, alternators, and starters are sold because battery-cable ends are dirty. A maladjusted or stuck automatic choke is cured by a new carburetor. Water pumps and alternators are sold to correct problems from loose fan belts. In the course of the replacement, the fan belt gets properly tightened, so the original problem disappears in the misguided cure, with mechanic and owner never the wiser.

I understand the venality° (and laziness and ignorance) of   25
mechanics, and I understand the shop owner's need to pay a salary to someone to keep up with the IRS and OSHA forms. The shop marks up parts by 50 to 100 percent. When the car with the faulty choke comes in the door, the mechanic must make a choice: he can spend fifteen minutes fixing it and charge a half-hour's labor, or he can spend a half-hour replacing the carburetor (and charge for one hour) with one he buys for $80 and sells for $135. If the shop is a profit-making enterprise, the mechanic can hardly be blamed for selling the unneeded new carburetor, especially if the customer will stand still to be fleeced. Whether the mechanic acts from ignorance or larceny° (the odds are about equal), the result is still a waste, one that arises from the driver's refusal to study the cause and effect of events that occur under the hood of his car.

The willingness of a people to accept responsibility for the   26
machines they depend on is a fair barometer of their sense of individual worth and of the moral strength of a culture. According to popular reports, the Russian working folk are a sorrowfully vodka-besotted lot; likewise, reports are that Russian drivers abuse their vehicles atrociously. In our unhappy country, as gauges for battery-changing (ammeters), cooling-water temperature, and oil

pressure disappeared from dashboards, they were replaced by a big-brotherly series of cacophonous° buzzers and flashing lights, buzzers and lights mandated° by regulatory edict° for the sole purpose of reminding the driver that the government considers him a hopeless fool. Concurrent with these developments has come social agitation and law known as "consumer protection," which is, in fact, an extension of the philosophy that people are morons for whom the government must provide outpatient care. People pay handsome taxes to be taught that they are not responsible and do not need to be.

27   What is astounding and dismaying is how quickly people came to believe in their own incompetence. In 1951, Eric Hoffer noted in *The True Believer* that a leader so disposed could make free people into slaves easier than he could turn slaves into free people (cf. Moses). Hoffer must be pained by the accuracy of his perception.

28   I do not claim that Everyman can be his own expert mechanic, for I know that precious few can. I do claim that disdain° for the beautiful series of cause-and-effect relationships that move machines, and particularly the automobile, measures not only a man's wit but also a society's morals.

DON SHARP

Don Sharp, the journalist, was born in New Mexico in 1938. He is a graduate of the University of Alaska, in Fairbanks. He taught English in several small colleges in the United States before becoming a free-lance writer and magazine editor. He has published articles in *Harper's* and *Commentary*, and is currently editor of *The Western Boatman*, published in California.

Paragraph Words and Meanings

2	hazard:	chance, risk
7	barring mishap:	unless something goes wrong, or there is an accident
8	mitigated:	lessened, diminished
10	peened:	hammered thin
12	dissertation bond:	typing paper
17	remiss: disclaims:	careless, negligent denies any knowledge of
18	qualm:	uneasiness, twinge of conscience
19	casuistic:	fine distinctions; quibbling

Herr Doktor:	highly educated man; university professor	21
Q.E.D.:	*quod erat demonstrandum*, Latin for "proved"	
post hoc fallacy:	error of assuming that because one event fol-	22
	lowed another, it was caused by the first event	
ilk:	like; people similar to him	23
venality:	lack of principle; greed	25
larceny:	theft	
cacophonous:	harsh-sounding	26
mandated:	required	
edict:	law	
disdain:	scorn, contempt	28

Structure and Strategy

1. What introductory strategy does the author use?
2. Study the DICTION of paragraph 5. How does it help to reveal Sharp's attitudes toward machines in general and the automobile in particular?
3. Explain the implied contrast in paragraph 2 that reveals Sharp's opinion of car manufacturers' most recent car designs.
4. Identify the definition Sharp provides in paragraph 10 that is further explained by a comparison in paragraph 11.
5. Identify two of the examples Sharp uses to show that ignorance of mechanical cause-effect relationships is expensive.
6. This essay may be divided into five parts: paragraphs 1 to 4, 5 to 13, 14 to 17, 18 to 25, and 26 to 28. Identify the main idea each part develops.

Content and Purpose

1. What is the basis of an "agreement" and what is the basis of a "contract"? Why does Sharp stress the difference between these two relationships in paragraphs 3 and 4?
2. Summarize the author's reasons for believing that both drivers and mechanics are guilty of ignoring the laws of cause and effect.
3. Who are the "lilies of the postindustrial field" (paragraph 22) and what is Sharp's attitude toward them?
4. What is the author's purpose in comparing mechanics to academics, bureaucrats, and education consultants? What, in Sharp's opinion, do these groups have in common?
5. Why does Sharp dislike "consumer protection" laws? (See paragraph 26.)

6. What is the implied thesis of this essay? (See paragraphs 26 to 28.) Summarize the thesis in your own words.
7. Sharp ends his essay with a credo, a statement of personal philosophy or belief. Summarize his credo. Do you agree or disagree with it?

Suggestions for Writing

1. Write a paper explaining the cause-effect relationship between any two things: two organisms, two parts of a machine, two chemicals, two emotions, two social conditions, or two environmental conditions.
2. We frequently hear that the quality of our school system is deteriorating. Do you think the average high school graduate today is less well-educated than one of twenty years ago? If so, what are some of the causes of this decline in quality? If you don't agree, what are some of the causes of the perceived decline?

Additional Suggestions for Writing: Causal Analysis

Choose one of the topics below and write a paper that explores its causes *or* effects. Write a clear thesis statement and plan the development of each main point before you begin to write the paper.

1. sibling rivalry
2. seat-belt legislation
3. the popularity of a current television series
4. the increasing number of working mothers
5. fascination with the lifestyles of the rich and famous
6. the tendency of people to distrust or dislike people different from themselves
7. the pressure on women to be thin
8. the appeal of television evangelists or preachers
9. peer pressure among adolescents
10. the increasing popularity of foreign-made cars
11. the increasing popularity of French-immersion schooling in Canada
12. the trend to postpone childbearing until a couple reaches their thirties
13. a specific phobia that affects someone you know
14. the attraction of religious cults
15. marriage breakdown
16. alcoholism
17. the popularity of Gordon Korman, or Judy Blume, or any other widely read writer of fiction for adolescents
18. the demand among employers for ever-increasing levels of literacy
19. guilt
20. "Happy families are all alike; every unhappy family is unhappy in its own way." (Tolstoy)

U N I T

Definition: Explaining "What"

What? The Definition

Communication between writer and reader cannot take place unless there is a shared understanding of the meaning of the writer's words. Knowing when and how to define terms clearly is one of the most useful skills a writer can learn. Through definition, a writer creates meaning.

In the Biblical creation myth, which has endured for millennia (a millennium is a period of a thousand years), the Creator presents the animals to Adam in order that he name them:

> And out of the ground the Lord God formed every beast of the field, and every fowl of the air; and brought them to Adam to see what he would call them: and whatsoever Adam called every creature, that was the name thereof.
> (Genesis 2:19)

Adam isn't asked to count or catalogue or describe or judge the beasts of creation. They are arrayed before him so that he might *name* them, *define* them, an act which is itself a kind of creation. This capacity to define things through words and to communicate thought by means of those words makes us unique as humans.

There are two basic ways to define terms: the short way and the long way. The short way is sometimes called **formal definition**. The writer very quickly, in a sentence or so, explains a word that may be unknown to the reader. An example of formal definition is the explanation of the word "millennium" in the paragraph above. You should include a definition whenever you introduce an unfamiliar word, or whenever you assign a particular meaning to a general term. If you do not define ambiguous words or phrases, you leave the reader wondering which of several possible meanings you intended. You should also provide definitions when using technical terms, since these are likely to be unfamiliar to at least some readers. For instance, a reader who is not familiar with the term "formal definition" might assume it means "elaborate" or "fancy," when in fact it means a one-sentence definition written in a particular form.

The second way to define a term is through **extended definition**, a form of expository writing in which the word, idea, thing, or phenomenon being defined is the subject of the entire essay or paper. Extended definition is required when the nature of the thing to be defined is complex, and explaining *what it is* in detail is the writer's goal.

Why? The Purpose

In your studies, you have probably already discovered that fully exploring a complex subject requires a detailed explanation of it. Definition papers answer the question, "What does S mean?" For example, the word "myth" used above to describe the creation story does not, in any way, mean "untrue," though that is often the way the word is used. A myth is better defined as a traditional or legendary story that attempts to explain a basic truth. Entire books have been written to define what myth is and how it works in our culture. Obviously, myth is a topic that lends itself to extended definition.

Extended definition is especially useful for three purposes: explaining the abstract, the technical, or the changed meanings of a word or concept. If you were asked in a history class, for example, to define an abstract idea such as "freedom" or "misogyny" or "justice," an extended definition would enable you to establish the meaning of the concept and also to explore your personal commitments and aspirations.

Whatever their professional background, all writers occasionally use technical terms that must be defined for readers who may be unfamiliar with them. For example, a Canadian businessperson with a large potential market in the United States may have to define "free trade" to prospective investors. A social worker would be wise to detail what she means by "substance abuse" in a brochure aimed at teenage drug users. An engineer could not explain concepts such as "gas chromatography" or "atomic absorption" to a nontechnical audience without first adequately defining them.

Extended definition can also be used to clarify the way in which a particular term has changed in meaning over the years. For instance, everyone is aware of the way in which the word "gay," which originally meant only "joyful" or "bright," has expanded to include "homosexual," even in its denotative, or dictionary, meaning. Tracking the evolution of a word's meaning can be both an effective and an interesting way to define the term for your readers.

Clearly, extended definition is ideal for explaining because it establishes the boundaries of meaning intended by the writer. In fact, the very word "define" comes from the Latin word *definire*, which means "to put a fence around." But definition is not restricted to its expository function. Defining something in a particular way sometimes involves persuading other people to accept and act on the definition. Our businessperson will probably want to take a stand on free trade after defining it; the social worker's definition of substance abuse might well form the basis of the arguments against drug use. Extended definition is thus a versatile rhetorical strategy that can accommodate the urge we all have to convince and influence the people with whom we're communicating.

How? The Method

Extended definition does not have a single, clear-cut rhetorical pattern unique to itself. Its development relies instead on one or more of the other patterns explained in this text. In other words, depending on the topic and the audience, an extended definition may use any of a variety of forms, or even a combination of forms. For instance, if you wanted to define the term "myth," one way would be by providing *examples* of different myths. Another way would involve *comparing* the terms "myth" and "legend." Or you might choose to explain some of the *effects* of a particular myth on a specific culture. An extended definition of gas chromatography, on the other hand, might focus on the *process* involved in using a chromatograph. An extended definition of substance abuse could *classify* the various addictive drugs. Sometimes a combination of patterns is the best approach. You need to put yourself in your reader's place to determine what questions he or she would be most likely to ask about your topic. Then you'll be able to choose the most appropriate pattern or patterns with which to organize your paper.

It is often helpful to begin your extended definition with a *formal definition*. To write a formal definition, first put the term you are defining into the general class of things to which it belongs; then identify the qualities that set it apart or distinguish it from the others in that class. Here are some examples of formal definitions:

TERM		CLASS	DISTINGUISHING FEATURES
A turtle	is	a shelled reptile	that lives in water.
A tortoise	is	a shelled reptile	that lives on land.
Misogyny	is	a feeling of hatred	against women.
Misanthropy	is	a feeling of hatred	against people in general.
The Gross National Product	is	an economic indicator	derived by establishing the total value of a country's goods and services.
A résumé	is	a written summary	of a job applicant's education, work experience, and personal background.

Constructing a formal definition is a logical way to begin any task of definition. It prevents vague formulations such as "a turtle lives in water" (so does a tuna), or "misanthropy is when you don't like people." (By the way, avoid using "is when" or "is where" in a formal definition—it's bound to be loose and imprecise.) Notice that a formal definition is sometimes a ready-made thesis statement, as in the last two examples given above. An extended definition of the Gross National Product would divide the GNP into its component parts—goods and services—and show how their value is determined. Similarly, an extended definition of a résumé would explain its three essential components: the applicant's education, work experience, and personal background.

There are two pitfalls to avoid when you are writing definitions. First, do not begin with a word-for-word definition copied straight out of the dictionary, even though you may be tempted to do so when you're staring at a piece of blank paper. Resist the temptation. As an introductory strategy, a dictionary definition is both boring and irrelevant. It's *your* meaning the reader needs to understand, not all the potential meanings of the word given in the dictionary. "*Webster's Third International Dictionary* defines love as 'a predilection or liking for anything' " is hardly a useful, let alone an attention-getting, introduction. Second, don't chase your own tail: avoid using in your definition a form of the term you're defining. A definition such as "adolescence is the state of being an adolescent" not only fails to clarify the meaning for your readers, but also wastes their time.

A good definition establishes clearly, logically, and precisely the boundaries of meaning. It communicates the meaning in an organizational pattern appropriate to the term and to the reader. To define is, in many ways, to create, and to do this well is to show respect for the ideas or things you're explaining as well as courtesy to your audience.

Here is an example of an essay that defines a term by exploring its etymological roots.

A Definition of Education

Introduction

Thesis statement ⟶

Words don't spring into being out of no-where: they grow out of other words. It is often useful and interesting to explore the etymology, or origins, of the words we use. The word "education," for ex-ample, has a meaningful history. It is derived from two different but related Latin words: *educare* and *educere*.

First point (developed by definition and quotation)

The Latin verb *educare* is most often translated as "to rear" or "to nourish." Originally, the word was applied to both children and animals, because "rear-ing" means providing food and basic ne-cessities. The *Oxford English Dictionary* tells us that one of the earliest recorded uses of the word was in the context of animal husbandry. In 1607 a man named Topsell wrote that "horses are not to be despised, if they [are] well bred and ed-ucated." The word is not used this way today—we teach a dog new tricks; we don't "educate" him. The word retains something of its earlier meaning, how-ever, in that parents and teachers nour-ish the young with knowledge, which is digested by relatively passive recipients.

Second point (also developed by definitions and quotation)

The Latin verb *educere*, on the other hand, has a different, more active mean-ing. It means "to lead out" or "to draw forth." The English word "educe," a di-rect descendant of *educere*, means to infer something, or to come up with ideas oneself. In other words, if I use my own faculties, combined with the knowledge I've gained, I can actively educe or de-velop new ideas on my own. The En-glish poet Samuel Taylor Coleridge asserted, "In the education of children, love is first to be instilled, and out of love obedience is to be educed." His use of the word "educed" implies that children can naturally develop obedience out of their own best instincts rather than remain passive receptacles into whom "obedience" is poured (or thrashed). Similarly, a teacher can lead her students or draw them out, but the students must respond actively to develop the behaviour or knowledge themselves. Basically, the *educare* root points to a passive experience in which the learner waits to be filled with facts, while the *educere* root points to a dynamic experience in which the learner interacts creatively with the teacher and the subject matter.

Conclusion (makes use of a short anecdote to make the general point specific)

This distinction was brought home to me recently as I listened to a hotline radio program in which a grade-ten dropout bemoaned his lack of a job: "Unless my education improves," he began, "I won't have a chance." Interestingly, his phrase lacked a "doer." He seemed to understand education only in the sense that derives from *educare*: the experience of being spoon-fed. To this young man, education was something separate from himself, outside his control—something which, like his chances, could only be altered by outside forces. This attitude is clearly self-defeating. It fails to recognize the meaning of education that derives from *educere*: the experience of actively responding to and developing what a teacher has initiated. The relationship between the learner and what is being learned must be an active one. The learner, in other words, must assume responsibility in the process.

Thus, the roots of the word "education" have something to teach us. We can educe useful knowledge from them even today—hundreds of years after the word itself first appeared in our language.

The Devil's Dictionary

AMBROSE BIERCE

1   ABSURDITY, n. A statement or belief manifestly inconsistent with one's own opinion.

2   BIGOT, n. One who is obstinately and zealously attached to an opinion that you do not entertain.

3   BORE, n. A person who talks when you wish him to listen.

4   BOUNDARY, n. In political geography, an imaginary line between two nations, separating the imaginary rights of one from the imaginary rights of the other.

5   BRIDE, n. A woman with a fine prospect of happiness behind her.

6   CALAMITY, n. A more than commonly plain and unmistakable reminder that the affairs of this life are not of our own ordering. Calamities are of two kinds: misfortune to ourselves, and good fortune to others.

7   CHRISTIAN, n. One who believes that the New Testament is a divinely inspired book admirably suited to the spiritual needs of his neighbor. One who follows the teachings of Christ in so far as they are not inconsistent with a life of sin.

8   COWARD, n. One who in a perilous emergency thinks with his legs.

9   DIPLOMACY, n. The patriotic art of lying for one's country.

10   EDUCATION, n. That which discloses to the wise and disguises from the foolish their lack of understanding.

11   EGOTIST, n. A person of low taste, more interested in himself than in me.

12   LOGIC, n. The art of thinking and reasoning in strict accordance with the limitations and incapacities of the human misunderstanding. The basic logic is the syllogism, consisting of a major and a minor premise and a conclusion—thus:
Major Premise: Sixty men can do a piece of work sixty times as quickly as one man.
Minor Premise: One man can dig a post hole in sixty seconds; therefore—

From *The Devil's Dictionary* by Ambrose Bierce. Copyright 1957. Reprinted by permission of Hill and Wang Publishers.

Conclusion: Sixty men can dig a posthole in one second.
This may be called the syllogism arithmetical, in which, by combining logic and mathematics, we obtain a double certainty and are twice blessed.

```
┌─────────────────────────────┐
│                             │
│                             │
└─────────────────────────────┘
```

AMBROSE BIERCE

Ambrose Bierce (1842–1914), the American journalist and short story writer, is best remembered for his short stories, collected in such books as *In the Midst of Life* and for *The Devil's Dictionary*. A contrary person, Bierce disappeared while on a visit to war-torn Mexico.

Structure and Strategy

1. What is the TONE of Bierce's definitions?
2. How many of Bierce's definitions are examples of formal definition? (See the introduction to this unit.)

Content and Purpose

1. Why do you think Bierce called his book *The Devil's Dictionary*? What is his purpose in inventing these definitions?
2. Explain the PUN (see FIGURES OF SPEECH) in Bierce's definition of a *bride* (paragraph 4).
3. Do you think Bierce was a misanthrope or a reformer? Consider his TONE, DICTION, and content in your answer.

Suggestions for Writing

1. Write formal definitions, serious or ironic, for five slang terms you use frequently or for the following terms:
   a college student
   a Big Mac (or any other burger)
   a censor
   rock music
   convocation
2. Write formal definitions for five technical terms from your professional field or from a subject you are currently studying.
3. The last sentence of Bierce's definition of "calamity" could serve as a thesis statement for a classification paper. Develop that thesis statement into a short paper.

How the Law of Raspberry Jam Applies to Culture

MAVOR MOORE

It would be better to stop using the word "culture."
—Sir Herbert Read

1   hat Read advises (and many of us might endorse°) is more easily said than done. The main reason for doing away with the word "culture" is that it means many things—but this is also the best reason for keeping it. Since most other words with an allied sense (such as "civilization," "the arts," "education," "heritage," "identity") are forced to be equally elastic these days, we would achieve little by dropping "culture" simply because it is confusing. Its replacement might be even more so. But what are we to do about it?

2   In recent weeks, I have received a number of letters asking me to define culture. How does it differ from the arts, or education, or entertainment? What does Prime Minister Brian Mulroney mean when he talks about our "cultural identity"? Is there some other kind? What does Joe Clark, our Minister for External Affairs, mean when he tells a U.S. audience that "What is entertainment for you is culture for us"? For that matter, what is a column on cultural affairs doing in the entertainment section of your newspaper?

3   The dictionaries are more bewildering than precise. We learn that culture can signify everything from refinement of the mind to manure, from good manners to a colony of viruses, from a particular school of art to boundary lines on a map. "In anthropology," one dictionary tells us, culture is "the sum total of the attainments and activities of any specific period, race, or people, including their implements, handicrafts, agriculture, economics, music, art, religious beliefs, traditions, language and story." At the other extreme is Quentin Crisp's definition of culture as "television programs so boring that they cannot be described as entertainment."

4   But entertainment fares little better in the dictionaries. To en-

"How the Law of Raspberry Jam Applies to Culture" by Mavor Moore. From *The Globe and Mail*. Copyright Jan. 11, 1986. Reprinted by permission of Mavor Moore.

tertain means to amuse or divert; but it also means to establish and maintain correspondence or conversation, to host a gathering, to consider ideas, to occupy time, to cherish beliefs and to hold the attention. On this basis, obviously, you can entertain (or fail to entertain) practically anybody or anything; but amusement is only one way of doing either, and diversion may not do the trick at all. It seems to me an open question, moreover, whether you can achieve much in the way of either education or civilization without first gaining and then continuing to hold the attention of others.

There was a time, perhaps, when each of these human activities had a separate meaning, or when one of them semantically° contained others. In Canada, it has been only 35 years since the Massey-Levesque Report spoke of culture as "that part of education which enriches the mind and refines the taste," and as "the development of intelligence through the arts, letters and sciences." More recently, a UNESCO paper announces, with more hope than evidence, that "there is now unanimity in favor of a socio-anthropological definition of culture as opposed to any esthetic approach, which is rejected on the grounds of its elitist character. . . . The socio-anthropological definition is typified by its global or exhaustive approach, according to which culture is the sum total of the material as well as the intellectual and spiritual distinctive features that characterize a society or a social group."

It becomes a matter of which word you want to stretch. Said Marshall McLuhan once: "Art is anything you can get away with." All of life can be seen as art, or science, or education, or communications, or religion, or entertainment, or whatever heading you want to put at the top of the page. "All the world's a stage" will do very well, as Shakespeare wrote in the aptly-titled *As You Like It*. But one's choice of a hold-all word tells us as much about the speaker as it does about the word. We read and manipulate each other through words used as symbols for ideas. Words with the glowing patina° of ancient authority as well as hot currency, especially, are prized for their power, and bent or stretched to serve a purpose. We owe it to ourselves to scrutinize the purpose instead of getting entangled in word-definitions.

We have two defences against the commandeering of a common word by special interests. One is simply to give it a sense and meaning of our own (as kids, sociologists and computer programmers do), which is exhilarating° but negative: it reduces a common word to private use. The other is to appeal to the basic sense in which it first received wide circulation, then take later variations into account. When we do so, we will often find that, despite obvious areas of overlap, the different meanings are necessary and complementary.

8   The root sense of "culture" is (late Latin *cultura*) preparation for growth. The root sense of "art" is (Latin *artem*) skill. The root sense of "science" is (Latin *scientia*) knowledge. The root sense of "education" is (Latin *educ[e]re*) to bring out. The root sense of "entertainment" is (Latin *intertenere*) to hold. So far as I can see, society needs all of these means of coping with each other and with the world. One can fiddle with the words, one can change current meanings or introduce new varieties, but the human requirement for the activity each describes is crucial to civilization—and together they are interdependent.

9   The area to be covered by general words is continually in dispute. Collectively, they wax and wane like moons. Today, for example, there are powerful forces at work persuading us that entertainment is a commercial industry, and that culture is a department of politics. It does not seem to bother either group that entertainment is often (a) an instrument of politics and (b) naturally uneconomic, or that culture is often (a) completely apolitical° and (b) naturally anarchistic°. When a word is pushed and pulled like this, it becomes subject to what Alvin Toffler calls The Law of Raspberry Jam: the wider it is spread the thinner it gets. Its value as verbal coin is debased, not increased.

10   So I prefer to keep the word "culture" in its valuable common sense (because there really is no other word) of collective preparation for, and maintenance of human development. This involves, above all, the use of our creative imagination. (Said Arthur Koestler: "Artists treat facts as stimuli for the imagination, while scientists use their imagination to co-ordinate facts.") This is quite broad enough, allowing us to throw in a well-designed kitchen sink. But we cannot develop creativity by consuming the products of others, or being entertained without entertaining.

11   In this sense, cultured is either something we make of ourselves, or a word for cheap pearls from smarter oysters. And if we find the process more palatable in the guise of entertainment, so be it—but for that, also, we need our own entertainment section.

MAVOR MOORE

Mavor Moore, man of the theatre, was born in 1919 in Toronto, the son of Dora Mavor Moore, a well-known theatre personality. Moore has acted on radio, television, the stage, and in films. As well, he has produced and directed. He taught theatre at York University in Toronto and contributes a weekly column on culture to the *Toronto Star*.

Words and Meanings

Paragraph

endorse:	support, agree with	1
semantically:	relating to the meaning of words	5
patina:	shine or gloss produced by age	6
exhilarating:	stimulating, making happy	7
apolitical:	without political reference or meaning	9
anarchistic:	chaotic, ungovernable	

Structure and Strategy

1. What is the function of the direct questions Moore asks in paragraphs 1 and 2?
2. How does the quotation from Quentin Crisp at the end of paragraph 3 reinforce the last sentence of paragraph 2 and prepare the reader for the essay's conclusion?
3. Do you see any similarity of tone between McLuhan's definition of art (paragraph 6) and Ambrose Bierce's definitions (see previous selection)?
4. What is the function of paragraph 8?
5. Do you think Moore's concluding paragraph is effective or ineffective? Why?

Content and Purpose

1. Why, according to Moore, is "culture" so difficult to define? Why can't we just look the word up in the dictionary?
2. What connections does Moore see between culture and entertainment? Are they the same thing?
3. Summarize the distinction between the "socio-anthropological" and the "esthetic" definitions of culture (paragraph 5).
4. Which definition of culture does Moore prefer? With that definition in mind, what relationship do you think Moore sees between culture and education?
5. What is the "Law of Raspberry Jam" and where does it come from? How does careful definition redeem the "debased value of individual words" (paragraph 9)?

Suggestions for Writing

1. Write an extended definition of the term "culture." You may use Moore's essay as a starting point, but develop ideas of your own.
2. Write an essay of extended definition that explains several possible meanings of one of these words: humour, establishment, state, holocaust, Black.

Don't You Think It's Time to Start Thinking?

NORTHROP FRYE

1   Astudent often leaves high school today without any sense of language as a structure.

2   He may also have the idea that reading and writing are elementary skills that he mastered in childhood, never having grasped the fact that there are differences in levels of reading and writing as there are in mathematics between short division and integral calculus.

3   Yet, in spite of his limited verbal skills, he firmly believes that he can think, that he has ideas, and that if he is just given the opportunity to express them he will be all right. Of course, when you look at what he's written you find it doesn't make any sense. When you tell him this he is devastated.

4   Part of his confusion here stems from the fact that we use the word "think" in so many bad, punning ways. Remember James Thurber's Walter Mitty who was always dreaming great dreams of glory. When his wife asked him what he was doing he would say, "Has it ever occurred to you that I might be thinking?"

5   But, of course, he wasn't thinking at all. Because we use it for everything our minds do, worrying, remembering, day-dreaming, we imagine that thinking is something that can be achieved without any training. But again it's a matter of practice. How well we can think depends on how much of it we have already done. Most students need to be taught, very carefully and patiently, that there is no such thing as an inarticulate° idea waiting to have the right words wrapped around it.

6   They have to learn that ideas do not exist until they have been incorporated into words. Until that point you don't know whether you are pregnant or just have gas on the stomach.

7   The operation of thinking is the practice of articulating ideas until they are in the right words. And we can't think at random either. We can only add one more idea to the body of something we have already thought about. Most of us spend very little time

"Don't You Think It's Time to Start Thinking?" by Northrop Frye from *The Toronto Star*. Copyright Jan. 25, 1986. Reprinted by permission of Northrop Frye.

doing this, and that is why there are so few people whom we regard as having any power to articulate at all. When such a person appears in public life, like Mr. Trudeau, we tend to regard him as possessing a gigantic intellect.

A society like ours doesn't have very much interest in literacy. 8 It is compulsory to read and write because society must have docile and obedient citizens. We are taught to read so that we can obey the traffic signs and to cipher so that we can make out our income tax, but development of verbal competency is very much left to the individual.

And when we look at our day-to-day existence we can see that 9 there are strong currents at work against the development of powers of articulateness. Young adolescents today often betray a curious sense of shame about speaking articulately, of framing a sentence with a period at the end of it.

Part of the reason for this is the powerful anti-intellectual drive 10 which is constantly present in our society. Articulate speech marks you out as an individual, and in some settings this can be rather dangerous because people are often suspicious and frightened of articulateness. So if you say as little as possible and use only stereotyped, ready-made phrases you can hide yourself in the mass.

Then there are various epidemics sweeping over society which 11 use unintelligibility° as a weapon to preserve the present power structure. By making things as unintelligible as possible, to as many people as possible, you can hold the present power structure together. Understanding and articulateness lead to its destruction. This is the kind of thing that George Orwell was talking about, not just in *Nineteen Eighty-Four*, but in all his work on language. The kernel of everything reactionary° and tyrannical° in society is the impoverishment of the means of verbal communication.

The vast majority of things that we hear today are prejudices 12 and clichés, simply verbal formulas that have no thought behind them but are put up as a pretence of thinking. It is not until we realize these things conceal meaning, rather than reveal it, that we can begin to develop our own powers of articulateness.

The teaching of humanities° is, therefore, a militant° job. Teach- 13 ers are faced not simply with a mass of misconceptions° and unexamined assumptions. They must engage in a fight to help the student confront and reject the verbal formulas and stock responses°, to convert passive acceptance into active, constructive power. It is a fight against illiteracy and for the maturation of the mental process, for the development of skills which once acquired will never become obsolete.

NORTHROP FRYE

Northrop Frye, the literary critic, was born in 1912 in Sherbrooke, Que., and raised in Moncton, N.B. For many years he taught English at Victoria College, University of Toronto. His theories of the relationship between myth and reality have had a wide literary and social influence. Among his books are *The Educated Imagination, Anatomy of Criticism,* and *The Great Code.*

Paragraph

Words and Meanings

5	inarticulate:	unexpressed; not put into words
11	unintelligibility:	lack of understandable meaning
	reactionary:	ultraconservative
	tyrannical:	like a dictator or tyrant
13	humanities:	the traditional liberal arts subjects, such as philosophy, history, and literature
	militant:	fighting; engaged in battle
	misconception:	mistaken belief
	stock responses:	standard, predictable expressions

Structure and Strategy

1. What is the function of paragraphs 1 to 3 and paragraphs 4 to 6?
2. Why is Frye's allusion to Walter Mitty particularly appropriate in this essay? (If you aren't familiar with the story, look up "The Secret Life of Walter Mitty" in an anthology of James Thurber's short stories.)
3. What metaphor (see FIGURES OF SPEECH) does Frye use in paragraph 6 to help reinforce his point? What connection does Frye imply between pregnancy and thinking?
4. Identify Frye's formal definition of "thinking."
5. What are the reasons Frye offers to support his opinion that thinking isn't often found in our society? How does he develop them (paragraphs 8 to 12)?

Content and Purpose

1. What does Frye mean by "language as structure" (paragraph 1)?
2. What does Frye mean by "literacy" and "verbal competency" (paragraph 8)?
3. According to Frye, is it possible for an inarticulate person to think? Why?
4. Which groups in our society use "unintelligibility as a weapon"? Why do you think Frye doesn't identify them for us? Why might these groups fear articulateness? (See paragraph 11.)

5. Why are clichés and prejudice enemies of thinking?
6. Explain in your own words what Frye means when he claims that teaching the humanities is "a militant job."

Suggestion for Writing

Write a formal definition of one of the following terms, and develop it by whatever expository techniques you choose into an extended definition: thoughtfulness, imagination, literacy, creativity.

Work, Labor, and Play

W.H. AUDEN

So far as I know, Miss Hannah Arendt was the first person to define the essential difference between work and labor. To be happy, a man must feel, firstly, free and, secondly, important. He cannot be really happy if he is compelled by society to do what he does not enjoy doing, or if what he enjoys doing is ignored by society as of no value or importance. In a society where slavery in the strict sense has been abolished, the sign that what a man does is of social value is that he is paid money to do it, but a laborer today can rightly be called a wage slave. A man is a laborer if the job society offers him is of no interest to himself but he is compelled to take it by the necessity of earning a living and supporting his family. 1

The antithesis° to labor is play. When we play a game, we enjoy what we are doing, otherwise we should not play it, but it is a purely private activity; society could not care less whether we play it or not. 2

Between labor and play stands work. A man is a worker if he is personally interested in the job which society pays him to do; what from the point of view of society is necessary labor is from his own point of view voluntary play. Whether a job is to be classified as labor or work depends, not on the job itself, but on the tastes of the individual who undertakes it. The difference does not, for example, coincide with the difference between a manual and a mental job; a gardener or a cobbler may be a worker, a bank clerk 3

"Work, Labor, and Play" from *A Certain World: A Commonplace Book* by W. H. Auden. Copyright 1970 by W. H. Auden. Reprinted by permission of Viking Penguin Inc.

a laborer. Which a man is can be seen from his attitude toward leisure. To a worker, leisure means simply the hours he needs to relax and rest in order to work efficiently. He is therefore more likely to take too little leisure than too much; workers die of coronaries and forget their wives' birthdays. To the laborer, on the other hand, leisure means freedom from compulsion, so that it is natural for him to imagine that the fewer hours he has to spend laboring, and the more hours he is free to play, the better.

4   What percentage of the population in a modern technological society are, like myself, in the fortunate position of being workers? At a guess I would say sixteen per cent, and I do not think that figure is likely to get bigger in the future.

5   Technology and the division of labor have done two things: by eliminating in many fields the need for special strength or skill, they have made a very large number of paid occupations which formerly were enjoyable work into boring labor, and by increasing productivity they have reduced the number of necessary laboring hours. It is already possible to imagine a society in which the majority of the population, that is to say, its laborers, will have almost as much leisure as in earlier times was enjoyed by the aristocracy. When one recalls how aristocracies in the past actually behaved, the prospect is not cheerful. Indeed, the problem of dealing with boredom may be even more difficult for such a future mass society than it was for aristocracies. The latter, for example, ritualized° their time; there was a season to shoot grouse, a season to spend in town, etc. The masses are more likely to replace an unchanging ritual by fashion which it will be in the economic interest of certain people to change as often as possible. Again, the masses cannot go in for hunting, for very soon there would be no animals left to hunt. For other aristocratic amusements like gambling, dueling, and warfare, it may be only too easy to find equivalents in dangerous driving, drug-taking, and senseless acts of violence. Workers seldom commit acts of violence, because they can put their aggression into their work, be it physical like the work of a smith, or mental like the work of a scientist or an artist. The role of aggression in mental work is aptly expressed by the phrase "getting one's teeth into a problem."

W.H. AUDEN

W.H. Auden (1907–1973), the distinguished poet and author, was born in England but lived for many years in the United States. He published many collections of poetry, notable for its wit and ideas, and a number of plays as well as literary and social criticism.

Words and Meanings

antithesis:	direct opposite	2
ritualized:	organized into fixed patterns of activity	5

Structure and Strategy

1. In what ORDER has Auden arranged his main points? How would the effect of the essay change if he had arranged them differently?
2. Why does Auden devote only two sentences (paragraph 2) to his definition of play?
3. How does Auden develop his definition of work (paragraph 3)? What expository techniques does he use?

Content and Purpose

1. Define "work," "labour," and "play," using only one sentence for each term.
2. For what reasons does Auden think that the percentage of "workers" is not likely to get bigger in our society? (See paragraphs 4 and 5.)
3. Why does Auden consider "workers" to be the luckiest people in the world?
4. For what reasons does Auden predict that violence will become an increasingly serious problem in our society?
5. Labourers, Auden maintains, will become increasingly troubled by boredom (see paragraph 5). To whom does he compare them? How are the amusements of both groups similar? Dissimilar? Why don't workers, in contrast to labourers, get bored?

Suggestions for Writing

1. Write a short paper in which you take a point of view opposite to Auden's: namely, that technology will prove to be more beneficial than harmful to society. Begin with a formal definition of technology, and then develop your definition using such patterns as example, cause and effect, comparison, or process.
2. Write an extended definition contrasting two kinds of workers: blue-collar, white-collar, pink-collar, professional, unskilled, tradespeople.

Wrong Ism

J. B. PRIESTLEY

1   There are three isms that we ought to consider very carefully—regionalism, nationalism, internationalism. Of these three the one there is most fuss about, the one that starts men shouting and marching and shooting, the one that seems to have all the depth and thrust and fire, is of course nationalism. Nine people out of ten, I fancy, would say that of this trio it is the one that really counts, the big boss. Regionalism and internationalism, they would add, are comparatively small, shadowy, rather cranky. And I believe all this to be quite wrong. Like many another big boss, nationalism is largely bogus°. It is like a bunch of flowers made of plastics.

2   The real flowers belong to regionalism. The mass of people everywhere may never have used the term. They are probably regionalists without knowing it. Because they have been brought up in a certain part of the world, they have formed perhaps quite unconsciously a deep attachment to its landscape and speech, its traditional customs, its food and drink, its songs and jokes. (There are of course always the rebels, often intellectuals and writers, but they are not the mass of people). They are rooted in their region. Indeed, without this attachment a man can have no roots.

3   So much of people's lives, from earliest childhood onwards, is deeply intertwined with the common life of the region, they cannot help feeling strongly about it. A threat to it is a knife pointing at the heart. How can life ever be the same if bullying strangers come to change everything? The form and colour, the very taste and smell of dear familiar things will be different, alien, life-destroying. It would be better to die fighting. And it is precisely this, the nourishing life of the region, for which common men have so often fought and died.

4   This attachment to the region exists on a level far deeper than that of any political hocus-pocus. When a man says "my country" with real feeling, he is thinking about his region, all that has made up his life, and not about that political entity, the nation. There can be some confusion here simply because some countries are so

"Wrong Ism" from *Essays of Five Decades* by J. B. Priestley. Copyright 1968 (in association with Little, Brown & Co. and Atlantic Monthly Press). Reprinted by permission of A. D. Peters & Co. Ltd.

small—and ours is one of them—and so old, again like ours, that much of what is national is also regional. Down the centuries, the nation, itself, so comparatively small, has been able to attach to itself the feeling really created by the region. (Even so there is something left over, as most people in Yorkshire or Devon, for example, would tell you.) This probably explains the fervent patriotism developed early in small countries. The English were announcing that they were English in the Middle Ages, before nationalism had arrived elsewhere.

If we deduct from nationalism all that it has borrowed or stolen   5 from regionalism, what remains is mostly rubbish. The nation, as distinct from the region, is largely the creation of power-men and political manipulators. Almost all nationalist movements are led by ambitious frustrated men determined to hold office. I am not blaming them. I would do the same if I were in their place and wanted power so badly. But nearly always they make use of the rich warm regional feeling, the emotional dynamo of the movement, while being almost untouched by it themselves. This is because they are not as a rule deeply loyal to any region themselves. Ambition and a love of power can eat like acid into the tissues of regional loyalty. It is hard, if not impossible, to retain a natural piety and yet be for ever playing both ends against the middle.

Being itself a power structure, devised by men of power, the   6 nation tends to think and act in terms of power. What would benefit the real life of the region, where men, women and children actually live, is soon sacrificed for the power and prestige of the nation. (And the personal vanity of presidents and ministers themselves, which historians too often disregard.) Among the new nations of our time innumerable peasants and labourers must have found themselves being cut down from five square meals a week to three in order to provide unnecessary airlines, military forces that can only be used against them and nobody else, great conference halls and official yachts and the rest. The last traces of imperialism and colonialism may have to be removed from Asia and Africa, where men can no longer endure being condemned to a permanent inferiority by the colour of their skins; but even so, the modern world, the real world of our time, does not want and would be far better without more and more nations, busy creating for themselves the very paraphernalia that western Europe is now trying to abolish. You are compelled to answer more questions when trying to spend half a day in Cambodia than you are now travelling from the Hook of Holland to Syracuse.

This brings me to internationalism. I dislike this term, which   7 I used only to complete the isms. It suggests financiers and dubious° promoters living nowhere but in luxury hotels; a shallow world of entrepreneurs° and impresarios°. (Was it Sacha Guitry who said that impresarios were men who spoke many languages but all with a foreign accent?) The internationalism I have in mind here is best described as world civilisation. It is life considered on a global scale. Most of our communications and transport already exist on this high wide level. So do many other things from medicine to meteorology. Our astronomers and physicists (except where they have allowed themselves to be hush-hushed) work here. The UN special agencies, about which we hear far too little, have contributed more and more to this world civilisation. All the arts, when they are arts and not chunks of nationalist propaganda, naturally take their place in it. And it grows, widens, deepens, in spite of the fact that for every dollar, ruble, pound or franc spent in explaining and praising it, a thousand are spent by the nations explaining and praising themselves.

8   This world civilisation and regionalism can get along together, especially if we keep ourselves sharply aware of their quite different but equally important values and rewards. A man can make his contribution to world civilisation and yet remain strongly regional in feeling: I know several men of this sort. There is of course the danger—it is with us now—of the global style flattening out the regional, taking local form, colour, flavour, away for ever, disinheriting future generations, threatening them with sensuous poverty and a huge boredom. But to understand and appreciate regionalism is to be on guard against this danger. And we must therefore make a clear distinction between regionalism and nationalism.

9   It is nationalism that tries to check the growth of world civilisation. And nationalism, when taken on a global scale, is more aggressive and demanding now than it has ever been before. This in the giant powers is largely disguised by the endless fuss in public about rival ideologies, now a largely unreal quarrel. What is intensely real is the glaring nationalism. Even the desire to police the world is nationalistic in origin. (Only the world can police the world.) Moreover, the nation-states of today are for the most part far narrower in their outlook, far more inclined to allow prejudice against the foreigner to impoverish their own style of living, than the old imperial states were. It should be part of world civilisation that men with particular skills, perhaps the product of the very regionalism they are rebelling against, should be able to move easily from country to country, to exercise those skills, in anything from teaching the violin to running a new type of factory to managing an old hotel. But nationalism, especially of the newer sort, would rather see everything done badly than allow a few non-nationals to get to work. And people face a barrage of passports, visas,

immigration controls, labour permits; and in this respect are worse off than they were in 1900. But even so, in spite of all that nationalism can do—so long as it keeps its nuclear bombs to itself—the internationalism I have in mind, slowly creating a world civilisation, cannot be checked.

Nevertheless, we are still backing the wrong ism. Almost all   10 our money goes on the middle one, nationalism, the rotten meat between the two healthy slices of bread. We need regionalism to give us roots and that very depth of feeling which nationalism unjustly and greedily claims for itself. We need internationalism to save the world and to broaden and heighten our civilisation. While regional man enriches the lives that international man is already working to keep secure and healthy, national man, drunk with power, demands our loyalty, money and applause, and poisons the very air with his dangerous nonsense.

┌─────────────────────────┐
│   │
│   │
└─────────────────────────┘

J.B. PRIESTLEY

J. B. Priestley (1894–1984), the English novelist and dramatist, wrote a number of essays on social and political themes. His best-known novel is *The Good Companions*, while a number of his plays, such as *Time and the Conways*, deal with the nature of time.

Words and Meanings   Paragraph

bogus:	sham, phony	1
dubious:	unreliable, of suspicious character	7
entrepreneur:	self-employed promoter, money-maker	
impresario:	producer, usually of some form of public entertainment	

Structure and Strategy

1. Where and what is Priestley's thesis statement?
2. What SIMILE does Priestley introduce to emphasize the difference between regionalism and nationalism?
3. What expository techniques does Priestley use to develop his definition of regionalism (paragraphs 2 to 4)? How does he develop his definition of nationalism (paragraphs 5 and 6)?
4. What SIMILE in paragraph 5 forcefully communicates Priestley's dislike of the nationalistic spirit?
5. Priestley sums up his attitude to the three "isms" in a METAPHOR in paragraph 10. What is it? How does it contribute to the effectiveness of his conclusion?

Content and Purpose

1. Why has Priestley titled this essay "Wrong Ism"?
2. In a single sentence for each, define "regionalism," "nationalism," and "internationalism."
3. Summarize Priestley's objections to nationalism.
4. Priestley claims that "the nation-states of today are for the most part far narrower in their outlook, far more inclined to allow prejudice against the foreigner to impoverish their own state of living, than the old imperial states were" (paragraph 9). What does he mean by this charge? Can you think of examples to support or to disprove this claim?
5. Canada is often described as "a nation of regions." Do you think this is an accurate description? In other words, has Canada managed to avoid the "rubbish" of nationalism (see paragraphs 5 and 6)?

Suggestions for Writing

1. Write a paper in which you define three fads, personality types, or leisure activities. As Priestley has done in his essay, use comparison and contrast to help make clear to your readers which of the three you favour most and which you like least.
2. Write an essay which defines the region of Canada in which you live (or have lived). Use examples, comparison and contrast, or any other expository technique to define the region and its unique characteristics.

Being a Man

PAUL THEROUX

1　　　　　　　　　　　here is a pathetic sentence in the chapter "Fetishism" in Dr. Norman Cameron's book *Personality Development and Psychopathology*. It goes, "Fetishists are nearly always men; and their commonest fetish° is a woman's shoe." I cannot read that sentence without thinking that it is just one more awful thing about being a man—and perhaps it is an important thing to know about us.

"Being a Man" from *Sunrise with Seamonsters* by Paul Theroux. Copyright © 1985 by Cape Cod Scriveners Company. Reprinted by permission of Houghton Mifflin Company.

I have always disliked being a man. The whole idea of manhood in America is pitiful, in my opinion. This version of masculinity is a little like having to wear an ill-fitting coat for one's entire life (by contrast, I imagine femininity to be an oppressive sense of nakedness). Even the expression "Be a man!" strikes me as insulting and abusive. It means: [b]e stupid, be unfeeling, obedient, soldierly and stop thinking. Man means "manly"—how can one think about men without considering the terrible ambition of manliness? And yet it is part of every man's life. It is a hideous and crippling lie; it not only insists on difference and connives° at superiority, it is also by its very nature destructive—emotionally damaging and socially harmful.

The youth who is subverted, as most are, into believing in the masculine ideal is effectively separated from women and he spends the rest of his life finding women a riddle and a nuisance. Of course, there is a female version of this male affliction. It begins with mothers encouraging little girls to say (to other adults) "Do you like my new dress?" In a sense, little girls are traditionally urged to please adults with a kind of coquettishness°, while boys are enjoined to behave like monkeys towards each other. The nine-year-old coquette proceeds to become womanish in a subtle power game in which she learns to be sexually indispensable, socially decorative and always alert to a man's sense of inadequacy.

Femininity—being lady-like—implies needing a man as witness and seducer; but masculinity celebrates the exclusive company of men. That is why it is so grotesque; and that is also why there is no manliness without inadequacy—because it denies men the natural friendship of women.

It is very hard to imagine any concept of manliness that does not belittle women, and it begins very early. At an age when I wanted to meet girls—let's say the treacherous years of thirteen to sixteen—I was told to take up a sport, get more fresh air, join the Boy Scouts, and I was urged not to read so much. It was the 1950s and if you asked too many questions about sex you were sent to camp—boy's camp, of course: the nightmare. Nothing is more unnatural or prison-like than a boy's camp, but if it were not for them we would have no Elks' Lodges°, no pool rooms, no boxing matches, no Marines.

And perhaps no sports as we know them. Everyone is aware of how few in number are the athletes who behave like gentlemen. Just as high school basketball teaches you how to be a poor loser, the manly attitude towards sports seems to be little more than a recipe for creating bad marriages, social misfits, moral degenerates, sadists, latent rapists and just plain louts. I regard high school sports as a drug far worse than marijuana, and it is the reason that the average tennis champion, say, is a pathetic oaf.

7   Any objective study would find the quest for manliness essentially right-wing, puritanical, cowardly, neurotic and fueled largely
by a fear of women. It is also certainly philistine°. There is no book-
hater like a Little League coach. But indeed all the creative arts are
obnoxious to the manly ideal, because at their best the arts are
pursued by uncompetitive and essentially solitary people. It makes
it very hard for a creative youngster, for any boy who expresses
the desire to be alone seems to be saying that there is something
wrong with him.

8   It ought to be clear by now that I have something of an objection
to the way we turn boys into men. It does not surprise me that
when the President of the United States has his customary weekend
off he dresses like a cowboy—it is both a measure of his insecurity
and his willingness to please. In many ways, American culture
does little more for a man than prepare him for modeling clothes
in the L.L. Bean° catalogue. I take this as a personal insult because
for many years I found it impossible to admit to myself that I
wanted to be a writer. It was my guilty secret, because being a
writer was incompatible with being a man.

9   There are people who might deny this, but that is because the
American writer, typically, has been so at pains to prove his manliness that we have come to see literariness and manliness as mingled qualities. But first there was a fear that writing was not a
manly profession—indeed, not a profession at all. (The paradox in
American letters is that it has always been easier for a woman to
write and for a man to be published.) Growing up, I had thought
of sports as wasteful and humiliating, and the idea of manliness
was a bore. My wanting to become a writer was not a flight from
that oppressive role-playing, but I quickly saw that it was at odds
with it. Everything in stereotyped manliness goes against the life
of the mind. The Hemingway personality is too tedious to go into
here, and in any case his exertions are well-known, but certainly
it was not until this aberrant° behavior was examined by feminists
in the 1960s that any male writer dared question the pugnacity° in
Hemingway's fiction. All the bullfighting and arm wrestling and
elephant shooting diminished Hemingway as a writer, but it is
consistent with a prevailing attitude in American writing: one cannot be a male writer without first proving that one is a man.

10   It is normal in America for a man to be dismissive or even
somewhat apologetic about being a writer. Various factors make it
easier. There is a heartiness about journalism that makes it acceptable—journalism is the manliest form of American writing and,
therefore, the profession the most independent-minded women
seek (yes, it is an illusion, but that is my point). Fiction-writing is
equated with a kind of dispirited failure and is only manly when
it produces wealth—money is masculinity. So is drinking. Being a

drunkard is another assertion, if misplaced, of manliness. The American male writer is traditionally proud of his heavy drinking. But we are also a very literal-minded people. A man proves his manhood in America in old-fashioned ways. He kills lions, like Hemingway; or he hunts ducks, like Nathanael West; or he makes pronouncements like, "A man should carry enough knife to defend himself with," as James Jones once said to a *Life* interviewer. Or he says he can drink you under the table. But even tiny drunken William Faulkner loved to mount a horse and go fox hunting, and Jack Kerouac roistered up and down Manhattan in a lumberjack shirt (and spent every night of *The Subterraneans* with his mother in Queens). And we are familiar with the lengths to which Norman Mailer is prepared, in his endearing way, to prove that he is just as much a monster as the next man.

When the novelist John Irving was revealed as a wrestler, peo-   11
ple took him to be a very serious writer; and even a bubble rep-
utation like Eric (*Love Story*) Segal's was enhanced by the news that he ran the marathon in a respectable time. How surprised we would be if Joyce Carol Oates were revealed as a sumo wrestler or Joan Didion active in pumping iron. "Lives in New York City with her three children" is the typical woman writer's biographical note, for just as the male writer must prove he has achieved a sort of mus-cular manhood, the woman writer—or rather her publicists—must prove her motherhood.

There would be no point in saying any of this if it were not   12
generally accepted that to be a man is somehow—even now in feminist-influenced America—a privilege. It is on the contrary an unmerciful and punishing burden. Being a man is bad enough; being manly is appalling (in this sense, women's lib has done much more for men than for women). It is the sinister silliness of men's fashions, and a clubby attitude in the arts. It is the subversion of good students. It is the so-called "Dress Code" of the Ritz-Carlton Hotel in Boston, and it is the institutionalized cheating in college sports. It is the most primitive insecurity.

And this is also why men often object to feminism but are   13
afraid to explain why: of course women have a justified grievance, but most men believe—and with reason—that their lives are just as bad.

PAUL THEROUX

Paul Theroux is an American-born novelist, travel writer, critic, and poet. After graduating from university, Theroux spent ten years travelling abroad, teaching in Malawi, Uganda, Italy, and Singapore before settling in England.

Much of his writing centres on characters whose experiences of a foreign culture have left them disillusioned and critical of the values of their own society. Among his best-known works are *The Mosquito Coast* (1981), *Picture Palace* (1977), *The Great Railway Bazaar* (1975), and *Kingdom by the Sea* (1983).

Words and Meanings

Paragraph

1	fetish:	object to which one is irrationally devoted or attached; here, in the sense of sexual arousal
2	connives:	schemes or co-operates secretly
3	coquettishness:	flirtatiousness
5	Elks' Lodges:	kind of club; fraternal society for men
7	philistine:	anti-intellectual
8	L. L. Bean catalogue:	American mail-order catalogue for fashionable sportswear, hunting and camping equipment
9	aberrant:	erratic or abnormal
	pugnacity:	quarrelsome tendency; desire to fight

Structure and Strategy

1. How successful is the first paragraph in catching the reader's interest?
2. What is the TONE of paragraphs 5 to 8?
3. What is the topic sentence of paragraph 9 and how is it developed in the next two paragraphs?
4. Do paragraphs 12 and 13 form a successful conclusion to this essay? Why or why not?

Content and Purpose

1. What idea or concept is Theroux defining in this essay? Is his definition successful or unsuccessful in your opinion?
2. What does Theroux mean when he says he has always "disliked being a man"? What is the distinction between "being a man" and "being manly"?
3. In what ways are both the masculine ideal and the feminine ideal damaging to one's identity and personality? (See paragraphs 3 and 4.)
4. What are the reasons Theroux objects to the way North American society rears male children, the way we "turn boys into men"?
5. Would you describe Theroux as a feminist? Why or why not?

Suggestions for Writing

1. Think of a particular man or some men whom you admire and write an essay defining what it means to be a man.
2. Theroux discusses the difficulty of being a man. Are there difficulties associated with being a woman? Write an essay defining what it means to be a woman.

Altruism

LEWIS THOMAS

Altruism has always been one of biology's deep mysteries. Why should any animal, off on its own, specified and labeled by all sorts of signals as its individual self, choose to give up its life in aid of someone else? Nature, long viewed as a wild, chaotic battlefield swarmed across by more than ten million different species, comprising unnumbered billions of competing selves locked in endless combat, offers only one sure measure of success: survival. Survival, in the cool economics of biology, means simply the persistence of one's own genes in the generations to follow.

At first glance, it seems an unnatural act, a violation of nature, to give away one's life, or even one's possessions, to another. And yet, in the face of improbability, examples of altruism abound. When a worker bee, patrolling the frontiers of the hive, senses the nearness of a human intruder, the bee's attack is pure, unqualified suicide; the sting is barbed, and in the act of pulling away the insect is fatally injured. Other varieties of social insects, most spectacularly the ants and higher termites, contain castes of soldiers for whom self-sacrifice is an everyday chore.

It is easy to dismiss the problem by saying that "altruism" is the wrong technical term for behavior of this kind. The word is a human word, pieced together to describe an unusual aspect of human behavior, and we should not be using it for the behavior of mindless automata°. A honeybee has no connection to creatures

"Altruism" from *Late Night Thoughts on Listening to Mahler's Ninth Symphony* by Lewis Thomas. Copyright © 1982 by Lewis Thomas. Reprinted by permission of Viking Penguin Inc.

like us, no brain for figuring out the future, no way of predicting the inevitable outcome of that sting.

4   But the meditation of the 50,000 or so connected minds of a whole hive is not so easy to dismiss. A multitude of bees can tell the time of day, calculate the geometry of the sun's position, argue about the best location for the next swarm. Bees do a lot of close observing of other bees; maybe they know what follows stinging and do it anyway.

5   Altruism is not restricted to the social insects, in any case. Birds risk their lives, sometimes lose them, in efforts to distract the attention of predators from the nest. Among baboons, zebras, moose, wildebeests, and wild dogs there are always stubbornly fated guardians, prepared to be done in first in order to buy time for the herd to escape.

6   It is genetically determined behavior, no doubt about it. Animals have genes for altruism, and those genes have been selected in the evolution of many creatures because of the advantage they confer for the continuing survival of the species. It is, looked at in this way, not the emotion-laden problem that we feel when we try to put ourselves in the animal's place; it is just another plain fact of life, perhaps not as hard a fact as some others, something rather nice, in fact, to think about.

7   J.B.S. Haldane, the eminent British geneticist, summarized the chilly arithmetic of the problem by announcing, "I would give up my life for two brothers or eight cousins." This calculates the requirement for ultimate self-interest: the preservation and survival of an individual's complement of genes. Trivers, Hamilton, and others have constructed mathematical models to account nicely for the altruistic behavior of social insects, quantifying the self-serving profit for the genes of the defending bee in the act of tearing its abdomen apart. The hive is filled with siblings, ready to carry the *persona* of the dying bee through all the hive's succeeding generations. Altruism is based on kinship; by preserving kin, one preserves one's self. In a sense.

8   Haldane's prediction has the sound of a beginning sequence: two brothers, eight (presumably) first cousins, and then another series of much larger numbers of more distant relatives. Where does the influence tail off? At what point does the sharing of the putative° altruist's genes become so diluted as to be meaningless? Would the line on a graph charting altruism plummet to zero soon after those eight cousins, or is it a long, gradual slope? When the combat marine throws himself belly-down on the live grenade in order to preserve the rest of his platoon, is this the same sort of altruism, or is this an act without any technically biological meaning? Surely the marine's genes, most of them, will be blown away

forever; the statistical likelihood of having two brothers or eight cousins in that platoon is extremely small. And yet there he is, belly-down as if by instinct, and the same kind of event has been recorded often enough in wartime to make it seem a natural human act, normal enough, even though rare, to warrant the stocking of medals by the armed services.

At what point do our genetic ties to each other become so remote that we feel no instinctual urge to help? I can imagine an argument about this, with two sides, but it would be a highly speculative discussion, not by any means pointless but still impossible to settle one way or the other. One side might assert, with total justification, that altruistic behavior among human beings has nothing at all to do with genetics, that there is no such thing as a gene for self-sacrifice, not even a gene for helpfulness, or concern, or even affection. These are attributes that must be learned from society, acquired by cultures, taught by example. The other side could maintain, with equal justification, since the facts are not known, precisely the opposite position: we get along together in human society because we are genetically designed to be social animals, and we are obliged, by instructions from our genes, to be useful to each other. This side would argue further that when we behave badly, killing or maiming or snatching, we are acting on misleading information learned from the wrong kinds of society we put together; if our cultures were not deformed, we would be better company, paying attention to what our genes are telling us.

For the purposes of the moment I shall take the side of the sociobiologists because I wish to carry their side of the argument a certain distance afield, beyond the human realm. I have no difficulty in imagining a close enough resemblance among the genomes° of all human beings, of all races and geographic origins, to warrant a biological mandate° for all of us to do whatever we can to keep the rest of us, the species, alive. I maintain, despite the moment's evidence against the claim, that we are born and grow up with a fondness for each other, and we have genes for that. We can be talked out of it, for the genetic message is like a distant music and some of us are hard-of-hearing. Societies are noisy affairs, drowning out the sound of ourselves and our connection. Hard-of-hearing, we go to war. Stone-deaf, we make thermonuclear missiles. Nonetheless, the music is there, waiting for more listeners.

But the matter does not end with our species. If we are to take seriously the notion that the sharing of similar genes imposes a responsibility on the sharers to sustain each other, and if I am right in guessing that even very distant cousins carry at least traces of this responsibility and will act on it whenever they can, then the whole world becomes something to be concerned about on solidly scientific, reductionist, genetic grounds. For we have cousins more than we can count, and they are all over the place, run by genes so similar to ours that the differences are minor technicalities. All of us, men, women, children, fish, sea grass, sandworms, dolphins, hamsters, and soil bacteria, everything alive on the planet, roll ourselves along through all our generations by replicating DNA° and RNA°, and although the alignments of nucleotides within these molecules are different in different species, the molecules themselves are fundamentally the same substance. We make our proteins in the same old way, and many of the enzymes most needed for cellular life are everywhere identical.

12   This is, in fact, the way it should be. If cousins are defined by common descent, the human family is only one small and very recent addition to a much larger family in a tree extending back at least 3.5 billion years. Our common ancestor was a single cell from which all subsequent cells derived, most likely a cell resembling one of today's bacteria in today's soil. For almost three-fourths of the earth's life, cells of that first kind were the whole biosphere°. It was less than a billion years ago that cells like ours appeared in the first marine invertebrates, and these were somehow pieced together by the joining up and fusion of the earlier primitive cells, retaining the same blood lines. Some of the joiners, bacteria that had learned how to use oxygen, are with us still, part of our flesh, lodged inside the cells of all animals, all plants, moving us from place to place and doing our breathing for us. Now there's a set of cousins!

13   Even if I try to discount the other genetic similarities linking human beings to all other creatures by common descent, the existence of these beings in my cells is enough, in itself, to relate me to the chestnut tree in my backyard and to the squirrel in that tree.

14   There ought to be a mathematics for connections like this before claiming any kinship function, but the numbers are too big. At the same time, even if we wanted to, we cannot think the sense of obligation away. It is there, maybe in our genes for the recognition of cousins, or, if not, it ought to be there in our intellects for having learned about the matter. Altruism, in its biological sense, is required of us. We have an enormous family to look after, or perhaps that assumes too much, making us sound like official gardeners and zookeepers for the planet, responsibilities for which we are probably not yet grown-up enough. We may need new technical terms for concern, respect, affection, substitutes for altruism. But at least we should acknowledge the family ties and, with them, the obligations. If we do it wrong, scattering pollutants, clouding the atmosphere with too much carbon dioxide, extinguishing the

thin carapace° of ozone, burning up the forests, dropping the bombs, rampaging at large through nature as though we owned the place, there will be a lot of paying back to do and, at the end, nothing to pay back with.

```
┌─────────────────────────┐
│                         │
└─────────────────────────┘
```

LEWIS THOMAS

Chancellor of New York's Sloan-Kettering Center, the largest cancer research hospital in the world, Dr. Lewis Thomas combines the careers of research scientist, physician, teacher, and writer. The recipient of many scientific and academic awards, Lewis Thomas strives in his essays to humanize science and to remind us that medicine is an art. A recurring theme in books such as *The Lives of a Cell* (1974), *The Medusa and the Snail* (1979) and *The Youngest Science* (1983) is the interrelatedness of all life forms.

Words and Meanings

Paragraph

automata:	unthinking, machinelike organisms	3
putative:	supposed	8
genomes:	chromosomal structures	10
mandate:	contract, requirement	
DNA	deoxyribonucleic acid; the molecule that carries genetic information	11
RNA	ribonucleic acid; the substance that transmits genetic information from the nucleus to the surrounding cellular material	
biosphere:	earth's zone of life—from crust to atmosphere— encompassing all living organisms	12
carapace:	outer shell, such as on a crab or tortoise	14

Structure and Strategy

1. What two ABSTRACT terms does Thomas define in his introductory paragraph? How does he do so?
2. The body of this essay can be divided into sections, as follows: paragraphs 2 to 5, 6 to 8, 9 to 10, 11 to 13. Identify the main idea Thomas develops in each of these four sections, and list some of the expository techniques he uses in his development.
3. From paragraphs 1 to 8, Thomas writes in the third person. Why does he shift to the first person in paragraph 9 and continue in first person until the end? To understand the different effects of

the two POINTS OF VIEW, try rewriting some of the sentences in paragraph 14 in the third person.

4. In paragraph 10, Thomas introduces and develops a SIMILE to explain his faith in the "genetic message." Identify the simile and explain how it helps prepare the reader for the conclusion.

5. What concluding strategy does Thomas use in paragraph 14? How does his conclusion contribute to the UNITY of the essay?

Content and Purpose

1. What is Thomas's thesis? Can you summarize it in a single sentence?

2. In paragraph 1, Thomas introduces the fundamental IRONY on which this essay is based. Explain in your own words the ironic connection between altruism and survival.

3. Identify six or seven specific examples of animals that, according to Thomas, display altruistic behaviour. What ILLUSTRATION does Thomas use to show the altruistic behaviour of human beings?

4. Explain in your own words Thomas's claim that altruism is not an "emotion-laden problem" but that it is based on self-interest (see paragraph 7).

5. In paragraph 9, Thomas identifies two opposing explanations for altruistic behaviour: the cultural and the sociobiological. Summarize these in your own words. Which side does Thomas take and why? (See paragraphs 10 to 13.)

Suggestions for Writing

1. Write an extended definition of the term "parenthood." Explain the reasons why people choose to have children, an act that involves a considerable amount of self-sacrifice.

2. Define another abstract term such as "wisdom," "integrity," "freedom," "evil," "success." Attempt to define it as clearly and concretely as Thomas does "altruism."

Additional Suggestions for Writing: Definition

Write an extended definition of one of the topics below.

addiction
team spirit
superstition
maturity
elitism
conspicuous
    consumption
wisdom
terrorism
creativity
censorship

physical fitness
juvenile delinquency
a typical Canadian
a Yuppie
chauvinism
sin
beauty
a conservative
a liberal
the ideal job (boss, employee, parent,
    roommate, friend, spouse, child)

U N I T

7

Argument and Persuasion: Appealing to Reason and Emotion

What? The Definition

We all know what is meant by the word **persuasion**. It's bringing someone over to our side, sometimes with a nod, a wink, usually with a word or two. The meaning of the word **argument** is reasonably clear as well. An argument is a disagreement, an altercation, a verbal brawl of sorts; an argument may occur when someone resists our attempts at persuasion. As Unit Six on definition pointed out, however, occasionally words have specific meanings different from their generally accepted meanings.

Persuasion is more than encouraging someone to come on side; argument means more than disagreement. In the context of writing, argument and persuasion refer to a kind of writing that has a particular purpose—one that differs in degree, if not in kind, from the purpose of expository prose.

The introductions to the first six units of this text have explained structural patterns commonly found in *exposition*—writing intended primarily to explain. It is true that many explanations contain some element of argument or persuasion: consider Berton's satire on divorce or Mitford's indictment of embalming in Unit Two, for instance. Nevertheless, the primary purpose of expository writing is to *inform* the reader.

Argument and persuasion have a different primary purpose; they attempt to lead the reader to share the writer's belief and, perhaps, even to act on this belief. Naturally, readers are not likely to be persuaded of anything unless the concept is first clearly explained to them. In this chapter, we will consider argument and persuasion as writing strategies designed to *convince* the reader of an opinion, judgment, or course of action.

There are two ways to convince people: through their minds or through their hearts. *Argument* is the term often applied to the logical approach, convincing a person by way of the mind. *Persuasion* is the term often applied to the emotional approach, convincing a person by way of the heart. Often we can use both routes. We decide which approach to use, logical or emotional—or a combination of the two—depending on the issue we are discussing. For instance, if we want to persuade someone to give money for famine relief, we might appeal to the reader's emotions with descriptions of blighted landscapes, emaciated adults, and starving children. We want our readers to feel the victims' plight and support the cause. However, if we want to argue that a highway needs widening, there is likely to be little emotional punch. In a case like this, we would appeal to the reader's mind by providing logical, well-developed reasons. The issue itself determines which approach is the best one to take.

An important part of convincing the reader is getting the facts straight. An argument is only as strong as the logic behind it. Even when appealing primarily to the reader's feelings, the writer must do so reasonably or risk producing a paper that is sentimental, bullying, or manipulative, and therefore not persuasive. Most of us have been pestered by "persuaders" who attempt to convince us that water fluoridation is a Communist plot, or that all Irish are drunkards, or that people who smoke marijuana inevitably get addicted to heroin. The reasoning that leads to such conclusions is faulty. To be convincing, the reasoning must be sound; if it is not, readers are likely to be confused or insulted rather than convinced.

There are two fundamental ways of reasoning: **induction** and **deduction**. Exploring these logical processes will help you to clarify your own ideas before you try to convince someone else.

Inductive reasoning is the logical process of examining a number of individual cases and coming to a general conclusion. For example, if you order pizza from Guido's Pizzeria once and it's cold when delivered, a one-time-only delay may have occurred. But if you get cold pizzas three times in a row from Guido's, and talk to four friends who have likewise got cold pizza from Guido's, it is fair to make a generalization: Guido's pizzas are usually cold by the time they get to you. You'd better phone another pizzeria. This simple example illustrates the straightforward, let's-look-at-the-facts approach of inductive reasoning. On a more lofty level, we find that induction is also the reasoning of the science laboratory and the law court. For example, if a microbiologist finds bacillus X in the bloodstreams of a significant number of flu victims, she may eventually generalize that bacillus X is the cause of that particular strain of flu.

To use inductive reasoning effectively, you must make sure that your evidence is solid, that it isn't just hearsay or unsupported opinion. You must also ensure that you have sampled enough evidence. You may know three teenage mothers who do not take good care of their babies, but three instances are not enough evidence to dismiss all teenagers as poor mothers.

Deductive reasoning is the flip side of inductive reasoning. Instead of considering specific cases to come up with a general statement, deduction applies a general statement to a specific instance and reasons through to a conclusion. Deduction is the formal logic of the syllogism, a traditional three-part formula:

MAJOR PREMISE: All humans are mortal.
MINOR PREMISE: Socrates[1] is human.
CONCLUSION: Socrates is mortal.

Deductive logic is only as solid as its premises. Deducing specifics from faulty generalizations is dangerous reasoning, as the next example shows:

MAJOR PREMISE: All Lebanese are terrorists.
MINOR PREMISE: Yusuf is Lebanese.
CONCLUSION: Yusuf is a terrorist.

Given the flawed nature of the major premise, the conclusion is erroneous. It is also the product of a bigoted mind.

In short, any writing intended to convince must be grounded in sound logic. Both inductive and deductive reasoning are only as sound as the observations or the premises on which they are based. If your readers are able to detect logical gaps, faulty premises, or

---

[1]Socrates (469–399 B.C.) was a Greek thinker and teacher who, along with his disciples Plato and Aristotle, is considered the founder of Western philosophy.

unsupportable generalizations in your reasoning, they will not be convinced of anything you say.

Why? The Purpose

Papers designed to convince the reader answer the question, "What are the reasons for—or against—S?" To answer this question, you must first critically assess the belief, proposal, or course of action on which your paper is based. Keep in mind that "critical" means to make a judgment—for or against—not just to "find fault." Once you have tested the logic of your viewpoint, you can use argument and persuasion to accomplish one of two purposes—and sometimes both.

You may simply want your readers to share your opinion, to agree with the argument you present. You may want to bring them over to your side. For instance, you could try to convince readers that Canada's involvement in space exploration is valuable both economically and technologically.

On the other hand, you may intend not only to convince your readers to agree with you but also to convince them to *do* something, to act in some way, based on your opinion. For example, you might argue that regular exercise promotes health and lengthens life expectancy; hence, the reader should get involved in a regular exercise program. Usually you need to accomplish the first aim, getting the reader's agreement (especially if the topic is a controversial one), before you attempt the second, moving the reader to act. For instance, a writer might argue for mandatory jail sentences for drunk drivers. The writer might then go on to urge readers to write letters, circulate petitions, and pressure legislators to enact such a law. Proposals such as this one require that you first convince your readers of the validity of your opinion and then motivate them to support your cause.

Learning about the logical processes that underlie argumentation and persuasion has another purpose, one that extends beyond the act of writing. The "hidden agenda" in mastering this rhetorical mode is that learning to reason well enables us to detect other people's attempts to pull persuasive wool over our eyes. If we know the rules of sound logical argument, we can see through the tricks of those who would like to manipulate or lie to us. We frequently meet relatively innocuous examples, such as the promises of television commercials: Drink Blue—you'll be part of the crowd; brush with Glitzodent—you'll get your man; buy a diamond—your marriage will last forever. At other times we encounter profoundly disturbing distortions and lies: Blacks are inferior—they should not be allowed to vote; the Holocaust never happened—the millions who were "murdered" never existed. It is imperative that we recognize the twisted logic of those who would persuade us to evil. It was, after all, Adolf Hitler who forewarned in *Mein Kampf*: "The broad mass of a nation . . . will more easily fall victim to a big lie than to a small one." A person aware of the principles of sound reasoning is not easily victimized by lies, big or small.

How? The Technique

Persuasive papers can be developed in a variety of ways. It is possible, as you will see in the readings for this unit, to use a number of different structural patterns to convince your readers. For instance, a *cause-effect* structure might be an ideal way to urge action to end the sulphur emissions that cause acid rain. *Comparison* might offer an opportunity to assess the efficiency of Canada's regulated airline industry as opposed to the deregulated industry in the United States and to argue in favour of one approach. Most of the expository patterns can be adapted to persuasive purposes.

Two patterns are specific to argument and persuasion. One is the classic *their side—my side* strategy, which is particularly useful when you are arguing a controversial position that will provoke serious dispute. This pattern involves presenting the "con" (or "against") points of your opponents first, then refuting them with the "pro" (or "for") side of your argument. For example, if a writer were to argue that women in the Canadian Armed Forces should participate in combat, she might choose to present the opposing view and then counter each point with well-reasoned arguments of her own. Such a strategy impresses readers with its fairness and tends to neutralize opposition.

The second structural pattern specific to argument and persuasion makes use of the familiar thesis statement. The first step in this procedure is discovering, examining, and stating an *opinion* about an issue. Of course, the logic of your opinion must be scrutinized carefully before the opinion can serve as the subject of a persuasive paper. Here are three examples of clearly stated opinions that could be expanded into thesis statements:

1. General education is an essential part of the college curriculum. (See "Why Are We Reading This Stuff, Anyway?")

2. Cheating is pervasive in college sports. (See Harry Bruce's essay, "May the Best Cheater Win.")

3. A married person has no right to pursue his or her own sexual gratification at the expense of a spouse's happiness. (See C.S. Lewis's essay, "We Have No 'Right to Happiness.' ")

The crucial test for a satisfactory statement of opinion is that someone could argue the contrary point of view: "General education is not an essential part of the college curriculum"; "Cheating is not often found in college sports"; "A married person has the right to pursue his or her own sexual gratification, despite the express wishes of a spouse."

Once the opinion is clearly stated, the second step is to assemble *reasons* to support it. Here again, logic is essential. Apply the rules of evidence, as they are called in courtrooms. Your reasons should be *accurate*, *relevant*, and *complete*. Facts, especially statistics, must be precise. For example, a recent letter to *The Globe and Mail* lamented that only 32 percent of the books purchased by the Toronto Public Library were written by women, while 48 percent of the fiction purchased by the Antigonish Public Library was written by women. Given that no totals were provided, that the categories of books are different, and that Toronto and Antigonish are hardly comparable in size and diversity of population, the statistic was misleading and made the writer's entire argument suspect. As Britain's eminently quotable Prime Minister, Benjamin Disraeli, once said, "There are three kinds of lies: lies, damned lies, and statistics." The writer of a persuasive paper, like the witness in a courtroom, should tell the truth, the whole truth and nothing but the truth.

Once you have ensured that your reasons are accurate, relevant (clearly related to the stated opinion), and complete (omitting no vital premise), the next step is to arrange these reasons in order. The usual arrangement is climactic order, which means building from least important to most important. In climactic order, you save your most compelling reasons for the end of the paper when the reader may already be inclined to accept your point of view. For example, you might argue that censorship of books is dangerous because it restricts an individual's right to read, it impedes artists' ability to create, and it jeopardizes an entire society's freedom of expression. Arranged in this order, the argument proceeds from the individual level to the threat to the artistic community and on to the larger implications of censorship for society as a whole. The reasons are separate, yet linked, and build upon each other convincingly.

The last step is to link the opinion to the reasons in a grammatically parallel thesis statement (**O** stands for your statement of opinion; **1**, **2**, and **3** represent your reasons):

> O because of 1, 2, and 3.

Example: Censorship of books is dangerous because it restricts the individual's right to read, impedes artists' ability to create, and jeopardizes society's freedom of expression.

Example: General education is an essential part of the college curriculum because it enhances one's ability to build a career and to live a full life.

Clearly, bringing someone over to our side through well-chosen words is a challenge. Argument and persuasion are probably the most formidable writing tasks that we undertake, yet they may also be the most important. When we are engaged in argument and persuasion, we distinguish ourselves from those who can only nod, grunt, wag a tail, or brandish a club over another's head. It is possible to convince others to agree with us and even prevail upon them to act, armed with nothing more than our logic, our feelings, our words and, ultimately, our integrity. Effective persuasion is an art that truly deserves to be called civilized.

The essay that follows expands one of the thesis statements given above into a convincing argument:

"Why Are We Reading This Stuff, Anyway?"

Introduction (uses an anecdote to ask an important question)

As an English teacher in a community college, I encounter large numbers of bright, highly motivated students who are committed to particular career paths. English is not their favourite subject. One of these students—a would-be microbiologist—challenged me as we worked our way through a Faulkner piece one gray, wintry Monday morning. "Why," he demanded, "are we reading this stuff, anyway?" Not being especially quick on my verbal feet so early in the morning, I burbled something about the value of literature and of empathy, the ability to see the world through someone else's eyes. I could tell by his glower that he was unconvinced.

Now I'd like to step back and answer the larger question inherent in my student's query. Why do colleges require anything other than skills training? Why bother with the seemingly unrelated, "ir-

Thesis statement

First point (the reason is developed through well-chosen examples)

relevant" part of the curriculum called "general education"? To my microbiology student and the many others who ask this question, I would like to respond: general education is an essential part of the curriculum because it enhances one's ability to build a career and to live a full life.

Skills training alone is enough to get you a job. College or university training will provide you with the entry-level professional skills that most employers require. The important word here, however, is "entry-level." Your degree or diploma does not entitle you to an executive suite; it enables you to find a footing on the very first rung of the ladder. To proceed up that ladder, to build a career, you must continue to learn and to develop numerous other skills. You must be able to read quickly and thoroughly, to analyze all kinds of information logically, to solve problems effectively, and to communicate both in speech and in writing in an articulate and reasonably sophisticated way. In addition, you will be expected to function in a world where people are comfortable with ideas. The latest television miniseries, fashion fad, or hockey brawl will not always be appropriate conversational fare. You may be expected to know who Sigmund Freud, John Maynard Keynes, or Dr. Samuel Johnson were. To be unaware of great cultural epochs or accomplishments, to fail to read significant new publications, to be ignorant of the difference between the Great War and the Black Death will mark you as uneducated and possibly unsuited to high career achievement. The skills and knowledge described here are developed in the "general education" portion of your education, in courses such as history, English, psychology, philosophy, and the natural sciences.

Second point (again,
note use of examples to
develop the reason)

Lastly, one pursues an education to improve the overall quality of life. Working is only one part of living. Most of us hope that it is the means to an end: a comfortable life shared with other people in a way that will bring happiness to ourselves and those around us. We may marry and have children; we will surely make friends; and we will want to contribute to the communities in which we live. The education we acquire will contribute to our family's well-being in a spiritual and cultural sense as well as an economic one. Our education will enable us to make thoughtful choices; it will arm us against manipulation by sham ideas and charlatans. It will even help us to acquire some measure of wisdom and courage and serenity as we face whatever joys and perils life holds for us.

Conclusion (ties the
essay together by citing
a quotation from the
writer mentioned
in the introductory
paragraph)

Grand promises? Perhaps. However, people with a solid, well-rounded education tend to thrive in the same way that civilizations that place a premium on education continue to flourish. With these thoughts in mind, I return to my young microbiology student and remind him of some lines by William Faulkner, the author whose text we were studying that dreary Monday:

I believe that man will not merely endure: he will prevail. He is immortal, not because he alone among creatures has an inexhaustible voice, but because he has a soul, a spirit capable of compassion and sacrifice and endurance. The poet's, the writer's, duty is to write about these things. It is his privilege to help man endure by lifting his heart, by reminding him of the courage and honor and hope and pride and compassion and pity and sacrifice which have been the glory of his past. The poet's voice need not merely be the record of man, it can be one of the props, the pillars to help him endure and prevail.[2]

[2]William Faulkner, Nobel prize acceptance speech, 1949.

Why the Old Dislike the Young

RICHARD J. NEEDHAM

All through history, one suspects, the young
and the old have been at loggerheads°. Shakespeare told it 400
years ago, "Crabbed age and youth cannot live together." In our
time, however, it's being said that the old have developed a genuine hatred for the young; not the bickering and nattering of the
past, but a detestation that's quite literally murderous.

June Callwood, the Toronto writer, says that in every community across the land, "adults are expressing hatred of the young
and hurt them wherever they can." Edgar Friedenberg says in his
little classic, *The Vanishing Adolescent*, that the youthful personality
of today "evokes in adults conflict, anxiety and an intense hostility—usually disguised as concern."

John Stickney is a young American long-hair who turned his
back on a wealthy family, a B.A. degree and a reporting job on
Life, to spend a year with his bedroll on the road, studying the so-
called youth counter-culture in the United States. His book about
it [is titled] *Streets, Actions, Alternatives, Raps*; and here is how he
found the youth situation during his wanderings:

> The journeys were not always easy, since there was a cold war in the
> land among generations, classes, and lifestyles. Indeed, to be young, no
> matter what your appearance, marked you as an enemy, an alien in your
> own country, always suspect. The long-hair quickly divined his base
> status in the cold relentless stares of straights passing him by on the road,
> the comments about his masculinity in small-town cafés—and the crude
> lip-licking lust for the free young women simultaneously hated and de-
> sired. And the police along the way, well, the threat of insurrection°, the
> potential for secreted drugs, the casual vagrancy, the cry of revolution
> bruited about in the streets, the rumour of sexual promiscuity, all grated
> against their sensibilities. I learned that if you did not have a job, a plan,
> a lot of money, a credit card, a home address, a friend nearby, and you
> were young, you just weren't worth a . . . in America. You hardly even
> existed, except as an outlaw.

Let's turn now to the current (November) issue of the *Atlantic*,
in which you'll find a striking article about young-old hostility by
Antonia Chayes, who teaches political science at Tufts University
in Massachusetts and is herself the mother of five children. Mrs.

"Why the Old Dislike the Young" by Richard J. Needham. Copyright Nov. 11, 12,
& 13, 1971. Reprinted by permission of *The Globe and Mail*, Toronto.

Chayes makes no bones about her anger with the young, including—and perhaps particularly—her own:

> Our daughter said she finished school only to please us, and then left home to live in a commune where a Jesus-autocrat with no teeth and a hillbilly accent told her to wash dishes and mind the little children. She was always a good baby-sitter, but she did the dishes only under duress° at home, and left the ghost of her midnight snack for us to face at breakfast. We told her not to go, and gave reasons. But we had no power.

5   Again:

> There were low, low youth fares to Europe this summer, and those spoiled children whose toys and peeled crayons we had picked up years ago went abroad. They left behind ashtrays for us to empty, and broken belts, odd socks, and little wilted heaps of underwear to pick up and wash.

6   And again:

> My face looks very stern to me. There is a sort of dignity there, an honest sadness that must command respect. It is born of hurt and not understanding, of loving without reserve and trying to please. My cheeks and eyes look hollow. I know I'm not alone. I hear stories worse than ours, and can pick out parents at parties whose children have wounded and disappointed them. Their eyes are hollow too, and some of them drink too much.

7   What this mother's protest boils down to is that young people, including her own, act to please themselves, not their parents. This is hardly a novel state of affairs. Haven't children always been ungrateful? Haven't they always refused to "understand," or "be understood" by, their parents? Haven't they generally disappointed and wounded their parents by their failure to meet parental expectations?

8   If there's some "problem" here, perhaps it's the expectations themselves. As Mark Twain said, "Blessed are they that expect nothing, for they shall not be disappointed." Wise parents might limit themselves to seeing that the kid grew up all in one piece, the rest being left to fate. But the part of wisdom is not always the part of love—the "loving without reserve" of which Mrs. Chayes writes, the endless "trying to please."

9   When this vast outpouring of love is rejected, when it doesn't "pay off" in the form of respect and respectability, obedience and returned affection, may the love not turn into hate? To reword Congreve, Hell hath no fury like a parent scorned.

10   There are other, equally antique, reasons for the battle between the generations.

11   For example, there's the North American worship of youthfulness—being and looking and acting "young"—coupled with the North American fear of age—being and looking and acting "old." Men dye their hair and wear wigs in order to look 10 years younger; women spend billions on guck which promises the same result. As Edgar Friedenberg says in *The Vanishing Adolescent*, people who

are so determined to stay young will naturally resent those who really *are* young—who don't *need* to wear wigs or put on guck.

Again, there's the matter of "success," whatever that is. Most   12
older people believe (whether they admit it or not) that they've botched up their lives, made wrong and irreversible decisions; they had their chance, as we all do, and blew it. They've failed and they're trapped in that failure; their future's behind them; all they can do is put in time until they retire or die. Feeling this way, they naturally cast a bleak eye on the young, who aren't trapped—yet.

As Friedenberg remarks,   13
> Young people, who really do have their lives ahead of them, and who have not yet begun in earnest to make the least of their opportunites, are bound to arouse mixed feelings in their elders. They arouse genuine concern; it is excruciating° to watch a youngster, especially one who refuses to listen to you, making what you are quite sure are serious mistakes. But at a deeper level, it may be even more painful when he does not make them, or when they turn out not to be mistakes; when he grasps and holds what eluded you, or what you dared not touch and have dreamed of ever since.

Next comes dat ole debbil sex. Youthful sexuality is certainly   14
more out in the open than it was 20, 30 or 40 years ago; but whether there actually is more of it, I don't know. I could tell you some gorgeous stories about my own romantic flings—and those of others my age—in the Toronto of the early 1930s. Oh, the things that went on in the back seats of the Alhambra Theatre at Bloor and Bathurst, with an ice cream soda at Peter's afterwards!

But most old and middle-aged people today think (whether it's   15
true or not) that there's been a great change. They think the young of today are making love every hour on the hour, and each time with a different partner, and this upsets them—(1) because they didn't get all these frolics when they were young and (2) because the penalty was much higher when they were young (no morning-after pill in those days) and (3) because they feel that in their 40 or 50 or 60 years' life, they haven't made much of a mark in the romance department, in the sex department, anyhow.

Hooked in with what you might call youth-envy, success-envy   16
and sex-envy, is what I'd call life-envy. The old entertain the illusion (and what an illusion it is) that the young are happy, carefree, adventurous, bursting with joie-de-vivre. "The best years of your life." Ha! They're the worst. But the older people don't know this, or else they've forgotten it, and that's another source of hostility. Unhappy people hate those who are—or appear to be, or "ought" to be—happy.

Finally, one perceives among older people the fear of change,   17
disorder, loss of control. This fear seems to me comical; the mass of young people I encounter are as square, as timid, as hide-bound

as the mass of their parents. But a small minority of the young make rebellious noises, and this alarms older people who cling so desperately to their homes, their jobs, their set ways and ideas, the tight framework they've worked hard and long to put around themselves.

18   Is there no sound reason, then, for the hostility which the old feel toward the young—and which is so enthusiastically returned? I think there is one sound reason—a big one. . . .

19   Human nature never changes. Every generation that comes into the world bears within it the white of good, the black of evil, and all sorts of greys in between. So it is with this generation. I refuse to believe that some 15 or 20 years ago, the women of Canada gave birth to an army of angels; or to an army of devils, either. What we got was the same old stuff as always.

20   Circumstances do change, however. The younger generation of present-day Canada has come up, by and large, in affluence°— the greatest affluence this country has ever known. It also has come up in a society which is crazy, besotted, lunatic, on the subject of "education." Everybody, everybody—no matter what their ability, no matter what the cost—must go to public school, high school and some sort of university or college, a process taking 16 or 17 years at a classroom cost alone of $20,000.

21   This has given us a completely new kind of human being, the teenager. It has given us a protracted° childhood, a protracted dependency, which no previous society was able to afford. People who are grown up sexually around 12, and grown up physically around 16, continue to be treated as children; continue to be supported, in most cases, by the labor of others. To put the matter bluntly, they are parasitic on their parents and on the taxpayers generally. They are a leisure class such as Thorstein Veblen° never dreamed of, little being required of them save to go through the motions (if that) of "being educated."

22   The young do not, by and large, resent this dependency, but rather enjoy it. As many have said to me, it beats working. Many of them remain dependent even after they're out of school or college; they just go on welfare. They believe the world owes them a living; they see no reason why they should work; and if pressed on the matter, reply—with some accuracy—that there's no work for them, anyhow. You could call these people irresponsible, I guess, but when was responsibility ever imposed upon them? When were they ever told they must sink or swim, shape up or ship out, work or starve?

23   A visiting foreigner might reach the conclusion that the older people in Canada have an immense love for the young—a love expressed by giving them so much, doing so much for them, look-

ing tenderly after them for so very, very long. But as he checked around, he might find a deep and growing hostility toward them; and here I'll answer the basic question posed by [this article]. I think the old dislike the young for being parasitic on them, riding on their backs, draining them of money when they should be out making it.

Out of this prolonged idleness, boredom, parasitism, irre-   24
sponsibility, come many other things which annoy the old—the drug thing, I suppose, is one of them; the aimless drifting around and hanging around; the child-like fads and crazes; the reversion, in many cases, to a sort of barbarism. These, I think, are only symptoms of the disease; the disease itself is dependency.

Much as many or most of the young enjoy having the disease,   25
much as they may wish to prolong it, it wasn't the young who invented it. That was done by the adult society of the last 25 years. It was the adults who forced kids to stay in school until 16, and coerced them into staying much longer. It was the adults who set up a welfare system which enables and encourages so many people, including young people, to live without working.

It was the adults who introduced minimum wage laws which   26
make it impractical for employers to hire inexperienced young people. It was the adults who set up labor laws and labor contracts which freeze young people out of industry. It was the adults who created the economic fiasco° Canada's floundering in today—a fiasco which finds some 210,000 Canadians between 16 and 24 unemployed. It was the adults, in short, who created the entire situation which now bothers or annoys or infuriates them.

If the offending situation is to be changed, it's the adults them-   27
selves who must change it. Most Canadians, it is true, now have the vote at 18; but there aren't enough of them to change it—even if they did want it changed. Will any of our political parties argue that most kids should get out of school and start work at 14 or 15 or even 16? Will any of them argue that kids starting work should be paid only what little they're worth? Will any of them argue that only a minority of kids can benefit from going to high school, and that only a small minority can benefit from going on to university?

Of course not; and so, I suppose, the old will become more   28
and more hostile toward the dependent young. The young will respond to this hostility with their own brands of it; a generation with so much time on its hands can think up all sorts of interesting ways to harry° its elders. In short, a civil (or incivil) war—and I've the feeling it's just starting.

RICHARD J. NEEDHAM

Richard J. Needham, humorist and essayist, was born in Gilbraltar and raised in India, Ireland, and England. He has lived in Toronto for many years and contributed a daily column to the editorial page of *The Globe and Mail.* Among the many collections of his columns are *A Friend in Needham* and *Needham's Inferno.*

Paragraph	# Words and Meanings

Paragraph		
1	at loggerheads:	fighting with each other
3	insurrection:	rebellion
4	duress:	threat of force
13	excruciating:	extremely painful
20	affluence:	great wealth
21	protracted: Thorstein Veblen:	stretched out in time sociologist and economist, author of *The Theory of the Leisure Class* (1899)
26	fiasco:	disastrous failure
28	harry:	to torment

Structure and Strategy

1. What introductory strategy does Needham use, and how does it lead to the statement of opinion that forms the basis for his argument in this article?
2. Study Needham's use of quotations as evidence. Pick out a quotation that you think is particularly appropriate and explain why you think it is effective.
3. Among the writers Needham quotes to support his argument are two relatively unknown ones, John Stickney and Antonia Chayes. What makes them credible as authorities on the subject of the hostility between young and old?
4. Underline the six main reasons Needham advances for his opinion that the old dislike the young. Identify the paragraphs devoted to the development of each reason.
5. What is the function of the first sentence of paragraph 16?
6. Why do you think Needham ends his article with a sentence fragment?

Content and Purpose

1. Needham has often been described as a curmudgeon, an ill-tempered, cynical, surly individual. Do you think his reputation is justified? Why?

2. Needham distinguishes between the problems in parent-child relationships and the problems in relations between young and old generally. What difference does he identify?
3. Needham is contemptuous of the fears the old have of the young. (See paragraph 17.) Do you agree with him?
4. Needham blames the old for creating the very reasons for their dislike of the young. Do you think he is fair in his assessment? Why?
5. Needham is over seventy. Do you think he shares the attitude of the old toward the young that he describes in this article? If not, why not? What could account for the difference between his attitude and that of "the old" in general?
6. This essay appeared in *The Globe and Mail* in 1971. Do you think that the young generation he describes is different from today's 16- to 24-year-olds? If so, how?

Suggestions for Writing

1. Following Needham's model, write a paper persuading your readers that the young dislike the old.
2. Traditional societies like the Chinese respect and venerate the old, but progressive societies in the West increasingly see the aged as an unwelcome burden. Write an essay in which you identify and explain two or three significant reasons why our society excludes or rejects the elderly.

The Ascetic° in a Canoe

PIERRE ELLIOTT TRUDEAU

I would not know how to instil a taste for adventure in those who have not acquired it. (Anyway, who can ever prove the necessity for the gypsy life?) And yet there are people who suddenly tear themselves away from their comfortable existence and, using the energy of their bodies as an example to

"The Ascetic in a Canoe" from *Wilderness Canada* by Borden Spears. © 1970 by Clarke, Irwin & Co. Ltd. Used by permission of Irwin Publishing Inc.

their brains, apply themselves to the discovery of unsuspected pleasures and places.

2   I would like to point out to these people a type of labour from which they are certain to profit: an expedition by canoe.

3   I do not just mean "canoeing." Not that I wish to disparage° that pastime, which is worth more than many another. But, looked at closely, there is perhaps only a difference of money between the canoeists of Lafontaine Park° and those who dare to cross a lake, make a portage°, spend a night in a tent and return exhausted, always in the care of a fatherly guide—a brief interlude momentarily interrupting the normal course of digestion.

4   A canoeing expedition, which demands much more than that, is also much more rewarding.

5   It involves a starting rather than a parting. Although it assumes the breaking of ties, its purpose is not to destroy the past, but to lay a foundation for the future. From now on, every living act will be built on this step, which will serve as a base long after the return of the expedition . . . and until the next one.

6   What is essential at the beginning is the resolve to reach the saturation point. Ideally, the trip should end only when the members are making no further progress within themselves. They should not be fooled, though, by a period of boredom, weariness or disgust; that is not the end, but the last obstacle before it. Let saturation be serene!

7   So you must paddle for days, or weeks, or perhaps months on end. My friends and I were obliged, on pain of death, to do more than a thousand miles by canoe, from Montreal to Hudson Bay. But let no one be deterred by a shortage of time. A more intense pace can compensate for a shorter trip.

8   What sets a canoeing expedition apart is that it purifies you more rapidly and inescapably than any other. Travel a thousand miles by train and you are a brute; pedal five hundred on a bicycle and you remain basically a bourgeois; paddle a hundred in a canoe and you are already a child of nature.

9   For it is a condition of such a trip that you entrust yourself, stripped of your worldly goods, to nature. Canoe and paddle, blanket and knife, salt pork and flour, fishing rod and rifle; that is about the extent of your wealth. To remove all the useless material baggage from a man's heritage is, at the same time, to free his mind from petty preoccupations, calculations and memories.

10   On the other hand, what fabulous and undeveloped mines are to be found in nature, friendship and oneself! The paddler has no choice but to draw everything from them. Later, forgetting that this habit was adopted under duress°, he will be astonished to find so many resources within himself.

Nevertheless, he will have returned a more ardent believer   11
from a time when religion, like everything else, became simple.
The impossibility of scandal creates a new morality, and prayer
becomes a friendly chiding of the divinity, who has again become
part of our everyday affairs. (My friend, Guy Viau, could say about
our adventure, "We got along very well with God, who is a damn
good sport. Only once did we threaten to break off diplomatic
relations if he continued to rain on us. But we were joking. We
would never have done so, and well he knew it. So he continued
to rain on us.")

The canoe is also a school of friendship. You learn that your   12
best friend is not a rifle, but someone who shares a night's sleep
with you after ten hours of paddling at the other end of a canoe.
Let's say that you have to be towed up a rapid and it's your turn
to stay in the canoe and guide it. You watch your friend stumbling
over logs, sliding on rocks, sticking in gumbo°, tearing the skin on
his legs and drinking water for which he does not thirst, yet never
letting go of the rope; meanwhile, safely in the middle of the cat-
aract, you spray your hauler with a stream of derision. When this
same man has also fed you exactly half his catch, and has made a
double portage because of your injury, you can boast of having a
friend for life, and one who knows you well.

How does the trip affect your personality? Allow me to make   13
a fine distinction, and I would say that you return not so much a
man who reasons more, but a more reasonable man. For, throughout this time, your mind has learned to exercise itself in the working
conditions which nature intended. Its primordial° role has been to
sustain the body in the struggle against a powerful universe. A
good camper knows that it is more important to be ingenious° than
to be a genius. And conversely, the body, by demonstrating the
true meaning of sensual pleasure, has been of service to the mind.
You feel the beauty of animal pleasure when you draw a deep
breath of rich morning air right through your body, which has been
carried by the cold night, curled up like an unborn child. How can
you describe the feeling which wells up in the heart and stomach
as the canoe finally rides up on the shore of the campsite after a
long day of plunging your paddle into rain-swept waters? Purely
physical is the joy which the fire spreads through the palms of
your hands and the soles of your feet while your chattering mouth
belches the poisonous cold. The pleasurable torpor° of such a moment is perhaps not too different from what the mystics of the East
are seeking. At least it has allowed me to taste what one respected
gentleman used to call the joys of hard living.

Make no mistake, these joys are exclusively physical. They   14
have nothing to do with the satisfaction of the mind when it im-

poses unwelcome work on the body, a satisfaction, moreover, which is often mixed with pride, and which the body never fails to avenge. During a very long and exhausting portage, I have sometimes felt my reason defeated, and shamefully fleeing, while my legs and shoulders carried bravely on. The mumbled verses which marked the rhythm of my steps at the beginning had become brutal grunts of "uh! uh! uh!" There was nothing aesthetic° in that animal search for the bright clearing which always marks the end of a portage.

15   I do not want you to think that the mind is subjected to a healthy discipline merely by worrying about simplistic problems. I only wish to remind you of that principle of logic which states that valid conclusions do not generally follow from false premises. Now, in a canoe, where these premises are based on nature in its original state (rather than on books, ideas and habits of uncertain value), the mind conforms to that higher wisdom which we call natural philosophy; later, that healthy methodology and acquired humility will be useful in confronting mystical and spiritual questions.

16   I know a man whose school could never teach him patriotism, but who acquired that virtue when he felt in his bones the vastness of his land, and the greatness of those who founded it.

[   ]

PIERRE ELLIOTT TRUDEAU

Pierre Elliott Trudeau (b. 1919), who served as the fifteenth prime minister of Canada, was born in Montreal and educated at Collège Brébeuf, the Université de Montréal, Harvard University, the École des Sciences Politiques in Paris, and the London School of Economics. He headed the government of Canada from 1968 to 1979 and from 1980 to 1984. Among his numerous books is *Federalism and the French Canadians* (1968), a collection of political essays. An outdoorsman of note, Trudeau is an expert canoeist and a black belt in Judo. The essay you have just read, first published in French, was written when Trudeau was twenty-five years old.

Paragraph   **Words and Meanings**

	ascetic:	the opposite of self-indulgent; someone who practises self-discipline and self-denial in solitude
3	disparage:	speak of in a negative way
	Lafontaine Park:	Montreal park with a large pond and canoe-rental facilities
	portage:	trip overland, carrying a canoe between bodies of water

duress:	constraint, compulsion	10
gumbo:	very sticky mud	12
primordial:	very earliest, from the beginning	13
ingenious:	clever, resourceful, inventive	
torpor:	numbness, sleepiness	
aesthetic:	sensitive to art and beauty	14

Structure and Strategy

1. Identify the paragraphs that form the introduction to this essay and those that form the conclusion. Together, how do they contribute to the UNITY of the whole?
2. Where does Trudeau most clearly state the opinion that forms the basis for his argument?
3. How would you describe the TONE of this essay?
4. Can you find evidence in DICTION and SYNTAX of the fact that this essay was originally written in French and later translated into English?
5. What stylistic device does Trudeau use in paragraph 8 to add EMPHASIS to his point?
6. Find the three one-sentence paragraphs in this essay and explain their function.
7. In what ORDER has Trudeau arranged the reasons to support his opinion that "an expedition by canoe" is physically, socially, and spiritually rewarding?

Content and Purpose

1. What is Trudeau's purpose in this essay: to convince his readers of the validity of his own opinion about wilderness canoeing or to persuade the readers to try it themselves? How do you know?
2. What is the difference between "canoeing" and "a canoeing expedition" according to Trudeau?
3. In Trudeau's opinion, what is the value of the mind exercising itself "in the working conditions which nature intended"? (See paragraph 13.)
4. In Trudeau's estimation, how does a canoeing expedition force the adventurer to confront not only geography but also history?
5. Given what you know of Pierre Trudeau's long years in public service—his successes, his failures, his unmistakable charisma—does this essay seem characteristic of the man? It was written when he was only 25. What does it say about the man he was to become?

Suggestions for Writing

1. Have you ever had an experience that tested you, forced you to stretch yourself physically, emotionally, and spiritually? Write a paper in which you prove that this experience profoundly affected you either because you accepted the challenge or because, for your own valid reasons, you did not accept the challenge.
2. Write an essay convincing your readers of the value of a particular kind of physical challenge.

And May the Best Cheater Win

HARRY BRUCE

1   Every youth knows he can get into deep trouble by stealing cameras, peddling dope, mugging winos, forging cheques or copying someone else's answers during an exam. Those are examples of not playing by the rules. Cheating. But every youth also knows that in organized sports across North America, cheating is not only perfectly okay, it's *recommended*. "The structure of sport . . . actually promotes deviance," says U.S. sport sociologist D.S. Eitzen.

2   The downy-cheeked hockey player who refuses to play dirty may find himself fired off the team. The boy soccer player who refuses to rough up a superior striker to "throw him off his game" may find himself writhing under a coach's tongue-lashing. The basketball player who refuses to foul a goal-bound enemy star in the last seconds of a close game may find himself riding the bench next week. Thus, we have that cynical paradox, "the good foul," a phrase that makes about as much sense as "a beneficial outbreak of bubonic plague."

3   If organized sports offer benefits to youngsters, they also offer a massive program of moral corruption. The recruiting of college athletes in the United States, and the use of academic fraud to maintain their "eligibility," stunk so powerfully in 1980 that *Newsweek* decided "cheating has become the name of the game," and spoke of the fear on U.S. campuses of "an epidemic of corruption."

"And May the Best Cheater Win" by Harry Bruce from *Quest Magazine*. Copyright November, 1984. Reprinted by permission of Bella Pomer Agency Inc.

But the epidemic had already arrived, and what really worried *Newsweek* was national acceptance of corruption as normal: "Many kids are admitting that they have tried to take the bribes and inducements on the sleazy terms with which they are offered. Their complaints are not so much that illegalities exist, but that they aren't getting their share of the goodies." Fans, alumni, coaches, college administrators, players and their parents all believed nothing could ever be more important than winning (or more disgraceful than losing), and that cheating in victory's cause was therefore commendable°.

"Candidates for big-time sport's Hall of Shame have seemed   4
suddenly to break out all over like an ugly rash," William Oscar Johnson wrote last year in *Sports Illustrated*. He constructed a dismal catalogue of assaults on cops, drunken brawls, adventures in the cocaine trade, credit-card frauds and other sordid activities by rich professional athletes who, in more naive times, might have earned the adulation° of small boys. Jim Finks, then Chicago Bears general manager, speculated that the trouble with the younger lawbreakers was that they had "been looked after all the way from junior high school. Some of them have had doctored grades. This plus the affluence [astronomical salaries] means there has never been any pressing need for them to work things out for themselves. They have no idea how to face reality."

No one in all their lives had taught them about fair play. "In   5
the early days of playground and high-school leagues, one of the key issues was moral regulation," says Alan Ingham, a teacher at the University of Washington. "You got sports, and you got Judeo-Christian principles thrown in, too." Now, however, "the majority of things taught in sports are performance things." John Pooley of the School of Recreation, Physical and Health Education at Dalhousie University, Nova Scotia, asked Calvin Hill, a former Dallas Cowboy, what percentage of all the football rookies he'd ever met had said that, as college players, they'd encountered no cheating. Hill's reply was short: "None."

So here we have the most powerful nation in the world, and   6
it blithely corrupts children so they'll mature as athletic machines without an ounce of the moral sense that might prevent their sniffing cocaine or complicate their lust for victory. Pray for nuclear disarmament, fans.

Still, Canadians are little better. We all know who invented the   7
game that inspired Paul Newman to star in *Slap Shot*, a black and bloody comedy about butchery on ice. We can't argue that it's only American coaches who teach peewees to draw tripping penalties rather than let an enemy player continue a breakaway on your goal. Moreover, I happen to live in Halifax, where only last winter

St. Mary's University was disgraced for allowing a ringer from Florida to play varsity basketball. The coach of a rival but inferior team ferreted out the truth about the player's ineligibility. In doing so, he imported one of the fine old traditions of amateur sports in the States: if you can't beat them, hire a private dick. Oh well, that's what universities are supposed to be all about: the pursuit of truth.

8   Pursuing another truth, Pooley of Dalhousie surveyed recent graduates of three down-east universities. The grads were both men and women, and they had all played intercollegiate field hockey, ice hockey, soccer or basketball. "With one exception [a woman field hockey player], all felt there was immense pressure to win," Pooley said. Typical responses: "Winning is everything in university sport. . . . The measure of success was not how well you played but the win-loss record. . . . There is incredible pressure to perform because there are always two or three guys on the bench ready to take your place."

9   Half said their coaches had urged "winning at any cost." One grad revealed, "Some coaches send their players 'out to get' a good player on the other team." Another described "goon coaches who stressed intimidation and rough play." Coaches had not only con- doned° tactical fouls, but had actually taught the arts of fouling during routine practice. A player who had competed against British and Bermudian teams said they played "intensely but fairly" while the Maritimers "sometimes used dirty tactics" or "blatantly tried to stop a player."

10   Pooley wondered if the grads, after years in intercollegiate sport, felt it had promoted fair play. Only the field-hockey players said yes. Answers from the others were shockers: "Everyone cheats and the best cheater wins. . . . Fair play and sportsmanship are *not* promoted. This is a joke. . . . You did whatever you could to win. . . . You are taught to gain an advantage, whatever it takes." Such cynicism, from people so young they've barely doffed their mortarboards°, confirms the sad opinion of one Kalevi Heinila, who told a world scientific congress in 1980 that fair play was "ripe to be dumped in the waste basket of sport history."

11   The irony in all this—and it's both ludicrous and nauseating— is that universities defend their expensive programs for intercol- legiate sports with lip service to the notion that keen teamwork in clean competition nurtures good citizens. Fair play in sports, don't you know, spawns fair players for the worlds of politics, the profes- sions and business. *Counter arg.*

12   That's a crock. What intercollegiate sport really teaches is how to get away with murder, how to be crooked within the law. Just listen to one of the fresh-faced grads in Pooley's survey as he sets out to make his way in the world, his eyes shining with idealism:

"University sport teaches you to play as close to the limits as possible; and this is the attitude that will get you ahead in the business world." Another acknowledged that his "concept of fair play decreased"; but, on the other hand, he had learned to "stretch the rules to my advantage." A young woman confided, "University sport has made me tough, less sensitive to other people's feelings." Still others stressed that college sport had prepared them for "the real world," for "real life," in which winning was all.

Cheating in amateur sport, Pooley says, "gives it a hollow   13
feeling. Many coaches do not have integrity. I'm still sickened by that. It upsets me, at all levels." A tall, talkative, forceful man with a bony face and a thick brush of steely hair, Pooley has coached soccer in six countries, once played for professional teams in Britain, and now, at 53, cavorts on a team for men over 35. "I'm still playing league soccer," he wrote in a paper for the 1984 Olympic Scientific Congress in Eugene, Oregon, "because: a) I helped to organize and plan my own youth soccer experiences; b) coming second or being beaten was okay; c) I was always much more interested in playing well than playing to win; d) I never minded playing less well than I'd earlier played; and e) I always felt successful at the level played."

Those are highly un-American reasons for playing any sport,   14
but Pooley is originally from northern England, the nation that invented "fair play" and knew that certain things just weren't cricket°. That was in a time long before Americans institutionalized cheating even in soap box derbies, before athletes gobbled steroids, before universities invented courses in weight lifting and raquetball so quarterbacks could qualify as "students." Moreover, Pooley believes that the few adults who stick with team sports until middle age do so because, as youngsters, "They preferred the feel of the ball, the pass well made, the sweetness of the stroke or the power in the shot, rather than whether they won or lost the game." Such people don't need to cheat.

Some scholars believe that the sleaziness of organized sports   15
simply reflects the sleaziness of our entire culture. Pooley points out, for instance, that one sociologist offers two reasons why cheating in sports shouldn't be "disproportionately reprimanded." The first is that it's "endemic° in society," and the second is that even more cheating probably occurs in other fields. Pooley disagrees. *counter arg.* He says this argument is like saying you should not disproportionately reprimand the clergy for being dishonest. Poor Pooley. He has such quaint ideas about sports. He actually believes they should not be immoral, and should be fun.

HARRY BRUCE

Toronto-born Harry Bruce began his career as a journalist with the *Ottawa Citizen* in 1955. He has written articles and columns for leading magazines and newspapers across the country. *Each Moment As It Flies* is a collection of articles and essays in which Bruce explores a number of subjects such as the lives of famous Canadians, recollections of his childhood experiences, environmental issues, and family life. Bruce now makes his home in Halifax.

Paragraph | ## Words and Meanings

Paragraph		
3	commendable:	praiseworthy, something to be congratulated for
4	adulation:	excessive praise; hero-worship
9	condoned:	excused, overlooked
10	doffed their mortarboards:	taken off the caps worn during graduation ceremonies
14	weren't cricket:	British expression for "socially unacceptable"
15	endemic:	widespread, pervasive

Structure and Strategy

1. What two methods of paragraph development has Bruce used in paragraph 1? What is the effect of the one-word sentence fragment in this paragraph?
2. In paragraph 3, Bruce claims that cheating in sports has become "an epidemic of corruption." Find three or four instances of this METAPHOR elsewhere in the essay and explain how it contributes to the UNITY of the whole piece.
3. What FIGURES OF SPEECH make the first sentence of paragraph 4 particularly effective?
4. What is the TOPIC SENTENCE of paragraph 12, and how does Bruce develop it?
5. Study the direct quotations Bruce uses as evidence in his essay. Why are they effective in supporting his argument?
6. Paragraph 6 consists of two seemingly unrelated sentences. Explain the connection between them that Bruce implies.

Content and Purpose

1. Summarize the opinion and supporting reasons that form the thesis of this essay.
2. What is Bruce's attitude toward cheating in college sports? Why does he take the matter so seriously?
3. What is wrong with the argument that "cheating in sports shouldn't be disproportionately reprimanded" because cheating is "endemic in society"? (See paragraph 15.)

4. What connection does Bruce establish between corruption in organized sports and the decline in moral standards of society as a whole?
5. Explain why Bruce sees organized sports at their best as a form of training for responsible citizenship.

Suggestions for Writing ⅃

1. Write a paper persuading your readers that Canadians are (or are not) the world's best hockey players, professional peace-keepers, or most devoted sports fans.
2. Write a paper arguing that some form of cheating is necessary (or unnecessary) in a particular situation, such as in a sport, a business, an exam, a personal relationship, preparing one's income tax, or filling out a job application.

Resisting the Revolution

DAVID SUZUKI

For years now, I have resisted the pressure   1
to buy a personal computer. I am not mesmerized° by technology, nor am I a technophobe° (as proof, I have two VCRs and love my stereo system). I do admit to being intimidated by the hackers° and the video parlor freaks. But having watched my secretary (I can't reveal her age lest she quit, but she is older than I and I'm almost 50) take to a word processor easily, the crunch has now come. I've rationalized my lack of interest in computers because I couldn't see a valid use for them, but word processing is definitely something I now need. By the time this article is out, I am absolutely sure I'll find a portable word processor, with modem, indispensable.

One of history's remarkable lessons is the incredible seduc-   2
tiveness of technology. At first it's just convenient; but once we overcome initial reticence° and conquer it, it becomes indispensable—it turns around and conquers us. I get annoyed as hell when my phone calls from Toronto to Vancouver don't go through right away—yet not long ago, I'd have had to go through an operator and wait quite a while to make a transcontinental call. Indeed, we

"Resisting the Revolution" from *Science Dimension* by David Suzuki. Copyright 1985. Reprinted by permission of The National Research Council of Canada.

now take direct overseas dialing for granted. Yet in 1945, there was no transatlantic telephone cable at all; and until communications satellites went up in the '60s, there were fewer than 300 channels for all transatlantic calls. Does anyone out there remember when we had to book them days in advance?

3   I was once waiting at the airport with a friend when his mother (originally an immigrant from Europe) arrived on the plane from New York. The jet had been full and the airport crowded, so it took almost an hour before her baggage arrived—and she spent the entire wait complaining bitterly about the inefficiency of the airlines. I found it amusing to think that it once took her two weeks to get from London to Montreal by boat; here she had just reached Vancouver in a 747 in six hours, yet felt enormously put out by an hour's inconvenience.

4   Once a technology is available, we rapidly forget what life was like before it, and simply take it as the norm. Today, we complain that amniocentesis° takes up to four weeks for a diagnosis; yet twenty years ago, it wasn't possible to do any such analysis before birth. I get furious at the CBC office because our videotape machine is so "old." I can't rewind and view a tape at the same time, and it takes "so long" (meaning 15 seconds or so) to go back and forth from shot to shot. When our copier breaks down, I rant and rave without remembering all those smudged hands from ink and gels and stencils.

5   These technologies have transformed society beyond recognition from the one I knew as a child. My children grow up thinking of my childhood as an ancient way of life, long extinct. (Why, their dad is so old, there was no television when he was a kid!) And in spite of ourselves, we have been changed by technology in our values, in our expectations, and in the 'needs' we feel.

6   In the summer of 1983, I spent time with the nomadic San people of the Kalahari Desert. One night, after they had slaughtered a cow we presented to them, they began to dance while we filmed the spectacle. As the camera zoomed in on a group of singers, we were astounded to find a huge, battery-driven cassette tape recorder blasting away. Where they got the machine, and how they got batteries for it, days away from the nearest settlement, is beyond me. But even they found value in its technology, thus ensuring that a chunk of their millennia-old culture will soon disappear.

7   We operate on simple faith that if we find any new technologies to have serious deleterious° effects, we can always prohibit them. But when in history have we ever done that? Some suggest supersonic transport was scrapped because of its potential effect on the ozone layer. Nonsense! The Americans saw the enormous deficits it would pile up, and the Concorde is certainly proving them wise.

Well, how about DDT? Yes, it was ultimately banned—in the industrialized countries—not so that we'd become less dependent on chemical technology, but only because there were alternative chemical pesticides. Technologies are too useful and convenient, and compel us ever onward. This leads us to depend on technological solutions to technological problems, thus assuring there will always be a price to be paid for the benefits.

And where does it all end? I am appalled at the effort that has   8
gone into the development of embryo transplants for women. In a time when overpopulation, malnutrition, and parasitic disease cause global problems, medical science pursues non-life-threatening "problems" to satisfy *desires*. And once the new technology is in place, it is impossible to resist its use. Aside from the issue of whether it's a worthwhile use of medical expertise, the technology of embryo transplants has a deep impact on the very nature of biological lineage, by separating the 'egg mother' from the 'uterine mother' from the 'social mother.' Where that leads I have no idea, but it's not a trivial problem. I have watched, in horror, as parents pled for a liver to transplant into their mortally ill child—horrified at how far humans are prepared to go to fight nature, but also at the realization that were my child to develop a lethal liver condition, I would feel the same urge as those other distraught parents, now that the technology exists.

So, cognizant° of and grateful for the utility of technology, I   9
nevertheless feel that we ought to spend far more time weighing its benefits against its possible social costs. Does anyone out there agree or disagree?

☐

DAVID SUZUKI

David Suzuki, geneticist and broadcaster, was born in Vancouver in 1936, and was interned with his family during World War II. He is both a scientist and a popularizer of science, contributing learned papers to scientific publications and articles of interest to magazines and newspapers. He is a popular radio and television performer who explains the mysteries of science and its influence on our daily lives.

Words and Meanings   Paragraph

mesmerized:	hypnotized	1
technophobe:	person who hates or fears technology	
hackers:	people with a passionate interest in computers	
reticence:	reservations, holding back	2

4	amniocentesis:	test performed on amniotic fluid to diagnose genetic disorders in a fetus and, incidentally, to identify the sex of the fetus
7	deleterious:	harmful
9	cognizant:	aware, knowledgeable

Structure and Strategy

1. Identify five examples Suzuki uses to explain the "incredible seductiveness" of technology.
2. What is the function of paragraph 5? How does it link together the two halves of this essay? Which half is primarily expository and which is primarily persuasive?
3. Explain how paragraphs 6 to 8 develop the last sentence of paragraph 5.
4. How does paragraph 9 contribute to the UNITY of this essay?

Content and Purpose

1. Suzuki's essay is both an argument and a warning. Is his primary purpose to convince his readers of the validity of his opinion or to move them to act in some way?
2. Summarize the main ideas advanced in the two major parts of this essay: paragraphs 2 to 4 and 6 to 8.
3. How would you answer the question Suzuki puts to his readers in the last paragraph?

Suggestions for Writing

1. Do you know the story of the genie and the bottle, or the story of the sorcerer's apprentice? Relate these stories to the history of man and technology and then write a paper proving that technology is the genie in the first story or that man is the apprentice in the second story.
2. Write a paper explaining why you agree or disagree with Suzuki that society ought to spend more time weighing the benefits of new technology against its possible disadvantages.

In Defence of the
Divine Right of Kings

ALDEN NOWLAN

Occasionally I astonish friends and frighten   1
strangers by telling them there are valid arguments in favour of
the principle of the divine right of kings°. I like to think that I'd
have supported Charles I against Parliament, and James II against
the Whig aristocracy; and I believe I understand why Yukio Mish-
ima, the Japanese writer who recently committed ritual suicide,
could argue that his emperor was divine.

Most of us first learned about divine right from high school   2
history books, the authors of which assumed the principle was too
ludicrous to merit discussion. Certainly divine right would be ridiculous if it meant that Providence had granted absolute power
to, say, an old fool like James I—but that's not what it meant at
all. Quintessentially, divine right meant that men were governed
by a moral authority greater than mere consensus°. In other words,
a society could be unanimous and yet be wrong, because there
existed a morality above and beyond the law.

Modern democracies are based on the opposite premise. Small   3
"l" liberals constantly remind us that the state can't legislate morality; sin is one thing and illegality quite another. Advocates of
liberalized abortion laws, for instance, assert that while individuals
are free to believe that abortion is immoral, they have no right to
impose their convictions on their fellow citizens—which means, in
effect, that you can believe what you like but where acts, as distinct
from mere beliefs, are concerned, the will of the state must be
supreme. That's generally regarded as the enlightened, as opposed
to the reactionary, viewpoint. Yet if followed through to its logical
conclusion it could be used to justify the race laws of Hitler's Germany. The German nurses put on trial after the Second World War
for administering lethal doses of drugs to victims of senility and
retardation pleaded that they were only obeying the laws of the
state. And so they were.

The old kaiser, Wilhelm II°, made a bit of an ass of himself by   4
espousing the principle of divine right long after it had ceased to

"In Defence of the Divine Right of Kings" from *Double Exposure* by Alden Nowlan.
Copyright 1978. Reprinted by permission of Brunswick Press.

be fashionable, or even respectable. And, like many such mon-
archs, he was inclined to confuse his whims with the will of God.
Still, he was always dimly aware that he was responsible to the
deity. It was his sense of that responsibility that made him try
unsuccessfully to prevent zeppelins from bombing London. Hitler
was responsible to nobody. Hitler, like Stalin, was an absolute ruler
in a sense in which no kaiser or czar could ever have been an
absolute ruler, because above the kaiser or the czar there was God.

5   Here, as everywhere else in human experience, the practice
seldom, if ever, lived up to the theory. It's doubtful if Ivan the
Terrible° was preferable in any way to Stalin°. The point is that, in
principle, there were once irrevocable limitations to the authority
of any tyrant. The czars believed until the very last that they derived
their authority from God. Well, so did Saul°, and when he offended
God, the shepherd boy, David, was anointed king in his stead.

6   Samuel Johnson° endorsed the principle of divine right as represented by the House of Stuart, not because he had any illusions
about the abilities or character of the ageing Bonnie Prince° then
nursing his brandy bottle in Rome, but because at that particular
point in time and space the Stuarts symbolized the principle that
there are certain laws that can't be altered by men, not even by an
overwhelming majority of men. Johnson lived during the Age of
Enlightenment when progressive thinkers were expounding the
theory of the Social Contract°, according to which human societies
were formed in much the same way as joint stock companies°. He
rejected that concept not because he was a reactionary looking only
toward the past, but because he was a very wise man looking
toward the distant future and foresaw where the Enlightenment
could lead.

7   It's important to remember that under divine right it was the
principle and not the person of the king that mattered. The king
possessed only such power as was delegated to him by God. Similarly, Parliaments possess only such power as is granted them by
the people—but the people, unlike God, are fallible. The kings who
ruled, or attempted to rule, by divine right have been swept into
what Marx called the "dustbin of history." That doesn't much
matter; they were a shabby lot, most of them. But the principle
they represented is probably more important today than it ever
was. Twentieth century man may yet discover that only God can
protect him from the state.

8   "All power to the people!" the New Leftists cry. Myself, I
suspect the people already possess more power than is good for
them. I agree with Miguel de Unamuno°, who said that one human
being is of more importance than all of humanity. For "humanity"
and "the people" are mere abstractions. What's required is more

power for the private man, and the private woman. Ironically, that may be what many of the young radicals really want: more power for the individual. It's a cliché of the critics of the radicals that if all power were actually given to the people the first act of the people would be to tear the radicals apart. We've all of us seen those old films of the Nazi rallies at Nuremberg: flags, torches, uniforms, bands, and tens of thousands of persons, old and young, screaming "Sieg Heil!" They were The People, too.

```
┌──────────────────────────┐
│                          │
│                          │
└──────────────────────────┘
```

ALDEN NOWLAN

Alden Nowlan (1933–1983), the poet, story writer, and essayist, was born in Windsor, N.S., and worked as a journalist before joining the University of New Brunswick, where he was writer-in-residence. His poems appear in numerous collections, including *Between Tears and Laughter*; his stories in *Miracle at Indian River*; and his journalism in *Double Exposure*.

Words and Meanings

Paragraph

principle of the divine right of kings:	theory that the monarch of a nation derives authority and power from God	1
consensus:	agreement among everyone involved in a decision	2
Wilhelm II:	the last autocratic kaiser, or ruler, of Germany, who abdicated in 1918	4
Ivan the Terrible:	sixteenth-century Russian czar and warlord	5
Stalin:	Soviet dictator who died in 1953	
Saul:	first king of Israel in the Old Testament	
Samuel Johnson:	eighteenth-century English man of letters, compiler of the first English dictionary	6
Bonnie Prince:	Prince Charles, Stuart contender for the throne of England	
theory of the Social Contract:	theory that society works because its members agree to make it work	
joint stock companies:	early form of business owned not by a single person but by a consortium or group	
Miguel de Unamuno:	Spanish philosopher and theorist of individual freedom	8

Structure and Strategy

1. Explain what makes the first sentence of Nowlan's essay particularly arresting.
2. Where does Nowlan define what he means by "divine right"?

3. In paragraph 3, how does the author use the issue of abortion to show the strengths and shortcomings of "enlightened" people?
4. In his concluding paragraph, what connection does Nowlan draw between the New Leftists, who want power for the people, and the Nazis, who wanted power for themselves?

Content and Purpose

1. Do you feel "astonished" or "frightened" by the principle of the divine right of kings?
2. Which is of greater importance, the notion of kingship or the individual king?
3. Does Alden Nowlan believe there are moral laws that apply to everyone, or does he believe that each individual is a law unto himself?
4. What does Nowlan mean when he writes, "Twentieth century man may yet discover that only God can protect him from the state"?
5. How would life in Canada be different if we were ruled by a monarch with the divine right to rule?

Suggestions for Writing

1. Write a paper in which you argue that Canada should or should not return to the principle of governance by divine right.
2. Write a paper in which you argue that the legal drinking age should or should not be raised.
3. Write a paper in which you argue that the legal driving age ought to be a matter decided between the individual and his or her parents.

We Have No "Right to Happiness"

C.S. LEWIS

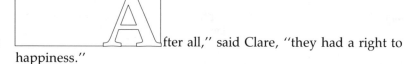

1   fter all," said Clare, "they had a right to happiness."

2   We were discussing something that once happened in our own neighbourhood. Mr. A. had deserted Mrs. A. and got his divorce

"We Have No 'Right to Happiness' " from *Undeceptions* by C. S. Lewis. Copyright 1971. Reprinted by permission of Collins Publishers.

in order to marry Mrs. B., who had likewise got her divorce in order to marry Mr. A. And there was certainly no doubt that Mr. A. and Mrs. B. were very much in love with one another. If they continued to be in love, and if nothing went wrong with their health or their income, they might reasonably expect to be very happy.

3 It was equally clear that they were not happy with their old partners. Mrs. B. had adored her husband at the outset. But then he got smashed up in the war. It was thought he had lost his virility°, and it was known that he had lost his job. Life with him was no longer what Mrs. B. had bargained for. Poor Mrs. A., too. She had lost her looks—and all her liveliness. It might be true, as some said, that she consumed herself by bearing his children and nursing him through the long illness that overshadowed their earlier married life.

4 You mustn't, by the way, imagine that A. was the sort of man who nonchalantly threw a wife away like the peel of an orange he'd sucked dry. Her suicide was a terrible shock to him. We all knew this, for he told us so himself. "But what could I do?" he said. "A man has a right to happiness. I had to take my one chance when it came."

5 I went away thinking about the concept of a "right to happiness."

6 At first this sounds to me as odd as a right to good luck. For I believe—whatever one school of moralists may say—that we depend for a very great deal of our happiness or misery on circumstances outside all human control. A right to happiness doesn't, for me, make much more sense than a right to be six feet tall, or to have a millionaire for your father, or to get good weather whenever you want to have a picnic.

7 I can understand a right as a freedom guaranteed me by the laws of the society I live in. Thus, I have a right to travel along the public roads because society gives me that freedom; that's what we mean by calling the roads "public." I can also understand a right as a claim guaranteed me by the laws, and correlative° to an obligation on someone else's part. If I have a right to receive £100 from you, this is another way of saying that you have a duty to pay me £100. If the laws allow Mr. A. to desert his wife and seduce his neighbour's wife, then, by definition, Mr. A. has a legal right to do so, and we need bring in no talk about "happiness."

8 But of course that was not what Clare meant. She meant that he had not only a legal but a moral right to act as he did. In other words, Clare is—or would be if she thought it out—a classical moralist after the style of Thomas Aquinas, Grotius, Hooker and Locke. She believes that behind the laws of the state there is a Natural Law.

9 I agree with her. I hold this conception to be basic to all

civilization. Without it, the actual laws of the state become an absolute, as in Hegel. They cannot be criticized because there is no norm against which they should be judged.

10 　　The ancestry of Clare's maxim, "They have a right to happiness," is august°. In words that are cherished by all civilized men, but especially by Americans, it has been laid down that one of the rights of man is a right to "the pursuit of happiness." And now we get to the real point.

11 　　What did the writers of that august declaration mean?

12 　　It is quite certain what they did not mean. They did not mean that man was entitled to pursue happiness by any and every means—including, say, murder, rape, robbery, treason and fraud. No society could be built on such a basis.

13 　　They meant "to pursue happiness by all lawful means"; that is, by all means which the Law of Nature eternally sanctions° and which the laws of the nation shall sanction.

14 　　Admittedly this seems at first to reduce their maxim° to the tautology° that men (in pursuit of happiness) have a right to do whatever they have a right to do. But tautologies, seen against their proper historical context, are not always barren° tautologies. The declaration is primarily a denial of the political principles which long governed Europe: a challenge flung down to the Austrian and Russian empires, to England before the Reform Bills, to Bourbon France. It demands that whatever means of pursuing happiness are lawful for any should be lawful for all; that "man," not men of some particular caste, class, status, or religion, should be free to use them. In a century when this is being unsaid by nation after nation and party after party, let us not call it a barren tautology.

15 　　But the question as to what means are "lawful"—what methods of pursuing happiness are either morally permissible by the Law of Nature or should be declared legally permissible by the legislature of a particular nation—remains exactly where it did. And on that question I disagree with Clare. I don't think it is obvious that people have the unlimited "right to happiness" which she suggests.

16 　　For one thing, I believe that Clare, when she says "happiness," means simply and solely "sexual happiness." Partly because women like Clare never use the word "happiness" in any other sense. But also because I never heard Clare talk about the "right" to any other kind. She was rather leftist in her politics, and would have been scandalised if anyone had defended the actions of a ruthless man-eating tycoon on the ground that his happiness consisted in making money and he was pursuing his happiness. She was also a rabid teetotaller; I never heard her excuse an alcoholic because he was happy when he was drunk.

17 　　A good many of Clare's friends, and especially her female

friends, often felt—I've heard them say so—that their own happiness would be perceptibly increased by boxing her ears. I very much doubt if this would have brought her theory of a right to happiness into play.

Clare, in fact, is doing what the whole western world seems   18
to me to have been doing for the last 40-odd years. When I was a youngster, all the progressive people were saying, "Why all this prudery°? Let us treat sex just as we treat all other impulses." I was simple-minded enough to believe they meant what they said. I have since discovered that they meant exactly the opposite. They meant that sex was to be treated as no other impulse in our nature has ever been treated by civilized people. All the others, we admit, have to be bridled°. Absolute obedience to your instinct for self-preservation is what we call cowardice; to your acquisitive impulse, avarice°. Even sleep must be resisted if you're a sentry. But every unkindness and breach of faith seems to be condoned° provided that the object aimed at is "four bare legs in a bed."

It is like having a morality in which stealing fruit is considered   19
wrong—unless you steal nectarines.

And if you protest against this view you are usually met with   20
chatter about the legitimacy and beauty and sanctity° of "sex" and accused of harbouring some Puritan prejudice against it as something disreputable or shameful. I deny the charge. Foam-born Venus° . . . golden Aphrodite° . . . I never breathed a word against you. If I object to boys who steal my nectarines, must I be supposed to disapprove of nectarines in general? Or even of boys in general? It might, you know, be stealing that I disapproved of.

The real situation is skilfully concealed by saying that the question   21
of Mr. A.'s "right" to desert his wife is one of "sexual morality." Robbing an orchard is not an offense against some special morality called "fruit morality." It is an offense against honesty. Mr. A.'s action is an offense against good faith (to solemn promises), against gratitude (toward one to whom he was deeply indebted) and against common humanity.   *thesis*

Our sexual impulses are thus being put in a position of pre-   22
posterous privilege. The sexual motive is taken to condone all sorts of behaviour which, if it had any other end in view, would be condemned as merciless, treacherous and unjust.

Now though I see no good reason for giving sex this privilege,   23
I think I see a strong cause. It is this.

It is part of the nature of a strong erotic passion—as distinct   24
from a transient fit° of appetite—that it makes more towering promises than any other emotion. No doubt all our desires make promises, but not so impressively. To be in love involves the almost irresistible conviction that one will go on being in love until one

dies, and that possession of the beloved will confer, not merely frequent ecstasies, but settled, fruitful, deep-rooted, lifelong happiness. Hence *all* seems to be at stake. If we miss this chance we shall have lived in vain. At the very thought of such a doom we sink into fathomless depths of self-pity.

25   Unfortunately these promises are found to be quite untrue. Every experienced adult knows this to be so as regards all erotic passions (except the one he himself is feeling at the moment). We discount the world-without-end pretensions of our friends' amours easily enough. We know that such things sometimes last—and sometimes don't. And when they do last, this is not because they promised at the outset to do so. When two people achieve lasting happiness, this is not solely because they are great lovers but because they are also—I must put it crudely—good people; controlled, loyal, fair-minded, mutually adaptable people.

26   If we establish a "right to (sexual) happiness" which supersedes° all the ordinary rules of behaviour, we do so not because of what our passion shows itself to be in experience but because of what it professes to be while we are in the grip of it. Hence, while the bad behaviour is real and works miseries and degradations, the happiness which was the object of the behaviour turns out again and again to be illusory°. Everyone (except Mr. A. and Mrs. B.) knows that Mr. A. in a year or so may have the same reason for deserting his new wife as for deserting his old. He will feel again that all is at stake. He will see himself again as the great lover, and his pity for himself will exclude all pity for the woman.

27   Two further points remain.

28   One is this. A society in which conjugal infidelity° is tolerated must always be in the long run a society adverse° to women. Women, whatever a few male songs and satires may say to the contrary, are more naturally monogamous° than men; it is a biological necessity. Where promiscuity° prevails, they will therefore always be more often the victims than the culprits. Also, domestic happiness is more necessary to them than to us. And the quality by which they most easily hold a man, their beauty, decreases every year after they have come to maturity, but this does not happen to those qualities of personality—women don't really care twopence about our *looks*—by which we hold women. Thus in the ruthless war of promiscuity women are at a double disadvantage. They play for higher stakes and are also more likely to lose. I have no sympathy with moralists who frown at the increasing crudity of female provocativeness. These signs of desperate competition fill me with pity.

29   Secondly, though the "right to happiness" is chiefly claimed for the sexual impulse, it seems to me impossible that the matter should stay there. The fatal principle, once allowed in that de-

partment, must sooner or later seep through our whole lives. We thus advance toward a state of society in which not only each man but every impulse in each man claims *carte blanche°*. And then, though our technological skill may help us survive a little longer, our civilization will have died at heart, and will—one dare not even add "unfortunately"—be swept away.

```
┌─────────────────────────────┐
│                             │
│                             │
└─────────────────────────────┘
```

C.S. LEWIS

C.S. Lewis (1898–1965), the English novelist, literary critic, and essay writer, taught for many years at Oxford University. He is the author of *The Screwtape Letters* as well as the Perelandra series of science-fiction novels and the Narnia series of fantasy adventures for young readers. Much of his work deals with Christian theology and moral problems.

Words and Meanings

Paragraph

virility:	sexual potency	3
correlative:	counterpart; something corresponding to	7
august:	venerable, awe-inspiring	10
sanctions:	authorizes, endorses, gives binding force to	13
maxim:	principle, saying, rule of conduct	14
tautology:	saying the same thing twice in different words	
barren:	unproductive, ineffectual, meaningless	
prudery:	excessive modesty, shyness about sexual matters	18
bridled:	restrained, controlled	
avarice:	greed	
condoned:	excused, forgiven	
sanctity:	purity, holiness, goodness	20
Venus:	Roman goddess of Love	
Aphrodite:	Greek goddess of Love	
transient fit:	passing phase; short-lived experience	24
supersedes:	replaces	26
illusory:	based on illusion, unreal	
conjugal infidelity:	adultery	28
adverse:	opposed to the interests of	
monogamous:	having one mate at a time	
promiscuity:	indiscriminate sexual behaviour; playing around	
carte blanche:	French for "blank paper"—given to a person so that he could write his own terms on it; complete freedom from restriction or regulation	29

Structure and Strategy

1. Study the TONE of paragraph 4. How does Lewis signal his disapproval to the reader?
2. Why are paragraphs 5, 11, 19, 23, and 27 so short? What function do they serve?
3. What definition of "right" does Lewis offer in paragraph 7? How does he develop that definition?
4. What is the function of paragraph 15? What does it contribute to the development of Lewis's argument?
5. What is the function of paragraph 26? Why is it crucial to Lewis's argument?
6. What concluding strategy does Lewis employ in paragraphs 19 to 21? How do you respond to the tone of these paragraphs?

Content and Purpose

1. What is the difference between a legal right and a moral right (paragraphs 9 and 10)? Summarize the difference in your own words.
2. What Natural Law does Lewis believe lies behind all the laws, rules, and regulations of our society?
3. Why does Lewis reject his friend Clare's concept of happiness (paragraph 16) and, by extension, that of the whole western world for the past 40 years (paragraph 18)?
4. Why does Lewis believe that our sexual impulses are not a solid basis for human happiness?
5. In your own words, summarize the reasons Lewis believes promiscuity should not be condoned (paragraph 21).
6. Consider Lewis's claims in paragraphs 28 and 29. Is he arguing from a feminist point of view? Would Gloria Steinem agree with what he says here (see her essay in Unit Four)? Do you think his argument is valid?

Suggestions for Writing

1. Some people in our society believe they have a "right" to deal drugs and make money, or to take drugs and get high. They believe that neither dealing nor consuming is immoral, and that neither dealing nor consuming should be illegal.

    Using Lewis's essay as a model, write an essay convincing your readers that drug dealers (or users) have a "right to happiness."
2. Do you feel it is morally right for a person to leave a spouse because he or she is no longer sexually attractive? Write a persuasive essay giving the reasons for your opinion.

The Huxleyan Warning

NEIL POSTMAN

There are two ways by which the spirit of   1
a culture may be shriveled. In the first—the Orwellian°—culture
becomes a prison. In the second—the Huxleyan°—culture becomes
a burlesque°.

No one needs to be reminded that our world is now marred   2
by many prison-cultures whose structure Orwell described accu-
rately in his parables. If one were to read both *1984* and *Animal
Farm*, and then for good measure, Arthur Koestler's *Darkness at
Noon*, one would have a fairly precise blueprint of the machinery
of thought-control as it currently operates in scores of countries
and on millions of people. Of course, Orwell was not the first to
teach us about the spiritual devastations of tyranny. What is irreplaceable about his work is his insistence that it makes little difference if our wardens are inspired by right- or left-wing ideologies.
The gates of the prison are equally impenetrable, surveillance equally
rigorous, icon-worship equally pervasive.

What Huxley teaches is that in the age of advanced technology,   3
spiritual devastation is more likely to come from an enemy with a
smiling face than from one whose countenance exudes suspicion
and hate. In the Huxleyan prophecy, Big Brother° does not watch
us, by his choice. We watch him, by ours. There is no need for
wardens or gates or Ministries of Truth. When a population becomes distracted by trivia, when cultural life is redefined as a perpetual round of entertainments, when serious public conversation
becomes a form of baby-talk, when, in short, a people become an
audience and their public business a vaudeville act, then a nation
finds itself at risk; culture-death is a clear possibility.

In America, Orwell's prophecies are of small relevance, but   4
Huxley's are well under way toward being realized. For America
is engaged in the world's most ambitious experiment to accommodate itself to the technological distractions made possible by the
electric plug. This is an experiment that began slowly and modestly
in the mid-nineteenth century and has now, in the latter half of

"The Huxleyan Warning" from *Amusing Ourselves to Death: Public Discourse in the
Age of Show Business* by Neil Postman. Copyright © 1985 by Neil Postman. Reprinted
by permission of Viking Penguin Inc.

the twentieth, reached a perverse maturity in America's consuming love-affair with television. As nowhere else in the world, Americans have moved far and fast in bringing to a close the age of the slow-moving printed word, and have granted to television sovereignty over all of their institutions. By ushering in the Age of Television, America has given the world the clearest available glimpse of the Huxleyan future.

5   Those who speak about this matter must often raise their voices to a near-hysterical pitch, inviting the charge that they are everything from wimps to public nuisances to Jeremiahs°. But they do so because what they want others to see appears benign°, when it is not invisible altogether. An Orwellian world is much easier to recognize, and to oppose, than a Huxleyan. Everything in our background has prepared us to know and resist a prison when the gates begin to close around us. We are not likely, for example, to be indifferent to the voices of the Sakharovs° and the Timmermans° and the Walesas°. We take arms against such a sea of troubles, buttressed by the spirit of Milton°, Bacon°, Voltaire°, Goethe° and Jefferson°. But what if there are no cries of anguish to be heard? Who is prepared to take arms against a sea of amusements? To whom do we complain, and when, and in what tone of voice, when serious discourse dissolves into giggles? What is the antidote° to a culture's being drained by laughter?

6   I fear that our philosophers have given us no guidance in this matter. Their warnings have customarily been directed against those consciously formulated ideologies that appeal to the worst tendencies in human nature. But what is happening in America is not the design of an articulated ideology. No *Mein Kampf*° or *Communist Manifesto*° announced its coming. It comes as the unintended consequence of a dramatic change in our modes of public conversation. But it is an ideology nonetheless, for it imposes a way of life, a set of relations among people and ideas, about which there has been no consensus, no discussion and no opposition. Only compliance. Public consciousness has not yet assimilated° the point that technology is ideology. This, in spite of the fact that before our very eyes technology has altered every aspect of life in America during the past eighty years. For example, it would have been excusable in 1905 for us to be unprepared for the cultural changes the automobile would bring. Who could have suspected then that the automobile would tell us how we were to conduct our social and sexual lives? Would reorient our ideas about what to do with our forests and cities? Would create new ways of expressing our personal identity and social standing?

7   But it is much later in the game now, and ignorance of the score is inexcusable. To be unaware that a technology comes equipped

with a program for social change, to maintain that technology is
neutral, to make the assumption that technology is always a friend
to culture is, at this late hour, stupidity plain and simple. Moreover,
we have seen enough by now to know that technological changes
in our modes of communication are even more ideology-laden than
changes in our modes of transportation. Introduce the alphabet to
a culture and you change its cognitive habits°, its social relations,
its notions of community, history and religion. Introduce the printing press with movable type, and you do the same. Introduce
speed-of-light transmission of images and you make a cultural revolution. Without a vote. Without polemics°. Without guerrilla resistance. Here is ideology, pure if not serene. Here is ideology
without words, and all the more powerful for their absence. All
that is required to make it stick is a population that devoutly believes in the inevitability of progress. And in this sense, all Americans are Marxists, for we believe nothing if not that history is
moving us toward some preordained paradise and that technology
is the force behind that movement.

Thus, there are near insurmountable difficulties for anyone   8
who has written such a book as this, and who wishes to end it
with some remedies for the affliction. In the first place, not everyone believes a cure is needed, and in the second, there probably
isn't any. But as a true-blue American who has imbibed the un-
shakable belief that where there is a problem there must be a
solution, I shall conclude with the following suggestions.

We must, as a start, not delude° ourselves with preposterous   9
notions such as the straight Luddite° position as outlined, for example, in Jerry Mander's *Four Arguments for the Elimination of Television*. Americans will not shut down any part of their technological
apparatus, and to suggest that they do so is to make no suggestion
at all. It is almost equally unrealistic to expect that nontrivial modi-
fications in the availability of media will ever be made. Many civilized nations limit by law the amount of hours television may
operate and thereby mitigate° the role television plays in public
life. But I believe that this is not a possibility in America. Once
having opened the Happy Medium to full public view, we are not
likely to countenance even its partial closing. Still, some Americans
have been thinking along these lines. As I write, a story appears
in *The New York Times* (September 27, 1984) about the plans of
the Farmington, Connecticut, Library Council to sponsor a "TV
Turnoff." It appears that such an effort was made the previous
year, the idea being to get people to stop watching television for
one month. The *Times* reports that the turnoff the previous January
was widely noted by the media. Ms. Ellen Babcock, whose family
participated, is quoted as saying, "It will be interesting to see if

the impact is the same this year as last year, when we had terrific media coverage." In other words, Ms. Babcock hopes that by watching television, people will learn that they ought to stop watching television. It is hard to imagine that Ms. Babcock does not see the irony in this position. It is an irony that I have confronted many times in being told that I must appear on television to promote a book that warns people against television. Such are the contradictions of a television-based culture.

10   In any case, of how much help is a one-month turnoff? It is a mere pittance°; that is to say, a penance°. How comforting it must be when the folks in Farmington are done with their punishment and can return to their true occupation. Nonetheless, one applauds their effort, as one must applaud the efforts of those who see some relief in limiting certain kinds of content on television—for example, excessive violence, commercials on children's shows, etc. I am particularly fond of John Lindsay's suggestion that political commercials be banned from television as we now ban cigarette and liquor commercials. I would gladly testify before the Federal Communications Commission as to the manifold merits of this excellent idea. To those who would oppose my testimony by claiming that such a ban is a clear violation of the First Amendment, I would offer a compromise: [r]equire all political commercials to be preceded by a short statement to the effect that common sense has determined that watching political commercials is hazardous to the intellectual health of the community.

11   I am not very optimistic about anyone's taking this suggestion seriously. Neither do I put much stock in proposals to improve the quality of television programs. Television, as I have implied earlier, serves us most usefully when presenting junk-entertainment; it serves us most ill when it co-opts° serious modes of discourse°— news, politics, science, education, commerce, religion—and turns them into entertainment packages. We would all be better off if television got worse, not better. "The A-Team" and "Cheers" are no threat to our public health. "60 Minutes," "Eye-Witness News" and "Sesame Street" are.

12   The problem, in any case, does not reside in *what* people watch. The problem is in *that* we watch. The solution must be found in *how* we watch. For I believe it may fairly be said that we have yet to learn what television is. And the reason is that there has been no worthwhile discussion, let alone widespread public understanding, of what information is and how it gives direction to a culture. There is a certain poignancy° in this, since there are no people who more frequently and enthusiastically use such phrases as "the information age," "the information explosion," and "the information society." We have apparently advanced to the point where we have

grasped the idea that a change in the forms, volume, speed and context of information *means* something, but we have not got any further.

What is information? Or more precisely, what *are* information? 13
What are its various forms? What conceptions of intelligence, wisdom and learning does each form insist upon? What conceptions does each form neglect or mock? What are the main psychic effects of each form? What is the relation between information and reason? What is the kind of information that best facilitates thinking? Is there a moral bias to each information form? What does it mean to say that there is too much information? How would one know? What redefinitions of important cultural meanings do new sources, speeds, contexts and forms of information require? Does television, for example, give a new meaning to "piety," to "patriotism," to "privacy"? Does television give a new meaning to "judgment" or to "understanding"? How do different forms of information persuade? Is a newspaper's "public" different from television's "public"? How do different information forms dictate the type of content that is expressed?

These questions, and dozens more like them, are the means 14
through which it might be possible for Americans to begin talking back to their television sets. For no medium is excessively dangerous if its users understand what its dangers are. It is not important that those who ask the questions arrive at my answers or Marshall McLuhan's° (quite different answers, by the way). This is an instance in which the asking of the questions is sufficient. To ask is to break the spell. To which I might add that questions about the psychic, political and social effects of information are as applicable to the computer as to television. Although I believe the computer to be a vastly overrated technology, I mention it here because, clearly, Americans have accorded it their customary mindless inattention; which means they will use it as they are told, without a whimper. Thus, a central thesis of computer technology—that the principal difficulty we have in solving problems stems from insufficient data—will go unexamined. Until, years from now, when it will be noticed that the massive collection and speed-of-light retrieval of data have been of great value to large-scale organizations but have solved very little of importance to most people and have created at least as many problems for them as they may have solved.

In any case, the point I am trying to make is that only through 15
a deep and unfailing awareness of the structure and effects of information, through a demystification of media, is there any hope of our gaining some measure of control over television, or the computer, or any other medium. How is such media consciousness

to be achieved? There are only two answers that come to mind, one of which is nonsense and can be dismissed almost at once; the other is desperate but it is all we have.

16   The nonsensical answer is to create television programs whose intent would be, not to get people to stop watching television but to demonstrate how television ought to be viewed, to show how television recreates and degrades our conception of news, political debate, religious thought, etc. I imagine such demonstrations would of necessity take the form of parodies, along the lines of "Saturday Night Live" and "Monty Python," the idea being to induce a nationwide horse laugh over television's control of public discourse. But, naturally, television would have the last laugh. In order to command an audience large enough to make a difference, one would have to make the programs vastly amusing, in the television style. Thus, the act of criticism itself would, in the end, be co-opted by television. The parodists would become celebrities, would star in movies, and would end up making television commercials.

17   The desperate answer is to rely on the only mass medium of communication that, in theory, is capable of addressing the problem: our schools. This is the conventional American solution to all dangerous social problems, and is, of course, based on a naive and mystical faith in the efficacy° of education. The process rarely works. In the matter at hand, there is even less reason than usual to expect it to. Our schools have not yet even got around to examining the role of the printed word in shaping our culture. Indeed, you will not find two high school seniors in a hundred who could tell you— within a five-hundred-year margin of error—when the alphabet was invented. I suspect most do not even know that the alphabet *was* invented. I have found that when the question is put to them, they appear puzzled, as if one had asked, When were trees invented, or clouds? It is the very principle of myth, as Roland Barthes pointed out, that it transforms history into nature, and to ask of our schools that they engage in the task of de-mythologizing media is to ask something the schools have never done.

18   And yet there is reason to suppose that the situation is not hopeless. Educators are not unaware of the effects of television on their students. Stimulated by the arrival of the computer, they discuss it a great deal—which is to say, they have become somewhat "media conscious." It is true enough that much of their consciousness centers on the question, How can we use television (or the computer, or word processor) to control education? They have not yet got to the question, How can we use education to control television (or the computer, or word processor)? But our reach for solutions ought to exceed our present grasp, or what's our dreaming for? Besides, it is an acknowledged task of the schools to assist

the young in learning how to interpret the symbols of their culture. That this task should now require that they learn how to distance themselves from their forms of information is not so bizarre an enterprise that we cannot hope for its inclusion in the curriculum; even hope that it will be placed at the center of education.

What I suggest here as a solution is what Aldous Huxley sug-   19
gested, as well. And I can do no better than he. He believed with H.G. Wells that we are in a race between education and disaster, and he wrote continuously about the necessity of our understanding the politics and epistemology° of media. For in the end, he was trying to tell us that what afflicted the people in *Brave New World* was not that they were laughing instead of thinking, but that they did not know what they were laughing about and why they had stopped thinking.

NEIL POSTMAN

Neil Postman, the American advocate of radical educational reform, lives in Flushing, New York, and is a professor of communication arts and sciences at New York University. Among his many books are *Teaching as a Subversive Activity*, *The Disappearance of Childhood*, and *Amusing Ourselves to Death*. In the chapters that precede the excerpt above, Postman argues that our society expects and requires its politics, religion, education, news and commerce to be delivered in the form of entertainment—a demand that ultimately trivializes them.

Words and Meanings
Paragraph

Orwellian:	reference to George Orwell's *1984*, a novel about dictatorship through thought-control	1
Huxleyan:	reference to Aldous Huxley's *Brave New World*, a contrasting view of future society	
burlesque:	farce	
Big Brother	dictator in *1984* whose image controls the masses	3
Jeremiahs:	prophets of doom	5
benign:	harmless, or even good	
the Sakharovs, Timmermans and Walesas:	Russian, Argentinian, and Polish dissidents	
Milton:	seventeenth-century English poet who celebrated liberty	
Bacon:	Francis Bacon, seventeenth-century English essayist	
Voltaire:	eighteenth-century French writer	

Goethe:	nineteenth-century German philosopher and poet
Jefferson:	Thomas Jefferson, one of the "fathers of America" who helped draft the Declaration of Independence
antidote:	remedy, cure

6   *Mein Kampf*:   Adolf Hitler's autobiography
      Communist Manifesto: Karl Marx's 1848 indictment of capitalism
      assimilated: digested, absorbed; fully understood

7   cognitive habits: ways of knowing
      polemics: controversial discussions; debates

9   delude: deceive
      Luddite: follower of eighteenth-century workman, Ned Ludd, who thought he could halt technological progress by destroying the machines threatening the workers' livelihood
      mitigate: moderate, diminish

10   pittance: small amount, trifle
      penance: self-imposed punishment

11   co-opts: adopts, absorbs
      discourse: verbal communication

12   poignancy: painful sharpness

14   Marshall McLuhan: philosopher of the media, coiner of the phrase "the medium is the message"

17   efficacy: power, effectiveness

19   epistemology: how we know what we know

Structure and Strategy

1. In paragraph 1, Postman introduces a contrast that forms the basis of the first section of this essay. How does he develop that contrast in paragraphs 2 to 5?
2. Identify the main point Postman develops in each of the following sections: paragraphs 6 to 8; 9 to 11; 12 to 14; 15. How does paragraph 15 serve as a TRANSITION?
3. Explore the ALLUSION in paragraph 5. (Hint: see *Hamlet*, III, i, 59.)
4. Identify three or four particularly effective examples of IRONY in this essay.
5. Postman attempts to appeal to his readers' emotions as well as to their reason in this essay. Identify two or three examples of his use of DICTION to affect our emotions.
6. What concluding strategy does Postman use? Is it effective?

Content and Purpose

1. Does Postman intend simply to convince his readers that his point of view is a valid one, or does he want his readers to act in some way as a result of his message? What are his purposes in writing this essay?
2. Why does Postman regard Huxley's prophecies as more dangerous to our culture than Orwell's (paragraph 3)?
3. In paragraph 4, Postman claims that Americans live in an Age of Television more than any other people in the world. To what extent do you think Canadians share the Americans' "consuming love-affair with television" and, therefore, share the risk of "culture-death"?
4. Explain what Postman means when he asserts that technology is not neutral. What examples does he use to support this contention? (See paragraphs 6 and 7.)
5. Why does Postman reject "Luddite" solutions in America and regard the campaign against television as ironic?
6. Why does Postman believe that "we would all be better off if television got worse, not better"?
7. What is Postman's solution? Why does he see the problem as "a race between education and disaster," as H.G. Wells described it?

Suggestions for Writing

1. Postman writes about the pervasive influence of television in America, but he does not mention the pervasive influence of America on the rest of the world, an influence which is largely attributable to American media. Many countries, Canada included, regard the influence of American television as cultural imperialism. However, some people in Canada want access to American television at all costs and are not in the least worried about Canada's identity as a nation. Write an essay in which you attempt to convince your readers that American television programs should (or should not) be severely restricted in Canada.
2. Write an essay in which you argue that television is a positive influence in our society.

Additional Suggestions for Writing: Argument and Persuasion

Choose one of the topics below and write an essay based on it. Think through your position carefully, formulate your opinion, and identify logical reasons for holding that opinion. Construct a clear thesis statement before you begin to write the paper.

1. Equal pay for work of equal value is (or is not) an impractical goal in Canada.
2. Canada Post should (or should not) provide home mail delivery to everyone.
3. The overall quality of Canadian life is improving (or declining).
4. Violence against an established government is (or is not) justified in certain circumstances.
5. Private religious schools should (or should not) receive government subsidies.
6. The federal government should (or should not) make significant changes to the u.i.c. (unemployment insurance) plan.
7. It is too easy (or too difficult) to get a divorce in Canada.
8. A teacher should (or should not) aim most of the course work at the weakest students in the class.
9. A couple should (or should not) live together before marriage.
10. Smoking should (or should not) be banned in all public buildings.
11. The government of Canada should (or should not) decriminalize the use of "soft" drugs.
12. Blondes do (or do not) have more fun.
13. Boys and girls should (or should not) play on the same sports teams.
14. Critically ill patients should (or should not) be permitted to end their lives if and when they choose.
15. The government of Canada is (or is not) helpless to deal effectively with acid rain (or any other environmental hazard).
16. Physical education should (or should not) be compulsory for all able-bodied students throughout the high school years.
17. Fully subsidized day-care is (or is not) in the best interests of the whole community.
18. A gay parent should (or should not) be eligible to gain custody of his or her children after a divorce.
19. Dishonesty is sometimes (is never) the best policy.
20. "It is a truth universally acknowledged that a single man in possession of a good fortune must be in want of a wife." (Jane Austen)

Further Reading

The Softball Was Always Hard

HARRY BRUCE

When I tell young softball players I played the game barehanded, they regard me warily. Am I one of those geezers who's forever jawing about the fact that, in *his* day, you had to walk through six miles of snowdrifts just to get to school? Will I tediously lament the passing of the standing broad jump, and the glorious old days when the only football in the Maritimes was English rugger, when hockey was an outdoor art rather than indoor mayhem and, at decent yacht clubs, men were gentlemen and women were *personae non grata*? No, but I will tell today's softball players that—with their fancy uniforms, batters' helmets, dugouts, manicured diamonds, guys to announce who's at bat over public-address systems and, above all, gloves for every fielder—the game they play is more tarted-up and sissy than the one I knew.

"The Softball Was Always Hard" from *Each Moment As It Flies: Writings by Harry Bruce*. Copyright 1984. Reprinted by permission of Bella Pomer Agency Inc.

Softball bloomed in the Dirty Thirties because it was a game the most impoverished deadbeat could afford to play. For schools, it had the edge that soccer still has over North American football: it required no expensive equipment. It was the people's game in the worst of times. Unlike baseball, which calls for a field the size of a town, softball could flourish in one corner of a city park, on a vacant lot, in any schoolyard. The only gear you needed was a ball, a bat, a catcher's glove and mask, and a first baseman's glove, a floppy affair which I knew as a "trapper." Two amiable teams might even use the same gloves—two gloves for eighteen players.

In the Toronto gradeschool league of the Forties, gloves for all other players were outlawed. This meant that early in the season the hands of a boy shortstop felt as though a 300-lb. vice-principal had given him the strap. Any team that lasted long enough to reach the city finals, however, boasted little infielders with palms like saddle-leather. They learned to catch a line drive with both hands, not by snaring it with a glove big enough to hold a medicine ball. They cushioned the ball by drawing back their cupped hands at the split-second of impact. They fielded sizzling grounders by turning sideways, dropping one knee to the ground, getting their whole bodies in front of the ball, then scooping it up, again with both small, bare hands.

A word about balls. The *New Columbia Encyclopedia* says, "Despite the name, the ball used is not soft," which may be the understatement of the tome's 3,052 pages. There were three kinds of softballs, and each was about as soft as anthracite. The best was simply a big baseball, with seams that were pretty well flush with the horsehide cover. Then there was a solid rubber ball with fake seams. After a while, this ball did soften up, but on grounds it no longer hurt enough for competition, it was then retired for use only in practice. Then there was the "outseam" ball. Perhaps it was not a sadist who invented it. Perhaps it was merely someone who sought durability in lean times. But the outseam was a quarter-inch ridge of leather so hard that, when you fielded a rifling, spinning grounder, the ball felt as though its real function was to rip the skin off your palms. The outseam ball was a character-builder.

We had no uniforms, but if you reached the city finals team sweaters might magically emerge from some secret cache in the school basement. Certain coaches had the stern theory that even these were bad news, that boys would be so captivated by their own spiffy appearance they'd lose that vital concentration on the game itself, and commit errors. Some boys played in the only shoes they owned, scampers or black oxfords. Others had beaten-up sneakers and, on most teams, some wore short pants and some long. But these youngsters, gangs of ragamuffins by today's standards of sartorial elegance in softball, played furiously competitive, heads-up ball.

If you played outside the school system, for a team sponsored by a camera shop, dairy, hardware store or greasy spoon, then you did get a sweater. You swaggered in it. You'd earned it. Not every kid was good enough to make a team with sweaters. They were advertisements of ability. Nowadays, of course, any kid with the money can buy an Expos' jacket or a Pirates' cap. They're merely advertisements of disposable income, much like the $25 million worth of gear that the chains of athletic-shoe stores expected to sell in Canada during recession-ridden 1982.

But as a celebrator of softball austerity, I am a pipsqueak beside an eighty-year-old tycoon I know. As a boy in a Nova Scotia coal-mining town, he played cricket and street baseball with home-made bats and balls. To make a ball, boys hoarded string and wrapped it around a rock, or if they were lucky a small rubber ball. "We made very good balls," he said, "and we had just as much fun as kids have today with all their expensive stuff." In line with Canada's hoariest hockey tradition, he added, "We used a piece of frozen manure for a puck. It worked just about as good." It wasn't as durable as rubber, but in those days there was no shortage of horse poop.

I once played with a home-made baseball myself. Indeed, I placed the order for its construction. In the summer of '46, when I turned twelve, my father exiled me from Toronto to spend two months at the Bruce homestead on a Nova Scotian shore. That shore, even now, is as sleepy a spot as you're ever likely to find. Not even most Nova Scotians know where it is. But in 1946, the community was not merely remote, it was an anachronism. It hadn't changed much since Victoria had been queen, and to a kid from what he fancied as a bustling, modern metropolis, its empty beauty was at first desolating. This was the ultimate sticks, the boondocks with a vengeance, and I worked off my loneliness by playing catch with myself. Hour after hour, I hurled a Toronto tennis ball against a bluenose barn, catching it on the rebound.

Then I discovered potential ballplayers.

They lived on the farm next door. They were a big, cheerful family, and my knowing them then started my lifelong love affair with the neighborhood. As things are unfolding now, I'll end up there for good. Anyway, several of these farm kids—the oldest was a gentle man of fifteen who, with one paralysing hand, pinned me to a hayfield while I endured the sweet, excruciating humiliation of having his giggling, thirteen-year-old sister plant saliva on my face—were old enough to play a form of softball. Amazingly, however, they'd never played it, nor seen it. They'd never even heard the word.

I told the fifteen-year-old a softball bat was *this* long, and *this* thick at one end, and *this* thin at the other. He made one in half an hour. It wasn't exactly a Louisville Slugger but it had heft to it, and at the same time it was light enough to enable the smaller kids to take a good cut at the ball. What ball? My tennis ball had split. When I knowledgeably declared that the heart of a real baseball was cork, the fifteen-year-old took me down to the stony shore to negotiate with a character I've preserved in memory as "the Ball-maker." He was a hermit who had just given up commercial fishing on his own. He would never again sail the small schooner he'd built, and she'd begun to rot where she lay, a few feet closer to Chedabucto Bay than the ramshackle hut where he somehow survived the seasons.

He was a "beach person," as surely as the salt-stunted spruce were beach trees, and therefore disreputable. If he had known women they had not been church-going women. He was thin, stooped, gnarled, and smelled as though he'd been embalmed in brine, rum, tar, tobacco juice, his own sweat and sinister doings. There was something wrong with one of his eyes and some of his fingers, and though he may only have been as old as I am now (forty-eight), I thought he was ancient enough, and certainly evil enough, to have slit throats for Blackbeard.

The Ball-maker conversed with grunts, snarls, illogical silences, and an accent so thick that, to me, it was a foreign language. But we struck a deal. He gave me a dime. If I would walk inland, following a brookside path through a forest of spruce and fir, and on past a sawmill to a general store, and if I would use the dime to buy him a plug of chewing tobacco and, further, if I would then take the tobacco to him . . . well, he would meanwhile sculpt a baseball-sized sphere of cork. And he did. He fashioned it from three pieces: a thick, round disc and two polar caps, all jammed together with a single spike. That ball was so flawless it was spooky. I can still see it and feel it in my hand, a brown globe so perfect I wondered if the Ball-maker was a warlock.

Back at my friends' farm, we encased the cork in scratchy manila twine till we had something bigger than a hardball but smaller than a softball. For bases, we dropped sweaters among the cowflaps in a pasture, and the lesson began. We would play the kind of teamless ball that's been known in a million schoolyards: as each batter went out, the fielders would all change positions to guarantee that every player got a crack at batting. As the ace from Toronto, I naturally led off. Trouble was, I adored the afternoon's first pitcher. It was she who'd kissed me in the hayfield.

She had hair like a blonde waterfall, eyes like dark chocolate, and skin I ached to touch and smell. Whenever we wrestled, she won. I still dislike that adult sneer, "puppy love." A boy of twelve can love a girl of thirteen with agonizing power. To make matters worse, he hasn't a hope in hell of even understanding the emotion that's racking his skinny being, much less satisfying it. All he knows is that she obsesses him, he yearns for her, he must always appear fine in her eyes.

She had never pitched in her life so it surprised me when she tossed her waterfall in the sunlight and floated the ball gently into the strike zone. Her first pitch. It crept towards me, letter-high. It could have been hanging there in front of me on a string from the sky, and I stepped into it with all the style I'd learned from a hundred Toronto afternoons. Thwack! A line drive so fast no one saw it, and down she went. She crumpled in a heap of blouse, skirt, hair and bare, beloved arms and legs. I had smacked her with the cursed, hairy ball square on her right eye. Her big brother got her sitting up, and we all huddled round her, with me bleating horrified apologies. She never cried. She managed a smile, got to her feet, and shakily went home.

When she turned up for our second game, she had the ugliest black eye I have ever seen on a child. To me, it was a beauty mark. She never blamed me for it. It became a bond, proof of a famous incident we'd shared. She was a tough, forgiving farm girl, and she and her brothers and sisters taught me something I'd not forget about the rough grace of the country folk down home. We played ball for weeks. We played till we pounded the ball to bits, till her eye was once more perfect, and summer was gone.

The car that drove me to the train station passed their farm. Sheets on the clothesline billowed in the usual southwesterly. With her brothers and sister, she was horsing around with their wolfish mutt. They stopped to watch the car moving along the dirt road, and then they all waved goodbye. I was glad they were too far away to see my face. I still lacked her control.

I have my own cabin on that shore now, and though most of those farmyard ballplayers of thirty-seven summers ago have moved away I still see one of them occasionally. He's a mere forty-six, and I like him now as I liked him then. Sometimes I walk along the gravel beach to a patch of grass, from which a footpath once led to a general store. The Ball-maker's shack is gone, but gray planks and ribs and rusty boat nails still endure the lashing of the salt wind that ceaselessly sweeps the bay. They're all that's left of his schooner. Wrecked by time, like bare-handed softball.

HARRY BRUCE

Harry Bruce, journalist and essayist, was born in Toronto. He has written for the country's leading magazines and newspapers. *Each Moment As It Flies* is a collection of articles and essays. Bruce now makes his home in Halifax.

The Game

KEN DRYDEN

The Forum is disturbingly empty: just a few players sit quietly cocooned away in a dressing room; twenty-five or thirty staff work in distant upstairs offices; throughout the rest of its vast insides a few dozen men are busy washing, painting, fixing, tidying things up. There is one other person. Entering the corridor to the dressing room, I hear muffled, reverberating sounds from the ice, and before I can see who it is, I know it's Lafleur. Like a kid on a backyard rink, he skates by himself many minutes before anyone joins him, shooting pucks easily off the boards, watching them rebound, moving skates and gloved hands wherever his inventive instincts direct them to go. Here, far from the expedience of a game, away from defenders and linemates who shackle him to their banal predictability, alone with his virtuoso skills, it is his time to create.

The Italians have a phrase, *inventa la partita*. Translated, it means to "invent the game." A phrase often used by soccer coaches and journalists, it is now, more often than not, used as a lament. For in watching modern players with polished but plastic skills, they wonder at the passing of soccer *genius*—Pele, di Stefano, Puskas—players whose minds and bodies in not so rare moments created something unfound in coaching manuals, a new and continuously changing game for others to aspire to.

It is a loss they explain many ways. In the name of team play, there is no time or place for individual virtuosity, they say; it is a game now taken over by coaches, by technocrats and autocrats who empty players' minds to control their bodies, reprogramming them with X's and O's, driving them to greater *efficiency* and *work rate*, to move *systems* faster, to move games faster, until achieving mindless pace. Others fix blame more on the other side: on smothering defenses played with the same technical sophistication, efficiency, and work rate, but in the nature of defense, easier to play. Still others argue it is the professional sports culture itself which says that games are not won on good plays, but by others' mistakes, where the safe and sure survive, and the creative and not-so-sure may not.

From *The Game* by Ken Dryden. © 1983. Reprinted by permission of Macmillan of Canada, A Division of Canada Publishing Corporation.

But a few link it to a different kind of cultural change, the loss of what they call "street soccer": the mindless hours spent with a ball next to your feet, walking with it as if with a family pet, to school, to a store, or anywhere, playing with it, learning new things about it and about yourself, in time, as with any good companion, developing an *understanding*. In a much less busy time undivided by TV, rock music, or the clutter of modern lessons, it was a child's diversion from having nothing else to do. And, appearances to the contrary, it was creative diversion. But now, with more to do, and with a sophisticated, competitive society pressing on the younger and younger the need for training and skills, its time has run out. Soccer has moved away from the streets and playgrounds to soccer fields, from impromptu games to uniforms and referees, from any time to specific, scheduled time; it has become an *activity* like anything else, organized and maximized, done right or not at all. It has become something to be taught and learned, then tested in games; the answer at the back of the book, the one and only answer. So other time, time not spent with teams in practices or games, deemed wasteful and inefficient, has become time not spent at soccer.

Recently, in Hungary, a survey was conducted asking soccer players from 1910 to the present how much each practi[s]ed a day. The answer, on a gradually shrinking scale, was three hours early in the century to eight minutes a day today. Though long memories can forget, and inflate what they don't forget, if the absolute figures are doubtful, the point is none the less valid. Today, except in the barrios of Latin America, in parts of Africa and Asia, "street soccer" is dead, and many would argue that with it has gone much of soccer's creative opportunity.

When Guy Lafleur was five years old, his father built a small rink in the backyard of their home in Thurso, Quebec. After school and on weekends, the rink was crowded with Lafleur and his friends, but on weekdays, rushing through lunch before returning to school, it was his alone for half an hour or more. A few years later, anxious for more ice time, on Saturday and Sunday mornings he would sneak in the back door of the local arena, finding his way unseen through the engine room, under the seats, and onto the ice. There, from 7:30 until just before the manager awakened about 11, he played alone; then quickly left. Though he was soon discovered, as the manager was also coach of his team Lafleur was allowed to continue, by himself, and then a few years later with some of his friends.

There is nothing unique to this story; only its details differ from many others like it. But because it's about Lafleur it is notable. At the time, there were thousands like him across Canada on other noon-hour rinks, in other local arenas, doing the same. It was when he got older and nothing changed that his story became special. For as others in the whirl of more games, more practices, more off-ice diversions, more travel and everything else gave up solitary time as boring and unnecessary, Lafleur did not. When he moved to Quebec City at fourteen to play for the Remparts, the ice at the big Colisée was unavailable at other times, so he began arriving early for the team's 6 p.m. practices, going on the ice at 5, more than thirty minutes before any of his teammates joined him. Now, many years later, the story unchanged, it seems more and more remarkable to us. In clichéd observation some would say it is a case of the great and dedicated superstar who is first on the ice, last off. But he is not. When practice ends, Lafleur leaves, and ten or twelve others remain behind, skating and shooting with Ruel. But every day we're in Montreal, at 11 a.m., an hour before Bow-man steps from the dressing room as signal for practice to begin, Lafleur goes onto the ice with a bucket of pucks to be alone.

Not long ago, thinking of the generations of Canadians who learned hockey on rivers and ponds, I collected my skates and with two friends drove up the Gatineau River north of Ottawa. We didn't know it at the time, but the ice conditions we found were rare, duplicated only a few times the previous decade. The combination of a sudden thaw and freezing rain in the days before had melted winter-high snow, and with temperatures dropping rapidly over-night, the river was left with miles of smooth glare ice. Growing up in the suburbs of a large city, I had played on a river only once before, and then as a goalie. On this day, I came to the Gatineau to find what a river of ice and a solitary feeling might mean to a game.

We spread ourselves rinks apart, breaking into river-wide openings for passes that sometimes connected, and other times sent us hundreds of feet after what we had missed. Against the wind or with it, the sun glaring in our eyes or at our backs, we skated for more than three hours, periodically tired, continuously renewed. The next day I went back again, this time alone. Before I got bored with myself an hour or two later, with no one watching and nothing to distract me, loose and daring, joyously free, I tried things I had never tried before, my hands and feet discovering new patterns and directions, and came away feeling as if something was finally clear.

The Canadian game of hockey was weaned on long northern winters uncluttered by things to do. It grew up on ponds and rivers, in big open spaces, unorganized, often solitary, only occasionally moved into arenas for practices or games. In recent generations, that has changed. Canadians have moved from farms and towns to cities and suburbs; they've discovered skis, snowmobiles, and southern vacations; they've civilized winter and moved it indoors.

A game we once played on rivers and ponds, later on streets and driveways and in backyards, we now play in arenas, in full team uniform, with coaches and referees, or to an ever-increasing extent we don't play at all. For, once a game is organized, unorganized games seem a wasteful use of time; and once a game moves indoors, it won't move outdoors again. Hockey has become suburbanized, and as part of our suburban middle-class culture, it has changed.

Put in uniform at six or seven, by the time a boy reaches the NHL, he is a veteran of close to 1,000 games—30-minute games, later 32-, then 45-, finally 60-minute games, played more than twice a week, more than seventy times a year between late September and late March. It is more games from a younger age, over a longer season than ever before. But it is less hockey than ever before. For, every time a twelve-year-old boy plays a 30-minute game, sharing the ice with teammates, he plays only about ten minutes. And ten minutes a game, anticipated and prepared for all day, travelled to and from, dressed and undressed for, means ten minutes of hockey a day, more than two days a week, more than seventy days a hockey season. And every day that a twelve-year-old plays only ten minutes, he doesn't play two hours on a backyard rink, or longer on school or playground rinks during weekends and holidays.

It all has to do with the way we look at free time. Constantly preoccupied with time and keeping ourselves busy (we have come to answer the ritual question "How are you?" with what we apparently equate with good health, "Busy"), we treat non-school, non-sleeping or non-eating time, unbudgeted free time, with suspicion and no little fear. For, while it may offer opportunity to learn and do new things, we worry that the time we once spent reading, kicking a ball, or mindlessly coddling a puck might be used destructively, in front of TV, or "getting into trouble" in endless ways. So we organize free time, scheduling it into lessons—ballet, piano, French—into organizations, teams, and clubs, fragmenting it into impossible-to-be-boring segments, creating in ourselves a mental metabolism geared to moving on, making free time distinctly unfree.

It is in free time that the special player develops, not in the competitive expedience of games, in hour-long practices once a week, in mechanical devotion to packaged, processed, coaching-manual, hockey-school skills. For while skills are necessary, setting out as they do the limits of anything, more is needed to transform those skills into something special. Mostly it is time—unencumbered, unhurried, time of a different quality, more time, time to find wrong answers to find a few that are right; time to find your own right answers; time for skills to be practi[s]ed to set higher limits, to settle and assimilate and become fully and completely yours, to organize and combine with other skills comfortably and easily in some uniquely personal way, then to be set loose, trusted, to find new instinctive directions to take, to create.

But without such time a player is like a student cramming for exams. His skills are like answers memorized by his body, specific, limited to what is expected, random and separate, with no overviews to organize and bring them together. And for those times when more is demanded, when new unexpected circumstances come up, when answers are asked for things you've never learned, when you must intuit and piece together what you already know to find new answers, memorizing isn't enough. It's the difference between knowledge and understanding, between a super-achiever and a wise old man. And it's the difference between a modern suburban player and a player like Lafleur.

For a special player has spent time with his game. On backyard rinks, in local arenas, in time alone and with others, time without short-cuts, he has seen many things, he has done many things, he has *experienced* the game. He understands it. There is *scope* and *culture* in his game. He is not a born player. What he has is not a gift, random and otherworldly, and unearned. There is surely something in his genetic make-up that allows him to be great, but just as surely there are others like him who fall short. He is, instead, *a natural.*

"Muscle memory" is a phrase physiologists sometimes use. It means that for many movements we make, our muscles move with no message from the brain telling them to move, that stored in the muscles is a learned capacity to move a certain way, and, given stimulus from the spinal cord, they move that way. We see a note on a sheet of music, our fingers move; no thought, no direction, and because one step of the transaction is eliminated—the information-message loop through the brain—we move faster as well.

When first learning a game, a player thinks through every step of what he's doing, needing to direct his body the way he wants it to go. With practice, with repetition, movements get memorized, speeding up, growing surer, gradually becoming part of the muscle's memory. The great player, having seen and done more things, more different and personal things, has in his muscles the memory of more notes, more combinations and patterns of notes, played in more different ways. Faced with a situation, his body responds. Faced with something more, something new, it finds an answer he didn't know was there. He *invents the game.*

Listen to a great player describe what he does. Ask Lafleur or Orr, ask Reggie Jackson, O. J. Simpson, or Julius Erving what makes them special, and you will get back something frustratingly unrewarding. They are inarticulate jocks, we decide, but in fact they can know no better than we do. For ask yourself how you walk, how your fingers move on a piano keyboard, how you do any number of things you have made routine, and you will know why. Stepping outside yourself you can think about it and decide what *must* happen, but you possess no inside story, no great insight unavailable to those who watch. Such movement comes literally from your body, bypassing your brain, leaving few subjective hints behind. Your legs, your fingers move, that's all you know. So if you want to know what makes Orr or Lafleur special, watch their bodies, fluent and articulate; let them explain. They know.

When I watch a modern suburban player, I feel the same as I do when I hear Donnie Osmond or René Simard sing a love song. I hear a skillful voice, I see closed eyes and pleading outstretched fingers, but I hear and see only fourteen-year-old boys who can't tell me anything.

Hockey has left the river and will never return. But like the "street," like an "ivory tower," the river is less a physical place than an *attitude*, a metaphor for unstructured, unorganized time alone. And if the game no longer needs the place, it needs the attitude. It is the rare player like Lafleur who reminds us.

KEN DRYDEN

Ken Dryden, the hockey player, was born in Hamilton, Ont. in 1947. He kept goal for the Montreal Canadiens and played for Team Canada in 1972 against the USSR. He is a lawyer and the author of *The Game*, a best-selling study of hockey.

St. Urbain Street Then and Now

MORDECAI RICHLER

Bad news. They're closing Baron Byng High School. Our Baron Byng. I speak of a legendary Montreal school, founded in 1921, that resembles nothing so much as a Victorian workhouse. Architecturally, the loss will be minimal (the building's a blight), but emotionally . . . ah, that's something else. If the Battle

"St. Urbain Street Then and Now" from *Home Sweet Home: My Canadian Album* by Mordecai Richler. Copyright 1984. Reprinted by permission of McClelland and Stewart Limited.

of Waterloo was won on the playing fields of Eton, then the character of Montreal's diminishing Jewish community was hammered into shape in the smelly classrooms of that big brown brick building.

> Themistocles, Thermopylae,
>   the Peloponnesian War,
> X^2, Y^2, H_2SO_4,
>   One, two, three, four,
> Who are we for?
>   Byng! Byng! Byng!

Today's Jewish community in Montreal is a group riddled with apprehension. Nobody is signing a long lease, every family has its own contingency plans. Once, however, many of us were at BBHS together. Everything possible. September 1944. Even as our elder brothers and cousins were thrusting into Holland, with the Canadian army battling on the Hitler Line, we stood in rows in the BBHS gym, raw and pimply, but shiny trousers freshly pressed. New boys we were. Rambunctious thirteen-year-olds, charged with hope. We were told, "I suppose most of you expect to go on to McGill University four years from now. Well, you will have to work hard. McGill entrance calls for a sixty-five percent average in the matriculations, but Jewish boys seeking admission will require seventy-five percent."

Baron Byng was being shut down because its student body, now largely Greek in origin, numbered only 405, but once those classrooms reverberated with the ambition of 1,000 strivers. Scrappy, driving boys and girls who led the province of Quebec in matriculation results year after year.

Baron Byng lies right out there on St. Urbain Street in what used to be the heart of Montreal's swirling Jewish quarter. In my day, St. Urbain Street was the lowest rung on a ladder we were all hot to climb. No, St. Urbain wasn't the lowest rung, for one street below came Clark, where they had no lane and had to plunk their garbage out on the street. Parked right before the front door. Immediately below Clark there came the fabled Main or, more properly, Boulevard St. Laurent. Levitt's delicatessen. Moishe's steak house. Richstone's bakery. The editorial offices of the *Canadian Jewish Eagle*. The Canada, where you could take in three movies for a quarter, but sometimes felt gray squishy things nibbling at your ankles. The Roxy and the Crystal Palace, where they showed only two movies, but offered a live show as well. A forlorn parade of pulpy strippers. "Put on your glasses, boys," the MC would say, "for here come the Hubba-Hubba Girls." It was to the Main we repaired for zoot trousers, ducktail haircuts, and free auto parts calendars that showed leggy girls, their skirts blown high by the wind. If the calendar was vintage, the real stuff, you could just make out the girl's nipples *straining against her blouse*, as they wrote in the best stories that appeared in *True Detective*.

Our world was largely composed of the five streets that ran between Park Avenue and the Main: Jeanne Mance, Esplanade, Waverly, St. Urbain, and Clark. Standing tippy-toe on St. Urbain's next-to-the-bottom rung, you could just peer over Park Avenue— Park Avenue, the dividing line—into blessed Outremont, with its tree-lined streets and parks and skating rinks and (oh my God) furnished basements. Outremont, where the girls didn't wear shiny discount dresses and gaudy shell necklaces, but frocks that had been bought retail and pearls, yes, strands of pearls that had not been pilfered from Kresge's grab-all counter, but paid for at Birks maybe. Outremont fathers, in their three-piece suits and natty fedoras, were in property or sweaters or insurance or (the coming thing) plastics. They were learning how to golf. They thought nothing of driving down to New York to "take in the shows" or of renting a summer cottage on the lakeside in Ste-Agathe-des-Monts. For the children's sake, they bought sets of *The Book of Knowledge*, sheltering them in a prominently displayed glass-doored bookcase. *King's Row* or *Forever Amber*, on the other hand, was kept in the bottom desk drawer. Locked.

Outremont, our heart's desire, was amazing. Kids our own age there didn't hang out at the corner cigar store or poolroom, they had their very own quarters. *Basement playrooms, Ping-Pong tables*. There were heated towel racks in the bathrooms. In each kitchen, a Mixmaster. No icebox, but a refrigerator. I had a school friend up there whose mother wore a *pince-nez*, and had hired a maid to answer the door, and even the telephone.

We would ring the house again and again, crowding round the receiver, stifling giggles, if only to hear the maid chirp, "This is the Feigelbaum residence."

But on St. Urbain, our fathers worked as cutters or pressers or scrap dealers and drifted into cold-water flats, sitting down to supper in their freckled Penman's long winter underwear, clipping their nails at the table. Mothers organized bazaars, proceeds for the Jewish National Fund, and jockeyed for position on the ladies' auxiliary of the Talmud Torah or the Folkshule, both parochial schools. Visiting aunts charged into the parlor, armed with raffle books, ten cents a ticket. Win an RCA Victor radio. Win a three-volume *History of the Jews*, slipcover case included. The ladies had a favorite record. It was Jan Peerce, one of ours, singing "The Bluebird of Happiness." "The poet with his pen/The peasant with his plow/It's all the same somehow."

We preferred Artie Shaw's "Stardust," which gave us a chance to dance close, or any boogie-woogie, an opportunity to strut. After supper, I had to sift the ashes before stoking the furnace for the night, emerging prematurely gray from the shed. I attended parochial school (studying English, modern Hebrew, and French), and after classes, three afternoons a week, I knuckled down to the Talmud with Mr. Yalofsky's class in the back room of the Young Israel Synagogue.

—If a man tumbles off the roof of an eight-story building and four stories down another man sticks a sword out of the window and stabs him, is that second man guilty of murder? Or not?

—Rabbi Menasha asks, did he fall or was he pushed off the roof?

—Rabbi Yedhua asks, was he already dead of heart failure before he was stabbed?

—Were the two men related?

—Enemies?

—Friends?

—Was the sword already sticking out of the window or was it thrust into the falling body?

—Would the man have died from the fall in any event?

Who cared? Concealed on our laps, below the table, at the risk of having our ears twisted by Mr. Yalofsky, was the *Herald*, opened at the sports pages. What concerned us, children of the new world, was would the Punch Line (Maurice "the Rocket" Richard, Elmer Lach, Toe Blake) finish one-two-three in the scoring race, and would the Canadiens thrash the dreaded Toronto Maple Leafs in the Stanley Cup Finals?

Our parents were counting on us—a scruffy lot, but, for all that, the first Canadian-born generation—to elbow our way into McGill, not so much Cardinal Newman's notion of a university as the block and tackle that would hoist the family into blessed Outremont. Many of us, but certainly not all, made it not only into Outremont, which turned out to be no more than a way station, but into the once *judenfrei* Town of Mount Royal, and even Westmount. *Above the Boulevard.*

Bliss, yes, but at a price.

En route, Schneider was anglicized to Taylor; Putterschnit was born again Patterson; Krashinsky, Kane. Children were no longer named Hershl or Muttel or Malke or Zippora, but, instead, Stuart, Byron, Melinda, and Vanessa. Rather than play jacks under a winding outside staircase after school, the girls in their trainer bras from New York, New York, were driven to the nose-job doctor and ballet class and the orthodontist in Mommy's Mercedes. The boys, instead of delivering for the drugstore after classes, saving up for their very own CCM bike, took tennis lessons, which would help them to meet the right people.

And then (surprise, surprise) suddenly the old neighborhood, *the starting line*, became modish and some of the children, the ungrateful ones, the know-it-alls, moved back into those yucky moldering cold-water flats on St. Urbain, nudging out the new tenants: Greeks, Italians, Portuguese. And there, on St. Urbain, where it was whispered that they smoked pot and didn't even remove their Frye boots to screw on those filthy sheets, they filled the front windows not with rubber plants of the old days, but with protest posters. Those play-poor kids in designer jeans were against nukes, acid rain, and herpes, and for organically grown, good multiple orgasms and the Parti Québécois.

The Parti Québécois?

"You exploited the French," they lectured grandfathers who used to eke out a living bent over a sewing machine, fathers who remembered flying into street battles against the followers of Adrian Arcand, armed with lengths of lead pipe.

"You've got to learn to identify with the real Québécois," they argued.

"What, at my age, I should acquire a taste for Mae Wests or sugar pie or french fries soaked in vinegar?"

"That's a racist remark."

"Listen, kid, they don't have to fast with me on Yom Kippur, I don't need to march in the St-Jean Baptiste parade."

Red-letter days on St. Urbain.

Sent to Jack and Moe's barbershop, corner of Park Avenue and Laurier, for my monthly haircut, a quarter clutched in my hand, I had grown accustomed to the humiliation of waiting for Moe to slide the board over the barber chair's arms, which raised me high enough to be shorn. But this day of glory, Moe merely jerked his head at me and snarled, "Siddown." There was no board. I was now tall enough to sit in the actual chair. On the St. Urbain Street standard, my manhood had been certified. From this day forward anything was possible.

Another day, at Baron Byng High School, I came of political age.

Ramsay MacDonald's number-one son Malcolm, the British colonial secretary, came to address us in the gym, but those of us who were members of the Labour Zionist Movement absolutely refused to stand up to sing "God Save the King." We greeted MacDonald with hostile silence. Why, that bastard had cut off immigration to Palestine. Leaking tubs overflowing with emaciated concentration-camp survivors were being turned back or led to Cyprus.

On St. Urbain, we were either very observant Orthodox Jews, dedicated Labour Zionists, or red-hot communists. There were a few suspected homosexuals in the neighborhood, that is to say, young men who read poetry and smoked cork-tipped cigarettes; there was at least one professional hooker that I knew of; but nobody, certainly, who would admit to being a member of the Conservative Party.

Communist conundrums on St. Urbain were sometimes resolved in a peculiar fashion.

A cousin of mine, then a communist firebrand but now a computer consultant, canvassed votes door-to-door for Labour-Progressive Party MP Fred Rose. Standing on one supposedly communist doorstep, expounding on Marx and Engels, the worker's sorry plight in Montreal, he was cut short by the irate housewife. "What you say may be true," she allowed, "but this time I don't vote for him, you can count on it."

"Why?"

"When his niece got married last April, we were invited to the ceremony but not to the dinner. The hell with him."

In my last year at Baron Byng High School, I worked nights in a Park Avenue bowling alley, spotting pins. A year later, enrolled at Sir George Williams College, I found work reporting on college events for the *Montreal Herald* on space rates. The bowling alley paid me three cents a line, the *Herald* only two, but I chucked being a pin boy and stuck with the *Herald*, revealing, I think, a precocious dedication to letters no matter what the cost.
St. Urbain.

Like many another old boy of my generation, I still wander down there on occasion, tramping through the lanes where we once played hockey—lanes still thick with garbage and abandoned mattresses bleeding stuffing. I make the obligatory stop at the Bagel Factory on St. Viateur near Park Avenue. In deference to the French Language Charter, Bill 101, it is now called La Maison du Bagel, Boulangerie. The YMHA, on Mount Royal, where we used to box, hoping to qualify for the Golden Gloves, has become the Pavillon Mont-Royal of the Université de Montréal. My old parochial school, the Talmud Torah, where we once stumbled over Hebrew grammar, has happily maintained a connection of sorts with Zion. It is now École Primaire Nazareth. Only a block away, on Laurier, the Stuart Biscuit Company, where we used to be able to buy a bag of broken biscuits for two cents, is still there. But immediately across the street, my father's favorite old cigar & soda, Schacter's, has become an overpriced antique shop, haunted—I like to think—by the ghosts of gin rummy games past. Laurier, above Park Avenue, is no longer a tacky street of bicycle and auto-parts shops. It has been transmogrified into a street of elegant restaurants, boutiques, fine-food shops, and bookstores. My God, my God, these days, only two blocks away from hot bagel heaven and Mehadrin's Marché de Viande Kosher, you can feast on hot croissants and espresso.

Jack and Moe's barbershop, where you could once also lay down two bucks on a horse, has been displaced by a more reliable investment house, a branch of the Banque Nationale de Grèce. The Young Israel synagogue is no longer on Park Avenue. The Regent Theatre—where I sat through at least four double features in the balcony before I dared slip my arm (slowly, slowly) around Riva Tannenbaum's bony shoulders, my heart thumping as I actually kissed her cheek in the dark—has, given such a start, slid into undreamed-of depravity. It has become le Beaver, where you can now catch HOT LEGS, "The Ups and Downs of the Stocking and Garter Industry Fully Exposed!" The Rialto, on the corner of Bernard, has also become a porn palace, this one showing the hot stuff in Greek. Indeed, this familiar chunk of Park Avenue, a street where our mothers used to comparison-shop for odd cups and saucers—an avenue where the nearest you could come to sin was to flip hastily through the latest *Esquire* at the corner newsstand, searching for the Vargas girl—is now totally disreputable. Where once it was a scandal for a neighborhood girl to be seen out for a stroll, wearing a tight sweater, acknowledging what she had there, you can now drop into SECRET SUPER SEXE, *danseuses nues*, as well as EXPO SEXE, both establishments serving hamburgers for lunch. To go with, as they say. But for all that, Park Avenue is still a street of Hasidic rabbis and their progeny. Immediately around the corner from Park Avenue, on Jeanne Mance, the two-fisted followers of the Satmar rabbi are rooted, and also in the neighborhood there are still many adherents of the Lubavitcher rabbi. Boys, wearing skullcaps and long sidecurls, who gather together to sing:

> "We only eat a kosher diet,
> Non-kosher food we'd never try it.
> To be healthy Jews is our main goal
> Non-kosher food is harmful for body and soul."

Nobody who was raised on St. Urbain ventures into the old neighborhood without stopping for a special at Wilensky's, corner of Clark and Fairmount. A special, I should point out, is made up of cuts of different kinds of salami, grilled in a delicious roll. Traditionally, it is washed down with a nonvintage cherry Coke, mixed at the fountain.

Wilensky's, which has been serving the neighborhood since 1931, is now presided over by Moe, son of the original proprietor. During World War II days, we gathered at the soda fountain for heated political disputes. Should the Allies OPEN UP A SECOND

FRONT NOW, relieving pressure on the hard-pressed Russians but risking the life of many a St. Urbain urchin who had enlisted?

St. Urbain Street old boys, running into each other at Wilensky's forty years on, still talk politics but now it isn't about the war over there, on the other side of the ocean, but about the trouble right here: the Parti Québécois. The boys I grew up with, parents themselves now, counting cholesterol rather than batting averages, drift off to whisper in the corners. "And what about you, are you staying on in Montreal?"

"What should I do? Take the chicken run to Toronto and make new friends at my age?"

In the quarrel between the English and French in Montreal, the Jews feel they are caught in the middle. "Look here," an old friend told me, "I don't think for a minute that the Parti Québécois is anti-Semitic. My God, you look at the faces on the front bench in the Assembly and they shine with intelligence. In a way, they're Zionists at home. I can understand everything they want. I can understand it in my head. But here," he continued, pounding his gut, "here, you know what I feel? If they don't get everything they want—we're the ones who are going to be blamed."

And now there are also the Italians, the Greeks, and the Portuguese, post-World War II immigrants for the most part, the inheritors of St. Urbain, Main, and Park Avenue, many of them with something like the old Jewish appetite.

Take feisty Jimmy Essaris, for instance. Forty-nine years old, dark, handsome, with flashing black eyes. Jimmy, sprung from a farming village near Athens, arrived here penniless in 1951, walking up and down the streets banging on doors before he finally surfaced with a job as a dishwasher in a Greek short-order restaurant in suburban Lachine. At the time, he spoke no English, no French, but within five months he was a counterman and had convinced the proprietor to stay open twenty-four hours a day, more than tripling his take. Jimmy stayed on there for three years, earning $100 weekly in 1954. "Don't mis-me-understand," he told me, "it was a lot of money at the time." But a year later, Jimmy had left to buy his own restaurant from an elderly Greek couple. They wanted $4,000; Jimmy offered them all the money he had saved, $3,000. " 'You will take it,' he said to the couple, 'because you are a Greek and I am a Greek and if not I will buy the place next door.' I laid the cash on the counter and the guy is shaking now. And you will pay the notary, too, I told him," Jimmy added.

"Soon I'm doing very good, I make maybe two hundred dollars a week net, but I don't like the place, it's too small for me, and I sell it for nine thousand dollars. It's 1955 now, and I have a little car, it cost me three hundred dollars. One night this girl phones me and she wants to go to a movie in Montreal. I still don't know what it means Montreal. But she wants Montreal, so we go. I can't park here, I can't park there. I have to go to a parking lot. The old man in the lot, he says to me one dollar. *One dollar parking*. I'm so polite I gave him the dollar and in the meantime I'm counting the cars. My head is pounding. I sit on the sidewalk and I think, hey, this is some fantastic business. One dollar parking, and you don't have to make club sandwiches or wash up. I can't concentrate on the movie. I tell the girl, hey, I will pay you twenty-five dollars a week, all I want is you find me a parking lot."

Early in 1956, Jimmy found one downtown, on Stanley Street, and rented it for $750 a month. But no sooner did he sign the papers in the landlord's office and stride down to the lot than the parking attendant said to him, welcome, sucker, you are the fifth man to rent this lot in two years. "The first night I made twenty dollars, the second, eighteen dollars. I multiply this by thirty and I see I can't even make the seven-hundred-fifty rent. Then one day I invite the cop on the street in for a coffee and I say to him, don't mis-me-understand, but now I will tell you a sad story. I am a poor Greek boy. I have nothing. I need help. Give tickets. Scare them. I can't do that, he says. But we become friendly, *very friendly*, and he says, I am going to help you. First night, one hundred tickets. Now everybody gets the medicine. My third week, I'm full. I start to make money. I'm grossing seventeen hundred dollars a month."

Now Jimmy Essaris owns fifty parking lots in Montreal, Quebec City, and Toronto; he employs 300 people and grosses $12 million annually.

"I am against separatism," he said, "but I do not run. If I have to fight, I will fight. English is necessary. It is the language of business, and they have to accept that. But I would be disappointed if my kids did not speak French also. Poor Greek families on St. Urbain feel threatened. They work hard. They came here looking for stability, now there is a quarrel here, it is terrible. We went through enough from 1939 to 1951 in Greece. The way Lévesque is running the economy, everybody is going to go bankrupt and they will have to close the doors."

MORDECAI RICHLER

Mordecai Richler, the novelist, was born in Montreal in 1931 and educated at Sir George Williams University (now Concordia University). Among his novels are *Cocksure*, *Joshua Then and Now*, and *The Apprenticeship of Duddy Kravitz*.

The Harvest, the Kill

JANE RULE

I live among vegetarians of various persuasions and moral meat eaters; therefore when I have guests for dinner, I pay rather more attention to the nature of food than I would, left to my own imagination.

The vegetarians who don't eat meat because they believe it to be polluted with cancer-causing hormones or because they identify their sensitive digestive tracts with herbivore ancestors are just cautious folk similar to those who cross the street only at the corner with perhaps a hint of the superstition found in those who don't walk under ladders. They are simply taking special care of their lives without further moral deliberation.

Those who don't eat meat because they don't approve of killing aren't as easy for me to understand. Yesterday, as I pried live scallops from their beautiful, fragile shells and saw them still pulsing in the bowl, ready to cook for friends for whom food from the sea is acceptable, it felt to me no less absolute an act of killing than chopping off the head of a chicken. But I also know in the vegetable garden that I rip carrots untimely from their row. The fact that they don't twitch or run around without their heads doesn't make them less alive. Like me, they have grown from seed and have their own natural life span which I have interrupted. It is hard for me to be hierarchical about the aliveness of living things.

There are two vegetarian arguments that bear some guilty weight for me. The first is the number of acres it takes to feed beef cattle as compared to the number of acres it takes to feed vegetarians. If there ever were a large plan to change our basic agriculture in order to feed everyone more equably, I would support it and give up eating beef, but until then my not eating beef is of no more help than my eating my childhood dinner was to the starving Armenians. The second is mistreatment of animals raised for slaughter. To eat what has not been a free-ranging animal is to condone the abuse of animals. Again, given the opportunity to support laws for more humane treatment of the creatures we eventually eat, I would do so, but I probably wouldn't go so far as to approve of chickens so happy in life that they were tough for my table.

"The Harvest, the Kill" from *A Hot-Eyed Moderate* by Jane Rule. © 1986. Reprinted by permission of Lester & Orpen Dennys Publishers Ltd., Toronto, Canada.

The moral meat eaters are those who believe that we shouldn't eat what we haven't killed ourselves, either gone to the trouble of stalking it down or raising it, so that we have proper respect for the creatures sacrificed for our benefit.

I am more at home with that view because my childhood summers were rural. By the time I was seven or eight, I had done my share of fishing and hunting, and I'd been taught also to clean my catch or kill. I never shot anything larger than a pigeon or rabbit. That I was allowed to use a gun at all was the result of a remarkably indulgent father. He never took me deer hunting, not because I was a girl but because he couldn't bear to shoot them himself. But we ate venison brought to us by other men in the family.

I don't remember much being made of the sacredness of the life we took, but there was a real emphasis on fair play, much of it codified in law, like shooting game birds only on the wing, like not hunting deer with flashlights at night, like not shooting does. But my kinfolk frowned on bait fishing as well. They were sportsmen who retained the wilderness ethic of not killing more than they could use. Strictly speaking, we did not need the food. (We could get meat in a town ten miles down the road.) But we did eat it.

Over the years, I became citified. I still could and did put live lobsters and crab in boiling water, but meat came from the meat market. Now that I live in the country again, I am much more aware of the slaughter that goes on around me, for I not only eat venison from the local hunt but have known the lamb and kid on the hoof (even in my rhododendrons, which is good for neither them nor the rhododendrons) which I eat. The killers of the animals are my moral, meat-eating neighbors. I have never killed a large animal, and I hope I never have to, though I'm not particularly tender-hearted about creatures not human. I find it hard to confront the struggle, smell, and mess of slaughter. I simply haven't the stomach for it. But, if I had to do it or go without meat, I would learn how.

It's puzzling to me that cannibalism is a fascinating abomination to vegetarian and meat eater alike, a habit claimed by only the most vicious and primitive tribes. We are scandalized by stories of the Donner Party or rumors of cannibalism at the site of a small plane crash in the wilderness, a boat lost at sea. Yet why would it be so horrifying for survivors to feed on the flesh of those who have died? Have worms and buzzards more right to the carcass?

We apparently do not think of ourselves as part of the food chain, except by cruel and exceptional accident. Our flesh, like the cow in India, is sacred and taboo, thought of as violated even when it is consigned to a mass grave. We bury it to hide a truth that still must be obvious to us, that as we eat so are we eaten. Why the lowly maggot is given the privilege (or sometimes the fish or the vulture) denied other living creatures is a complex puzzle of hygiene, myth and morality in each culture.

Our denial that we are part of nature, our sense of superiority to it, is our basic trouble. Though we are not, as the producers of margarine would make us believe, what we eat, we are related to what we harvest and kill. If being a vegetarian or a moral meat eater is a habit to remind us of that responsibility, neither is to be disrespected. When habit becomes a taboo, it blinds us to the real meaning. We are also related to each other, but our general refusal to eat our own flesh has not stopped us from slaughtering each other in large and totally wasted numbers.

I am flesh, a flesh eater, whether the food is carrot or cow. Harvesting and killing are the same activity, the interrupting of one life cycle for the sake of another. We don't stop at eating either. We kill to keep warm. We kill for shelter.

Back there in my rural childhood, I had not only a fishing rod and rifle, I had a hatchet, too. I cleared brush, cut down small trees, chopped wood. I was present at the felling of a two-thousand-year-old redwood tree, whose impact shook the earth I stood on. It was a death more simply shocking to me than any other I've ever witnessed. The house I lived in then was made of redwood. The house I live in now is cedar.

My ashes may nourish the roots of a living tree, pitifully small compensation for the nearly immeasurable acres I have laid waste for my needs and pleasures, even for my work. For such omnivorous creatures as we are, a few frugal habits are not enough. We have to feed and midwife more than we slaughter, replant more than we harvest, if not with our hands, then with our own talents to see that it is done in our name, that we own to it.

The scallop shells will be finely cleaned by raccoons, then made by a neighbor into wind chimes, which may trouble my sleep and probably should until it is time for my own bones to sing.

JANE RULE

Jane Rule, the novelist and essayist, was born in 1931 in Plainfield, N.J. and educated at Mills College, California, and University College, London. She moved to Vancouver in 1956 and in 1976 settled on Galiano Island, B.C. Among her novels are *Desert of the Heart*, *The Young in One Another's Arms*, and *Contract with the World*.

The Greater Evil

MARGARET LAURENCE

I have a troubled feeling that I may be capable of doublethink, the ability to hold two opposing beliefs simultaneously. In the matter of censorship, doublethink seems, alas, appropriate. As a writer, my response to censorship of any kind is that I am totally opposed to it. But when I consider some of the vile material that is being peddled freely, I want to see some kind of control. I don't think I am being hypocritical. I have a sense of honest bewilderment. I have struggled with this inner problem for years, and now, with the spate of really bad video films and porn magazines flooding the market, my sense of ambiguity grows. I am certain of one thing, though. I cannot be alone in my uncertainty.

I have good reason to mistrust and fear censorship. I have been burned by the would-be book censors. Not burned in effigy, nor suffered my books being burned, not yet anyhow. But burned nonetheless, scorched mentally and emotionally. This has happened in more than one part of Canada, but the worst experience for me was in my own county of Peterborough a few years ago, when a group of people, sincere within their limited scope, no doubt, sought to have my novel, *The Diviners*, banned from the Grade 13 course and the school libraries. The book was attacked as obscene, pornographic, immoral and blasphemous. It is, I need hardly say, none of these things. Open meetings of the school board were held. Letters, pro and con, appeared in the local newspaper. Some awful things were said about the book and about me personally, mostly by people who had not read the book or met me. In retrospect, some of the comments seem pretty funny, but at the time I was hurt and furious. One person confidently stated that "Margaret Laurence's aim in life is to destroy the home and the family." In an interview, another person claimed that the novel contained a detailed account, calculated to titillate, of the sex life of the housefly. I couldn't recollect any such scene. Then I remembered that when Morag, as a child, is embarrassed by the sad, self-deprecating talk of her stepmother, the gentle, obese Prin, the girl seeks anything at all to focus on, so she need not listen. "She looked at two flies fucking, buzzing as they did it." Beginning and

"The Greater Evil" by Margaret Laurence. Copyright Sept., 1984. Reprinted by permission of *Toronto Life*.

end of sensational scene. The reporter asked if the fundamentalist minister himself had found the scene sexually stimulating. "Oh no," was the reply. "I am a happily married man." At one open meeting, a man rose to condemn the novel and said that he spoke for a delegation of seven: himself, his wife, their four children— and God. In another county, a bachelor pharmacist accused me of adding to the rate of venereal disease in Canada by writing my books. He claimed that young people should not be given any information about sex until they are physically mature—"at about the age of 21." I hoped his knowledge of pharmacy was greater than his knowledge of biology.

Many readers, teachers and students did speak out for the novel, which was ultimately restored to the Grade 13 course. But the entire episode was enough to make me come down heavily against censorship, and especially against self-appointed groups of vigilantes. At the time I made a statement, which said, in part: "Surely it cannot do other than help in the growing toward a responsible maturity, for our young people to read novels in which many aspects of human life are dealt with, by writers whose basic faith is in the unique and irreplaceable value of the human individual."

I hold to that position. Artists of all kinds have been persecuted, imprisoned, tortured and killed, in many countries and at many times throughout history, for portraying life as they honestly saw it. Artistic suppression and political suppression go hand in hand, and always have. I would not advocate the banning of even such an evil and obscene book as Hitler's *Mein Kampf*. I think we must learn to recognize our enemies, to counter inhuman ranting with human and humane beliefs and practices. With censorship, the really bad stuff would tend to go underground and flourish covertly, while works of genuine artistic merit might get the axe (and yes, I know that "genuine artistic merit" is very difficult to define). I worry that censorship of any kind might lead to the suppression of anyone who speaks out against anything in our society, the suppression of artists, and the eventual clamping down on ideas, human perceptions, questionings. I think of our distinguished constitutional lawyer and poet F.R. Scott. In an essay written in 1933, he said: " 'The time, it is to be hoped, has gone by,' wrote John Stuart Mill, 'when any defence would be necessary of the principle of freedom of speech.' His hope was vain. The time for defending freedom never goes by. Freedom is a habit that must be kept alive by use."

And yet—my ambiguity remains. The pornography industry is now enormous, and includes so-called "kiddie porn." Most of us do not look at this stuff, nor do we have any notion how widespread it is, nor how degrading and brutal toward women and children, for it is they who are the chief victims in such magazines and films. Let me make one thing clear. I do not object to books or films or anything else that deals with sex, if those scenes are between two adults who are entering into this relationship of their own free will. (You may well say—what about *Lolita*? I hated the book, as a matter of fact, and no, I wouldn't advocate banning Nabokov. Ambiguity.) I do not object to the portrayal of social injustice, of terrible things done to one human by another or by governments or groups of whatever kind, as long as this is shown for what it is. But when we see films and photographs, *making use of real live women and children*, that portray horrifying violence, whether associated with sex or simply violence on its own, as being acceptable, on-turning, a thrill a minute, then I object.

The distinction must be made between erotic and pornographic. Eroticism is the portrayal of sexual expression between two people who desire each other and who have entered this relationship with mutual agreement. Pornography, on the other hand, is the portrayal of coercion and violence, usually with sexual connotations, and, like rape in real life, it has less to do with sex than with subjugation and cruelty. Pornography is not in any sense life-affirming. It is a denial of life. It is a repudiation of any feelings of love and tenderness and mutual passion. It is about hurting people, mainly women, and having that brutality seen as socially acceptable, even desirable.

As a woman, a mother, a writer, I cannot express adequately my feelings of fear, anger and outrage at this material. I have to say that I consider visual material to be more dangerous than any printed verbal material. Possibly I will be accused of being elitist and of favoring my own medium, the printed word, and possibly such a charge could be true. I just don't know. The reason I feel this way, however, is that these films and photographs make use of living women and children—not only a degradation of them, but also a strong suggestion to the viewer that violence against women and children, real persons, is acceptable. One of the most sinister aspects of these films and photographs is that they frequently communicate the idea that not only is violence against women OK—women actually *enjoy* being the subject of insanely brutal treatment, actually enjoy being chained, beaten, mutilated and even killed. This aspect of pornography, of course, reinforces and purports to excuse the behavior of some men who do indeed hate women. I could weep in grief and rage when I think of this attitude. As for the use of children in pornography, this is unspeakable and should be forbidden by law. The effect of this material is a matter of some dispute, and nothing can be proved either way, but many people believe that such scenes have been frighteningly re-enacted in real life in one way or another.

But is censorship, in any of the media involved, the answer? I think of John Milton's *Areopagitica; A Speech for the Liberty of Unlicensed Printing to the Parliament of England*, in 1644, in which these words appear: "He that can apprehend and consider vice with all her baits and seeming pleasures, and yet abstain, and yet distinguish, and yet prefer that which is truly better, he is the true wayfaring Christian. I cannot praise a fugitive and cloistered virtue, unexercised and unbreathed, that never sallies out and sees her adversary, but slinks out of the race, where that immortal garland is to be run for, not without dust and heat." Obviously, Milton was not thinking of the sort of video films that anyone can now show at home, where any passing boy child can perhaps get the message that cruelty is OK and fun, and any passing girl child may wonder if that is what will be expected of her, to be a victim. All the same, we forget Milton's words at our peril.

The situation is not without its ironies. It has created some very strange comrades-in-arms. We find a number of feminists taking a strong stand *for* censorship, and being praised and applauded by people whose own stance is light-years away from feminism, the same people who would like my books, Alice Munro's books, W.O. Mitchell's books, banned from our high schools. We see civil libertarians who are *against* censorship and for free expression arguing that "anything goes," a view that must rejoice the hearts of purveyors of this inhumane material, but certainly distresses mine.

I consider myself to be both a feminist and a strong supporter of civil liberties and free speech, but there is no way I want to be on the same team as the would-be book-banning groups who claim that no contemporary novels should be taught or read in our schools. There is no way, either, that I want to be on the same team as the pornographers.

What position can a person like myself honestly take? The whole subject is enormously complex, but I must finally come down against a censorship board, whether for the visual media or for the printed word. I think that such boards tend to operate by vague and ill-defined standards. What can "acceptable community standards" possibly mean? It depends on which community you're talking about, and within any one community, even the smallest village, there are always going to be wide differences. Censorship boards tend to be insufficiently accountable. I believe that in cases of obscenity, test cases have to be brought before the courts and tried openly in accordance with our federal obscenity laws. The long-term solution, of course, is to educate our children of both sexes to realize that violence against women and children, against anyone, is not acceptable, and to equalize the status of women in our society.

What about Section 159 of the Criminal Code, "Offences Tending to Corrupt Morals"? My impression of federal law in this area is that its intentions are certainly right, its aims are toward justice, and it is indeed in some ways woefully outdated and in need of clarification. Clarification and amendment have not been and will not be easy. The clause that is most widely known to the general public is Section 159(8): "For the purpose of this Act, any publication a dominant characteristic of which is the undue exploitation of sex, or of sex and any one or more of the following subjects, namely, crime, horror, cruelty and violence, shall be deemed to be obscene." I think the first use of the words "of sex" could be deleted. How much sex between consenting adults is too much? Are three scenes OK but ten excessive? Frankly, among the many things I worry about in my life, as a citizen and as a writer, this is not one of them. But how are we to enshrine in our laws the idea that the degradation and coercion of women and children, of anyone, is dreadful, without putting into jeopardy the portrayal of social injustice seen as injustice? How are we to formulate a law that says the use of real women and children in situations of demeanment and violence, shown as desirable fun stuff, is not acceptable, while at the same time not making it possible for people who don't like artists questioning the status quo to bring charges against those who must continue to speak out against the violation of the human person and spirit?

In one case cited in the Criminal Code, the judge declares: "The onus of proof upon the Crown may be discharged by simply producing the publication without expert opinion evidence. Furthermore, where, although the book has certain literary merit particularly for the more sophisticated reader, it was available for the general public to whom the book was neither symbolism nor a psychological study the accused cannot rely on the defence of public good." "Public good" is later defined as "necessary or advantageous to religion or morality, to the administration of justice, the pursuit of science, literature or art, or other objects of general interest." If this precedent means what it appears to say, it alarms me. It appears to put works of "literary merit" into some jeopardy, especially as expert opinion evidence need not be heard. If a book of mine were on trial, I would certainly want expert opinion evidence. I do not always agree with the views of the literary critics, or of teachers, but at least, and reassuringly, many of them know how to read with informed skill.

Realizing the difficulty of accurate definitions, I think that violence itself, shown as desirable, must be dealt with in some way in this law. It is *not* all right for men to beat and torture women. *It is wrong.* I also think that the exploitation of real live children for "kiddie porn" should be dealt with as a separate issue in law and should not be allowed, ever.

The more I think about it, the more the whole question becomes disturbingly complicated. Yet I believe it is a question that citizens, Parliament and the legal profession must continue to grapple with. It is not enough for citizens to dismiss our obscenity laws as inadequate and outdated, and then turn the whole matter over to censorship boards. Our laws are not engraved on stone. They have been formulated carefully, although sometimes not well, but with a regard to a general justice. The law is not perfect, but it *is* public. It can be changed, but not upon the whim of a few. An informed and alert public is a necessary component of democracy. When laws need revision, we must seek to have them revised, not toward any narrowing down but toward a greater justice for all people, children, women and men, so that our lives may be lived without our being victimized, terrorized or exploited. Freedom is more fragile than any of us in Canada would like to believe. I think again of F.R. Scott's words: "Freedom is a habit that must be kept alive by use." Freedom, however, means responsibility and concern toward others. It does not mean that unscrupulous persons are permitted to exploit, demean and coerce others. It is said, correctly, that there is a demand for pornography. But should this demand be used to justify its unchallenged existence and distribution? Some men are said to "need" pornography. To me this is like saying some men "need" to beat up their wives or commit murder. Must women and children be victims in order to assuage the fears and insecurities of those men who want to feel they are totally powerful in a quite unreal way? I don't think so. If some men "need" pornography, then I as a woman will never be a party to it, not even by the tacit agreement of silence. We and they had better try together to control and redirect those needs. I think that citizens can and should protest in any nonviolent way possible against the brutalities and callousness of pornography, including one area I haven't even been able to deal with here, the demeanment of women in many advertisements.

In the long run, it is all-important to raise our children to know the reality of others; to let them know that sex can and should be an expression of love and tenderness and mutual caring, not hatred and domination of the victor/victim kind; to communicate to our daughters and our sons that to be truly human is to try to be loving and responsible, strong not because of power but because of self-respect and respect for others.

In *Areopagitica*, Milton said: "That which purifies us is trial, and trial is by what is contrary." In the final analysis, we and our society will not stand or fall by what we are "permitted" to see or hear or read, but by what we ourselves choose. We must, however, have some societal agreement as to what is acceptable in the widest frame of reference possible, but still within the basic concept that *damaging people is wrong*. Murder is not acceptable, and neither is the abasement, demeanment and exploitation of human persons, whatever their race, religion, age or gender. Not all of this can be enshrined in law. Laws can never make people more understanding and compassionate toward one another. That is what individual people try to do, in our imperfect and familial ways. What the law *can* do is attempt to curb, by open process in public courts, the worst excesses of humankind's always-in-some-way-present inhumanity to humankind.

This is as close as I can get to formulating my own beliefs. It is an incomplete and in many ways a contradictory formulation, and I am well aware of that. Perhaps this isn't such a bad thing. I don't think we can or should ever get to a point where we feel we know, probably in a simplistic way, what all the answers are or that we ourselves hold them and no one else does. The struggle will probably always go on, as it always has in one way or another. The new technology has brought its own intricacies. I doubt that the human heart and conscience will ever be relieved of their burdens, and I certainly hope they are not. This particular struggle, *for* human freedom and *against* the awfulness that seeks to masquerade as freedom but is really slavery, will not ever be easy or simple, but it is a struggle that those of us who are concerned must never cease to enter into, even though it will continue to be, in Milton's words, "not without dust and heat."

MARGARET LAURENCE

Margaret Laurence (1926–1987) was born in the prairie town of Neepawa, Man., which appears in her fiction as Manawaka. Her best-known novels include *The Stone Angel*, *A Jest of God*, and *The Fire-Dwellers*. Her articles and essays are collected in *Heart of a Stranger*.

Convocation Address

GEORGE FALUDY

For an exile who has spent the better part of his life taking refuge from the sadistic east in the masochistic west, it is an almost overwhelming honour to be recognized in this fashion.

I have made my home in Canada for the past 11 years, and have found here, as nowhere else, the peace and security of a marvelously decent society. . . .

If there [were] time, I would consider it my duty to speak on a subject which has long occupied my mind as much as poetry itself: on the survival of humanistic learning in a world where affluence has joined hands with destruction; a world in which absolutist ethics has given way to relativistic, then to utilitarian and finally to no ethics at all; a world in which education increasingly means vocational training, the diffusion of facts and data; in which comfort has become the measure of civilization; in which our greatest intellectual achievement, our science, has abjured the concept of wisdom, just as philosophy has come to renounce love; a world, in short, with one foot firmly on the foundation of an incredible advance in knowledge and technique, and the other foot dangling in a spiritual vacuum. But my purpose this evening is not to depress you with the fate of humanistic learning, but to tell you briefly how that learning on one occasion ensured the physical and spiritual survival of several hundred people, including myself.

Some years ago in Hungary I found myself, for the second time in my life, in a concentration camp. There were some thirteen hundred inmates: democrats, Catholics, liberals, socialists and people without any political preferences, most sentenced to hard labour on trumped-up charges, though a few were there without having been sentenced or even charged. We could neither write nor receive letters and parcels; we had no books, newspapers, radios, or visitors. We cut stones from dawn to dusk 365 days a year, except for May Day. We did this on a diet of 1,200 calories a day. Our situation was thus better than in a Nazi concentration camp, but much worse than in the present-day Soviet camps recently described by Bukovsky and others.

"Convocation Address" upon being awarded an honorary doctorate by the University of Toronto, Nov. 29, 1978, by George Faludy. Copyright Dec. 18, 1978. Reprinted by permission of Dr. George Faludy.

At first we returned to the barracks at night deadly tired, with no strength even to pull off our army boots and fall asleep on the rotten straw sacks. Our lives seemed not to differ from those of the slaves that built the pyramids, and our futures seemed equally bleak. But already on the day of my arrest, in the Black Maria that took me away, I had met young friends who had been denied a university education because of the war. Their faces had lit up: "You can lecture us in the camp," they said, "and we'll get our university education that way."

After about a week in the camp two of them approached me and insisted that I start my lectures immediately after lights out. We were by then even more exhausted than on the day of our arrival. At first four men sat beside my pallet, and we were jeered at by the others. Eventually twelve prisoners gathered beside my straw sack every night for an hour or two. We recited poems— Hungarian poems and foreign poems in translation. Among the English ones the "Ode to the West Wind" became the favourite. Then I would speak on literature, history or philosophy and my lecture would be discussed by all.

I was by no means the only prisoner to deliver such lectures. A former member of the short-lived democratic government knew *Hamlet* and *A Midsummer Night's Dream* by heart, and recited both to an enthusiastic audience. There were lectures on Roman law, on the history of the Crusades, narrations of large parts of *War and Peace*, courses in mathematics and astronomy avidly listened to, sometimes by men who had never entered a secondary school. There was even a former staff colonel who whistled entire operas. Those of us who lectured ransacked our memories to keep alive a civilization from which we were hopelessly—and, it seemed, permanently—cut off.

There were prisoners who looked on all this with disgust, maintaining that we were insane to spend our sleeping time in lectures when we were all going to die anyway. These men, intent on survival, retreated into themselves, becoming lonely, merciless with others, shutting out thought and even speech.

By the second winter of our imprisonment it began to happen when we were working that once, twice or even three times in the course of a day a prisoner would suddenly stop work and stagger off through the deep snow. After twenty or thirty yards of running he would collapse. In each case the man would die a day or two later, usually without regaining consciousness. Those who died in this way were always the men who had been most determined to survive, those who had concentrated on nothing but food, sleep and warmth. For my part, owing perhaps to large doses of pragmatism and positivism in my youth I was reluctant to admit the obvious: that delighting in a good poem or discussing Plato's Socratic dialogues could somehow arm the spirit to the point that it could prevent the body's collapse.

But then I was presented with proof. While I was washing myself in the snow before the barracks one evening, one of my pupils, a former government official, a strong young man, came up to tell me that he would not attend the lecture that night, nor indeed any other night. He wanted to survive and was going to sleep rather than talk; he was going, he said, to live the life of a tree or a vegetable. He waited before me as if expecting my objection. I was indescribably tired, and closing my eyes I saw scenes from my childhood, the sort of hallucinations one has in a state of semi-starvation. Suddenly it occurred to me that I must dissuade the man. But he was already gone. He slept perhaps twenty yards from me, but I never summoned the strength to argue with him. Five days later we saw him stop work, begin to run towards the trees, and then collapse in the snow. His death has been on my conscience ever since. But without exception all those who lectured, and all those who listened, survived.

It does not seem to me to be so far-fetched to apply this lesson in the infinitely more pleasant society of this country. It justifies, I think, the Platonic view that man as given by nature owes it to himself to obey the dictates of his higher nature to rise above evil and mindlessness. Those in the camp who attempted this, survived, although physical survival had not been their aim. And those who for the sake of physical survival vegetated, perished in large numbers. It seems to me that the mentality of these latter is, *mutatis mutandis*, analogous to the mentality of the consumer societies of the world, of those who seem obsessed with producing and consuming an ever-growing mountain of things to ensure comfort and survival; who have addicted themselves to energy as if to morphine until they are ready to destroy all nature to increase the dosage; who have, indeed, increased our life-span but have failed to mention that the brain requires jogging even more than the heart if that life-span is to mean anything.

The other conclusion I have drawn from my camp experience, and have tried to embody in my own poetry, is that our whole fragile tradition of art and thought is neither an amusement nor a yoke. For those who steep themselves in it, it provides both a guide and a goal far surpassing all the half-baked ideologies that have blown up at our feet in this century like landmines. Sitting comfortably in the present and looking forward to longevity in an unknown future does nothing to ensure our survival nor even to make it desirable. In any case we do not live in the future; we live in the present, and all we have to guide us in this present is the accumulated thought and experience of those who have lived before us.

For all the deficiency of my own learning, then, this is what I have attempted to voice in my work, and at this point in my life I feel safe in echoing the words of Petronius: *"Pervixi: neque enim fortuna malignior umquam eripiet nobis quod prior hora dedit*—I have lived, and no evil fate can ever take away from us what the past has given." I believe we will do ourselves a favour if we extend the meaning of the author of the *Satyricon* to include the past of all humanity.

GEORGE FALUDY

George Faludy, the poet and man-of-letters, was born in Budapest, Hungary, in 1910. He was imprisoned twice in his native land, first by the Nazis and then by the Communists. He settled in Toronto in 1967 and became a Canadian citizen. Among his numerous publications are *My Happy Days in Hell* and *Selected Poems*.

The Double-Headed Coin of Rights and Duties

MORRIS C. SHUMIATCHER

 country in which everybody demands his rights is like a house in which everyone is shouting for his supper with no one in the kitchen to cook it.

The International Year of the Child spawned a rash of rights that look much like the pimples of puberty on the faces of the pupils of at least one Canadian public school.

The object of the exercise was to create a "tribute to the International Year of the Child that would be everlasting." Here are some of the debts said to be owed to children by teachers, parents and others—all framed and enshrined on a prominent wall in the M.J. Coldwell School in Regina.

"The Double-Headed Coin of Rights and Duties" by Morris C. Shumiatcher. Copyright May, 1980. Reprinted by permission of Morris C. Shumiatcher.

"The Right to an Education"
There is scarcely a child of the past half a century who has not had
this right served up to him on heaping platters. Indeed for years,
truancy laws have served to remind children and their parents that
the doors of the schoolhouse are open wide to all, and that they
not only have the right to enter, but the duty to learn. No one but
they themselves can ever do that. What needs restating is not the
right to an education, but the *duty* of every child to learn. Whatever
pedagogues may claim, there is no such thing as teaching; there
is only such a thing as learning. If the aery-fairy Year of the Child
is to lead the young [person] into the real world where he may
become a mature adult, he must meet duty face to face. He must
discover his first duty is to learn, because to be ignorant is a shameful state. Without that duty, all of the education in the world will
drain from his brain like rain off a duck.
"The Right to Develop His Potential to the Fullest"
Everyone has the right to develop his muscles so that he can lift a
hundred and fifty pounds, the right to strengthen his brain so he
can understand Einstein's mass-energy theory, the right to stretch
his legs so he can run the four-minute mile like Bannister, and the
right to acquire the skill to play the violin like Yehudi Menuhin.
But what do those rights mean until the individual recognizes that
the responsibility of improving his body and his mind, his legs and
his fingers are his alone? Nothing can happen to realize any of those
wonderful results until the individual applies effort and hard work
to achieve what he genuinely wants. The right to develop without
the will to grow is a seed that is neither planted nor cultivated, but
is cast on a concrete road and dries and disintegrates for lack of
nutriment, and so is lost to the world at the end of the day.
"The Right to be a Useful Member of Society"
Every community hungers for competent, educated and energetic
people to take on the responsibilities of caring for its parks and
public places, of beautifying the dumps, of producing clear cold
water for the dwellers of the tenements, of bringing light to the
slums and letting pure air into the caverns of the city. Everyone
has a right to improve himself and his community. The smallest
child can keep his yard and neighborhood clean, can refrain from
heaving rocks through windows and drag-racing on main street
and breaking beer bottles on the sidewalk. He will then become a
useful member of society. It is not a "right" to adopt a life style
that is civilized, it is a duty. Every new generation that is born into
this world is a fresh barbarian invasion that will seize and grasp
and demand and consume everything in sight, until it is civilized
into understanding its duty to give and yield and respond and
produce.

"The Right to be Raised in the Spirit of Peace, Understanding,
Cooperation and Friendship"
Peace, understanding, cooperation, friendship. These are not gifts
that fall from heaven to those who sit idly by awaiting their bless-
ings. Peace is not a right: it is a duty, the burden of which men
and women of good will must carry upon their shoulders knowing
it to be a treasure beyond all measure. Cooperation is not conduct
that one may demand of another; it is a quality of the human state
that one can give and, in offering it, learn that it is returned like
the smile in a girl's eyes or a handshake when the fingers linger
long, carving the memory of a moment into the lines of your hand
and heart. Friendship is not a bank account established by a stranger
to pick your lucky ticket in a lottery. It is a bundle of duties and
obligations that may bud and blossom into a rose for those you
love, that one day may be returned to you with all of its fragrance
gone, but shorn of every thorn.
"The Right to Affection, Love and Understanding from Teachers
and Fellow Students"
To consider "affection and love" our right is to misunderstand the
individual's humanity. Love is not taken like an apple from a tree,
but only given. And understanding is not a right, but a pilgrimage
on a long and tortuous road that has no end. No one can demand
affection, no one can elicit love—not even with the most complex
machine man's ingenuity can create. To claim love as a right is as
foolish as to demand that the rain cease to fall upon you. The
greater the demand, the greater will be your disappointment.

The simple fact of life is that there are no rights that bloom in
the human state. There are only obligations; it is they that are the
seeds which, planted and laboriously nurtured, may one day blossom into rights.

Bills of Human Rights and laws that pretend unconditionally
to distribute "rights" are illusions like the commercials that advertise free money, or effortless muscle building, fat melting or
wrinkle routing. They exist only in one's imagination.

To my young friends so preoccupied with the *gimmies* that
masquerade as rights, may I suggest this: If you hope to enjoy the
right to a hot bowl of soup at lunch time, you will be doomed to
disappointment and will never have it unless someone assumes
the duty of finding the meat and vegetables to cook it, and takes
the time and trouble in the kitchen to produce it, and with affection
(or out of a sense of duty) places that bowl of soup on a plate on
the table for you to eat and enjoy. Without duty there is no soup.
And no one has a right to expect to enjoy soup unless he also is
prepared to perform his duty to cook it!

You may think you have a right to walk down the street at

night in safety. But simply to declare that such a right exists will give you neither safety nor comfort. It is only if I and every other citizen assume the duty to give you free passage and not molest you, that you can walk in safety on the city street you claim to be your own.

A "right" is a coin with only one side. Unless it has another side on which the word "duty" appears, the coin is as worthless as a Czarist ruble. You may have the right to pass it on to buy an apple, but if your grocer thinks it worthless, he has not obligation to accept it for his fruit, and you will go hungry. How valuable, then, is your one-sided coin that reads "right," without the other side that spells "duties"?

Have you ever thought that the Ten Commandments, older than the hills of Galilee and as durable as Mount Sinai, speak not a single word about human rights? They do not suggest you have a right to God's love, but rather, that you have a duty to love your God.

They do not create a right to make demands upon your parents, but they speak of the duty of every child to love and cherish and honor his mother and father: the duty to care for them as they grow old and feeble.

The United Nations Declaration of Human Rights was written in 1948 in the belief it would make us all more mindful of our duty to act justly toward our neighbors, whatever their color, creed or origin. Ever since, we have heard more and more about human rights, and less and less about personal duties. It was once considered enough for legislatures to declare, "let light abound that right be found." But laws can no more grant the smallest right to Peter without imposing a corresponding duty on Paul. If Peter is to be a pumpkin eater, Paul must be a pumpkin picker.

Let us then place alongside the Declaration of the Rights of the Children of the M. J. Coldwell School, a Proclamation of the Duties of the young to themselves, their parents and teachers, their friends and their neighbors. And let us not forget how large a part simple courtesy and good manners make up the basket of our duties.

MORRIS C. SHUMIATCHER

Morris C. Shumiatcher, lawyer and civil rights spokesperson, was born in Calgary in 1917. He is a graduate of the University of Alberta and the University of Toronto. In 1948 he became the youngest King's Counsel in the Commonwealth and now practises law in Regina. Among his books are *Welfare: Hidden Backlash* and *Man of Law: A Model*.

Once More to the Lake

E.B. WHITE

One summer, along about 1904, my father rented a camp on a lake in Maine and took us all there for the month of August. We all got ringworm from some kittens and had to rub Pond's Extract on our arms and legs night and morning, and my father rolled over in a canoe with all his clothes on; but outside of that the vacation was a success and from then on none of us ever thought there was any place in the world like that lake in Maine. We returned summer after summer—always on August 1 for one month. I have since become a salt-water man, but sometimes in summer there are days when the restlessness of the tides and the fearful cold of the sea water and the incessant wind that blows across the afternoon and into the evening make me wish for the placidity of a lake in the woods. A few weeks ago this feeling got so strong I bought myself a couple of bass hooks and a spinner and returned to the lake where we used to go, for a week's fishing and to revisit old haunts.

I took along my son, who had never had any fresh water up his nose and who had seen lily pads only from train windows. On the journey over to the lake I began to wonder what it would be like. I wondered how time would have marred this unique, this holy spot—the coves and streams, the hills that the sun set behind, the camps and the paths behind the camps. I was sure that the tarred road would have found it out, and I wondered in what other ways it would be desolated. It is strange how much you can remember about places like that once you allow your mind to return into the grooves that lead back. You remember one thing, and that suddenly reminds you of another thing. I guess I remembered clearest of all the early mornings, when the lake was cool and motionless, remembered how the bedroom smelled of the lumber it was made of and of the wet woods whose scent entered through the screen. The partitions in the camp were thin and did not extend clear to the top of the rooms, and as I was always the first up I would dress softly so as not to wake the others, and sneak out into the sweet outdoors and start out in the canoe, keeping close along the

"Once More to the Lake" from *Essays of E.B. White* by E.B. White. Copyright 1941 by E.B. White. Reprinted by permission of Harper & Row, Publishers, Inc.

shore in the long shadows of the pines. I remembered being very careful never to rub my paddle against the gunwale for fear of disturbing the stillness of the cathedral.

The lake had never been what you would call a wild lake. There were cottages sprinkled around the shores, and it was in farming country, although the shores of the lake were quite heavily wooded. Some of the cottages were owned by nearby farmers, and you would live at the shore and eat your meals at the farmhouse. That's what our family did. But although it wasn't wild, it was a fairly large and undisturbed lake and there were places in it that, to a child at least, seemed infinitely remote and primeval.

I was right about the tar: it led to within half a mile of the shore. But when I got back there, with my boy, and we settled into a camp near a farmhouse and into the kind of summertime I had known, I could tell that it was going to be pretty much the same as it had been before—I knew it, lying in bed the first morning, smelling the bedroom and hearing the boy sneak quietly out and go off along the shore in a boat. I began to sustain the illusion that he was I, and therefore, by simple transposition, that I was my father. This sensation persisted, kept cropping up all the time we were there. It was not an entirely new feeling, but in this setting it grew much stronger. I seemed to be living a dual existence. I would be in the middle of some simple act, I would be picking up a bait box or laying down a table fork, or I would be saying something, and suddenly it would be not I but my father who was saying the words or making the gesture. It gave me a creepy sensation.

We went fishing the first morning. I felt the same damp moss covering the worms in the bait can, and saw the dragonfly alight on the tip of my rod as it hovered a few inches from the surface of the water. It was the arrival of this fly that convinced me beyond any doubt that everything was as it always had been, that the years were a mirage and that there had been no years. The small waves were the same, chucking the rowboat under the chin as we fished at anchor, and the boat was the same boat, the same color green and the ribs broken in the same places, and under the floorboards the same fresh-water leavings and débris—the dead helgramite, the wisps of moss, the rusty discarded fishhook, the dried blood from yesterday's catch. We stared silently at the tips of our rods, at the dragonflies that came and went. I lowered the tip of mine into the water, tentatively, pensively dislodging the fly, which darted two feet away, poised, darted two feet back, and came to rest again a little farther up the rod. There had been no years between the ducking of this dragonfly and the other one—the one that was part of memory. I looked at the boy, who was silently watching his fly, and it was my hands that held his rod, my eyes watching. I felt dizzy and didn't know which rod I was at the end of.

We caught two bass, hauling them in briskly as though they were mackerel, pulling them over the side of the boat in a businesslike manner without any landing net, and stunning them with a blow on the back of the head. When we got back for a swim before lunch, the lake was exactly where we had left it, the same number of inches from the dock, and there was only the merest suggestion of a breeze. This seemed an utterly enchanted sea, this lake you could leave to its own devices for a few hours and come back to, and find that it had not stirred, this constant and trustworthy body of water. In the shallows, the dark, water-soaked sticks and twigs, smooth and old, were undulating in clusters on the bottom against the clean ribbed sand, and the track of the mussel was plain. A school of minnows swam by, each minnow with its small individual shadow, doubling the attendance, so clear and sharp in the sunlight. Some of the other campers were in swimming, along the shore, one of them with a cake of soap, and the water felt thin and clear and unsubstantial. Over the years there had been this person with the cake of soap, this cultist, and here he was. There had been no years.

Up to the farmhouse to dinner through the teeming, dusty field, the road under our sneakers was only a two-track road. The middle track was missing, the one with the marks of the hooves and the splotches of dried, flaky manure. There had always been three tracks to choose from in choosing which track to walk in; now the choice was narrowed down to two. For a moment I missed terribly the middle alternative. But the way led past the tennis court, and something about the way it lay there in the sun reassured me; the tape had loosened along the backline, the alleys were green with plantains and other weeds, and the net (installed in June and removed in September) sagged in the dry noon, and the whole place steamed with midday heat and hunger and emptiness. There was a choice of pie for dessert, and one was blueberry and one was apple, and the waitresses were the same country girls, there having been no passage of time, only the illusion of it as in a dropped curtain—the waitresses were still fifteen; their hair had been washed, that was the only difference—they had been to the movies and seen the pretty girls with the clean hair.

Summertime, oh, summertime, pattern of life indelible, the fade-proof lake, the woods unshatterable, the pasture with the sweetfern and the juniper forever and ever, summer without end; this was the background, and the life along the shore was the design, their tiny docks with the flagpole and the American flag floating against the white clouds in the blue sky, the little paths over the roots of the trees leading from camp to camp and the paths leading back to the outhouses and the can of lime for sprinkling, and at the souvenir counters at the store the miniature birch-bark canoes and the postcards that showed things looking a little better than they looked. This was the American family at play, escaping the city heat, wondering whether the newcomers in the camp at the head of the cove were "common" or "nice," wondering whether it was true that the people who drove up for Sunday dinner at the farmhouse were turned away because there wasn't enough chicken.

It seemed to me, as I kept remembering all this, that those times and those summers had been infinitely precious and worth saving. There had been jollity and peace and goodness. The arriving (at the beginning of August) had been so big a business in itself, at the railway station the farm wagon drawn up, the first smell of the pine-laden air, the first glimpse of the smiling farmer, and the great importance of the trunks and your father's enormous authority in such matters, and the feel of the wagon under you for the long ten-mile haul, and at the top of the last long hill catching the first view of the lake after eleven months of not seeing this cherished body of water. The shouts and cries of the other campers when they saw you, and the trunks to be unpacked, to give up their rich burden. (Arriving was less exciting nowadays, when you sneaked up in your car and parked it under a tree near the camp and took out the bags and in five minutes it was all over, no fuss, no loud wonderful fuss about trunks.)

Peace and goodness and jollity. The only thing that was wrong now, really, was the sound of the place, an unfamiliar nervous sound of the outboard motors. This was the note that jarred, the one thing that would sometimes break the illusion and set the years moving. In those other summertimes all motors were inboard; and when they were at a little distance, the noise they made was a sedative, an ingredient of summer sleep. They were one-cylinder and two-cylinder engines, and some were make-and-break and some were jump-spark, but they all made a sleepy sound across the lake. The one-lungers throbbed and fluttered, and the twin-cylinder ones purred and purred, and that was a quiet sound, too. But now the campers all had outboards. In the daytime, in the hot mornings, these motors made a petulant, irritable sound; at night, in the still evening when the afterglow lit the water, they whined about one's ears like mosquitoes. My boy loved our rented out-board, and his great desire was to achieve single-handed mastery over it, and authority, and he soon learned the trick of choking it a little (but not too much), and the adjustment of the needle valve.

Watching him I would remember the things you could do with the old one-cylinder engine with the heavy flywheel, how you could have it eating out of your hand if you got really close to it spiritually. Motorboats in those days didn't have clutches, and you would make a landing by shutting off the motor at the proper time and coasting in with a dead rudder. But there was a way of reversing them, if you learned the trick, by cutting the switch and putting it on again exactly on the final dying revolution of the flywheel, so that it would kick back against compression and begin reversing. Approaching a dock in a strong following breeze, it was difficult to slow up sufficiently by the ordinary coasting method, and if a boy felt he had complete mastery over his motor, he was tempted to keep it running beyond its time and then reverse it a few feet from the dock. It took a cool nerve, because if you threw the switch a twentieth of a second too soon you would catch the flywheel when it still had speed enough to go up past center, and the boat would leap ahead, charging bull-fashion at the dock.

We had a good week at the camp. The bass were biting well and the sun shone endlessly, day after day. We would be tired at night and lie down in the accumulated heat of the little bedrooms after the long hot day and the breeze would stir almost imperceptibly outside and the smell of the swamp drift in through the rusty screens. Sleep would come easily and in the morning the red squirrel would be on the roof, tapping out his gay routine. I kept remembering everything, lying in bed in the mornings—the small steamboat that had a long rounded stern like the lip of a Ubangi, and how quietly she ran on the moonlight sails, when the older boys played their mandolins and the girls sang and we ate doughnuts dipped in sugar, and how sweet the music was on the water in the shining night, and what it had felt like to think about girls then. After breakfast we would go up to the store and the things were in the same place—the minnows in a bottle, the plugs and spinners disarranged and pawed over by the youngsters from the boys' camp, the Fig Newtons and the Beeman's gum. Outside, the road was tarred and cars stood in front of the store. Inside, all was just as it had always been, except there was more Coca-Cola and not so much Moxie and root beer and birch beer and sarsaparilla. We would walk out with the bottle of pop apiece and sometimes the pop would backfire up our noses and hurt. We explored the streams, quietly, where the turtles slid off the sunny logs and dug their way into the soft bottom; and we lay on the town wharf and fed worms to the tame bass. Everywhere we went I had trouble making out which was I, the one walking at my side, the one walking in my pants.

One afternoon while we were there at that lake a thunderstorm came up. It was like the revival of an old melodrama that I had seen long ago with childish awe. The second-act climax of the drama of the electrical disturbance over a lake in America had not changed in any important respect. This was the big scene, still the big scene. The whole thing was so familiar, the first feeling of oppression and heat and a general air around camp of not wanting to go very far away. In mid-afternoon (it was all the same) a curious darkening of the sky, and a lull in everything that had made life tick; and then the way the boats suddenly swung the other way at their moorings with the coming of a breeze out of the new quarter, and the premonitory rumble. Then the kettle drum, then the snare, then the bass drum and cymbals, then crackling light against the dark, and the gods grinning and licking their chops in the hills. Afterward the calm, the rain steadily rustling in the calm lake, the return of light and hope and spirits, and the campers running out in joy and relief to go swimming in the rain, their bright cries perpetuating the deathless joke about how they were getting simply drenched, and the children screaming with delight at the new sensation of bathing in the rain, and the joke about getting drenched linking the generations in a strong indestructible chain. And the comedian who waded in carrying an umbrella.

When the others went swimming, my son said he was going in, too. He pulled his dripping trunks from the line where they had hung all through the shower and wrung them out. Languidly, and with no thought of going in, I watched him, his hard little body, skinny and bare, saw him wince slighty as he pulled up around his vitals the small, soggy, icy garment. As he buckled the swollen belt, suddenly my groin felt the chill of death.

E.B. WHITE

E.B. White (1899–1985) was for many years an editor of *The New Yorker*. Best known for his essays and short stories, White also wrote *Stuart Little* and *Charlotte's Web*, popular children's books, and edited William Strunk, Jr.'s *The Elements of Style*.

Politics and the English Language

GEORGE ORWELL

Most people who bother with the matter at all would admit that the English language is in a bad way, but it is generally assumed that we cannot by conscious action do anything about it. Our civilization is decadent and our language—so the argument runs—must inevitably share in the general collapse. It follows that any struggle against the abuse of language is a sentimental archaism, like preferring candles to electric light or hansom cabs to aeroplanes. Underneath this lies the half-conscious belief that language is a natural growth and not an instrument which we shape for our own purpose.

Now, it is clear that the decline of a language must ultimately have political and economic causes: it is not due simply to the bad influence of this or that individual writer. But an effect can become a cause, reinforcing the original cause and producing the same effect in an intensified form, and so on indefinitely. A man may take to drink because he feels himself to be a failure, and then fail all the more completely because he drinks. It is rather the same thing that is happening to the English language. It becomes ugly and inaccurate because our thoughts are foolish, but the slovenliness of our language makes it easier for us to have foolish thoughts. The point is that the process is reversible. Modern English, especially written English, is full of bad habits which spread by imitation and which can be avoided if one is willing to take the necessary trouble. If one gets rid of these habits one can think more clearly, and to think clearly is a necessary first step towards political regeneration: so that the fight against bad English is not frivolous and is not the exclusive concern of professional writers. I will come back to this presently, and I hope that by that time the meaning of what I have said here will have become clearer. Meanwhile, here are five specimens of the English language as it is now habitually written.

"Politics and the English Language" from *Shooting an Elephant and Other Essays 1950-1978* by George Orwell. Copyright 1950, 1978. Reprinted by permission of A.M. Heath & Company Limited on behalf of the estate of the late Sonia Brownell Orwell and Secker and Warburg Limited.

These five passages have not been picked out because they are especially bad—I could have quoted far worse if I had chosen—but because they illustrate various of the mental vices from which we now suffer. They are a little below the average, but are fairly representative samples. I number them so that I can refer back to them when necessary:

(1) I am not, indeed, sure whether it is not true to say that the Milton who once seemed not unlike a seventeenth-century Shelley had not become, out of an experience ever more bitter in each year, more alien [sic] to the founder of that Jesuit sect which nothing could induce him to tolerate.

Professor Harold Laski (Essay in *Freedom of Expression*)

(2) Above all, we cannot play ducks and drakes with a native battery of idioms which prescribes such egregious collocations of vocables as the Basic *put up with* for *tolerate* or *put at a loss* for *bewilder*.

Professor Lancelot Hogben (*Interglossa*)

(3) On the one side we have the free personality: by definition it is not neurotic, for it has neither conflict nor dream. Its desires, such as they are, are transparent, for they are just what institutional approval keeps in the forefront of consciousness; another institutional pattern would alter their number and intensity; there is little in them that is natural, irreducible, or culturally dangerous. But *on the other side*, the social bond itself is nothing but the mutual reflection of these self-secure integrities. Recall the definition of love. Is not this the very picture of a small academic? Where is there a place in this hall of mirrors for either personality or fraternity?

Essay on psychology in *Politics* (New York)

(4) All the "best people" from the gentlemen's clubs, and all the frantic fascist captains, united in common hatred of Socialism and bestial horror of the rising tide of the mass revolutionary movement, have turned to acts of provocation, to foul incendiarism, to medieval legends of poisoned wells, to legalize their own destruction of proletarian organizations, and rouse the agitated petty-bourgeoisie to chauvinistic fervor on behalf of the fight against the revolutionary way out of the crisis.

Communist pamphlet

(5) If a new spirit *is* to be infused into this old country, there is one thorny and contentious reform which must be tackled, and that is the humanization and galvanization of the B.B.C. Timidity here will bespeak cancer and atrophy of the soul. The heart of Britain may be sound and of strong beat, for instance, but the British lion's roar at present is like that of Bottom in Shakespeare's *Midsummer Night's Dream*—as gentle as any sucking dove. A virile new Britain cannot continue indefinitely to be traduced in the eyes or rather ears, of the world by the effete languors of Langham Place, brazenly masquerading as "standard English." When the Voice of Britain is heard at nine o'clock, better far and infinitely less ludicrous to hear

aitches honestly dropped than the present priggish, inflated, inhibited, school-ma'amish arch braying of blameless bashful mewing maidens!

Letter in *Tribune*

Each of these passages has faults of its own, but, quite apart from avoidable ugliness, two qualities are common to all of them. The first is staleness of imagery; the other is lack of precision. The writer either has a meaning and cannot express it, or he inadvertently says something else, or he is almost indifferent as to whether his words mean anything or not. The mixture of vagueness and sheer incompetence is the most marked characteristic of modern English prose, and especially of any kind of political writing. As soon as certain topics are raised, the concrete melts into the abstract and no one seems to think of turns of speech that are not hackneyed: prose consists less and less of *words* chosen for the sake of their meaning, and more and more of *phrases* tacked together like the sections of a prefabricated henhouse. I list below, with notes and examples, various of the tricks by means of which the work of prose-construction is habitually dodged:

Dying Metaphors

A newly invented metaphor assists thought by evoking a visual image, while on the other hand a metaphor which is technically "dead" (e.g., *iron resolution*) has in effect reverted to being an ordinary word and can generally be used without loss of vividness. But in between these two classes there is a huge dump of worn-out metaphors which have lost all evocative power and are merely used because they save people the trouble of inventing phrases for themselves. Examples are: *ring the changes on, take up the cudgels for, toe the line, ride roughshod over, stand shoulder to shoulder with, play into the hands of, no axe to grind, grist to the mill, fishing in troubled waters, rift within the lute, on the order of the day, Achilles' heel, swan song, hotbed.* Many of these are used without knowledge of their meaning (what is a "rift", for instance?), and incompatible metaphors are frequently mixed, a sure sign that the writer is not interested in what he is saying. Some metaphors now current have been twisted out of their original meaning without those who use them even being aware of the fact. For example, *toe the line* is sometimes written *tow the line*. Another example is *the hammer and the anvil*, now always used with the implication that the anvil gets the worst of it. In real life it is always the anvil that breaks the hammer, never the other way about: a writer who stopped to think what he was saying would be aware of this, and would avoid perverting the original phrase.

Operators or Verbal False Limbs

These save the trouble of picking out appropriate verbs and nouns, and at the same time pad each sentence with extra syllables which give it an appearance of symmetry. Characteristic phrases are: *render inoperative, militate against, make contact with, be subjected to, give rise to, give grounds for, have the effect of, play a leading part (role) in, make itself felt, take effect, exhibit a tendency to, serve the purpose of,* etc., etc. The keynote is the elimination of simple verbs. Instead of being a single word, such as *break, stop, spoil, mend, kill,* a verb becomes a *phrase,* made up of a noun or adjective tacked on to some general-purpose verb such as *prove, serve, form, play, render.* In addition, the passive voice is wherever possible used in preference to the active, and noun constructions are used instead of gerunds (*by examination of* instead of *by examining*). The range of verbs is further cut down by means of the *-ize* and *de-* formation, and the banal statements are given an appearance of profundity by means of the *not un-* formation. Simple conjunctions and prepositions are replaced by such phrases as *with respect to, having regard to, the fact that, by dint of, in view of, in the interests of, on the hypothesis that;* and the ends of sentences are saved from anticlimax by such resounding commonplaces as *greatly to be desired, cannot be left out of account, a development to be expected in the near future, deserving of serious consideration, brought to a satisfactory conclusion,* and so on and so forth.

Pretentious Diction

Words like *phenomenon, element, individual* (as noun), *objective, categorical, effective, virtual, basic, primary, promote, constitute, exhibit, exploit, utilize, eliminate, liquidate,* are used to dress up simple statements and give an air of scientific impartiality to biased judgments. Adjectives like *epoch-making, epic, historic, unforgettable, triumphant, age-old, inevitable, inexorable, veritable,* are used to dignify the sordid processes of international politics, while writing that aims at glorifying war usually takes on an archaic color, its characteristic words being: *realm, throne, chariot, mailed fist, trident, sword, shield, buckler, banner, jackboot, clarion.* Foreign words and expressions such as *cul de sac, ancien régime, deus ex machina, mutatis mutandis, status quo, gleichschaltung, weltanschauung,* are used to give an air of culture and elegance. Except for the useful abbreviations *i.e., e.g.,* and *etc.,* there is no real need for any of the hundreds of foreign phrases now current in English. Bad writers, and especially scientific, political and sociological writers, are nearly always haunted by the notion that Latin or Greek words are grander than Saxon ones, and unnecessary words like *expedite, ameliorate, predict, extraneous, deracinated, clandestine, subaqueous* and hundreds of others constantly gain ground from their Anglo-Saxon opposite numbers.[1] The jargon peculiar to Marxist writing (*hyena, hangman, cannibal, petty bourgeois, these gentry, lackey, flunkey, mad dog, White Guard,* etc.) consists largely of words and phrases translated from Russian, German, or French; but the normal way of coining a new word is to use a Latin or Greek root with the appropriate affix and, where necessary, the -*ize* formation. It is often easier to make up words of this kind (*deregionalize, impermissible, extramarital, nonfragmentatory* and so forth) than to think up the English words that will cover one's meaning. The result, in general, is an increase in slovenliness and vagueness.

Meaningless Words

In certain kinds of writing, particularly in art criticism and literary criticism, it is normal to come across long passages which are almost completely lacking in meaning.[2] Words like *romantic, plastic, values, human, dead, sentimental, natural, vitality,* as used in art criticism, are strictly meaningless in the sense that they not only do not point to any discoverable object, but are hardly ever expected to do so by the reader. When one critic writes, "The outstanding feature of Mr. X's work is its living quality," while another writes, "The immediately striking thing about Mr. X's work is its peculiar deadness," the reader accepts this as a simple difference of opinion. If words like *black* and *white* were involved, instead of the jargon words *dead* and *living,* he would see at once that language was being used in an improper way. Many political words are similarly abused. The word *Fascism* has now no meaning except in so far as it signifies "something not desirable." The words *democracy, socialism, freedom, patriotic, realistic, justice,* have each of them several different meanings which cannot be reconciled with one another. In the case of a word like *democracy,* not only is there no agreed definition, but the attempt to make one is resisted from all sides. It is almost universally felt that when we call a country democratic we are praising it: consequently the defenders of every kind of régime claim that it is a democracy, and fear that they might have to stop using the word if it were tied down to any one meaning.

---

[1]An interesting illustration of this is the way in which the English flower names which were in use till very recently are being ousted by Greek ones, *snapdragon* becoming *antirrhinum, forget-me-not* becoming *myosotis,* etc. It is hard to see any practical reason for this change of fashion: it is probably due to an instinctive turning-away from the more homely word and a vague feeling that the Greek word is scientific.

[2]Example: "Comfort's catholicity of perception and image, strangely Whitmanesque in range, almost the exact opposite in aesthetic compulsion, continues to evoke that trembling atmospheric accumulative hinting at a cruel, an inexorably serene timelessness. . . . Wrey Gardiner scores by aiming at simple bull's-eyes with precision. Only they are not so simple, and through this contented sadness runs more than the surface bitter-sweet of resignation." (*Poetry Quarterly*)

Words of this kind are often used in a consciously dishonest way. That is, the person who uses them has his own private definition, but allows his hearer to think he means something quite different. Statements like *Marshal Pétain was a true patriot*, *The Soviet Press is the freest in the world*, *The Catholic Church is opposed to persecution*, are almost always made with intent to deceive. Other words used in variable meanings, in most cases more or less dishonestly, are: *class, totalitarian, science, progressive, reactionary, bourgeois, equality*.

Now that I have made this catalogue of swindles and perversions, let me give another example of the kind of writing that they lead to. This time it must of its nature be an imaginary one. I am going to translate a passage of good English into modern English of the worst sort. Here is a well-known verse from *Ecclesiastes*:

> I returned and saw under the sun, that the race is not to the swift, nor the battle to the strong, neither yet bread to the wise, nor yet riches to men of understanding, nor yet favour to men of skill; but time and chance happeneth to them all.

Here it is in modern English:

> Objective consideration of contemporary phenomena compels the conclusion that success or failure in competitive activities exhibits no tendency to be commensurate with innate capacity, but that a considerable element of the unpredictable must invariably be taken into account.

This is a parody, but not a very gross one. Exhibit (3), above, for instance, contains several patches of the same kind of English. It will be seen that I have not made a full translation. The beginning and ending of the sentence follow the original meaning fairly closely, but in the middle the concrete illustrations—race, battle, bread—dissolve into the vague phrase "success or failure in competitive activities." This had to be so, because no modern writer of the kind I am discussing—no one capable of using phrases like "objective consideration of contemporary phenomena"—would ever tabulate his thoughts in that precise and detailed way. The whole tendency of modern prose is away from concreteness. Now analyze these two sentences a little more closely. The first contains forty-nine words but only sixty syllables, and all its words are those of everyday life. The second contains thirty-eight words of ninety syllables: eighteen of its words are from Latin roots, and one from Greek. The first sentence contains six vivid images, and only one phrase ("time and chance") that could be called vague. The second contains not a single fresh, arresting phrase, and in spite of its ninety syllables it gives only a shortened version of the meaning contained in the first. Yet without a doubt it is the second kind of sentence that is gaining ground in modern English. I do not want to exaggerate. This kind of writing is not yet universal, and outcrops of simplicity will occur here and there in the worst-written page. Still, if you or I were told to write a few lines on the uncertainty of human fortunes, we should probably come much nearer to my imaginary sentence than to the one from *Ecclesiastes*.

As I have tried to show, modern writing at its worst does not consist in picking out words for the sake of their meaning and inventing images in order to make the meaning clearer. It consists in gumming together long strips of words which have already been set in order by someone else, and making the results presentable by sheer humbug. The attraction of this way of writing is that it is easy. It is easier—even quicker once you have the habit—to say *In my opinion it is a not unjustifiable assumption that* than to say *I think*. If you use ready-made phrases, you not only don't have to hunt about for words; you also don't have to bother with the rhythms of your sentences, since these phrases are generally so arranged as to be more or less euphonious. When you are composing in a hurry—when you are dictating to a stenographer, for instance, or making a public speech—it is natural to fall into a pretentious, Latinized style. Tags like *a consideration which we should do well to bear in mind* or *a conclusion to which all of us would readily assent* will save many a sentence from coming down with a bump. By using stale metaphors, similes and idioms, you save much mental effort, at the cost of leaving your meaning vague, not only for your reader but for yourself. This is the significance of mixed metaphors. The sole aim of a metaphor is to call up a visual image. When these images clash—as in *The Fascist Octopus has sung its swan song, the jackboot is thrown into the melting pot*—it can be taken as certain that the writer is not seeing a mental image of the objects he is naming; in other words he is not really thinking. Look again at the examples I gave at the beginning of this essay. Professor Laski (1) uses five negatives in fifty-three words. One of these is superfluous, making nonsense of the whole passage, and in addition there is the slip *alien* for *akin*, making further nonsense, and several avoidable pieces of clumsiness which increase the general vagueness. Professor Hogben (2) plays ducks and drakes with a battery which is able to write prescriptions, and, while disapproving of the everyday phrase *put up with*, is unwilling to look *egregious* up in the dictionary and see what it means. (3), if one takes an uncharitable attitude towards it, is simply meaningless: probably one could work out its intended meaning by reading the whole of the article in which it occurs. In (4), the writer knows more or less what he wants to say, but an accumulation of stale phrases chokes him like tea leaves blocking a sink. In (5), words and meaning have almost parted company.

People who write in this manner usually have a general emotional meaning—they dislike one thing and want to express solidarity with another—but they are not interested in the detail of what they are saying. A scrupulous writer, in every sentence that he writes, will ask himself at least four questions, thus: What am I trying to say? What words will express it? What image or idiom will make it clearer? Is this image fresh enough to have an effect? And he will probably ask himself two more: Could I put it more shortly? Have I said anything that is avoidably ugly? But you are not obliged to go to all this trouble. You can shirk it by simply throwing your mind open and letting the ready-made phrases come crowding in. They will construct your sentences for you—even think your thoughts for you, to a certain extent—and at need they will perform the important service of partially concealing your meaning even from yourself. It is at this point that the special connection between politics and the debasement of language becomes clear.

In our times it is broadly true that political writing is bad writing. Where it is not true, it will generally be found that the writer is some kind of rebel, expressing his private opinions and not a "party line." Orthodoxy, of whatever color, seems to demand a lifeless, imitative style. The political dialects to be found in pamphlets, leading articles, manifestos, White Papers and the speeches of under-secretaries do, of course, vary from party to party, but they are all alike in that one almost never finds in them a fresh, vivid, home-made turn of speech. When one watches some tired hack on the platform mechanically repeating the familiar phrases—*bestial atrocities, iron heel, bloodstained tyranny, free peoples of the world, stand shoulder to shoulder*—one often has a curious feeling that one is not watching a live human being but some kind of dummy, a feeling which suddenly becomes stronger at moments when the light catches the speaker's spectacles and turns them into blank discs which seem to have no eyes behind them. And this is not altogether fanciful. A speaker who uses that kind of phraseology has gone some distance towards turning himself into a machine. The appropriate noises are coming out of his larynx, but his brain is not involved as it would be if he were choosing his words from himself. If the speech he is making is one that he is accustomed to make over and over again, he may be almost unconscious of what he is saying, as one is when one utters the responses in church. And this reduced state of consciousness, if not indispensable, is at any rate favorable to political conformity.

In our time, political speech and writing are largely the defense of the indefensible. Things like the continuance of British rule in India, the Russian purges and deportations, the dropping of the atom bombs on Japan, can indeed be defended, but only by arguments which are too brutal for most people to face, and which do not square with the professed aims of political parties. Thus political language has to consist largely of euphemism, question-begging and sheer cloudy vagueness. Defenseless villages are bombarded from the air, the inhabitants driven out into the countryside, the cattle machine-gunned, the huts set on fire with incendiary bullets: this is called *pacification*. Millions of peasants are robbed of their farms and sent trudging along the roads with no more than they can carry: this is called *transfer of population* or *rectification of frontiers*. People are imprisoned for years without trial, or shot in the back of the neck or sent to die of scurvy in Arctic lumber camps: this is called *elimination of unreliable elements*. Such phraseology is needed if one wants to name things without calling up mental pictures of them. Consider for instance some comfortable English professor defending Russian totalitarianism. He cannot say outright, "I believe in killing off your opponents when you can get good results by doing so." Probably, therefore, he will say something like this:

"While freely conceding that the Soviet régime exhibits certain features which the humanitarian may be inclined to deplore, we must, I think, agree that a certain curtailment of the right to political opposition is an unavoidable concomitant of transitional periods, and that the rigors which the Russian people have been called upon to undergo have been amply justified in the sphere of concrete achievement."

The inflated style is itself a kind of euphemism. A mass of Latin words falls upon the facts like soft snow, blurring the outlines and covering up all the details. The great enemy of clear language is insincerity. When there is a gap between one's real and one's declared aims, one turns as it were instinctively to long words and exhausted idioms, like a cuttlefish squirting out ink. In our age there is no such thing as "keeping out of politics." All issues are political issues, and politics itself is a mass of lies, evasions, folly, hatred and schizophrenia. When the general atmosphere is bad, language must suffer. I should expect to find—this is a guess which I have not sufficient knowledge to verify—that the German, Russian and Italian languages have all deteriorated in the last ten or fifteen years, as a result of dictatorship.

But if thought corrupts language, language can also corrupt thought. A bad usage can spread by tradition and imitation, even among people who should and do know better. The debased language that I have been discussing is in some ways very convenient. Phrases like *a not unjustifiable assumption, leaves much to be desired, would serve no good purpose, a consideration which we should do well to bear in mind*, are a continuous temptation, a packet of aspirins always at one's elbow. Look back through this essay, and for certain you will find that I have again and again committed the very faults I am protesting against. By this morning's post I have received a pamphlet dealing with conditions in Germany. The author tells me that he "felt impelled" to write it. I open it at random, and here is almost the first sentence that I see: "(The Allies) have an opportunity not only of achieving a radical transformation of Germany's social and political structure in such a way as to avoid a nationalistic reaction in Germany itself, but at the same time of laying the foundations of a co-operative and unified Europe." You see, he "feels impelled" to write—feels, presumably, that he has something new to say—and yet his words, like cavalry horses answering the bugle, group themselves automatically into the familiar dreary pattern. This invasion of one's mind by ready-made phrases (*lay the foundations, achieve a radical transformation*) can only be prevented if one is constantly on guard against them, and every such phrase anaesthetizes a portion of one's brain.

I said earlier that the decadence of our language is probably curable. Those who deny this would argue, if they produced an argument at all, that language merely reflects existing social conditions, and that we cannot influence its development by any direct tinkering with words and constructions. So far as the general tone or spirit of a language goes, this may be true, but it is not true in detail. Silly words and expressions have often disappeared, not through any evolutionary process but owing to the conscious action of a minority. Two recent examples were *explore every avenue* and *leave no stone unturned*, which were killed by the jeers of a few journalists. There is a long list of flyblown metaphors which could similarly be got rid of if enough people would interest themselves in the job; and it should also be possible to laugh the *not un-*formation out of existence,[3] to reduce the amount of Latin and Greek in the average sentence, to drive out foreign phrases and strayed scientific words, and, in general, to make pretentiousness unfashionable. But all these are minor points. The defense of the English language implies more than this, and perhaps it is best to start by saying what it does *not* imply.

To begin with it has nothing to do with archaism, with the salvaging of obsolete words and turns of speech, or with the setting up of a "standard English" which must never be departed from. On the contrary, it is especially concerned with the scrapping of

---

[3]One can cure oneself of the *not un-* formation by memorizing this sentence: *A not unblack dog was chasing a not unsmall rabbit across a not ungreen field.*

every word or idiom which has outworn its usefulness. It has nothing to do with correct grammar and syntax, which are of no importance so long as one makes one's meaning clear, or with the avoidance of Americanisms, or with having what is called a "good prose style." On the other hand, it is not concerned with fake simplicity and the attempt to make written English colloquial. Nor does it even imply in every case preferring the Saxon word to the Latin one, though it does imply using the fewest and shortest words that will cover one's meaning. What is above all needed is to let the meaning choose the word, and not the other way about. In prose, the worst thing one can do with words is to surrender to them. When you think of a concrete object, you think wordlessly, and then, if you want to describe the thing you have been visualizing you probably hunt about till you find the exact words that seem to fit. When you think of something abstract, you are more inclined to use words from the start, and unless you make a conscious effort to prevent it, the existing dialect will come rushing in and do the job for you, at the expense of blurring or even changing your meaning. Probably it is better to put off using words as long as possible and get one's meaning as clear as one can through pictures or sensations. Afterwards one can choose—not simply *accept*—the phrases that will best cover the meaning, and then switch round and decide what impression one's words are likely to make on another person. This last effort of the mind cuts out all stale or mixed images, all prefabricated phrases, needless repetitions, and humbug and vagueness generally. But one can often be in doubt about the effect of a word or a phrase, and one needs rules that one can rely on when instinct fails. I think the following rules will cover most cases:

(i) Never use a metaphor, simile or other figure of speech which you are used to seeing in print.

(ii) Never use a long word where a short one will do.

(iii) If it is possible to cut a word out, always cut it out.

(iv) Never use the passive where you can use the active.

(v) Never use a foreign phrase, a scientific word or jargon word if you can think of an everyday English equivalent.

(vi) Break any of these rules sooner than say anything outright barbarous.

These rules sound elementary, and so they are, but they demand a deep change in attitude in anyone who has grown used to writing in the style now fashionable. One could keep all of them and still write bad English, but one could not write the kind of stuff that I quoted in those five specimens at the beginning of this article.

I have not here been considering the literary use of language, but merely language as an instrument for expressing and not for concealing or preventing thought. Stuart Chase and others have come near to claiming that all abstract words are meaningless, and have used this as a pretext for advocating a kind of political quietism. Since you don't know what Fascism is, how can you struggle against Fascism? One need not swallow such absurdities as this, but one ought to recognize that the present political chaos is connected with the decay of language, and that one can probably bring about some improvement by starting at the verbal end. If you simplify your English, you are freed from the worst follies of orthodoxy. You cannot speak any of the necessary dialects, and when you make a stupid remark, its stupidity will be obvious, even to yourself. Political language—and with variations this is true of all political parties, from Conservatives to Anarchists—is designed to make lies sound truthful and murder respectable, and to give an appearance of solidity to pure wind. One cannot change this all in a moment, but one can at least change one's own habits, and from time to time one can even, if one jeers loudly enough, send some worn-out and useless phrase—some *jackboot, Achilles' heel, hotbed, melting pot, acid test, veritable inferno* or other lump of verbal refuse—into the dustbin where it belongs.

GEORGE ORWELL

George Orwell (1903–1950), the essayist and novelist, was born in India and died in London. He was a critic of colonialism and an advocate of clear thinking and writing. His two famous works of fiction are *Animal Farm* and *Nineteen Eighty-Four*. Also highly readable are such autobiographical books as *Down and Out in Paris and London* and *The Road to Wigan Pier*.

GLOSSARY

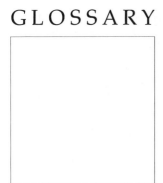

List of Useful Terms

ABSTRACT and CONCRETE are terms used to describe two kinds of language. *Abstract* words are for ideas, terms, feelings, qualities, measurements—concepts we understand through our minds. For example, *idea*, *term*, *feeling*, *quality* and *measurement* are all abstract words. *Concrete* words, on the other hand, are for things we perceive through our senses: we can see, hear, touch, taste, or smell what they stand for. *Knee*, *song*, *carburetor*, *apple*, and *smoke* are all concrete words.

ALLUSION is a reference to something—a person, a concept, a quotation, or a character—from literature, history, mythology, politics, or any other field familiar to your readers. For instance, in an essay on different kinds of employees, we might call one individual "the Woody Allen type." Immediately the reader can picture a slight, indecisive, funny character.

The secret of the effective use of allusions is to allude to events, books, people, or quotations that are known to your readers. Suppose one of the references in an essay on employee types is to a Morel type. Can you picture this type? Are you any better informed? If not, the allusion is a poor one.

Be sure your allusions are clear, single, and unambiguous. A reference to "King" could mean Mackenzie King, King Hussein (or any other male monarch), or Martin Luther King. Or perhaps it refers to the King of Rock. Who knows? Imagine the confusion if the reader has the wrong King in mind.

AMBIGUITY: An ambiguous statement is one that has at least two different and conflicting interpretations. Similarly, an ambiguous action is one that can be understood in various ways. When it's used deliberately and carefully, ambiguity can add richness of meaning to your writing; however, most of the time ambiguity is not planned. It is the result of imprecise use of language.

For instance, the statement, "He never has enough money" could mean that he is always broke, or that he is never satisfied no matter how much money he has. As a general rule, it is wise to avoid ambiguity in your writing.

ANALOGY is an extended comparison. Writers explain complicated or unfamiliar concepts by comparing them to simple or familiar ones. For instance, one could draw an analogy between life's experience and a race: the stages in life—infancy, childhood, adolescence, maturity, old age—become the laps of the race, and the problems or crises of life become the hurdles of an obstacle course. If we "fall down," we have let a problem get the better of us; if we "get up again," we are refusing to let a problem beat us. (See Tom Wolfe's "O Rotten Gotham" in Unit Five for an example of an extended analogy.)

ANALYSIS means looking at the parts of something individually and considering how they contribute to the whole. In essay writing, the common kinds of analysis are process analysis and causal analysis. See the introduction to Unit Two and Unit Five for a more detailed explanation.

ANECDOTE is a little story—an account of an incident—often humorous, that is used to catch the reader's interest. Writers frequently use this technique to introduce an essay. See the introduction to Atwood's "Canadians: What Do They Want?" in Unit Five for an example of the effective use of anecdote.

ARGUMENT: See RHETORICAL MODES.

AUDIENCE is the writer's intended reader or readers. Knowledge of their level of understanding, their expectations, is critically important to the writer. Tone, level of vocabulary, the amount of detail included, even the organizational structure, will all be influenced by the needs of the audience.

You know instinctively that when you speak or write to children, you use simple, direct language and, usually, short sentences. You adapt your style to suit your listeners. Before you begin to write, think about their knowledge of your subject, their educational background, their probable age level. Never talk down to your readers; but don't talk over their heads either, or they will stop reading in frustration.

For example, suppose you were preparing an article on the appeal of sports cars to the public. For a popular women's magazine, you would probably stress style, economy, comfort, and reliability, and you would support your thesis with examples of well-known women who love the sports cars they drive. You would not include much technical automotive jargon. If you were writing about the same topic for a general-audience consumers' magazine, however, you would include more specifics about price, ease of maintenance and cost, gas consumption, reliability under various weather and road conditions, with detailed figures comparing several popular makes. But if you were writing for a publication such as *Popular Mechanics* or *Road and Track*, you would stress performance, handling under high speed or unusual road conditions, and the ease or difficulty with which owners could maintain their cars themselves.

CHRONOLOGICAL ORDER means time order; items or ideas that are introduced chronologically are discussed in order of *time sequence*. Historical accounts are usually presented chronologically. In a chronological sequencing, connectives such as *first, second, third, next, then, after that*, and *finally*, are helpful to keep your reader on track. See the introduction to Unit Two for further details.

CLICHÉ is a trite and familiar expression that was once colourful and original; now it's so familiar it's boring. Clichés often appear in similes or comparisons: for example, your writing will be as "dull as dishwater" and your reader will be "bored stiff" if you are "as stubborn as a mule" and keep on using them. See also STEREOTYPES.

CLIMACTIC ORDER means order of importance. In this ordering pattern, writers arrange their main points so that the most important or strongest point comes last. Thus, the paper builds up to a *climax*.

COHERENCE means a clear connection among the ideas or parts of a piece of writing. In a coherent paper, one paragraph leads logically to the next: ideas are clearly sequenced; the subject is consistent throughout; and the writer has supplied carefully chosen and logical TRANSITIONS such as *also, however, nevertheless, on the other hand, first, second, thus*, etc. If a paper is coherent, it is probably unified as well. (See UNITY.)

COLLOQUIALISM: Colloquial language is the language we speak. Expressions such as *well, okay, a lot*, or *kids* are perfectly acceptable in informal speech but are not appropriate in essays, papers, or reports. Contractions (such as *they're, isn't, it's*, or *let's*) and abbreviations *(*such as *TV, ads*, or *photos*) that are often used in speech are appropriate in writing only if the writer is consciously trying to achieve a casual, informal effect.

CONCLUSION: The conclusion of any piece of writing determines what will stay with your reader; therefore, it should be both logical and memorable. A good conclusion contributes to the overall UNITY of the piece. This is no place to throw in a new point you just thought of, or a few minor details. Your conclusion should reinforce your THESIS, but it should not simply restate it, or repeat it word for word, which is even more boring. Here are five effective strategies you can choose from when writing a conclusion:

1.   *Refer back to your introduction.* This does *not* mean simply repeating the opening lines of your paper; instead, allude to its content and draw the connections for your reader. See the conclusion of "The Value of Education" in Unit One.

2.   *Conclude with a relevant, thought-provoking quotation.* See the conclusion of "Why Are We Reading This Stuff, Anyway?" in Unit Seven.

3.   *Ask a rhetorical question*—one that is asked to emphasize a point, not to elicit an answer. See the concluding paragraph of "Bumblers, Martinets, and Pros" in Unit Three.

4.   *Issue a challenge.* See the conclusion of "Flunking with Style" in Unit Two.

5. *Highlight the value or significance of your subject.* See the last paragraph of "Why Do They Fail?" in Unit Five.

There are still other techniques you can use to conclude effectively: by providing a suggestion for change, offering a solution, making a prediction, or ending with an ANECDOTE that perfectly illustrates your thesis. Whatever strategy you choose, you should leave your reader with a sense of your paper's unity and completeness.

CONNOTATION and DENOTATION: The *denotation* of a word is its literal or dictionary meaning. *Connotation* refers to the emotional overtones the word has in the reader's mind. Some words have only a few connotations, while others have many. For instance, "house" is a word whose denotative meaning is familiar to all and which has few connotations. "Home," on the other hand, is also denotatively familiar, but has a rich connotative meaning that differs from reader to reader.

To take another example, the word "prison" is denotatively a "place of confinement for lawbreakers who have been convicted of serious crimes." But the connotations of the word are much deeper and broader: when we hear or read the word "prison" we think of colours like grey and black; we hear sounds of clanging doors, jangling keys, or wailing sirens; and we associate with the word emotions like anger, fear, despair, or loneliness. A careful writer will not use this word lightly: to refer to your job as a "prison" is a strong statement. It would not be appropriate to use this phrase simply because you don't like the location or the lunch break.

CONTEXT is the verbal background of a word or phrase—the words that come before and after it and fix its meaning. For example, the word "happiness" in the context of Lewis's essay, "We Have No 'Right to Happiness,'" means sexual freedom. The word "manual," which in most contexts means an instruction book, means a non-electric typewriter in Peter Gzowski's essay.

When a word or phrase is taken *out of context*, it is often difficult to determine what it originally meant. Therefore, when you are quoting from another writer, be sure to include enough of the context so the meaning is clear to your reader.

DEDUCTION is the logical process of applying a general statement to a specific instance and reasoning through to a conclusion about that instance. See the introduction to Unit Seven.

DESCRIPTION: See RHETORICAL MODES.

DICTION refers to the selection and arrangement of words in a piece of writing. Effective diction depends upon the writer's careful choice of a level of vocabulary suited to both the reader and the subject. A careful writer does not mix formal with colloquial language; standard English with dialect or slang; or informal language with technical jargon or archaisms (outmoded, antique phrases). Good diction is that which is appropriate to the subject, the reader, and the writer's purpose. Writing for a general audience about the closing of the local A&P store, a careful writer would not say, "The retail establishment for the purveyance of merchandise relative to the sustaining of life has cemented its portals," which is pretentious nonsense. "The corner grocery store is closed" conveys the same meaning more appropriately and more concisely.

EMPHASIS: A writer can emphasize or highlight key points in several ways: by repetition; by placement (the essay's first and last sections are the most prominent positions); or by phrasing. Careful phrasing can call attention to a particular point. Parallel structure, a very short sentence or paragraph, even a deliberate sentence fragment are all emphatic devices. A writer can also add emphasis by developing an idea at greater length, or by calling attention to its significance directly, by inserting expressions such as *most important is* or *significantly*. TONE, particularly IRONY or even sarcasm, can be used to add emphasis. Finally, distinctive diction is an emphatic device. (See Wolfe's piece, "O Rotten Gotham," in Unit Five for a good example of the use of distinctive diction.)

EVIDENCE in a piece of writing functions the same way it does in a court of law: it proves the point. Evidence can consist of statistical data, examples, references to authorities in the field, surveys, illustrations, quotations, or facts. Charts, graphs, and maps are also forms of evidence and are well suited to particular kinds of reports.

A point cannot be effectively explained, let alone proved, without evidence. For instance, it is not enough to say that computers are displacing many office workers. You need to find specific examples of companies, jobs, and statistics to prove the connection. After all, the number of dogs in Ontario has increased almost as much as the number of computers. Does that prove that dogs breed computers? What makes a paper credible and convincing is the evidence presented and the COHERENCE with which you present it.

EXPOSITION: See RHETORICAL MODES

FIGURES of SPEECH are words or phrases that mean something more than the literal meanings of the individual words or phrases. Writers choose to use figurative language when they want the reader to associate one thing with another. Some of the more common figures of speech include similes, metaphors, personifications, and puns.

A *simile* is a comparison in which the author uses "like" or "as." For example, "She is as slow as an arthritic turtle" is a simile. Effective similes are both appropriate and imaginative: trotting out old clichés such as "cool as a cucumber" or "busy as a bee" will only bore, not enlighten, your reader.

A *metaphor* does not use "like" or "as": it claims one thing *is* another. For example, if you write, "My supervisor wallowed in his chair," you are implicitly comparing your boss to a pig. "My boss is a pig" is a metaphor, but it is unoriginal and inappropriate. Choose your metaphors with care: they should enlighten your readers with fresh and original insight, not confuse or tire them with an inappropriate comparison or a cliché.

Personification is a figure of speech in which the writer gives human qualities to an inanimate object or an abstract idea. For instance, if you write, "The brakes screeched when he hit them," you are comparing the sound of the car's brakes to a human voice. Strive for original and insightful personifications; otherwise, you will be trapped by clichés such as "The solution to the problem was staring me in the face."

A *pun* is the use of language so that one word or phrase brings to the reader's mind two different meanings. Max Eastman, in *Enjoyment of Laughter*, classifies puns into three sorts: atrocious, witty, and poetic. The person who wrote, "How does Dolly Parton stack up against Mae West?" was guilty of an atrocious pun. Barry Callaghan's title, "Canadian Wry," contains a witty pun. Poetic puns go beyond the merely humorous double meaning and offer the reader a concise, pointed, original comparison of two entities, qualities, or ideas. Dylan Thomas's "Do not go gentle into that good night" is an example of a poetic pun. See Callaghan's "Canadian Wry" in Unit One for numerous examples of puns.

GENERAL and SPECIFIC: *General* words refer to classes or groups of things. "Animal" is a general word; so is "fruit." *Specific* words limit or narrow down the class of things to something very specific such as "wolf" or "lemon." Good writing is a careful blend of general and specific language. (See also ABSTRACT/CONCRETE.)

GOBBLEDYGOOK is a type of JARGON distinguished by language that is both pretentious and wordy and highly ABSTRACT and vague. George Orwell's famous essay "Politics and the English Language" (Unit Eight) contains several examples of gobbledygook.

ILLUSTRATION: See the introduction to Unit One.

INDUCTION is the logical process of looking at a number of specific instances and reasoning through to a general conclusion about them. See the introduction to Unit Seven.

INTRODUCTION: The introduction to any piece of writing is crucial to its success. A good introduction indicates the THESIS of the piece, establishes the TONE, and secures the reader's attention. The introduction is the "hook" with which you catch your reader's interest and make him want to read what you have to say. Here are five different "attention-getters" you can use:

1. *Begin with a story of an interesting incident.* The story or ANECDOTE should be related to your subject. See the first paragraph of "Why Are We Reading This Stuff, Anyway?" in Unit Seven.

2. *Offer a dramatic statistic or striking fact.* See "Why Do They Fail?" in Unit Five.

3. *Begin with a relevant quotation.* Make it interesting but keep it short. See the first paragraph of "Bumblers, Martinets, and Pros" in Unit Three.

4. *Begin by stating a commonly held opinion that you intend to challenge.* See "Flunking with Style" in Unit Two.

5. *Set up a contrast to "hook" your reader.* The opening paragraph of

"College or University?" contrasts the post-secondary educational scene in the United States with that in Canada. See Unit Four.

Other strategies you might want to experiment with include posing a question, offering a definition—make sure it's yours, not the dictionary's— or even telling a joke. You know how important first impressions are when you meet someone. Treat your introductory paragraph with the same care you would take when you want to make a good first impression on a person. If you bait the hook attractively, your reader will want to read on—and that, after all, is your goal.

IRONY is a statement or situation that means the opposite of what it appears to mean. To call a hopelessly ugly painting a masterpiece is ironic—it's an example of verbal irony, to be exact. Irony of situation occurs when a twist of fate reverses an expected outcome: for example, a man defers all the pleasure in his life to scrimp and save for his retirement but wins a million-dollar lottery at age 65.

Irony is an effective technique because it forces readers to think about the relationship between seemingly different things or ideas. Notice how Russell Baker's "A Nice Place to Visit" in Unit Four really compliments Toronto as a civilized place to live, though it seems to instruct Torontonians on how they can transform their city into a "world-class" urban center like the relatively barbaric New York Baker describes.

JARGON is the specialized language used within a particular trade, discipline, or profession. Among members of that trade or profession, jargon is perfectly appropriate; indeed, such highly technical language is an efficient, time-saving means of communication. Outside the context of the trade or profession, however, jargon is inappropriate, because it inhibits rather than promotes the reader's understanding. Another meaning of jargon, the meaning usually intended when the word is used in this text, is GOBBLEDYGOOK.

METAPHOR: See FIGURES OF SPEECH.

NARRATION: See RHETORICAL MODES.

ORDER refers to the arrangement of information or points in a piece of prose. While you are still in the planning stages, choose the order most appropriate to your subject. There are four main ways to arrange your points:

1. *Chronological order* means in order of time, from first to last.

2. *Climactic order* means in order of importance, leading up to the climax. Usually you would present your strongest or most important point last, your second-strongest point first, and the others in between, where they will attract less attention.

3. *Causal* or *logical* order means that the points are connected in such a way that one point must be explained before the next can be understood. Often used in cause/effect patterns, this order is appropriate when there is a direct and logical connection between one point and the next.

4. *Random* order is a shopping-list kind of arrangement: the points can be presented in any order. Random order is appropriate only when the points are all equal in significance and not logically or causally linked. Goddard's "How to Spot Rock Types" (Unit Three) is an example of an article organized in random order; he could have presented the different classes of fans in another arrangement because they are all separate and distinct.

PARAGRAPH refers to a unit of composition, usually from five to ten sentences long, all dealing with one topic. In an essay you present several main ideas, all related to your subject. The main ideas are broken down into points or topics, each of which is developed in a paragraph.

Every paragraph should have a *topic sentence*—a sentence that states clearly what the paragraph is about. It is often the first or second sentence of the paragraph. The rest of the paragraph consists of sentences that develop the topic, perhaps with examples, a description, a definition, a quotation, a comparison—or a combination of these strategies. There should be no sentence in the paragraph that is not clearly related to its topic. A paragraph should lead smoothly into the next (see TRANSITION), and it must also possess internal COHERENCE and UNITY. The essays in this text by Bertrand Russell and Martin Luther King (Unit Three) deserve careful analysis: their paragraphs are models of form.

PARALLEL STRUCTURE means similarity of grammatical form. In a sentence, for example, all items in a series would be written in the same grammatical form: single words, phrases, or clauses. Julius Caesar's famous pronouncement, "I came; I saw; I conquered" is a classic example of parallelism.

Parallelism creates symmetry that is pleasing to the reader. Lack of parallelism, on the other hand, can be jarring: "His favourite sports are skiing, skating, and he particularly loves sailing." Such potholes in your prose should be fixed up before you hand in a paper. For example, "What Carol says, she means; and she delivers what she promises, too" would be much more effective if rewritten in parallel form: "What Carol says, she means; what she promises, she delivers."

Because the human mind responds favourably to the repetition of rhythm, parallelism is an effective device for adding EMPHASIS. King's "Dimensions of a Complete Life" (Unit Three) contains many examples of emphatic parallel structure. See also the concluding sentence in E.M. Forster's "My Wood" (Unit Five).

PARAPHRASE is putting another writer's ideas into your own words. Of course, you acknowledge the original writer as the source of the idea—if you don't, you are guilty of plagiarism.

You will find paraphrasing very useful when you are writing a research paper. Once you have gathered the information you need from your various sources and organized your ideas into an appropriate order, you then write the paper, drawing on your sources for supporting ideas, but expressing them in your own words.

A paraphrase should reflect both the meaning and the general TONE of the original. It may be the same length or shorter than the original, but it is not a PRÉCIS.

PERSONIFICATION: See FIGURES OF SPEECH.

PERSUASION: See RHETORICAL MODES and the introduction to Unit Seven.

POINT OF VIEW, in exposition, means the grammatical angle of the essay. (In persuasion, point of view can mean either the grammatical angle or an opinion.)

If the writer identifies himself as "I", we have the first-person point of view; in this case, we expect to find the writer's own opinions and first-hand experiences. Leacock's "Humour As I See It" (Unit Three) and Gzowski's "People and Their Machines and Vice Versa" (Unit Four) are written in the first person.

If the writer addresses the readers as "you," we have the second-person point of view, as in Berton's "Baked Beans," or Goddard's "How to Spot Rock Types" (Units Two and Three). Second person lends itself to a fairly informal style.

If the writer—or reader—is not grammatically "present" in the material, we have the third-person point of view. Malcolmson's "After Hiroshima: The Shift to Nuclear Technology" (Unit Three) is an example. The writer uses "one," "he," "they," and the result is a more formal essay than one written in the first or second person.

A careful writer maintains point of view consistently throughout an essay; if a shift occurs, it should be for a good reason, with a particular effect in mind. Careless shifts in point of view throw the reader off track. See paragraph 9 of Lewis Thomas's "Altruism" (in Unit Six) for an example of a purposeful change in point of view.

PRÉCIS is a condensed summary of an article or essay. It is one-quarter to one-third the length of the original. The examples and illustrations are omitted, and the prose is tightened up as much as possible. All the main ideas are included; most of the development is not.

PROCESS ANALYSIS: See the introduction to Unit Two.

PUN: See FIGURES OF SPEECH.

PURPOSE means the writer's intent: to inform, to persuade, or to amuse, or a combination of these. See RHETORICAL MODES.

RHETORICAL MODES: The word "rhetoric" simply means the art of using language effectively. There are four classic modes, or kinds, of writing: exposition, narration, description, and argument. The writer's choice of mode is often dependent on his or her PURPOSE.

Exposition is writing intended to inform or explain. If the writer's purpose is to inform, this mode is a likely choice. Expository writing can be personal or impersonal, serious or light-hearted. The various methods of exposition (such as exemplification, definition, comparison, and the rest) are sometimes called rhetorical forms.

Narration tells a story. It is the mode used for fiction. Examples of narrative writing are sometimes found within expository prose: in anecdotes or illustrations, for example.

Description is used to make a reader see, hear, taste, smell, or feel something. Good descriptive writing recreates a sensory experience in the reader's imagination. Descriptive writing is also sometimes found in expository prose. See the essays by E.B. White, Ken Dryden, and Harry Bruce in Unit Eight for examples of effective description.

Argument, sometimes called *persuasion*, is writing that sets out not to explain something, but to convince the reader of the validity of the writer's opinion on an issue. Sometimes its purpose goes even further, and the writer attempts to motivate the reader to act in some way. Like exposition, argument conveys information to the reader, but not solely for the purpose of making a subject clear. Argument seeks to reinforce or to change a reader's opinion about an issue.

SATIRE is a form of humour, sometimes light-hearted, sometimes biting, in which the writer deliberately attacks and ridicules something: a person, a political decision, an event, an institution, a philosophy, or a system. The satirist uses exaggeration, ridicule, and IRONY to achieve his or her effect. There is often a social purpose in satire: the writer points to the difference between the ideal—a world based on common sense and moral standards— and the real, which may be silly, vicious, alienating, or immoral, depending on the object of the satirist's attack. The essays by Atwood, Mitford, and Baker (Units Five, Two, and Four) in this text are examples of satire.

SIMILE: See FIGURES OF SPEECH.

STEREOTYPE refers to a character, situation, or idea that is trite, unoriginal, and conventional. Stereotypes are based on automatic, widely known, and usually incorrect assumptions: all women are poor drivers; all truck drivers are illiterate; all teenagers are boors; all Scots are tight with money. Stereotypical notions about races and nationalities are particularly dangerous: think of the well-known "Newfie" jokes, for example.

A careful writer avoids stereotypes, unless he or she is using them for satiric purposes. Unthinking acceptance of others' assumptions is a sure sign of a lazy mind.

STYLE refers to the distinctive way a person writes. When two writers approach the same subject, even if they share many of the same ideas, the resulting works will be different. That difference is the result of personal style. DICTION, sentence structure, sentence length, TONE, and level of formality all contribute to an individual's style. Compare Wolfe's "O Rotten Gotham: Sliding Down the Behaviorial Sink" (Unit Five) and Galbraith's "Writing, Typing, and Economics" (Unit Two) as examples of unique styles.

Good writers adapt their style to their audience; one doesn't write the same way in the business world as one does in the academic world, for example. In this sense, "good style" means one that suits the writer's PURPOSE, subject, and AUDIENCE. An informal and humorous style full of slang expressions would be inappropriate in a paper on teenage suicide. Similarly, a stiff, formal style would hardly be suitable for an article on new toys for the Christmas season.

SUMMARY is a brief statement, in sentence or paragraph form, of the main ideas of an article or essay. See also PRÉCIS and PARAPHRASE.

SYNTAX means the arrangement of words in a sentence. Good syntax means not only grammatical correctness, but also an effective word order and a variety of sentence patterns. Good writers use short sentences and long ones, simple sentences and complex ones, and natural-order sentences and inverted-order ones. The choice depends on the meaning the writer wishes to convey.

THESIS is the main idea or point the writer wants to communicate to the reader in an essay. It is often expressed in a *thesis statement*. (See "How to Write to Be Understood.") Sometimes the thesis is not stated, but implied. Whether stated or implied, however, the thesis is the central idea that everything in the essay is designed to support and explain.

TONE reflects the writer's attitude to the subject and to the presumed audience. For instance, a writer who is looking back with longing to the past will use a nostalgic tone. An angry writer might use an indignant, outraged tone, or an understated, ironic tone—depending on the subject and purpose of the piece.

Through DICTION, POINT OF VIEW, sentence structure, PARAGRAPH development, and STYLE, a writer modulates the message to suit the knowledge, attitudes, and taste of the people who will read it. Contrast the carping, negative tone of Atwood's "Canadians: What Do They Want?" with the poignant, yet somehow positive tone of Finn's "Reflections on My Brother's Murder" in Unit Five. Other examples of superb control of tone are Mitford's scathing "Behind the Formaldehyde Curtain," Needham's curmudgeonly "Why the Old Dislike the Young," and Malcolmson's calm yet passionate treatment of the nuclear threat in "After Hiroshima: The Shift to Nuclear Technology." (See Units Two, Seven, and Three.)

TOPIC SENTENCE is a sentence that identifies the topic, or main idea, of a paragraph; it is usually found at or near the beginning of the paragraph.

TRANSITIONS are linking words or phrases. They help connect a writer's sentences and paragraphs so that the whole piece flows smoothly and logically. Here are some of the most common transitions used to show relationships between ideas:

1. *to show a time relation*: first, second, third, next, before, during, after, now, then, finally, last
2. *to add an idea or example*: in addition, also, another, furthermore, similarly, for example, for instance
3. *to show contrast*: although, but, however, instead, nevertheless, on the other hand, in contrast, on the contrary
4. *to show a cause-effect relation*: as a result, consequently, because, since, therefore, thus
   See also COHERENCE.

UNITY: A piece of writing has unity if all its parts work together; each part contributes to the ultimate effect. The unified work has one subject and one tone. Unity is an important quality of a good paragraph: each sentence must be related to and develop the central idea expressed or implied in the TOPIC SENTENCE.

AUTHOR INDEX

To the Owner of This Book:

We are interested in your reaction to *Canadian Content: Essays for Composition from Canada, Britain and the United States* by Norton and Waldman.

  With your comments, we can improve this book in future editions. Please help us by completing this questionnaire.

1. What was your reason for using this book?

  _____ University Course

  _____ College Course   _____ Personal Interest

  _____ Continuing Education Course   _____ Other (Specify)

2. Which school do you attend? _____

3. What is the best aspect of the book? _____

_____

4. Please give your reaction to the selections listed by author in the order of their appearance in the book. (Refer to the Author Index for assistance if necessary.)

Author	Liked best				Liked least	Didn't read	Author	Liked best				Liked least	Didn't read
MacLennan	5	4	3	2	1	_____	Wolfe	5	4	3	2	1	_____
Sagan	5	4	3	2	1	_____	Forster	5	4	3	2	1	_____
Ward	5	4	3	2	1	_____	Sharp	5	4	3	2	1	_____
Pearson	5	4	3	2	1	_____	Bierce	5	4	3	2	1	_____
Callaghan	5	4	3	2	1	_____	Moore	5	4	3	2	1	_____
Tuchman	5	4	3	2	1	_____	Frye	5	4	3	2	1	_____
Berton	5	4	3	2	1	_____	Auden	5	4	3	2	1	_____
Berton	5	4	3	2	1	_____	Priestley	5	4	3	2	1	_____
Stoffman	5	4	3	2	1	_____	Theroux	5	4	3	2	1	_____
Mitford	5	4	3	2	1	_____	Thomas	5	4	3	2	1	_____
Galbraith	5	4	3	2	1	_____	Needham	5	4	3	2	1	_____
Eastman	5	4	3	2	1	_____	Trudeau	5	4	3	2	1	_____
Goddard	5	4	3	2	1	_____	Bruce	5	4	3	2	1	_____
Russell	5	4	3	2	1	_____	Suzuki	5	4	3	2	1	_____
Kettle	5	4	3	2	1	_____	Nowlan	5	4	3	2	1	_____
Malcolmson	5	4	3	2	1	_____	Lewis	5	4	3	2	1	_____
King	5	4	3	2	1	_____	Postman	5	4	3	2	1	_____
Leacock	5	4	3	2	1	_____	Bruce	5	4	3	2	1	_____
Gzowski	5	4	3	2	1	_____	Dryden	5	4	3	2	1	_____
Baker	5	4	3	2	1	_____	Richler	5	4	3	2	1	_____
MacLennan	5	4	3	2	1	_____	Rule	5	4	3	2	1	_____
Fulford	5	4	3	2	1	_____	Laurence	5	4	3	2	1	_____
Fairlie	5	4	3	2	1	_____	Faludy	5	4	3	2	1	_____
Steinem	5	4	3	2	1	_____	Shumiatcher	5	4	3	2	1	_____
Finn	5	4	3	2	1	_____	White	5	4	3	2	1	_____
Atwood	5	4	3	2	1	_____	Orwell	5	4	3	2	1	_____

5. Are there any authors not included whom you would like to see represented?

_____

6. Please add any comments or suggestions. _____

_____

Fold here

- -

**Business
Reply Mail**

No Postage Stamp
Necessary if Mailed
in Canada

43652

POSTAGE WILL BE PAID BY

    SUSAN LILHOLT
    Publisher
College Editorial Department
HOLT, RINEHART AND WINSTON
OF CANADA, LIMITED
55 HORNER AVENUE
TORONTO, ONTARIO
M8Z 9Z9

Tape shut